Professional Diploma in Marketing

STUDY TEXT

Managing Marketing

For exams up to December 2011

Second edition August 2010

ISBN 9780 7517 8941 6
(Previous ISBN 9780 7517 6814 5)

e-IBSN 9780 7517 9149 5

British Library Cataloguing-in-Publication Data
A catalogue record for this book
is available from the British Library

Published by

BPP Learning Media Ltd
Aldine House, Aldine Place
London W12 8AA

www.bpp.com/learningmedia

Printed in United Kingdom

We are grateful to the Chartered Institute of Marketing for permission to reproduce in this text the syllabus, tutor's guidance notes and past examination questions.

Authors: Barry Walsh, Claire Wright and Dr Kellie Vincent
CIM Publishing Manager: Rebecca Hart
Template design: Yolanda Moore
Photography: Terence O'Loughlin

Your learning materials, published by BPP Learning Media Ltd, are printed on paper sourced from sustainable, managed forests.

A note about copyright

Dear Customer

What does the little © mean and why does it matter?

Your market-leading BPP books, course materials and e-learning materials do not write and update themselves. People write them: on their own behalf or as employees of an organisation that invests in this activity. Copyright law protects their livelihoods. It does so by creating rights over the use of the content.

Breach of copyright is a form of theft – as well as being a criminal offence in some jurisdictions, it is potentially a serious breach of professional ethics.

With current technology, things might seem a bit hazy but, basically, without the express permission of BPP Learning Media:

- Photocopying our materials is a breach of copyright
- Scanning, ripcasting or conversion of our digital materials into different file formats, uploading them to facebook or emailing them to your friends is a breach of copyright

You can, of course, sell your books, in the form in which you have bought them – once you have finished with them. (Is this fair to your fellow students? We update for a reason.) But the e-products are sold on a single user licence basis: we do not supply 'unlock' codes to people who have bought them second-hand.

And what about outside the UK? BPP Learning Media strives to make our materials available at prices students can afford by local printing arrangements, pricing policies and partnerships which are clearly listed on our website. A tiny minority ignore this and indulge in criminal activity by illegally photocopying our material or supporting organisations that do. If they act illegally and unethically in one area, can you really trust them?

Contents

Introduction

Aim of the Study Text • Studying for CIM qualifications • The Professional Diploma Syllabus • The CIM's Magic Formula • Assessment format • A guide to the features of the Study Text • A note on Pronouns • Additional resources • Your personal study plan v

Chapters

1 The marketing organisation 1
2 Quality in marketing 35
3 Measuring marketing performance 69
4 Management and leadership 99
5 Designing and recruiting marketing teams 135
6 Managing team working 175
7 Managing team performance 209
8 Managing team challenges 243
9 Managing marketing finances 271
10 The budgeting process 287
11 Cost management 311
12 Other tools and approaches 335

Key concepts 355

Index 357

Review form & free prize draw

1 Aim of the Study Text

This book has been deliberately referred to as a 'Study Text' rather than text book , because it is designed to help you though your specific CIM Professional Diploma in Marketing studies. It covers Unit 3 Managing Marketing.

So, why is it similar, to but not actually a text book? Well, the CIM has identified key texts that you should become familiar with. The purpose of this workbook is not to replace these texts but to pick out the important parts that you will definitely need to know in order to pass, simplify these elements and, to suggest a few areas within the texts that will provide good additional reading but that are not absolutely essential. We will also suggest a few other sources and useful press and CIM publications which are worth reading.

We know some of you will prefer to read text books from cover to cover whilst others amongst you will prefer to pick out relevant parts or dip in and out of the various topics. This Study Text will help you to ensure that if you are a 'cover to cover' type, then you will not miss the emphasis of the syllabus. If you are a 'dip in and out' type, then we will make sure that you find the parts which are essential for you to know. Unlike a standard text book which will have been written to be used across a range of alter native qualifications, this Study Text has been specifically for your CIM course. Throughout the study text you will find real examples of marketing in practice as well as key concepts highlighted.

2 Studying for CIM qualifications

There are a few key points to remember as you study for your CIM qualification:

(a) You are studying for a **professional** qualification. This means that you are required to use professional language and adopt a business approach in your work.

(b) You are expected to show that you have 'read widely'. Make sure that you read the quality press (and don't skip the business pages), read Marketing, The Marketer, Research and Marketing Week avidly.

(c) Become aware of the marketing initiatives you come across on a daily basis, for example, when you go shopping look around and think about why the store layout is as it is, consider the messages, channel choice and timings of ads when you are watching TV. It is surprising how much you will learn just by taking an interest in the marketing world around you.

(d) Get to know the way CIM write their exam papers and assignments. CIM uses a specific approach which is referred to as The Magic Formula to ensure a consistent approach when designing assessment materials. Make sure you are fully aware of this as it will help you interpret what the examiner is looking for (a full description of the Magic Formula appears later and is heavily featured within the chapters).

(e) Learn how to use Harvard referencing. This is explained in detail in our CIM Professional Diploma Assessment Workbook.

(f) Ensure that you read very carefully all assessment details sent to you from CIM. They are very strict with regard to deadlines and completing the correct paperwork to accompany any assignment or project. Failing to meet any assessment entry deadlines or completing written work on time will mean that you will have to wait for the next round of assessment dates and will need to pay the relevant assessment fees again.

3 The Professional Diploma Syllabus

The Professional Diploma in Marketing is aimed at anyone who is employed in marketing management role such as Brand Manager, Account Manager or Marketing Executive etc. If you are a graduate, you will be expected to have covered a minimum of a third of your credits in marketing subjects. You are therefore expected at this level of the qualification to be aware of the key marketing theories and be able to apply them to different organisational contexts.

The aim of the qualification is to provide the knowledge and skills for you to develop an 'ability to do' in relation to marketing planning. CIM qualifications concentrate on applied marketing within real work-places.

The complete qualification is made from four units:

- Unit 1 Marketing Planning Process
- Unit 2 Delivering Customer Value Through Marketing
- **Unit 3 Managing Marketing**
- Unit 4 Project Management in Marketing

The CIM stipulate that each module should take 50 guided learning hours to complete. Guided learning hours refer to time in class, using distance learning materials and completing any work set by your tutor. Guided learning hours do not include the time it will take you to complete the necessary reading for your studies.

The syllabus, as provided by CIM, can be found below with reference to our coverage within this Study Text.

Unit characteristics

The focus of this unit is about developing the marketer as a manager, including giving them the knowledge and understanding required to develop and manage the marketing infrastructure and the organisation's talent development, capability and capacity. This includes developing effective quality systems and processes to support compliance and approaches to measuring and monitoring marketing activities.

The unit also includes developing and managing marketing teams, which includes co-ordinating the human, financial and physical resources within the team effectively.

Finally, the unit includes developing a detailed understanding of managing the financial aspects of the marketing function and its associated activities in order to ensure that the financial performance of the function is consistent, reliable and effective.

By the end of this unit, students should be able to demonstrate how they would approach the management of the marketing function and its associated marketing teams, including effective resource and financial management.

Overarching learning outcomes

By the end of this unit students should be able to:

- Recommend how a marketing function should be structured to deliver competitive advantage, marketing and organisational success
- Assess a range of approaches that can be used to manage the marketing function on a day-to-day basis
- Prepare plans for showing how a team should be structured, selected, formed, managed and developed to demonstrate effective performance against objectives
- Critically assess the organisation's resource needs and capabilities for the marketing team and manage its marketing activities effectively and efficiently
- Prepare appropriate budgets and accounting documentation to support the financial management of the marketing function and associated marketing activities
- Critically assess the ongoing financial situation including manageability of the budget, financial stability and success of the marketing function.

SECTION 1 – The marketing infrastructure (weighting 30%)

		Covered in chapter(s)
1.1	Critically evaluate the importance of organisational structures in delivering marketing value, focus and creativity including consideration of how the work of the marketing operations is going to be undertaken: • Functional structure • Product/market structure • Brand structure • Territory structure • Matrix structure • International and multinational organisational structures	1
1.2	Critically assess the requirements of developing effective and efficient quality systems and processes to support compliance including evaluating and assessing the relevance of key quality concepts: • The importance of quality systems to the organisation • A range of quality models e.g. Total Quality Management, European Foundation of Quality Management, ISO 9001, Six Sigma, ISO 14001, PAS2050, benchmarking • PDCA Cycle – Plan, Do, Check, Act • Deming 14 Steps for improving quality	2
1.3	Determine innovative and effective methods of measuring and monitoring marketing performance for marketing operation, marketing activities and effective resource management: • Accounting measures of performance – profit and loss, balance sheets, cash flow and budgetary control • Productivity measures of performance – inputs versus outputs • Relationship marketing and customer related measures – retention, satisfaction and communication • Internal measures of performance – recruitment, retention, attitude, performance, communications • Innovation and learning measures of performance	3
1.4	Critically analyse monitoring information and recommend ways in which to improve marketing performance: • Productivity analysis – inputs versus outputs • Comparative analysis – measuring changes over time • Segmental analysis – analysis of markets • Innovation audit – organisational climate, current performance, policies, practices and cognitive styles • Competitor comparisons and benchmarking	3

SECTION 2 – Managing marketing teams (weighting 40%)

		Covered in chapter(s)
2.1	Critically evaluate the differences between management and leadership and identify the role of an 'operational marketing manager': • Leadership traits, skills and attitude • Leadership and management styles e.g. Action-Centred Leadership, Transactional Leadership, Transformational Leadership, Situational Leadership, the management styles continuum • The scope of leadership – providing strategic direction • The manager's role – planning, organising, coordinating, controlling, communication, teambuilding, coaching networking, development the functions of the marketing manager – information, value creation, communications • Reflect on personal approach to management and leadership and produce a personal development plan	4
2.2	Determine the needs for and show how to establish and build synergistic and harmonious marketing teams including preparing a plan to show how teams should be structured to deliver organisational and marketing objectives: • Structuring the team – the team audit, functional roles, team roles • Team development and talent management – stages in team development, team cohesiveness, high performance teams, the manager's role • Job analysis, job design, job enlargement, job enrichment • Competency development requirements • Flexible working practices • Assess and apply a range of team theories e.g. Belbin's team roles, Tuckman's stages of team development	5, 6
2.3	Propose a range of approaches for the sourcing of a team, including consideration of recruitment, training and development to provide the right balance of competency and skills: • Recruitment channels – internally and externally • Selection tools – job description, person specification • Selection techniques – assessment centres, interviews • On-boarding – induction • Training and development • Outsourcing of jobs/projects • Recruitment evaluation – determining recruitment effectiveness • Legal considerations when recruiting	5, 7
2.4	Plan how the work of the team will be undertaken establishing priorities and critical activities required to meet marketing and organisational objectives and with customers in mind: • Performance management and measurement – marketing strategy and individual objectives, communicating standards, techniques to measure performance against objectives and standards • Internal marketing – aligning internal communications with external communications, managing knowledge	7

2.5	Propose approaches to manage and co-ordinate the work of teams and individuals to create effective working relations including appropriate levels of consultation, taking into account the balance of skills and activities available: • Characteristics of effective teamwork/high performing teams • Management skills and techniques – communication, motivation, empowerment, involvement, delegation, task allocation, feedback, running effective meetings, listening, assertiveness, group decision making • Assess and apply a range of management theories e.g. McGregor's Theory X/Y, Maslow's Hierarchy of Needs, Herzberg's Motivation-Hygiene Theory, McClelland's Motivation Needs Theory, Vroom's Expectancy Theory • Job enrichment/enlargement • Preventing discrimination and valuing diversity – equal opportunities and employment law • Reflect on personal approach to team management and produce a personal development plan • Flexible working practices	6, 8
2.6	Propose approaches to manage and co-ordinate the work of remote teams to create effective working relations • Managing international teams, cultural considerations e.g. Hofstede's Cultural Dimensions, Trompenaar's Cross Cultural Communication • Managing virtual teams – benefits and constraints	8
2.7	Identify potential areas of team conflict, identifying causes and making recommendations for ways in which to overcome it: • Sources of conflict – interpersonal, change, organisational, external environment • Cultural differences • Assess the impact of conflict both positively and negatively • Conflict resolution and management • Change management strategies	8
2.8	Critically assess levels of performance in order to identify poor performance and, reasons for it and recommendations of how to overcome it including consideration of loyalty and motivation programmes: • Performance management – measuring performance against objectives and standards and providing feedback • Appraisal and peer review including 360 feedback • Internal marketing – employee motivation and satisfaction, customer orientation and satisfaction, inter-functional coordination. • Competency assessment and achievement	7, 8

SECTION 3 – Operational finances for marketing (weighting 30%)

		Covered in chapter(s)
3.1	Assess the different requirements of managing the finances of the marketing function and associated marketing activities: • The manager's role – control, managing information, cross-functional communication • The purpose of budgeting – planning, coordination of activities, motivation, control, relationship to management of the marketing team • Budget considerations – fixed, semi-fixed, variable and semi-variable costs	9
3.2	Critically evaluate the different approaches to setting the marketing and communications budget and associated marketing activities: • Top-down budgets, bottom-up budgets • The financial approach to setting budget – the budgeting process, percentage of sales/profit, competitive parity, affordable method • The marketing approach – the planning and control process, objective and task approach, Share of Voice, cost-volume-profit • Forecasting, financial analysis, balance scorecard, resourcing	10
3.3	Evaluate the different information sources required to determine the marketing budget for marketing operations and activities: • Data, information, intelligence and knowledge • Internal data sources - sales figures, headcount, outsourcing costs, consultant costs, EPOS system, MkIS external data sources including exchange rates variances arising from international trading	10
3.4	Negotiate delegated budgets with colleagues and agree provisional budgets: • Preparing a budget bid/business case to obtain priority budget for marketing activities • Negotiation tactics for bidding internally for budget to senior management	10
3.5	Undertake cost benefit analysis of marketing activities establishing priorities and best value approaches to operations: • The balanced scorecard – learning and growth perspective, business process perspective, customer perspective, financial perspective • Value chain analysis • Cost control, cost improvement • Cost-volume-profit analysis • Break-even analysis • Sensitivity analysis	12
3.6	Establish effective cost management processes for marketing operations to ensure that costs are managed effectively to achieve viability in the long-term: • Variance analysis – sales variance, cost variance • Cost control • Activity-based costing • business process re-engineering	11, 12

3.7	Assess budget variances, identify causes and recommend corrective actions where appropriate: • Internal variance – organisational, impact of marketing strategy, internal constraints, product portfolio, international exchange rates • External variance – the macro environment, customers, competitors, partners, suppliers, external stakeholders • Reconciling variances	11
3.8	Establish systems to monitor, evaluate and report on the financial performance of marketing operations and associated activities against the delegated budget: • Stated standards of performance, KPIs, qualitative and quantitative standards • Internal sources of data – operating statements, expenditure, profit forecasts, cash flow statements, MIS, MkIS • Actual versus forecast • Plans to improve performance – cost reduction, marketing activities	10, 11

4 CIM's Magic Formula

The Magic Formula is a tool used by the CIM to help both examiners write exam and assignment tasks and you to interpret what you are being asked to write about. It is useful for helping you to check that you are using an appropriate balance between theory and practice for the qualification level.

Contrary to the title, there is nothing mystical about the Magic Formula and simply by knowing it (or even mentioning it in an assessment) will not automatically secure a pass. What it does do however is to help you to check that you are presenting your answers in an appropriate format, including enough marketing theory and applying it to a real marketing context or issue. Students working through the range of CIM qualifications, are expected to evaluate to a greater extent and apply a more demanding range of marketing decisions as they progress from the lower to the higher levels. At the Chartered Postgraduate Diploma level, there will be an emphasis on evaluation whilst at the Introductory Certificate level the emphasis is on developing concepts.

Graphically, the Magic Formula for the Professional Diploma in Marketing is shown below:

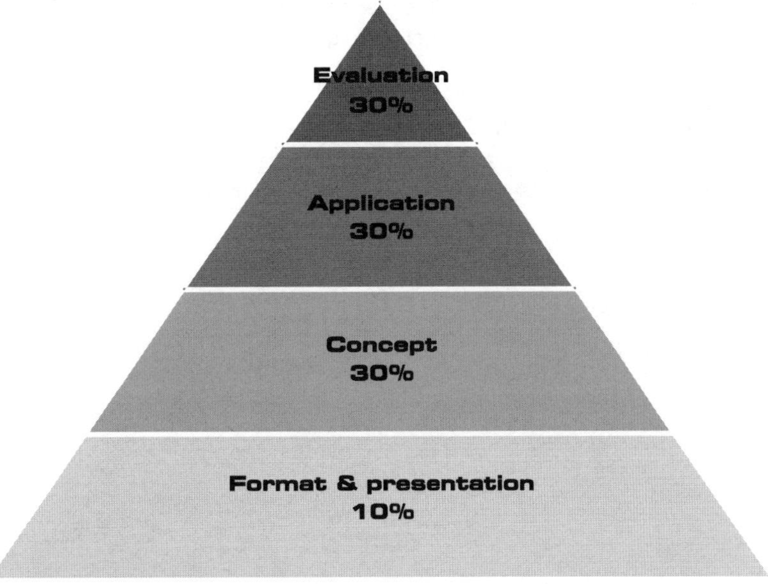

The Magic Formula for the Professional Diploma in Marketing

You can see from pyramid that for the Professional Diploma marks are awarded in the following proportions:

- ### Presentation and format – 10%

  Remember you are expected to present your work professionally which means that it should ALWAYS be typed and attention should be paid to making it look as visually appealing as possible even in an exam situation. It also means that CIM will stipulate the format that you should present your work in. The assessment formats you will be given will be varied and can include things like reports to write, slides to prepare, emails, memos, formal letters, press releases, discussion documents, briefing papers, agendas, and newsletters.

- ### Concept – 30%

  Concept refers to your ability to state, recall and describe marketing theory. The definition of marketing is a core CIM syllabus topic. If we take this as an example, you would be expected to recognise, recall, and write this definition to a word perfect standard to gain the full marks for concept. Understanding marketing concepts is clearly the main area where marks will be given within your assessment.

- ### Application – 30%

  Application based marks are given for your ability to apply marketing theories to real life marketing situations. For example, you may be asked to discuss the definition of marketing, and how it is applied within your own organisation. Within this sort of question 40% of the marks would have been awarded within the 'concept' aspect of the Magic Formula. You will gain the rest of the marks through your ability to evaluate to what extent the concept is applied within your own organisation. Here you are not only using the definition but are applying it in order to consider the market orientation of the company.

- ### Evaluation – 30%

  Evaluation is the ability to asses the value or worth of something sometimes through careful consideration of related advantages and disadvantages or weighing up of alternatives. Results from your evaluation should enable you to discuss the importance of an issue using evidence to support your opinions.

  Using the example of being asked whether or not your organisation adopts a marketing approach, if you were asked to 'evaluate' this, you should provide reasons and specific examples of why you think they might take this approach, as well as considering why they may not take this approach, before coming to a final conclusion.

  You should have noticed that for the Professional Diploma, you are expected to consider the equal weightings of concept, application and evaluation in order to gain maximum marks in assessments.

5 Assessment format

The Managing Marketing unit is assessed by a choice of assignment (one from two) each with six set tasks.

6 A guide to the features of the Study Text

Each of the chapter features (see below) will help you to break down the content into manageable chunks and ensure that you are developing the skills required for a professional qualification.

Chapter feature	Relevance and how you should use it	Corresponding icon
Chapter topic list	Study the list, each numbered topic denotes a numbered section in the chapter.	
Introduction	Shows why topics need to be studied and is a route guide through the chapter	
Syllabus linked Learning Objectives	Outlines what you should learn within the chapter based on what is required within the syllabus	
Format & Presentation	Outlines a key marketing presentation format with reference to the Magic Formula	10%
Concept	A key concept to learn with reference to the Magic Formula	30%
Application	An example of applied marketing with reference to the Magic Formula	30%
Evaluation	An example of evaluation with reference to the Magic Formula	30%
Activity	An application-based activity for you to complete	
Key text links	Emphasises key parts to read in a range of other texts and other learning resources	
Marketing at work	A short case study to illustrate marketing practice	NEWS
Exam/ Assessment tip	Key advice based on the assessment	
Quick quiz	Use this to check your learning	
Objective check	Use this to review what you have learnt	

7 A note on Pronouns

On occasions in this Study Text, 'he' is used for 'he or she', 'him' for 'him or her' and so forth. Whilst we try to avoid this practice it is sometimes necessary for reasons of style. No prejudice or stereotyping according to gender is intended or assumed.

8 Additional resources

8.1 The CIM's supplementary reading list

We have already mentioned that CIM requires you to demonstrate your ability to 'read widely'. The CIM issue an extensive reading list for each unit. For this unit they recommend supplementary reading. Within the Study Text we have highlighted in the wider reading links specific topics where these resources will help. The CIM's supplementary reading list for this unit is:

Adair, J. (2002) Inspiring leadership: learning from great leaders. London, Thorogood.

Adair, J. (2009) Effective leadership: how to be a successful leader. Revised edition. Pan Books.

Armstrong, M. (2009) Armstrong's handbook of human resource management practice. 11th edition.

Belbin, R. (2003) Management teams: why they succeed or fail. 2nd edition, Oxford, Butterworth Heinemann.

Bourne, M. (2007) Balanced scorecard. London, Hodder Education.

BPP (2009) CIM Professional Diploma Assessment Workbook. London, BPP Publishing.

BPP (2009) CIM – Professional Diploma in marketing: passcards. London, BPP Publishing.

Christopher, M., Payne, A. and Ballantyne, D. (2002) Relationship marketing: creating shareholder value. 3rd edition. Oxford, Butterworth Heinemann.

Collier, P.M. (2006) Accounting for managers. 2nd edition. Chichester, John Wiley & Sons.

Cole, G.A. (2004) Management: theory and practice. 6th edition. London, Thomson Learning.

Davidson, H (2004) The committed enterprise: making vision, values and branding work. 2nd edition. Oxford, Butterworth Heinemann.

Dibb, S. et al (2005) Marketing concepts and strategies.5th European edition. Boston, Houghton-Mifflin.

Note: Dibb, S. and Simkin, L. (2009) Marketing essentials. 1st edition. London, Cengage may replace the 5th edition above.

Palmer, R., Cockton, J. and Cooper, G. (2007) Managing marketing: a practical guide for marketers. Oxford, Elsevier.

Walsh, C. (2008) Key management ratios: The 100+ ratios every manager needs to know. 4th edition. Harlow, FT Prentice Hall.

8.2 Assessment preparation materials from BPP Learning Media

To help you pass the entire Professional Certificate in Marketing we have created a complete study package. **The Professional Diploma Assessment Workbook** covers all four units for the Professional Certificate level. Practice question and answers, tips on tackling assignments and work-based projects are written to help you succeed in your assessments.

Our A6 set of spiral bound **Passcards** are handy revision cards are ideal to reinforce key topics for the Delivering Customer Value through Marketing pre-seen case study exam.

9 Your personal study plan

Preparing a Study Plan (and sticking to it) is one of the key elements to learning success.

The CIM have stipulated that there should be a minimum of 50 guided learning hours spent on each unit. Guided learning hours will include time spent in lessons, working on fully prepared distance learning materials, formal workshops and work set by your tutor. We also know that to be successful, students should spend *at least* an additional 50 hours conducting self study. This means that for the entire qualification with four units you should spend 200 hours working in a tutor guided manner and at least an additional 200 hours completing recommended reading, working on assignments, and revising for exams. This study text will help you to organise this 50 hour portion of self study time.

Now think about the exact amount of time you have (don't forget you will still need some leisure time!) and complete the following tables to help you keep to a schedule.

	Date	Duration in weeks
Course start		
Course finish		Total weeks of course:
Submission	Assignment prep to commence on	Total weeks to complete assignment

Content chapter coverage plan

Chapter	To be completed by	Integrated into assignment
1 The marketing organisations		
2 Quality in marketing		
3 Measuring marketing performance		
4 Management and leadership		
5 Designing and recruiting marketing teams		
6 Managing team working		
7 Managing team performance		
8 Managing team challenges		
9 Managing marketing finances		
10 The budgeting process		
11 Cost management		
12 Other tools and approaches		

Chapter 1

The marketing organisation

Topic list

1 Organisation and organisation structure

2 Departmental and divisional structures

3 Flexible and adaptive organisation

4 Cross-functional co-ordination

5 Inter-organisational and international structures

6 Organisational culture

Introduction

This chapter sets the scene for the management of marketing performance (section 1 of the syllabus), marketing teams (section 2 of the syllabus) and marketing finance (section 3 of the syllabus) – by focusing on the organisational structure within which these systems and processes take place.

We start in section 1 by outlining the functions and elements of formal organisational structure, and its impact on work organisation, authority, relationships and job roles. We consider the various influences that shape organisation structure over time, and how structures can be intentionally designed and developed to support the delivery of marketing value, focus and creativity.

In section 2, we explain and evaluate various approaches to organisation and marketing structure: how functions and accountabilities can be divided up, via departmentation and divisionalisation, and which type of structure might be most effective for marketing.

In sections 3-5, we explore various contemporary issues in organisation structure: how to enhance organisational adaptability and responsiveness in the face of fast-changing environments and customer demands; how to encourage cross-functional communication and collaboration in support of marketing focus; and how to organise international and multi-national operations.

Finally, in section 6, we briefly outline the topic of organisation culture. Although not explicitly stated in the syllabus, culture is an influential part of the marketing infrastructure, expressing the *values and assumptions* behind all organisational activity and the *style* in which it is carried out.

Syllabus linked learning objectives

By the end of the chapter you will be able to:

	Learning objectives	Syllabus link
1	Evaluate the importance of organisational structures in delivering marketing value, focus and creativity	1.1
2	Recommend how a marketing function should be structured to deliver competitive advantage, marketing and organisational success	1.1
3	Evaluate a range of structural forms at the departmental, business unit and corporate level	1.1
4	Appreciate the impact of organisational culture on marketing performance	–

1 Organisation and organisation structure

KEY CONCEPT

concept

Organisation structure may be defined as 'the pattern of relationships among positions in the organisation and among members of the organisation. Structure makes possible the application of the process of management and creates a framework of order and command through which the activities of the organisation can be planned, organised, directed and controlled.' (Mullins, 1999).

Mintzberg (1983) defines an organisation's structure as: *'The sum total of the ways in which it divides its labour into distinct tasks and then achieves co-ordination among them'*. Organisation structure thus implies a framework intended to:

- Define **work roles and relationships**, so that areas and flows of authority and responsibility are clearly established.
- Define **work tasks and responsibilities**, grouping and allocating them to suitable individuals and groups.
- Channel **information flows** (communication) efficiently through the organisation.
- **Co-ordinate** the objectives and activities of different units, so that overall aims are achieved without gaps or overlaps in the flow of work.
- Control the **flow of work**, information and resources, through the organisation.
- Support **flexibility** and **adaptability** to changing internal and external demands.
- Support the **commitment, involvement and satisfaction** of the people who work for the organisation, by offering opportunities for participation, responsibility, team working etc.
- Support **value-adding, customer-focused business processes.**
- Support and improve **organisational performance** through all of the above.

1.1 Aspects of organisation structure

Some of the decisions that will have to be made in designing (or evaluating) an organisation structure (Huczyinski & Buchanan, 2001) include:

- **Specialisation**: how should the work of the organisation be divided up? Should tasks be grouped to allow units to specialise (allowing efficient focusing of training, equipment and management) – or should specialisation be minimised (to simplify communication and allow units and individuals to be versatile and flexible)?
- **Hierarchy**: should the overall structure be 'tall' (with many levels or tiers of management) or 'flat' (fewer tiers – meaning that each manager has to control more people: a wider 'span of control')? Tall organisations allow closer managerial control (due to narrower spans of control), while flat organisations save on managerial costs and empower and satisfy workers (who are given more authority and discretion).
- **Grouping**: how should jobs and departments be grouped together? Options include departmentation by the specialist expertise and resources required (function), or the services/products offered (product/market/brand), or the geographical area being targeted (territory).
- **Co-ordination**: how can the organisation foster integration between its different units, in order to maximise the 'horizontal' flow of business processes from one to the other? This will involve mechanisms such as rules and policies, carefully aligned goals and plans, liaison/co-ordinator roles, cross-functional team-working and so on.
- **Control:** should decisions be mainly 'centralised' (taken at the top) or 'decentralised' (delegated to lower levels) – or a mixture of both? Centralisation allows swift, decisive control and co-ordination, while decentralisation empowers and satisfies workers, and can support organisational responsiveness by having decisions taken closer to the customer or local market.

1.2 Power and authority

One of the most important aspects of formal organisation structure is the allocation of formal authority to perform tasks and make decisions.

KEY CONCEPT

Power is the ability to do something or get things done.

Authority is the right do something or to ask someone else to do it and expect it to be done.

French & Raven (1958) identified five types or sources of power in organisations.

- **Coercive power**: the power of physical or psychological force or intimidation. (This should be rare in business organisations, for ethical reasons.)
- **Reward (or resource) power**: based on access to or control over valued resources. Marketing managers, for example, have access to information, contacts and financial rewards for team members. The amount of resource power a person has depends on the scarcity of the resource, how much the resource is valued by others, and how far the resource is perceived as being under the manager's control.
- **Legitimate (or position) power**: formally conferred by the organisation, by virtue of the individual's position in the organisation structure. For example, a marketing manager has the authority to make certain decisions, and to command his or her team.
- **Expert power**: based on knowledge and expertise. For example, marketers have expert power because of their knowledge of the market and marketing techniques. Expert power depends on others recognising the expertise in an area which they need or value.
- **Referent (personal) power**: based on force of personality, 'charisma' or being a role model, which can attract, influence and inspire other people.

The organisation structure confers authority (legitimate or positional power) on individuals and teams. Note, however, that it need not directly convey other sorts of power, which may be wielded by people with no designated authority position: think about the most knowledgeable or experienced people in your team, for example, or individuals that other team members look up to.

1.2.1 Line, staff and functional authority

Expert power may be acknowledged in an organisation structure in various ways, in the concept of line, staff and functional authority:

- **Line authority** is the authority a manager has over a subordinate, flowing done the vertical chain (or line) of command in the organisation hierarchy.
- **Staff authority** is the influence one manager or unit may have in giving specialist advice or assistance to another manager or unit, over which they have no direct line authority. Staff authority does not entail the right to make or influence decisions or procedures: line managers may (or may not) accept the advice or assistance purely because of the perceived value of the staff unit's expertise. An example would be the HR department advising the marketing manager on selection interviewing techniques.
- **Functional authority** is the formalisation of staff authority, where a staff department management is given the authority, in certain circumstances, to direct, design or control the decisions or procedures of another unit. An example is where the finance manager has authority to enforce budgetary control disciplines in the marketing function.

These distinctions are a frequent cause of organisational problems, due to the ambiguity of the authority exercised in practice by staff/functional units such as HR, finance, market research and so on.

Power/authority issue	Possible solution
Staff units attempt to build influence in line units. This can be resented as 'interference' by line managers, especially if staff experts are perceived as 'ivory tower' theorists, distanced from the operational realities of line functions – and not being accountable for the success of their advice.	Ensure that staff units are fully aware of operational issues. Improve two-way communication. Encourage staff units to position themselves as internal consultants, with line units as internal clients.
Unclear boundaries of authority for line and functional managers.	Clarify areas in which functional managers have authority.
Functional managers 'empire building' to enforce their authority in line departments: eg causing the proliferation of rules, policies and red tape.	Encourage communication and collaboration between line/functional managers in the pursuit of shared objectives.

1.2.2 Centralisation

Another key power and authority issue, expressed in the organisation structure, is the extent of centralisation or decentralisation. We can look at centralisation in two ways:

- **Geography**: some functions may be centralised rather than dispersed in different offices, departments or locations. So, for example, secretarial support, IT support and human resources may be centralised in specialist departments (whose services are shared by other functions) rather than carried out by staff/equipment duplicated in each departmental office.
- **Authority**: centralisation also refers to the extent to which people have to refer decisions upwards to their superiors. Decentralisation therefore implies increased delegation, empowerment and autonomy at lower levels of the organisation.

The following table summarises some of the arguments in favour of centralisation and decentralisation.

Arguments for centralisation	Arguments for decentralisation
Decisions flow down from a central point, and so co-ordinate lower levels of activity more efficiently.	Avoids overburdening top managers, in terms of workload and stress.
Senior managers can take a wider view of problems and consequences, for better 'big picture' decisions.	Improves motivation of lower levels of management and staff, who are given more challenge and responsibility.
Senior managers can balance the interests of different functions (eg in resource allocations).	Greater awareness of local and front-line problems by decision makers (as opposed to top management 'distant' from the market and customers).
Quality of decisions is potentially higher due to senior managers' skill and experience.	Greater speed of decision making, and response to changing events, without the need to refer decisions upwards: particularly important in fast-change markets.
Crisis decisions are taken more quickly at the centre.	Separate spheres of responsibility can be identified: controls, performance measurement and accountability are better.
Policies, procedures and documentation can be standardised organisation-wide.	ICT supports decentralised decision-making, with the sharing of central decision-support data and tools.

This is obviously a very brief overview of some of the issues in organisation structure, power and authority. If you need to follow this up in more detail for an assignment, see Cole: 'Management', from the core reading list for this paper ■

1.3 Roles and relationships

1.3.1 Job roles

The division of labour and specialisation of work activities is an inevitable feature of large, complex organisations. The organisation's tasks are broken down into sub-tasks which can be allocated to individuals and teams in the form of 'jobs'. The organisation structure defines:

- How the organisation's work is divided up – and therefore what the appropriate content of each team's and person's job should be.
- Whether skills and specialisms are gathered together (eg in specialised or centralised departments) or dispersed and duplicated throughout the organisation.
- Where there are flows or overlaps in tasks from one organisational unit to another – and therefore how this flow of work should be co-ordinated or integrated.

There are a number of related issues here. We will look at the topic of **departmentation** (dividing up the tasks of the organisation in various ways) in section 2 below, and at **job design** in Chapter 5 (in the context of designing a marketing team).

1.3.2 Relationships

The formal organisation expresses the inter-relationship between job roles and organisational units, in terms of:

- The nature and structure of the **authority** they wield in relation to each other: line, staff and functional relationships, as discussed in paragraph 1.2.1 above.
- The lines of **communication** between them, by which information flows downwards (in the form of plans, briefings and instructions), side-ways (in the form of co-ordinating information) and upwards (in the form of feedback, reports and perhaps suggestions).
- The **flow of work** between them through 'horizontal' business processes and internal supply and value chains.

1.4 Elements of organisation structure

Henry **Mintzberg** (1983) provided a framework and language for discussing organisation structure, by categorising the building blocks of organisation. He suggested that all organisations can be analysed into five components, according to how they relate to the work of the organisation.

Mintzberg's organisational components

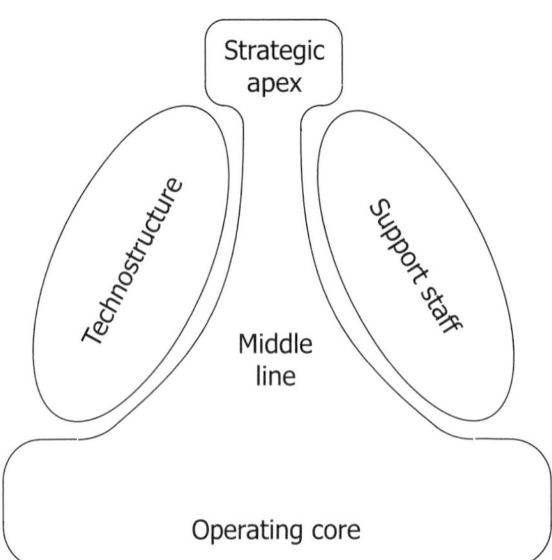

The components can be explained as follows.

Component	Function
Strategic apex	Ensures the organisation follows its mission and services the needs of its key stakeholders. Manages the organisation's relationship with the environment (boundary management). Acts as a force for **direction** (shared vision and goals).
Operating core	People *directly* involved in the process of obtaining inputs, and converting them into outputs (goods and services). Acts as a force for **proficiency** (competence).
Middle line	Conveys the goals set by the strategic apex and controls the work of the operating core in pursuit of those goals: ie middle management. Acts as a force for **concentration** (technical or product specialisation and accountability).
Technostructure	Analyses, determines and standardises work processes, techniques, skills and outputs. (Examples include strategic planners, quality controllers, human resource management: specialist advice and analysis.) Acts as a force for **efficiency**.
Support staff	Ancillary and administrative services such as PR, legal counsel, building maintenance and security. Support staff do not plan or standardise production, but function independently of the operating core. Acts as a force for **learning**.

These various components serve to **co-ordinate** the activities of the organisation in different ways:

- **Direct supervision**: favoured by the strategic apex and middle line. Power is directly applied to control and co-ordinate activity.
- **Mutual adjustment**: the integration of goals by communication and negotiation, favoured by the operating core and support staff.
- **Standardisation** of work processes, outputs and/or skills and knowledge, favoured by the technostructure.

The organisation also has a sixth component, which Mintzberg calls **ideology**: its paradigm or set of guiding assumptions and beliefs. This is identified with organisation **culture**, which we discuss in section 6 of this chapter.

ASSIGNMENT TIP

concept

Mintzberg's components are particularly useful when discussing issues of organisational structure. The vocabulary is precise and well-established.

By configuring these components in various ways, Mintzberg thus divides organisations into five broad types.

- **Simple (or entrepreneurial) structures**: small, hierarchical organisations based on centralised control by a single leader – eg a salon owner and a team of hairdressers. Because of their small size and strong hands-on leadership, they are characterised by coherent direction, informal relationships and flexibility. This structure is suited to small, entrepreneurial owner-managed firms. It consists mainly of the strategic apex and operating core.
- **Machine structure**: hierarchical, bureaucratic organisations, suited to stable environments and tasks requiring strict standardisation and compliance. This structure tends to have many layers of middle line, and an enlarged technostructure (to standardise work procedures) and staff support.
- **Professional structure**: eg a medical, legal or accountancy practice: hierarchical, but recognising the expectations and abilities of professional staff, and therefore flatter and more participative. This structure has little middle line or technostructure (since the operating core is comprised of experts), but a substantial staff support element for administrative and clerical support.
- **Divisional structure**: a number of more or less autonomous divisions, coordinated by centralised strategic and support functions. This is suitable for devolved structures (such as regionally or internationally dispersed divisions), where central direction is required for brand identity, investment strategy and so on. Each division effectively duplicates the whole middle line/operating core/technostructure/support staff structure, while reporting to the centralised strategic apex. The centralised technostructure and support structures may appear relatively small.
- **Ad hoc structure**: an organic, decentralised structure of temporary, flexible project teams and networks. This is suitable for new technology (IT, R&D) businesses, consultancies, small media companies and other organisations

focused on creativity and innovation. The structure tends to mostly technostructure and support staff, flexibly banding together and acting as an operating core where required.

1.5 Influences on organisation structure

Organisational structure is shaped by many factors. As we saw earlier, there are certain internal principles and dynamics of work organisation: how far power and authority are held at the top (centralised) or given to lower levels (decentralised); the span of control (the number of subordinates that can be supervised by any one superior); the division of labour; the grouping of people into working units; the need for communication channels, and so on. These determine some elements of structure, to an extent, according to internal logic.

According to contingency theory, however, there are still **managerial choices** to be made in order to optimise the structure. A number of contingent variables may influence structural choices and organisational development.

- The **strategic objectives** or **mission** of the organisation, and how these are broken down to define and guide the work of sub-units. Diversified organisations, for example, may require more decentralised structures.
- The **task** or 'business' of the organisation, which will determine which line or task functions are required (development, production, marketing, finance) and which support or staff functions (HR, planning, quality control, maintenance).
- The **technology** of the task may necessitate certain forms of organisation to maximise its efficiency (eg assembly line organisation of mass production) and the needs of people (eg team working to enhance human involvement in highly automated tasks).
- The **size** of the organisation. As it gets larger, its structure will get more complex: specialisation, subdivision and formalisation are required in order to control and coordinate performance (typically leading to the bureaucratisation of large organisations).
- **Geographical dispersion** may require federalised structures to take into account relevant factors at local, regional, national, international or global levels of operation.
- The **environment** of the organisation. Factors (and especially changes) in the legal, commercial, technical and social environment represent demands and constraints on organisational activity, and opportunities and threats to which organisation structure must adapt. As one example, information and communication technology (ICT) has enabled organisations to adopt looser, more network-style units or 'virtual teams'.
- The **culture and management** style of the organisation: eg the willingness of management to delegate authority and adopt more fluid facilitate-and-empower roles; organisational values about team working, formality, flexibility and so on.

1.5.1 Information and Communication Technology (ICT) and organisation structure

ICT, in particular, has enabled organisations to:

- **Outsource** areas of organisational activity to other organisations and freelance workers (even 'off-shore' in countries where skilled labour is cheaper), while minimising loss of control and co-ordination.
- **Decentralise** activity and decision-making to lower levels of management, and/or to dispersed offices, without loss of co-ordination, communication and control: ICT supports communication, data-sharing, results monitoring and so on.
- **Centralise** shared functions and services (like IT support) without loss of responsiveness to dispersed units: databases and communication tools create genuine interactive sharing of, and access to, common data.
- **Adopt flexible cross-functional and multi-skilled working**, by making expertise available across the organisation. A 'virtual team' (linked mainly or solely by ICT networks) co-opts the best people for the task – regardless of location.
- **Delayer and flatten** organisation structures: replacing some of the communication, performance monitoring and decision-making functions of middle management; and widening the spans of control by enabling managers to co-ordinate data-sharing and collaboration more efficiently.

1.6 Evaluating organisation structures for marketing

Drucker (1955) argued that: '**good organisation structure** does not by itself produce good performance. But a **poor organisation structure** makes good performance impossible, no matter how good the individual managers may be. To improve organisation structure... will therefore always improve performance.'

Signs that a structure may be **ineffective or dysfunctional** include problems such as:

- Slow decision/response times, due to the need to refer decisions via overly lengthy formal communication channels
- Inter-departmental conflicts, due to ambiguities or overlaps of responsibility
- Excessive layers of management (often in the middle line), which slows communication, increases overheads, and often requires work creation (or initiative-stifling micro-management) to justify the positions
- Lack of co-ordination between units, seen in customer complaints, production bottlenecks, inconsistent communications and the proliferation of special co-ordinating mechanisms (liaison officers, committees etc)
- High labour turnover among skilled junior staff, suggesting lack of delegation, challenge and/or development opportunities
- Lack of identifiable accountabilities for key tasks or results.

1.6.1 Supporting marketing value and focus

Kotler *et al* (1999) note that there has been both an absolute and a relative rise in the importance of marketing in the organisation. The responsibility of marketing has increased due to the increasingly complex environment, the slowing of demand in existing product fields and the rise in global competition. Meanwhile, companies have been forced to move from a product or production orientation (in which the priority was product quality or production efficiency) to a marketing orientation (in which the priority is anticipating and satisfying customer needs and wants), making marketing one of the critical management functions.

Kotler *et al* (1999) suggests that as a business grows, it will adopt an increasingly evolved and integrated view of marketing which supports the delivery of marketing value, and the development of marketing focus: that is, an extension of marketing influence throughout the organisation, so that all units cultivate a customer-focused marketing orientation.

The evolution of marketing organisation

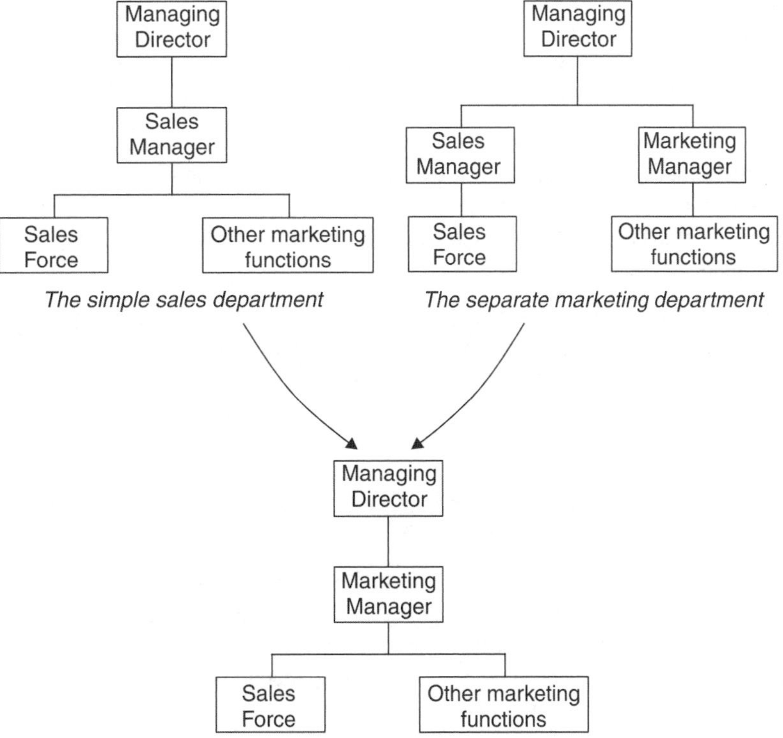

Marketing value and focus can be supported in an organisation structure by:

- **Positioning** the marketing function centrally, at a strategic level, so that strategy flows down from a marketing-oriented strategic apex.
- **Business process alignment** (or realignment): taking a horizontal process view of the organisation (facilitating the flow of work, information and value towards the customer) and aligning all business processes (research and development; purchasing, supply and distribution; production; sales and marketing) so that they service the same objectives of customer satisfaction.
- Establishing **communication mechanisms** for internal marketing: supporting the sharing of marketing values and information throughout the organisation.
- Establishing mechanisms for **cross-functional collaboration**: supporting the involvement and influence of marketing personnel in areas (such as product development and quality management) which potentially impact on customer satisfaction, and therefore benefit from marketing's understanding of customer needs.

We will discuss these issues further in Section 4 of this chapter.

1.6.2 Supporting creativity

As we saw from Mintzberg's concept of 'ad hocracy' (in paragraph 1.4 above), organisation structure can support creativity and innovation by:

- Encouraging high-frequency **multi-directional communication** (particularly lateral and upward) for information- and ideas-sharing. This is commonly achieved through cross-functional team-working, meetings (eg for ideas brainstorming) and data-sharing.
- Encouraging **flexibility**, by removing rigid controls in the form of tight job descriptions, detailed rules and procedures, close supervision, status barriers between managers and staff and so on. Structural flexibility supports cultural flexibility, or flexible thinking. Temporary project or task force teams may be formed as and when required for particular tasks, taking advantage of available expertise and ideas. All structures and arrangements should ideally be regarded as subject to alteration in response to changing conditions, since their purpose is to facilitate learning, innovation and performance.
- Encouraging **initiative, experimentation and risk-taking**, by devolving genuine authority to lower levels of staff: removing layers of control, supervision and upward referral. This will have to be supported by actual managerial behaviours as well: for example, not 'punishing' mistakes made while learning or taking initiative, but regarding them as 'learning opportunities'.
- **Softening boundaries** – not just within the organisation (status boundaries between levels in the hierarchy, and boundaries between functions) but between the organisation and the environment. 'Boundary workers' who have contacts outside the organisation should be encouraged to gather and share information to broaden the knowledge base. Opportunities should be sought to learn from other organisations (including customers and competitors) eg by benchmarking and imitation.

These kinds of 'enabling structures' are considered a key characteristic of '**learning organisations**' (Pedler *et al*, 1991): organisations which facilitate the acquisition and sharing of knowledge, and the learning of all their members, in order continuously and strategically to transform themselves in response to rapidly changing and uncertain environments.

1.7 Organisation charts

Organisation charts act as a guide to explain how different task roles and positions related to each other, and how they are co-ordinated and integrated. They typically show:

- '**Shape**': whether the organisation perceives itself as hierarchical (top down), or in some other way. A chart may take the form of concentric circles radiating out from a central leader, for example; or a 'web' or network of interrelationships and communication; or an upside-down pyramid with the pointy (senior management) end at the bottom (showing that management sees its role as supporting operational staff in serving the customer, rather than imposing its wishes on them).

- **Hierarchy**: the number of tiers (or circles) of authority in the organisation – and so, depending on the span of control, whether the organisation is tall or flat
- **Communication channels:** the lines connecting different levels (vertical) and units (horizontal) in the organisation, through which information flows in all directions. Horizontal lines are particularly important, as they reflect cross-functional or inter-group communication: a crucial mechanism of co-ordination.
- **Line, staff and functional authority relationships**. Staff relationships are often shown by a horizontal dotted line between the advisory and client units. Functional authority relationships are shown as a horizontal line joining the vertical chain of command, to show that the unit has authority 'over' aspects of line departments' work. An example is shown below.

Excerpt from a simple organisation chart.

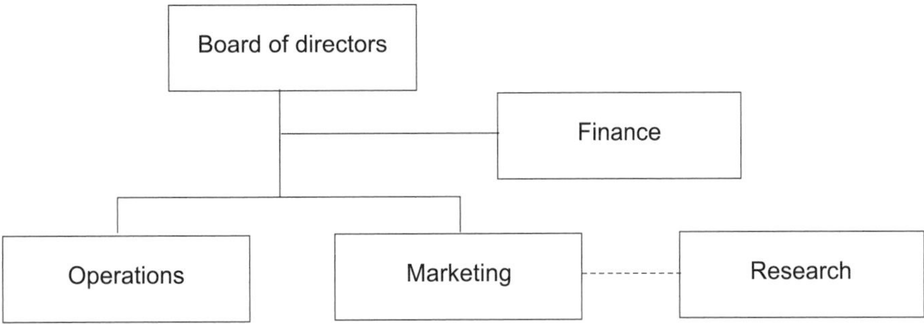

Note that an organisation chart is only a static 'snapshot' of the planned formal structure of an organisation at a moment in time. It cannot express the *quality* of management or relationships, or whether information flows *effectively* via formal channels. It does not attempt to show the true, complex pattern of relationships and communication in the organisation, taking into account *informal* contacts through 'grapevine'. It can show authority relationships, but not power or leadership relationships. It can show formally designated job roles – but not what people actually do, especially if jobs are loosely defined to allow for initiative, growth and flexible contribution.

Nevertheless, drawing an organisation chart may be a helpful way of:

- **Clarifying basic features** of the organisational structure
- **Highlighting potential inefficiencies and dysfunctions**, such as: long lines of communication, lack of cross-functional communication, duplications of activity, unclear boundaries of authority or unclear authority relationships.

ACTIVITY 1

application

Draw an organisation chart for your own organisation *and* marketing function, in any way that expresses, for you, both the structure and the self-perception (shape) of the organisation.

Get hold of the formal organisation chart (if any) of your organisation and marketing function.

Compare the two versions, perhaps in discussion with a colleague or fellow student. Evaluate:

- How far the formal organisation chart expresses the self-image and nature of the organisation.
- The effectiveness of the organisation and marketing structure: what potential strengths and weaknesses are highlighted by the chart.

2 Departmental and divisional structures

In most organisations, tasks and people are grouped together in some rational way: on the basis of specialisation, say, or shared technology or customer base. This is known as **departmentation**. Different patterns of departmentation are possible, and the pattern selected will depend on the goals and dynamics of the organisation.

2.1 Functional structure

Functional organisation involves grouping together people who do similar tasks (and therefore require similar skills, facilities and equipment). Functions in the organisation as a whole might be production, sales, finance, and general administration. Sub-sections of the marketing function might include: communications (or advertising and public relations), market research and sales. Functional specialists such as a market research manager or PR manager will take responsibility for all activities in their specialist discipline across all products and markets.

Functional departmentation

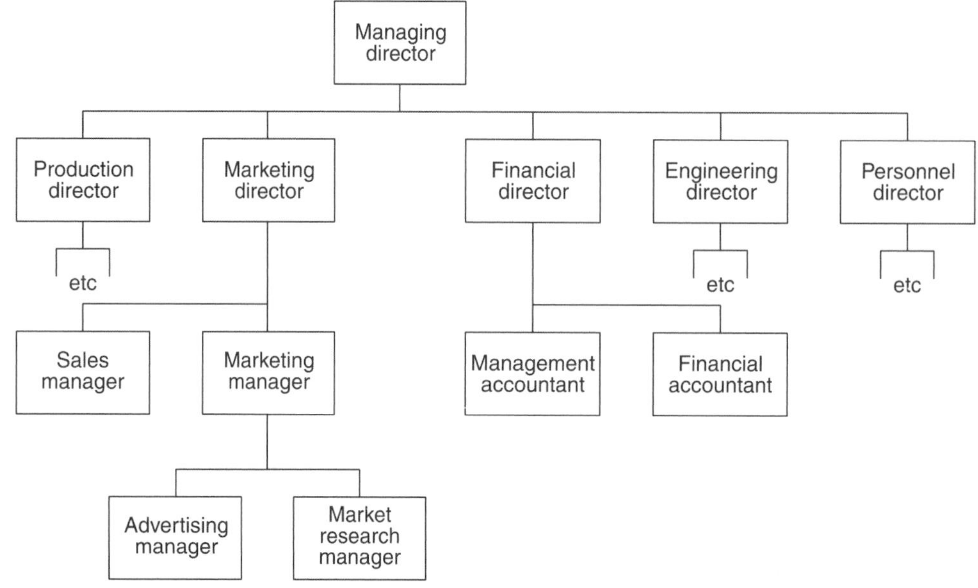

There are several advantages to such a structure.

- **Specialist expertise** is pooled and focused. Individuals and units can develop their specialisms, while the marketing director co-ordinates their plans and budgets to ensure the development of a coherent and consistent (integrated) marketing mix.
- It **avoids duplication** (eg having a marketing manager for each geographic area or product group).
- It enables **economies of scale** and **efficient sharing** of equipment and facilities.
- It facilitates the **recruitment, management and development** of functional specialists.

There are also a number of disadvantages, including:

- Tendency to **focus internally on** functional specialisms, processes and inputs, rather than on business processes, the customer and outputs, which are what ultimately drive a business. Inward-looking businesses are less able to adapt to changing demands.
- Lack of **'big picture' awareness** of whole-business, value-creating processes.
- **Poor co-ordination** and communication between functions, due to formal vertical channels of communication and specialist focus (and jargon).
- The creation of **vertical barriers** to information and work flow. Management writer Tom Peters suggests that efficient business processes and effective customer service requires 'horizontal' flow between functions – rather than passing the customer from one functional department to another.
- **Loss of control** once the organisation's range of products and markets expands: the functional manager may not be able to stay on top of the full range of products, markets or brands, and the burden of co-ordination between functional units may become too great.

2.2 Product, market or brand structure

2.2.1 Product structure

Some organisations group activities on the basis of **products** or product groups or 'lines'. Some functional departmentation remains (eg manufacturing, distribution, marketing and sales) but a divisional manager is given responsibility for the product or product line, with authority over personnel of different functions.

Product/brand organisation

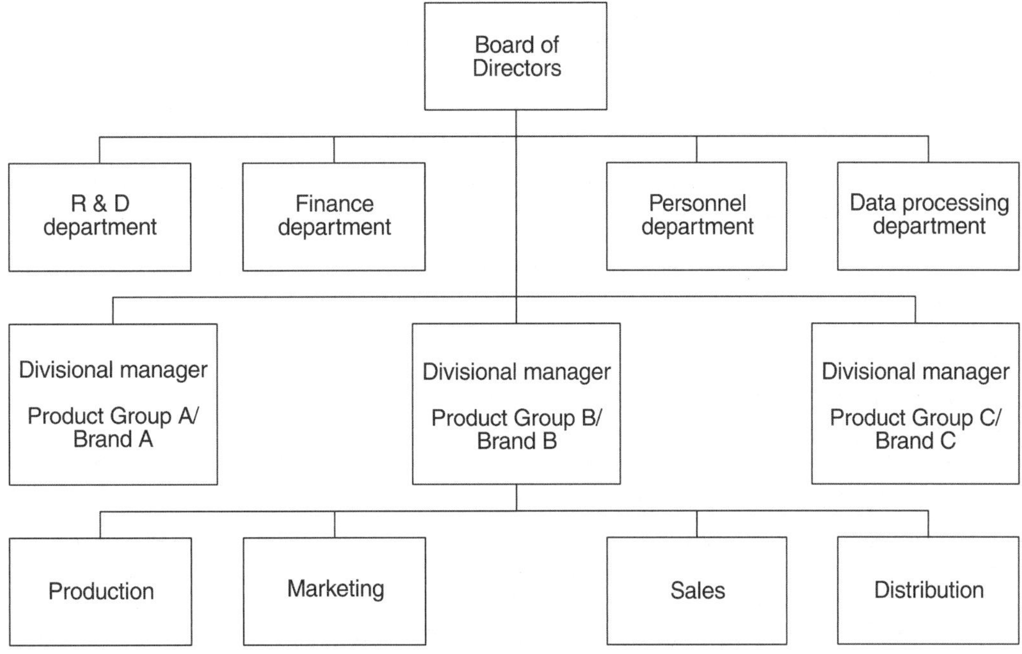

Product management involves adding an additional tier of management with responsibilities for: developing and implementing marketing plans for particular products or lines; gathering feedback on the products' performance; and initiating product modifications to meet market and competitive pressures. **Within a marketing function**, the structure may be seen as follows.

Product management within a marketing structure

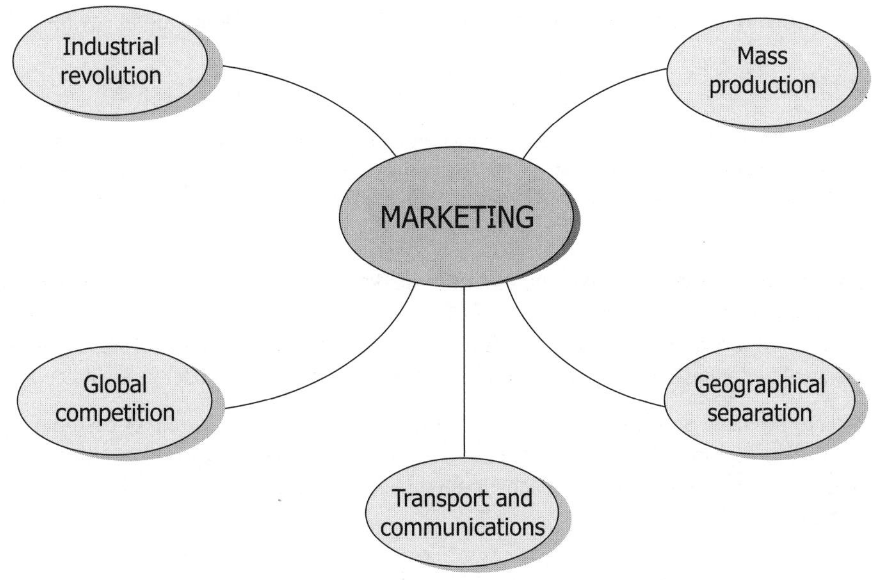

This type of approach may be particularly appropriate for organisations with a very diverse or very large range of products – especially if some of them are direct or indirect competitors with each other. Advantages include:

- **Accountability.** Individual managers can be held accountable for the profitability of individual products or lines.
- **Specialisation**. Product managers can build up considerable experience and understanding of their product groups and markets, which is valuable in a rapidly changing competitive environment. Salespeople may be trained to sell a specific product in which they may develop technical expertise, for example, and thereby offer a better sales service to customers.
- **Co-ordination.** The different functional activities and efforts required to make and sell each product can be co-ordinated and integrated by the divisional/product manager.

Disadvantages include:

- **Increased overhead costs** and managerial complexity.
- The risk that different product divisions may become competitive, **fragmenting objectives, markets and resources** in a way that is sub-optimal for the organisation as a whole.

The product-based approach is becoming increasingly popular, however, because the benefits of managers having accountability and expertise in specific product areas outweigh the costs associated with a loss of functional specialisation.

2.2.2 Brand structure

Brand structure is a variant of product structure (common in B2B marketing), focusing managerial authority and accountability on brands rather than product groups: this is common for FMCG producers with a range of potentially competing brands. As with product and market management, some functional organisation remains but brand managers have responsibility for the brand's marketing across all functional activities.

As you should be aware, a **brand** is a name (eg 'Cornflakes') or design which **identifies** the products or services of a provider and **distinguishes** them from those of competitors. Large organisations may produce a number of different brands of the same basic product: think Kellogg's cereals or Colgate dental care products, for example. Branding brings the product to the attention of buyers and is aimed at creating **recognition**, **differentiation, engagement** and **loyalty**: consumers need not realise that two 'rival' brands (Cornflakes or Rice Bubbles) are in fact produced by the same manufacturer.

Brand management may be particularly effective, because:

- Brands are packaged, promoted and sold in distinctive ways: there is arguably a need for specialisation of customer research and marketing effort.
- Brands may compete with each other, so it will be helpful to focus performance measurement (profitability, contribution) on a brand-by-brand basis – and to focus managerial accountability for performance accordingly.

2.2.3 Market or customer type (market management)

In a variant on the product-based approach, managers may take responsibility for particular **markets** or **customer segments:** in banking, for example, corporate, personal or high-net-worth customers; or in manufacturing, retail, industrial and export customers; or in book marketing, child, young adult and adult markets, or fiction and non-fiction markets; and so on.

In the case of services and B2B marketing, customer/market management would support **relationship marketing**: enabling the developing of on-going and continually deepening contacts and relationships with customers and clients. The segment, customer or account manager can develop a familiarity with the needs of his or her target market, and can develop targeted offerings, drawing flexibly on the organisation's whole product range as appropriate to meet those needs.

Where the buying motives, buying behaviour or media consumption of one group of customers **differ radically** from those of another group (as, most obviously, in the case of business customers and consumers), there is a strong case for market management – often to the extent that each type will have its own targeted marketing mix and its own dedicated marketing and sales teams.

2.3 Territorial structure

Where the organisation is structured according to geographic area, some authority is retained at Head Office but day-to-day operations are handled on a **territorial** basis (eg Southern region, Western region).

Territorial structure

A simple geographical organisation for a marketing department is an extension of the functional organisation in which responsibility for some or all functional activities is devolved to a regional level.

Territorial marketing structure

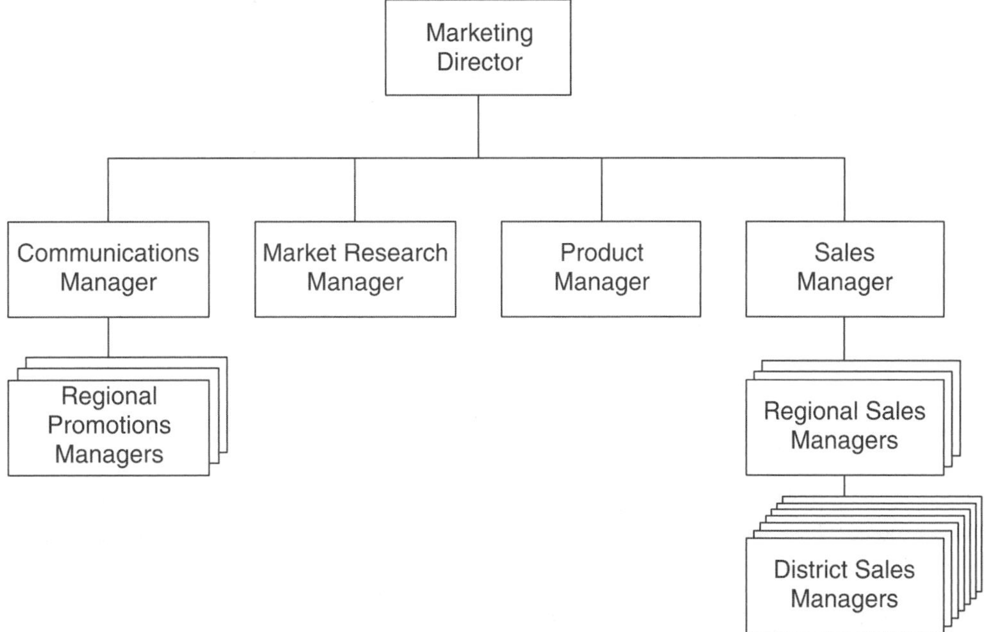

This type of organisation would be suitable for firms operating **internationally**, where the various functional activities would be required for *each* national market or group of national markets, in order to remain close to local customers, suppliers and contacts. The structure also tends to be adopted by larger companies where there are strong **regional differences**, for the same reason. **Sales departments** are often organised territorially, so that sales forces can focus travel time and resources, and build relationships, within defined areas.

There are advantages to geographic departmentation.

- There is **local decision-making** at the interface between the organisation and its customers, suppliers and other stakeholders (who may have distinctive needs).
- Cost-effective (because shorter) lines of supply, travel and communication to local markets, plants or offices.

But there are disadvantages too.

- **Duplication** and possible loss of economies of scale might arise. For example, a national organisation divided into ten regions might have a customer liaison department in each regional office. If the organisation did all customer liaison work from head office (centralised) it might need fewer managerial staff.
- **Inconsistency** in methods or standards may develop across different areas.

2.4 Divisionalisation

KEY CONCEPT

concept

Divisionalisation involves the formation of a number of more or less autonomous business units (divisions), co-ordinated by a centralised strategic apex (head office or holding company) each with its own revenues, expenditures and capital asset purchase programmes, and therefore each with its own profit and loss responsibility.

A division might take the form of a subsidiary company (under the umbrella of a holding company), or a profit or investment centre within a single company. Divisions may form on the basis of regions (particularly in multi-national firms or groups) or products, brands, or markets (think Virgin Records, Virgin Mobile, Virgin Airlines etc). Each may effectively duplicate another whole functional, market or regional organisation structure within itself. Marketing will often be devolved to the divisional level: some activities (eg corporate identity ad communications) may be centralised, but the extent of head office involvement can vary greatly.

KEY CONCEPT

concept

A Strategic Business Unit (SBU) is a section, usually a division within a larger organisation, that has a significant degree of autonomy, typically being responsible for developing and marketing its own products or services.

Divisionalisation is particularly suitable for **diversified and devolved** organisations (serving **distinct** customer groups, market segments or geographical regions, or using distinct technologies) – where **centralised strategic direction** is nevertheless required, to maintain core corporate identity, investment strategy and so on.

The advantages and disadvantages of divisionalisation may be summarised as follows.

Advantages	Disadvantages
Clear accountability for each division as a profit/investment unit.	In some businesses, it is impossible to identify completely independent products or markets for which separate divisions can be set up.
Focuses the attention of managers below the strategic apex on business performance.	Potential conflict between head office and divisional specialists.
Sensitivity to region/product specific demands and business opportunities and threats.	Potential fragmentation of overall objectives and markets, leading to sub-optimality.

2.5 Hybrid structures

'Hybrid' simply means 'mixed'. As you may have noticed from the various organisation charts shown above, business generally combined a variety of organisational forms. Hybrid structures allow the advantages of each form of organisation to be leveraged in appropriate ways: brand identity to be reinforced by a brand division, for example, with regional knowledge to be capitalised on by territorial sales departments, and economics of scale to be gained by specialised marketing or purchasing functions.

ACTIVITY 2

evaluation

How might a hybrid structure be appropriate in your organisation?

2.6 Matrix structures

Where hybrid organisation 'mixes' organisation types, **matrix** organisation actually *crosses* functional and product/customer/project organisation. The idea of the matrix emerged at US aerospace company Lockheed in the 1950s, when its customer (the US government) became frustrated at dealing separately with a number of functional specialists when negotiating defence contracts. The concept of the 'project co-ordinator' or 'customer account manager' was born.

The essence of matrix structure is **dual authority**: staff in different functions or regions are responsible *both* to their departmental managers, in regard to the activities of the department, and to a product, project or account manager, in regard to the activities of the department related to that particular product, project or account.

Matrix structure

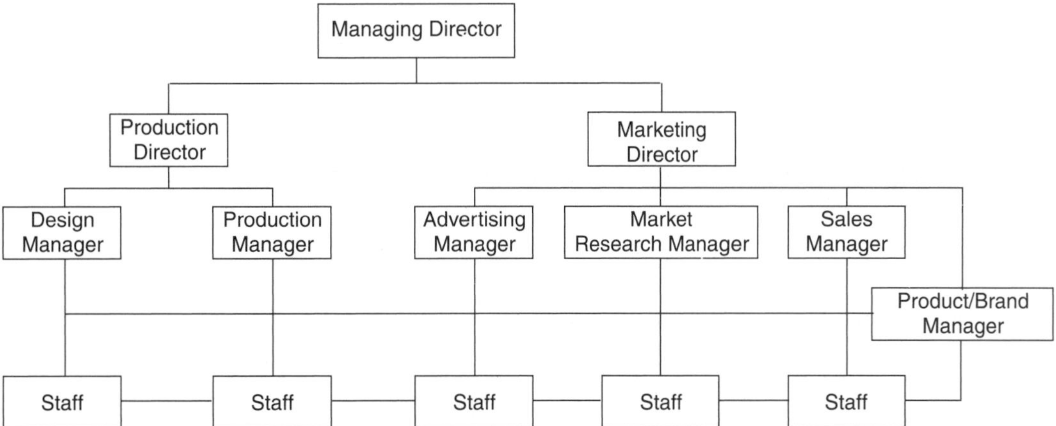

Cross-functional **project management** (which may be used for new product development, or to implement a customer care programme, say) is another example of multi-disciplinary team working under the authority of a co-ordinating manager – in this case, on a temporary basis.

Tom Peters (1994) called this a form of **horizontal structure**, which facilitates the flow of work across department/function boundaries, overlaid on the **vertical structure** of organisational authority (down the chain of command). Horizontal structures, such as cross-functional or project teams, are important in customer service, Peters argues, because the experience of a customer is horizontal, moving from one function to another (marketing, sales, accounts, after-sales service, relationship marketing etc).

Advantages of matrix organisation include:

- Greater **flexibility** of:
  - **People**. Employees develop an attitude geared to accepting change, and departmental monopolies are broken down.
  - **Workflow and decision-making**. Direct contact between staff encourages problem solving and big picture thinking.
  - **Tasks and structure**. The matrix structure may be readily amended, once projects are completed.
- **Inter-disciplinary co-operation** and a mixing of skills and expertise, along with **improved communication** and **co-ordination**.
- **Motivation and employee development**: providing employees with greater participation in planning and control decisions.
- **Market awareness**: the organisation tends to become more customer/quality focused.
- **Horizontal workflow**: bureaucratic obstacles are removed, and departmental specialisms become less powerful.

Again, there are disadvantages, however.

- **Dual authority** threatens a **conflict** between functional managers and project (or other co-ordinating) managers.
- An individual with two or more bosses may suffer stress from **conflicting demands** or **ambiguous roles**.
- **Cost**: management posts are added, meetings have to be held, and so on.
- **Slower decision making** due to the added complexity.

2.7 Choice of structure

We have suggested that each of the options so far discussed has advantages and disadvantages and may be appropriate in different circumstances. Lancaster & Withey (2005, p 68) argue that *'There is no one method of organising the implementation of marketing plans which is always and inevitably superior... It is impossible and downright dangerous to be prescriptive about the form which management and organisational structures should take. Having said that... they should be selected and designed ideally so as to provide:*

- *Company-wide customer orientation*
- *Organisational flexibility and speed of response*
- *Innovation*
- *Co-ordination and integration between different functional areas of the business and outside the organisation*
- *Effective communication*
- *Motivation and leadership.'*

Having raised the issue of flexibility, responsiveness, co-ordination and integration, let's go on to look at them in more detail.

3 Flexible and adaptive organisation

3.1 Mechanistic and organic organisation

The terms 'mechanistic and 'organic' were coined by Burns and Stalker (1961) to describe forms of organisation which are:

- Stable, efficient and suitable for slow-changing operating environments (mechanistic or 'machine-like' organisations: also called 'bureaucracies'), and
- Flexible, adaptive and suitable for fast-changing or dynamic operating environments (organic or 'organism-like' organisations).

The characteristics of these organisations can be summarised as follows.

Factor	Mechanistic	Organic
The job	Tasks are **specialised** and broken down into sub-tasks.	Specialist knowledge and expertise is understood to contribute to the **common task** of the organisation.
How the job fits in	People are concerned with completing the task **efficiently**, rather than how the task can be made to improve organisational **effectiveness**.	Each task is seen and understood to be set by the **total situation** of the firm: focus is on the task's contribution to **organisational effectiveness**.
Co-ordination	**Managers** are responsible for co-ordinating tasks.	People adjust and redefine their tasks through interaction and **mutual adjustment** with others.
Job description	There are **precise** job descriptions and delineations of responsibility.	Job descriptions are **less precise**: people do what is necessary to complete the task.
Commitment	**Doing the job** takes priority over serving the interests of the organisation.	**Commitment to the organisation** spreads beyond any technical definition of competence.
Legal contract vs common interest	**Hierarchical** structure of control. An individual's performance and conduct derive from a **contractual relationship** with an impersonal organisation.	**Network structure** of control. An individual's performance and conduct derive from a supposed **community of interest** between the individual and the organisation, and the individual's colleagues.
Decisions	Decisions are taken by **senior managers** who are assumed to know everything.	Relevant technical and commercial knowledge can be located **anywhere**.
Communication patterns	Communication is mainly **vertical** (up and down the scalar chain), and takes the form of **commands** and obedience.	Communication is **lateral** or networked, and communication between people of different rank represents **consultation**, rather than command.
Content of communications	Operations and working behaviour are governed by **instructions** issued by superiors.	Communication consists of **information and advice** rather than instructions and decisions.
Mission	Insistence on **loyalty** to the concern and **obedience** to superiors.	Commitment to the organisation's **mission** is more highly valued than loyalty as such.
Internal vs external expertise	**Internal knowledge** (eg of the organisation's specific activities) is more highly valued than general knowledge.	Importance and prestige attach to affiliations and expertise valid in the industrial, technical and commercial milieux **external** to the firm.

Burns and Stalker (1961) argue that while **bureaucracy** can be highly efficient in stable, slow-change environments, which do not require sensitivity to customer or external environmental demands, **organic structures** are better suited to conditions of change – particularly where there is a need to respond to change by continuous innovation and creativity, as is arguably the case in most marketing environments. They are typified by:

- A 'contributive' culture of information and skill sharing, encouraging versatility (rather than specialisation) and team working (rather than functional departmentation)
- A 'network' structure of authority and communication, allowing decentralisation and a range of lateral relationships (crossing functional boundaries) for co-ordination and self-control
- Focus on goals and outputs rather than processes
- Job design that allows flexible definition of tasks according to the needs of the team and changing demands.

Note that the two approaches represent two ends of a spectrum: there are intermediate stages between bureaucratic and organic organisations. Different departments of a business may be run on different lines. For example, the payroll department of a firm has a well defined task with little variation: controls are needed to ensure processing accuracy and to avoid fraud. A mechanistic system might be applied here. On the other hand, the marketing department, employing professional experts and creatives, requiring sensitivity to environmental changes and customer trends, and needing to network widely within and outside the organisation, may be run on an organic basis.

3.2 The new organisation

Some recent trends have emerged from the focus on **responsiveness and flexibility** as key organisational values.

- **Flat structures.** The flattening of hierarchies does away with levels of organisation which lengthened lines of communication and decision-making and encouraged ever-increasing specialisation. Flat structures are more responsive, because there is a more direct relationship between the organisation's strategic centre and the operational units serving the customer.
- **Horizontal structures**. What Peters (1994) calls 'going horizontal' is a recognition that functional versatility (through multi-functional project teams and multi-skilling, for example) is the key to flexibility. In the words (quoted by Peters) of a Motorola executive: 'The traditional job descriptions were barriers. We needed an organisation soft enough between the organisational disciplines so that ... people would run freely across functional barriers or organisational barriers with the common goal of getting the job done, rather than just making certain that their specific part of the job was completed.'
- **'Chunked' and 'unglued' structures**. So far, this has meant teamworking and decentralisation, or empowerment, creating smaller and more flexible units within the overall structure. Charles Handy's **'shamrock organisation'** (with a three-leafed structure of core, subcontractor and flexible part-time labour) is gaining ground as a workable model for a leaner and more flexible workforce, within a controlled framework (Handy, 1989).
- **Output-focused structures**. The key to all the above trends is the focus on results, and on the customer, instead of internal processes and functions for their own sake. A project management orientation and structure, for example, is being applied to the supply of services within the organisation (to internal customers) as well as to the external market, in order to facilitate listening and responding to customer demands.
- **'Jobless' structures**. Meanwhile, the employee becomes not a job-holder but the vendor of a portfolio of demonstrated outputs and competencies (Bridges, 1994). However daunting, this is a concrete expression of the concept of employability, which says that a person needs to have a portfolio of skills which are valuable on the open labour market: employees need to be mobile, moving between organisations rather than settling in to a particular job.
- **Boundaryless structures** (Milkovich & Boudreau, 1996; Welsh, 2005). Horizontal (status) barriers are removed or softened by delayering and participative decision-making, and vertical (functional) barriers by empowered cross-functional team working – in order to align business processes. The boundaries of the organisation are also softened, by co-opting suppliers, distributors, business allies and customers as collaborators in the value-adding process, creating an 'extended' or 'networked' enterprise.

- **Ad hocracy** (Huzcynski & Buchanan, 2001) is 'a type of organisation design which is temporary, adaptive, creative – in contrast to bureaucracy, which tends to be permanent, rule-driven and inflexible'. It is associated with creative thinking, innovation and organisational learning. It would typically involve the use of a loose network of flexible, temporary, cross-functional project teams or networks of specialists, banding together and disbanding as required to seize business opportunities. While ideally suited to turbulent, innovative markets, it presents a challenge for managers and employees, since it means living with disorder, ambiguity and uncertainty on an on-going basis.

ACTIVITY 3

application

You might like to consider how elements of such structures could fruitfully be built into your marketing organisation.

3.3 The flexible firm

Attention has focused on both functional and numerical flexibility, in order to help organisations to respond to changes and fluctuations in demand.

Functional flexibility or versatility may be achieved by methods such as:

- Multidisciplinary teamworking (eg multifunctional project or procurement strategy teams, bringing together individuals with different skills and specialisms, across functional boundaries, so that their competencies and resources can be pooled or exchanged)
- Multi-skilling (where each individual within a team is functionally versatile, and able to perform a number of different tasks as required)

We will look at these aspects further in Chapter 5 on structuring teams.

Numerical flexibility: the ability to shrink or enlarge the labour force in response to fluctuations in demand. This may be done by: using non-standard-contract and subcontracted labour (temporary, short-contract or freelance workers); outsourcing functions to other organisations; or introducing flexible working hours schemes. In practice, an organisation may adopt a 'core-periphery' model.

Handy (1989) proposes a '**Shamrock**' (four-leaf clover) configuration, with various 'leaves'.

- A small, stable **professional core** of full-time permanent labour, who represent the distinctive knowledge and competences of the firm: qualified professionals, technicians and managers, whose commitment is focused on their work and career within the organisation.
- A **periphery** of part-time and temporary labour (the 'flexible labour force') which can be deployed flexibly according to work flow peaks and troughs. Their commitment is typically focused on the immediate job and work group, rather than career or the organisation. However, they are crucial in maintaining standards of service – so it is important for the firm not to treat them 'casually': they should receive fair and equitable treatment (now enshrined in employment law), adequate training and status.
- The **option of contracting out** areas of work to a 'contractual fringe': external providers (freelancers, consultants and sub-contractors) who are able to undertake non-core activities and/or provide specialist services, more economically than the firm could manage internally. Their commitment is typically to achieving specified results in return for fees.

These represent three distinct labour forces, each with its own type of psychological (and legal) contract with the firm.

The Shamrock organisation

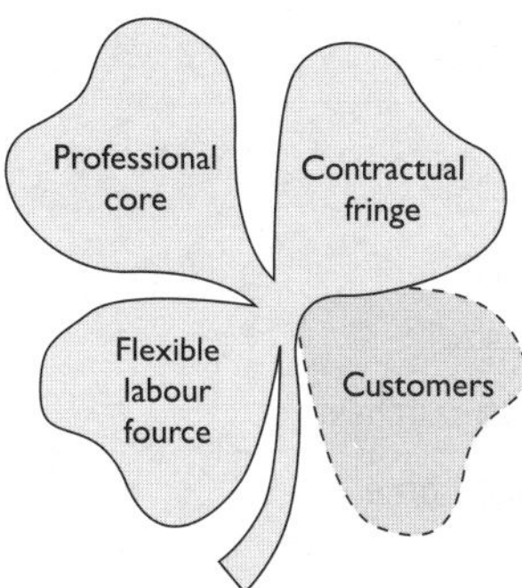

In addition, Handy (1989) notes the 'lucky' fourth leaf of the clover: the organisation may be able to 'sub-contract' some sales, service and supply tasks – for free – to **customers**. Information and communication technology (ICT) has supported a wide range of 'self service' applications such as: Internet/phone banking and automated teller machines (ATMs); Internet/telephone reservations and ticketing, in entertainment and travel; on-line information services and so on – in addition to traditional self-service retail and catering outlets, self-assembly products and so on. This should allow labour savings in other 'leaves' of the organisation.

4 Cross-functional co-ordination

4.1 The value of cross-functional co-operation

One of the main purposes of internal communication is co-ordination, co-operation or integration between different functions and units of the organisation.

KEY CONCEPT

concept

Co-ordination is planning, or taking action to improve, the inter-relationships (especially of timing and methods of communication) between a number of various activities, which contribute to the achievement of a single objective, so that they do not conflict and the objective is achieved with a minimal expenditure of time and effort.

The marketing department needs to ensure that other departments that depend on its work, or on which its work depends, are kept informed. At the most basic, information should include: plans and schedules, any *changes* to plans and schedules, and any feedback on the results of plans and schedules. This may seem like common sense. It should be obvious that you should check with the design or production team before you advertise product specifications, and inform them of the planned date of a new product launch, and monitor their readiness as the date approaches. However, failure to do these things presents common problems, sources of conflict – and even chaos!

4.1.1 Potential for conflict in interdepartmental relations

'In principle, business functions should mesh harmoniously to achieve the overall objectives of the firm. In practice, departmental interfaces are often characterised by deep rivalries and misunderstandings... Some inter-departmental conflict stems from differences of opinion about what lies in the best interests of the firm; some from real trade-offs between departmental well-being and company well-being; and some from unfortunate departmental stereotypes and prejudices.' (Kotler, 2002)

The **marketing concept** is designed to foster a deeper appreciation by all departments of the value and benefits of a customer orientation, but how much influence should marketing have over other functions to bring about coordinated effort in customer service, say, or product development? Other functions naturally stress their own special contribution to company goals, and view problems and opportunities in the light of their own expertise and culture.

Kotler (2002) summarises the potential for conflict as follows.

Other functions	Their emphasis	Marketing's emphasis
Research & Development (R & D)	Basic research	Applied (customer) research
	Intrinsic quality	Perceivable quality
	Functional features	Sales features
Purchasing	Narrow product line	Broad product line
	Price of materials	Quality of materials
	Economical lot size	Large lot size to avoid stock-out
	Infrequent batch purchase	Immediate purchase on demand
Manufacturing	Long product lead time	Short production lead time
	Long runs with few models	Short runs with many models
	No model changes	Frequent model changes
	Standard orders	Custom orders
	Ease of fabrication	Aesthetic appearance, features
	Average quality control	Zero-defects quality control
Finance and accounting	Strict rationale for spending	Intuitive arguments for spending
	Fixed budgets	Flexible budgets
	Pricing to cover costs	Pricing for demand, competition
	Standard transactions	Special terms and discounts
	Tough credit terms and debt collection	Easy credit terms and debt collection

One of the key principles of **relationship marketing** is the need to foster a deeper appreciation by all functions and departments of the need to add customer value and build relationships. *'**Internal marketing** is seen as a way of **integrating various functions** to enable staff to work together across functional boundaries, and aligning those cross-functional teams with **internal and external customer needs** and expectations, so that their work is attuned to the company's **mission, strategy and goals**.'* (Peck *et al*, 2004, p 315).

4.1.2 Whole-organisation marketing

Egan (2004, p 158) argues that one of the key causes of customer service problems is poor teamwork. Different functions in the organisation often operate as isolated towers or 'silos': unconnected to each other, acting independently and with little co-ordination or sense of shared goals. This causes problems because activities in the value chain are interrelated.

Customers experience the organisation '**horizontally**': that is, they deal in sequence with marketing, sales, order processing, accounts, deliveries, after-sales service – being passed from one department to another. Customers want this experience to be seamless: they don't want to come up against 'vertical' barriers or gaps between the units and functions of the organisation, where one department isn't talking to another, or has different systems and policies, or gives completely different messages.

Effective marketing and customer service therefore depends on cross-functional sharing of goals, values and information. It also requires all employees to see themselves as 'part time marketers': as direct or indirect contributors to customer relations, customer satisfaction and customer value.

4.2 Tools of inter-departmental relations

4.2.1 Formal communication and co-ordination mechanisms

Formal mechanisms for improving cross-functional relationships include the following.

- **Communication channels and flows**: using available channels and tools of communication (conferences, team/project meetings, email, intranet, newsletters and briefings, forms and reports, plans and schedules, shared access to a central database) to share and exchange information with other functions.

- **Communication and liaison positions**. Dedicated communications or liaison officers may be appointed to act as a 'hub' for cross-functional communication. Managers may also act as a 'cross-over' point for communication, where they have responsibility for two or more departments.
- **Cross-functional project teams, task-forces or committees**. Cross-functional teams include representatives from different functions and departments. Joint planning and on-going collaboration require them to share and exchange information on a regular, task-focused basis. This builds 'bridges' and interpersonal networks between functions.
- **Matrix organisation:** cross-functional working which is permanently embedded in the organisation structure, as discussed earlier.

4.2.2 Networking

The more marketers have contact with other departments, learn what they do and show that they appreciate their problems and capabilities, the more likely they are to develop co-operative relationships. Cross-functional networking, or informal communications, are very important in internal marketing. Marketers may:

- Attend organisation-wide and inter-departmental meetings and events.
- Join quality circles or other multi-disciplinary teams and committees that focus on shared objectives.
- Use contacts in other departments to arrange visits and briefings to learn about each other's objectives, culture and issues.

4.2.3 Internal marketing

KEY CONCEPT

concept

Internal marketing may be defined as a variety of approaches and techniques by which an organisation acquires, motivates, equips and retains customer-conscious employees (George & Grönroos, 1989), in order to help retain customers through achieving high quality service delivery and increased customer satisfaction.

The nature of internal marketing has been well summarised by Peck *et al* (2004, p 313):

'Internal marketing is concerned with creating, developing and maintaining an ***internal service culture and orientation****, which in turn assists and supports the organisation in the achievement of its goals. The internal service culture has a vital impact on how service-oriented and customer-oriented employees are, and, thus, how well they perform their tasks... The development and maintenance of a customer-oriented culture is a critical determinant of long-term success in relationship marketing...*

The basic premise behind the development of internal marketing is the acknowledgement of the ***impact of employee behaviour and attitudes*** *on the relationship between staff and external customers. This is particularly true where employees occupy boundary-spanning positions in the organisation... The skills and customer orientation of these employees are, therefore, critical to the customers' perception of the organisation and their future loyalty to the organisation.*

In other words, it is through internal marketing that all employees can develop an understanding of how their tasks, and the way they perform them, create and deliver customer value and build relationship.

We will discuss this process in more detail in Chapter 7.

ASSIGNMENT TIP

concept

It is worth bearing the internal marketing dimension in mind if you are asked to make proposals for marketing performance improvements in your assignment. What will be the internal market implications of your proposal? What internal human resources will be required? What training and communication will they need to adapt to the change or perform the task? What sources of resistance might there be – and how can these be changed into support and commitment? This may not be a major (or even explicit) part of the assignment brief, but by considering the internal marketing implications, you will be demonstrating your grasp of the syllabus, and of the interconnected nature of stakeholder marketing.

MARKETING AT WORK

Breakfast cereal manufacturer Jordans Cereals wanted all employees to appreciate the rationale behind a 'whole range' brand update. It was essential that employees fully understood the importance to the business of the changes they were being asked to support. To generate support internally, an exhibition and 'working lunch' event was held, hosted by sales and marketing managers.

5 Inter-organisational and international structures

5.1 Inter-organisational structures

Inter-organisational structures are structured relationships between two or more organisations, in which 'two or more organisations share resources and activities and pursue a common strategy' (Huczynski and Buchanan, 2001). Common approaches to extending the enterprise in this way include:

- **Merger** (where two companies voluntarily pool the ownership interests of their shareholders) or **acquisition** (where one firm buys the equity stake or assets of another company): either way, the assets of two organisations are integrated and jointly managed. This may offer a range of benefits: synergy and economies of scale arising from pooled activities; access to and ownership control over resources such as brand names, products, technology, customer bases or new national markets. An organisation may be able to reposition itself in the supply chain, by gaining control of a supplier (backwards integration) or distribution channel (forward integration), reducing the risk and cost of activities previously conducted by market transaction.
- **Joint venture**: a formal arrangement whereby two independent companies establish a new company which they jointly own and manage. (Where more than two companies enter such an arrangement, this is called a '**consortium**'.) Joint ventures are commonly used to overcome barriers to entry into international markets: eg Western companies forming joint ventures with local partners in Eastern Europe or China. One party provides technical and managerial expertise and investment, while the other supplies access to labour and local markets.
- **Strategic alliance:** a formally structured relationship in which two companies legally contract to co-operate in specific ways, to achieve specific commercial objectives that are of benefit to both parties. Huczynski & Buchanan (2001) summarise the relationship as follows. 'In a strategic alliance, companies merge a limited part of their domain with each other and attempt to achieve, with their existing respective value chains, the competitive advantage that might have... eluded them independently'. Examples include the Star Alliance group of airlines; the promotional alliances between credit card companies and other brands; and the co-development of micro-processors (such as Intel) and personal computers.
- **Subcontracting, outsourcing, licensing and franchising**: a variety of arrangements in which the organisation contracts or licences some of its functions or activities to other organisations. Many companies are currently outsourcing a range of support functions (such as cleaning, catering, warehousing and logistics) and even core functions such as sales and customer service (eg in outsourced call centres). Although these are market-style contracts, they involve close collaboration between partners. A franchise is a co-operative arrangement under which one party sells to another party the right to market its products or services, using the company's mane, trademarks and technology: examples include, McDonalds, Pizza Express, Kall Kwik printers and Kodak Express photo labs.
- **Network organisation:** a looser dynamic, more informal affiliation of autonomous and broadly equal organisations, which exchange information and pursue on-going (typically long-term) relationships for mutual benefit. There are no direct contractual or financial obligations: the relationships are purely based on collaboration, communication, trust and mutual advantage. An example might be the extended supply and distribution network of a given firm. The term '**virtual organisation**' is given to networks which collaborate using ICT links as their main – or only – means of contact.

MARKETING AT WORK

application

Many charities working towards similar or shared goals make use of networks especially if individually they are relatively small. NESSR is a Springer Spaniel rescue and re-homing service which operates mainly through a network of members who communicate via an online forum. The website www.nessr.net also hosts an area for other animal rescue organisations and lost dog websites.

Inter-organisational structures and relationships are a significant feature of the modern business environment, because of the rise of **relationship marketing** and the recognition that whole supply networks (not just individual firms) deliver customer value, and therefore offer competitive advantage. Inter-organisational relationships can offer:

- Access to **overseas** supply markets, distribution channels, customers, expertise and technology, where the partner has an established presence in the area
- Reduction in the effects of **competition**: competitors can join forces as allies, to enhance market share, defend against new entrants to the market and so on
- **Economies of scale** through pooling activities
- **Sharing the risk**, financial and operational, of new ventures and new products/markets
- **Synergy**, where core competencies and brand values of each firm enhance the other (2 + 2 = 5).

5.2 International and multinational structures

Local conditions and the scale and nature of operations will influence the organisation structure of companies trading and/or operating internationally. Structures range from the inclusion of an export department; through variations on a combination of functional and geographic responsibility areas (eg geographical divisions); to wholly-owned subsidiary operations, or joint ventures with local partners, in other countries.

- An 'international' company is one that **trades with** countries outside its domestic environment. **International marketing** implies that a firm takes its export activities seriously: an export department might be set up to develop export markets. A 'multi-domestic' strategy may be pursued, in which each country is regarded as a separate market. Arguably, this is sensible market segmentation, but it relies mainly on exports: only a few activities are conducted overseas.
- A 'multi-national company' (MNC) is thus one that **operates from bases** in several different countries. **Multi-national marketing** implies that the company has a large number of activities in different countries, having 'off-shored' both marketing and production facilities: the firm allocates and locates its resources according to opportunities arising in different countries. This can result in complex configurations: many multinational car manufacturing companies, like Toyota, for example, have moved from manufacturing a particular car at a particular location to manufacturing different *parts* of cars in different locations. 'The logistics problems of co-ordinating such operations are immense, requiring sophisticated control systems and management skills far removed from those in the smaller firm.' (Johnson, Scholes & Whittington, 2005).

Organisation by divisionalisation is common for multi-nationals, because of their size and the potential variation of conditions in different off-shore markets. If the diversity of the product group is perceived as more important than the diversity of the markets, a firm may organise globally by product, with each operating division having a geographic structure suited to its own needs.

Divisionalised international structure

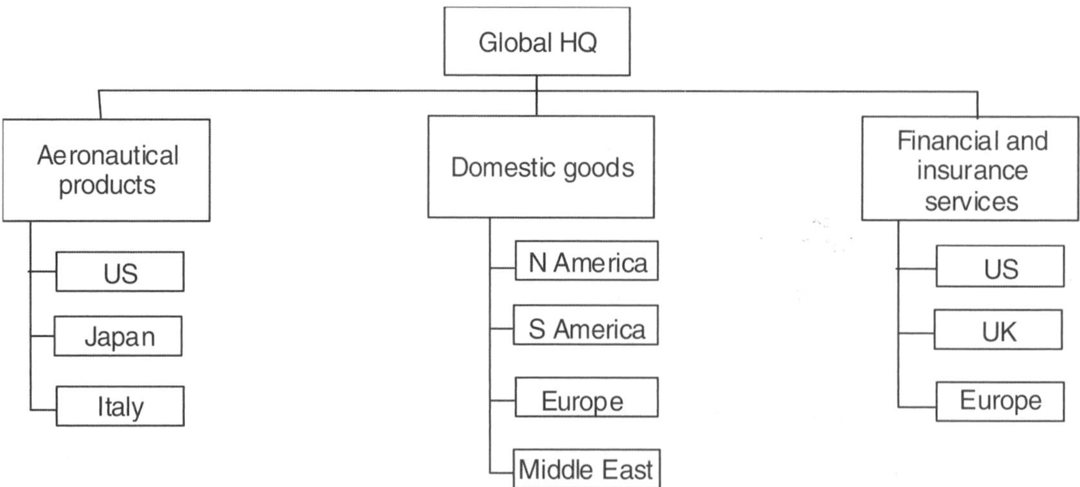

Companies placing a higher priority on market diversity may prefer their top-level structure to be broken down geographically, with product management conducted locally. Essentially the decision will depend on whether the international marketing strategy is one of:

- **Globalisation** (or standardisation): a company operating in international markets seeks to provide essentially the same offering and branding worldwide, *or*
- **Adaptation**: the company seeks to change its product and marketing mix to suit local needs and conditions. Johnson, Scholes & Whittington (2005) refer to this as a 'multi-domestic' strategy.

Very large and complex companies may be organised as a **hierarchy**: a less hierarchical, more organic structure with significant local control.

- Some **headquarters functions** are geographically dispersed. For example, R & D might be in the UK, marketing in the US. Or certain products may be made in one country and others elsewhere, according to the technology and materials available most competitively.
- **Subsidiary/divisional managers** have a strategic role for the corporation as a whole (eg through bargaining and coalition-forming).
- **Co-ordination** is achieved through corporate culture and shared values, rather than structural control mechanisms.
- **Alliances** can be formed with other strategic business units and other firms, perhaps in joint ventures or consortia.

ASSIGNMENT TIP

application

This is a vast topic, and may not apply directly to your work organisation for the purposes of assignment. If yourassignment focus is on an international or multi-national organisation, you can use the principles of organisation structure already discussed to evaluate your organisation structure. You might also widen your reading in appropriate areas.

6 Organisational culture

6.1 The informal organisation

An **informal organisation** exists side by side with the formal one. When people work together, they establish social relationships and customary ways of doing things. Unlike the formal organisation, the informal organisation is loosely structured, flexible and spontaneous. It embraces such mechanisms as:

- Social relationships and groupings (eg cliques) within – or across – formal structures.
- The 'grapevine', 'bush telegraph', or informal communication which by-passes the formal reporting channels and routes.
- Behavioural norms and ways of doing things, both social and work-related, which may circumvent formal procedures and systems (for good or ill). New members must 'learn the ropes' and get used to 'the way we do things here'.
- Power/influence structures, irrespective of organisational authority: informal leaders are those who are trusted and looked to for advice.

The informal organisation can offer some significant benefits for management.

- **Employee commitment**. The meeting of employees' social needs may contribute to morale and job satisfaction, with benefits in reduced absenteeism and labour turnover.
- **Knowledge sharing.** The availability of information through informal networks can give employees a wider perspective on their role in the task and the organisation, potentially stimulating 'big picture' problem-solving, cross-boundary co-operation and innovation.
- **Speed.** Informal networks and methods may sometimes be more efficient in achieving organisational goals, where the formal organisation has rigid procedures or lengthy communication channels, enabling decisions to be taken and implemented more rapidly.
- **Responsiveness**. The directness, information-richness and flexibility of the informal organisation may be particularly helpful in conditions of rapid environmental change, facilitating both the mechanisms and culture of anti-bureaucratic responsiveness.
- **Co-operation**. The formation and strengthening of interpersonal networks can facilitate teamworking and co-ordination across organisational boundaries. It may reduce organisational politics – or utilise it positively by mobilising effective decision-making coalitions and by-passing communication blocks.

Each of the positive attributes of informal organisation could as easily be detrimental if the power of the informal organisation is directed towards goals unrelated to, or at odds with, those of the formal organisation.

- Social groupings may act collectively against organisational interests, strengthened by collective power and information networks. Even if they are aligned with organisational goals, group/network maintenance may take a lot of time and energy away from tasks.
- The grapevine is notoriously inaccurate and can carry morale-damaging rumours.
- The informal organisation can become too important in fulfilling employees' needs: individuals can suffer acutely when excluded from cliques and networks.
- Informal work practices may 'cut corners', violating safety or quality assurance measures.

Managers can **minimise problems** by:

- Meeting employees' **needs** as far as possible via the *formal* organisation: providing information, encouragement, social interaction and so on.
- Harnessing the **dynamics** of the informal organisation – for example by using informal leaders to secure employee commitment to goals or changes.
- **Involving themselves** in the informal structure, so that they support information sharing, the breaking down of unhelpful rules and so on.

6.2 Organisation culture

KEY CONCEPT

Organisation culture may be defined as:

- *'The collection of traditions, values, policies, beliefs and attitudes that constitute a pervasive context for everything we do and think in an organisation'* (Mullins, 1999)
- *'A pattern of beliefs and expectations shared by the organisation's members, and which produce norms which powerfully shape the behaviour of individuals and groups in the organisation'* (Schwartz & Davies, 1981)
- *'The way we do things around here'* (Schein, 1985)

Trompenaars (1993) suggested that there are different levels at which culture can be understood.

- The **observable**, expressed or 'explicit' elements of culture include:
  - **Behaviour**: norms of personal and interpersonal behaviour; customs and rules about behaviours that are 'acceptable' or 'unacceptable'.
  - **Artefacts**: concrete expressions such as art and literature, architecture and interior design (eg of office premises), dress codes, symbols and 'heroes' or role models.
  - **Rituals**: patterns of collective behaviour which have traditional or symbolic value, such as greeting styles, business formalities, social courtesies and ceremonies.
- Beneath these observable phenomena lie **values and beliefs** which give the behaviours, artefacts and rituals their special meaning and significance. For example, the design of office space (artefact) may imply status and honour, or reflect the importance of privacy, or reflect spiritual beliefs (as in feng shui) within a culture: it 'means' more than the observable features. Values and beliefs may be overtly expressed in sayings, mottos and slogans.
- Beneath values and beliefs lie **assumptions**: foundational ideas that are no longer consciously recognised or questioned by the culture, but which 'programme' its ways of thinking and behaving. Examples include the importance of the individual in many Western cultures: this is taken for granted in designing HR (human resources) policies, for example.

Cultural assumptions, values and beliefs influence the behaviour of individuals, groups and organisations. They create a shared 'style' of operating within a given culture.

Strategy gurus Johnson, Scholes & Whittington (2005) introduce the concept of the **cultural web**, as a way of representing 'the taken-for-granted assumptions, or paradigm, of an organisation, and the behavioural manifestations of organisational and culture'. The elements of the web, which can be used as a framework to analyse organisational culture in a wide range of settings, are:

- Stories
- Symbols
- Power structures
- Organisational structures
- Control systems
- Rituals and routines

The way in which these elements interact and complement one another form the paradigm of an organisation.

6.2.1 What shapes organisation culture?

Handy (1995) noted that 'Organisations are as different and varied as nations and societies of the world. They have differing cultures... affected by events of the past and climate of the present, by the technology of the type of work, by their aims and type of people who work in them'.

Influences on organisational culture include:

- The organisation's **founder** or strong leader (eg a Henry Ford or Richard Branson). A strong set of values and assumptions is set up by such individuals, and these have their own momentum: an organisation might find it hard to shake off its original culture.
- The organisation's **history**. Culture reflects the era when the organisation was founded, and also the shared history of successes and failures, changes, great leaders and so on. (Think about the traditions built up in a long-established company such as Marks & Spencer, for example.)
- **Leadership and management style**. An organisation with a strong culture recruits and develops managers who naturally conform to – and perpetuate – it. Intentional leadership can, however, shape and change the culture.
- The **organisation's environment**. Nations, regions, occupations and business types have their own distinctive cultures, and these will affect the organisation's style.

6.2.2 Value of a strong positive culture

In their influential book *In Search of Excellence*, Peters & Waterman (1981) found that a defining feature of excellent (responsive and innovative) companies was their use of cultural values to guide business processes and motivate employees.

Deal & Kennedy (1982) likewise argued that cultural strength is a powerful tool for shaping the behaviour and success of an organisation. Not all organisation cultures are 'strong' – but those that *are* contribute to improved business performance. This school of thought defines 'strong' cultures as those in which key values are widely shared and intensely held, and in which employees allow themselves to be guided by them. In other words, as summarised by Huczynski and Buchanan (op cit): 'Strength refers to the degree to which employees share a commitment to a range of goals and values espoused by management, and have a high level of motivation to achieve them.'

It is argued that strong culture can improve business performance in various ways.

- Strong cultural norms can replace rules, guidelines and close supervision, focusing employees' attention on values such as quality and customer service, and empowering them to make more flexible decisions in pursuit of those values.
- Strong culture can increase employee loyalty and commitment. People need both to feel part of something meaningful and to 'shine' as stars in their own right: strong culture can satisfy both needs, by emphasising the 'family' nature of the enterprise, by building myths to reinforce the 'heroic' nature of the enterprise and by using value-laden symbols as rewards and incentives.
- Cultural values can be used to drive organisational change, on the basis that if values change, behaviour will follow.

6.2.3 How do you change a culture?

Cultures which are negative, unsuited to changing requirements or otherwise failing or dysfunctional can be changed. The key tools of cultural change include the following.

- Consistent **expression and modelling** of the new values by management (from the top down), leaders and influencers (who may need to be co-opted to the initiative by those in authority).
- Changing **underlying values and beliefs**, through communication, education and involvement of employees in discussing the need for new ideas and behaviours: spreading new values and beliefs and encouraging employees to 'own' them (through incentives, co-opting people to teach others and so on); and reinforcing the change (through implementation, recognition and rewards).
- Use of **human resource management mechanisms** to reinforce the changes: making the new values and behaviours criteria for recruitment and selection, appraisal and reward; including them in competency profiles and learning needs assessments for training and development planning; and so on. (These mechanisms are important because the organisation may need to bring in new people who will 'fit' the new culture – and squeeze out those who don't 'fit'.)

Learning objective review

Learning objectives	Covered
1 Evaluate the importance of organisational structures in delivering marketing value, focus and creativity	☑ Definition of organisation structure ☑ Elements or organisation structure: authority structures, job roles and relationships ☑ Elements or organisation structure: Mintzberg's structural components applied to different organisation types ☑ How to use organisation charts
2 Recommend how a marketing function should be structured to deliver competitive advantage, marketing and organisational success	☑ How to evaluate organisation structures, and how structural decisions contribute to marketing value, focus and creativity ☑ Description and evaluation of various departmental structures for marketing
3 Evaluate a range of structural forms at the departmental, business unit and corporate level	☑ Description and evaluation of various departmental structures: functional structure; product/market structure; brand structure; territory structure ☑ Description and evaluation of various flexible and adaptive structures: matrix structure, horizontal structure, flexible working models ☑ Description and evaluation of various mechanisms for encouraging cross-functional (horizontal) co-ordination ☑ Description and evaluation of various options for international and multi-national organisation structure
4 Appreciate the impact of organisational culture on marketing performance	☑ Elements of organisational culture: the cultural web ☑ Benefits of a strong positive culture ☑ How to change a dysfunctional culture

Quick quiz

1. Organisational structure refers to what?
2. What are the components of Mintzberg's organisational structure?
3. ICT has enabled organisations to outsource and decentralise. What else has been possible?
4. Matrix structures offer more flexibility. True or false?
5. What are the three labour forces represented in the Shamrock organisation?
6. What is represented by the cultural web?

Activity debriefs

1 This will depend on your own organisation.

2 Imagine an international food producer who specialises in both branded and own label chilled ready meals. It may be more appropriate for the product/brand structure or territorial structure to be adopted, so that the organisation has different territory groups each with their own branded and own label departments to deal with their respective markets.

3 This will depend on the context of your own organisation.

Quiz answers

1 Ways to divide labour into distinct co-ordinated tasks.

2 Operating core, technostructure, support staff, strategic apex, middle line and operating core.

3 Centralise shared functions, create virtual teams, delayer and flatten.

4 True.

5 Professional core, flexible labour force, contractual fringe.

6 The taken for granted assumptions or paradigms of an organisation, and how they are manifest in an organisation's culture.

References

Boddy, D. (2005) Management: An Introduction, (3rd edition), FT Prentice Hall, Harlow.

Bridges, W. (1994) Jobshift: How to prosper in a workplace without jobs, Allen & Unwin, London.

Burns, T. & Stalker, G.M. (1961) The Management of Innovation, Tavistock, London.

Deal, T.E. & Kennedy, A.A. (1982) Organisation Cultures: The Rites and Rituals of Organisation Life, MA Addison-Wesley, Reading.

Drucker, P (1955) The Practice of Management, Heinemann, London.

Egan, J (2004) Relationship Marketing: Exploring Relational Strategies in Marketing, (2nd edition), Pearson Education, Harlow.

French, J. & Raven, B. (1958) 'The bases of social power' in Studies in Social Power, Cartright D (ed). Institute for Social Research, Ann Arbor, MI.

George, W.R. & Grönroos, C. (1989) 'Developing customer-conscious employees at every level – internal marketing' in Handbook of Services Marketing, Congram & Friedman (eds). AMACOM, New York.

Handy, C. (1989) The Age of Unreason, Penguin, Harmondsworth.

Handy, C. (1995) Gods of Management: The Changing Work of Organisations, Random House Business, London.

Huczynski, A. & Buchanan, D. (2001) Organizational Behaviour: An Introductory Text, (4th edition), FT Prentice Hall, Harlow.

Jobber, D. (2007) Principles and Practice of Marketing, (5th edition), McGraw Hill Education, Maidenhead.

Johnson, G. Scholes K. & Whittington R. (2005) Exploring Corporate Strategy: Text and Cases, (7th edition), Pearson Education, Harlow.

Kotler, P. (2002) Marketing Management, (11th edition), US Imports and PHIPES.

Kotler, P. Armstrong, G. Meggs, D. Bradbury, E. & Grech, J. (1999) Marketing: An Introduction, Prentice Hall, Sydney.

Lancaster, G. & Withey, F. (2005) Marketing Fundamentals, Butterworth-Heinemann, Oxford.

Milkovitch, G.T. & Boudreau, J.W. (1996) Human Resource Management, (8th edition), McGraw Hill, New York.

Mintzberg, H. (1983) Structure in Fives: Designing Effective Organisations, Prentice Hall, New Jersey.

Mullins, L. (1999) Management & Organisation Behaviour, (5th edition), FT Prentice Hall, Harlow, Essex.

Peck, H.L. Payne, A. Christopher, M. & Clark, M. (2004) Relationship Marketing: Strategy and Implementation, Elsevier Butterworth-Heinemann, Oxford.

Pedler, M. Burgoyne, J. & Boydell, T. (1991) The Learning Company, McGraw Hill, Maidenhead.

Peters, T.J. (1994) Liberation Management, Pan, New York.

Peters, T.J. & Waterman, R.H. (1981) In Search of Excellence, Harper Collins, New York.

Schein, E.H. (1985) Organisational Culture and Leadership, Jossey-Bass, San Francisco.

Schwartz, H. & Davies, S.M. (1981) 'Matching Corporate Culture and Business Strategy' in Organisational Dynamics, Vol. 9, Pp30 - 48

Trompenaars, F. (1993) Riding the Waves of Culture. Nicholas Brealey, London.

Welch, J. (2005) Winning. Harper Business, New York.

Chapter 2
Quality in marketing

Topic list

1 Quality concepts
2 Quality systems and processes
3 Total Quality Management
4 Quality management standards
5 Quality improvement approaches
6 Service quality
7 Quality and relationship marketing

Introduction

This chapter explores the concept of 'quality', and its application to marketing.

This may seem like an odd topic to include in this syllabus, but quality is an important focus for any business – particularly a marketing-oriented one which seeks to satisfy (and if possible, delight) customers with high performance and service. Quality and service promises may also be a key selling point for marketing communications, so marketers have a strong interest in ensuring that the organisation's processes are capable of living up to such promises on a consistent basis. 'Quality management systems' are *not* just the province of operations managers!

We start in section 1 by outlining some key quality concepts, including various definitions of quality, and the dimensions or aspects of quality.

In section 2, we put forward the business case for quality: the reasons why it is important for organisations to build and maintain quality, and systems for pursuing and controlling quality. We then introduce some of the main quality strategies which an organisation might adopt, highlighting the distinction between quality control (or defect detection) and quality assurance (or defect prevention). In section 3, we focus on the popular – but radical – concept of Total Quality Management: a strategy which views quality as a total' way of life' for an organisation, and its operational implications.

In section 4, we look at a range of quality management standards and awards specified in the syllabus, designed to support organisations in assessing and improving their quality systems. In section 5, we go on to outline a range of approaches to quality improvement also raised by the syllabus, from statistical methods like Six Sigma to more universal problem-solving approaches such as the Plan-Do-Check-Act cycle and benchmarking.

Although not explicitly mentioned in the syllabus, measuring and maintaining the quality of *services* (and customer service) presents particular challenges, so we explore these in some detail in section 6.

Finally, we draw together some of the marketing implications of the topic by examining the importance of quality in relationship marketing, and the need to integrate quality, service and marketing in order to support customer loyalty.

Syllabus linked learning objectives

By the end of the chapter you will be able to:

	Learning objectives	Syllabus link
1	Evaluate and assess the relevance of key quality concepts	1.2
2	Assess what is required to develop effective and efficient quality systems and processes to support compliance	1.2
2	Outline and evaluate a range of quality management standards	1.2
4	Outline and evaluate a range of quality improvement approaches and processes	1.2
5	Appreciate the particular demands of managing service quality	1.2
6	Appreciate the role of quality in relationship marketing	1.2

1 Quality concepts

Product and service quality are critical success factors for marketing-oriented businesses, because they determine **customer satisfaction** – the ultimate source of competitive survival and advantage. The ability of a company to **differentiate** its products and services in the marketplace substantially rests on the quality of its total offering: its ability consistently not just to satisfy, but to delight – and hence retain, and potentially gain the loyalty of – its customers. So what is 'quality'? What makes a 'quality product' or offering?

1.1 Defining quality

KEY CONCEPT

Quality is a measure of the features and characteristics of a product or service which affects their ability to meet stated or implied needs.

Definitions of quality have focused on dimensions such as:

- **Quality of design:** the potential customer satisfactions built into a product
- **Fitness for use or fitness for purpose**: that is, the extent to which a product does what it is intended and expected to do, or meets the customer's needs. (This is sometimes called the 'user-based' approach to quality.)
- **Conformance to requirement** (or **meeting specification**): that is, the product complies with the features, attributes, performance and other aspects set out as a requirement in the product specification. (This is the 'product-based' approach.)
- **Acceptable quality and value for money**: customers may be willing to sacrifice some performance and features for a lower price, as long as fitness for use is still acceptable. (This is the 'value-based' approach.)

1.2 Dimensions of quality

Garvin (1987) identifies eight generic dimensions of product quality.

- **Performance**: the operating characteristics of the product
- **Features**: value-adding characteristics and service elements (eg warranties, after-sales service)
- **Reliability**: the ability of the product to perform consistently over time
- **Durability**: the length of time a product will last without deterioration
- **Conformance**: whether agreed specifications and standards are met
- **Serviceability**: the ease and availability of service support
- **Aesthetics**: customer perceptions of how pleasing the product looks, sounds, tastes etc
- **Perceived quality**: the subjective expectations and perceptions developed by customers, as a result of marketing, brand identity, price and so on.

Essentially and inevitably, however, quality means different things to different operations. For example, think what it might mean for a toy manufacturer, a medical practice and a professional body like the CIM.

It is also important to note that customers may perceive quality in different ways – and that quality must always be understood from the customer's perspective! Marketers need to identify 'quality gaps': shortfalls between what customers expect or perceive, and what the organisation provides.

Slack et al (2004) suggest that there may be a gap between the customer's specification and the organisation's specification; between the concept and the specification; between quality specification and actual quality; or between actual quality and the quality promised to the customer. Different strategies may be necessary to reduce or eliminate different gaps, embracing product specification and development, materials and production quality – *and* marketing.

1.3 The views of some quality 'gurus'

A number of writers have been influential on quality thinking in recent decades.

- **Juran** (1988) argued that quality should not be seen merely in terms of meeting specification (a measure of conformance from the producer's point of view), but should focus on the needs of internal and external **customers**. He advocated a **user-based** approach, focused on fitness for use or fitness for purpose. Juran emphasised the importance of management's role in quality improvement and the need to motivate the work force and involve them in quality improvement initiatives. He also emphasised that quality management should aim to ensure that the way in which work is performed (ie systems and processes) facilitated high quality output. Juran believed that 85% of quality problems were the result of **ineffective systems**.
- **Deming** (1986) argued that the only judge of quality is, ultimately, the customer**.** Quality means finding out what the customer needs, wants and values – and providing it, with the aim of meeting customer expectations (customer satisfaction) or going further and exceeding customer expectations (customer delight). Deming is credited with developing the Total Quality Management approach (discussed in section 3): emphasis shifted to quality as a **managerial philosophy** and underlying organisation-wide systems. Deming also took the view that as process variability (the amount of unpredictability in a process) decreases, quality and productivity increase: quality can therefore be improved by reducing process variability. His 'Fourteen points for quality improvement' (discussed in section 5) stressed the need for statistical control methods, participation, education, openness and improvement.
- **Ishikawa** (1991) stressed the importance of people and participation in the process of solving quality problems. He devised the idea of **quality circles** to achieve participation and overcome resistance to quality control, which workers tend to dislike because of its emphasis on statistics and rigid standards. He also introduced the use of 'fishbone' diagrams to diagnose quality problems.
- **Taguchi** (1986) argued that quality issues begin at the product design stage, and promoted the idea of team meetings between managers and workers to discuss product design. He also suggested that it was important for managers to understand the true costs of poor quality, to the organisation and to society, including factors such as warranty costs, customer complaints and the loss of customer goodwill.
- **Crosby** (1979) likewise focused on the costs of quality, the need for worker participation and the need to motivate individuals to improve quality. His 'absolutes of quality management' were:
  - Quality as conformance to requirements
  - Effort direct at prevention rather than detection of defects
  - Zero defects in production
  - Systematic measurement of the cost or price of non-conformance
  - No such thing as a 'quality problem'.

1.4 Costs of quality

The cost of quality is defined (BS 6143) as: *'The cost of ensuring and assuring quality, as well as the loss incurred when quality is not achieved'.* It is important for management to assess the true costs of quality, in order to make a compelling case for quality management and improvement.

The **costs of ensuring and assuring quality** include:

- **Prevention costs**: costs incurred prior to producing the product or delivering the service – to prevent or reduce defects or failures produced by the process.

  Examples include: the time and cost of building quality into the product/service design, implementing quality circles, preparing detailed specifications, training staff, maintaining equipment, setting up processes and systems, designing or purchasing prevention devices (eg fail-safe features) and so on.
- **Appraisal costs**: costs incurred *after* the product has been made or service delivered, to evaluate its conformance to quality requirements or agreed service levels.

Examples include: inspection and testing costs, supplier vetting and monitoring, designing and using customer feedback forms and so on.

Losses incurred when quality is not achieved include:

- **Internal failure costs**: costs arising from quality failure, where the problems is identified *before* the product or service reaches the customer.

  Examples include: costs of materials scrapped due to obsolescence or damage; cost of materials and components lost during production/delivery; cost of output rejected during inspection; cost of re-working faulty output; losses due to having to sell faulty output at lower prices; and so on.

- **External failure costs**: costs arising form quality failure discovered *after* the product/services has been delivered to the customer.

  Examples include: cost of product liability and warranty claims; cost of repairing or replacing products returned by customers; other costs of complaint adjustment (eg cost of the customer complaints unit); loss of customer loyalty and future sales; reputational damage arising from word-of-mouth about poor quality or product recalls (especially on safety grounds); and so on.

The costs and risks incurred as a result of poor quality are generally perceived to be higher than the costs of securing quality, and this is the rationale behind quality management systems and approaches.

2 Quality systems and processes

2.1 Why is it important to maintain quality?

The business case for quality management can be summarised as follows.

- **Cost**: as we mentioned above, the potential costs and risks of quality failure are more extensive, and higher, than the controllable costs of managing quality.
- **Competitive advantage**: quality is a key dimension on which products can be meaningfully differentiated from their competitors. The ability to offer consistently high quality may be a core distinguishing competence for an organisation. At the micro-level, quality comparison is likely to be a key decision factor for a customer choosing between competing products, and quality failures may be sufficient to cause brand switching.
- **Brand positioning**: quality is one of the main dimensions on which a marketing organisation may seek to position a brand in the perception of the market. High quality, premium or luxury brands deliberate engage customers on a brand platform focused on quality attributes. Quality failures may significantly damage the identity and positioning of such brands.
- **Relationship marketing**: quality is a tool of customer acquisition, but the consistent quality of goods and service encounters is also extremely important in customer retention, the building and maintenance of trust, and the engagement of customer loyalty – the main focus of relationship marketing. (We will discuss this aspect in a little more detail in Section 6 of this chapter.) Repeated disappointments (however well managed) will ultimately be fatal to the maintenance of on-going customer relationships – and reduce customer lifetime profitability.
- **Price**: quality is related to customer perceptions of value for money. The market will often bear higher or premium pricing for products and services perceived to be (or marketed as) of high quality.
- **Compliance**: in some areas, quality is an issue of legal compliance. If goods are not of satisfactory quality or are not fit for their purpose, or are actually or potentially unsafe, the supplier may be liable:
  - For breach of contract under the Sale of Goods Act 1979
  - For negligence, or a breach of the common law duty of reasonable care owed by a manufacturer or supplier to a consumer
  - For breach of consumer protection law (eg in the UK, the Consumer Protection Act, Food Safety Act, Enterprise Act 2002 and so on).

- **Reputation management**: quality – and more particularly, safety – failures can be highly damaging to the organisation's corporate reputation and standing, if goods are exposed as 'shoddy' or are forced to be recalled for safety reasons. (You might think of examples such as the mass recall of Mattel toys manufactured in China, which were found to include toxic lead paint.)
- **Culture and morale:** a culture built on values such as customer satisfaction, excellence and quality (whether 'premium/prestige' or 'value for money') is more compelling and positive than a culture of indifference, customer exploitation and 'corner cutting'. Pride in the organisation and brand can be a strong source of employee morale and team spirit.
- **Employee satisfaction and loyalty**: employee satisfaction and loyalty are linked to product and service quality in complex ways. The **loyalty-based cycle of growth** (Reichheld, 1996) suggests that superior quality and service creates satisfied and loyal customers – but, at the same time:
  - Satisfied and loyal customers generate revenue which can be invested in employees (eg through superior rewards)
  - Consistent delivery of superior value to customers gives employees pride and satisfaction in their work (and avoids the stress and frustration of complaint handling etc).

  A simplified version of this virtuous cycle can be depicted as follows.

Reichheld's loyalty-based cycle of growth (simplified)

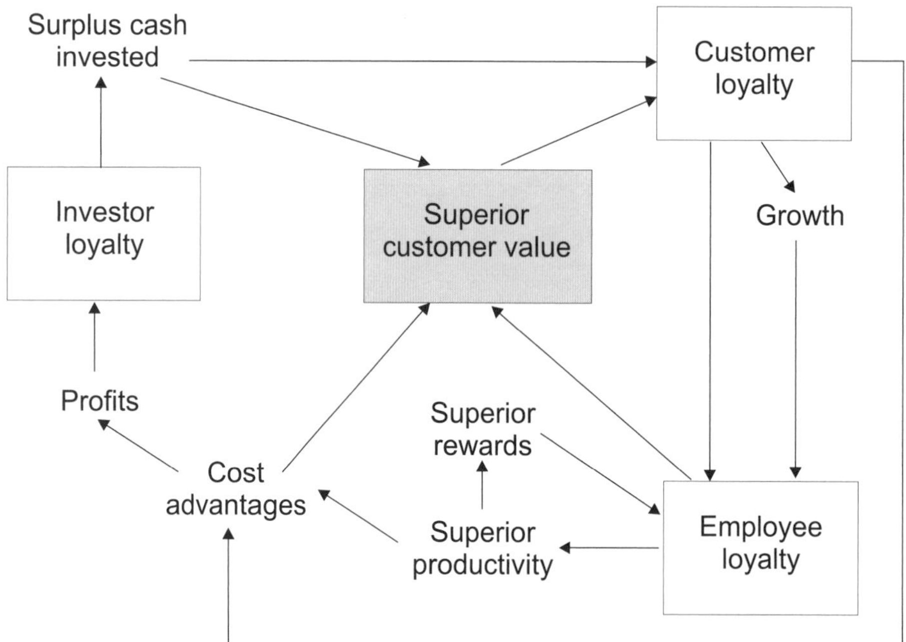

2.2 Quality management strategies

KEY CONCEPT

concept

Quality management is concerned with controlling activities with the aim of ensuring that products or services are fit for their purpose, and meet specifications. Quality management encompasses a variety of approaches, including quality assurance and quality control.

2.2.1 Quality control

KEY CONCEPT

Quality control is based on the concept of **defect detection**: checking and reviewing work that has already been done.

Quality control is the most traditional approach to the management of quality. It embraces a range of techniques and activities to:

- **Establish specifications**, standards and tolerances for work inputs and outputs
- **Monitor or inspect** items at various stages of the supply and production process: pre-despatch inspection by suppliers; inspection by the buyer on receiving delivery (receiving inspection); inspection during manufacturing or assembly processes (floor or process inspection); and inspection on completion of manufacturing or assembly (final inspection or testing)
- **Identify items that are defective** or do not meet specification
- **Scrap or rework items** that do not pass inspection
- **Pass acceptable items** on to the next stage of the process.

Various degrees of inspection 'tolerances' may be specified: 100% inspection may be used on critical features, where zero defects are required, while sampling may be used on less sensitive features.

The inspection-based approach has certain limitations.

- A very large number of items has to be inspected to prevent defective items from reaching customers. Deming (1986) argued that this ties up resources – and does not add value (or indeed 'improve' quality).
- Defect tolerances may be unacceptably high due to budget and schedule pressures (especially with modern supply techniques such as Just In Time supply): defects may well slip through to the customer, and be sufficient to cause dissatisfaction.
- The process identifies and reject outputs which have already incurred significant – wasted – costs (of design, raw materials, processing, overheads and so on):'locking the door after the horse has bolted'. In a service industry, the damage to customer satisfaction may already have been done before or during inspection.

Inspection activity tends to be duplicated at each stage of the process – magnifying the inefficiencies and wastes.

2.2.2 Quality assurance

KEY CONCEPT

concept

Quality assurance is based on the concept of **defect prevention**: focusing on analysing and designing the processes by which a product or service is produced, in order to improve their effectiveness and consistency in producing quality conformance.

Quality assurance is thus a more integrated approach than quality control. It includes a range of activities used within a quality system to 'assure' or give the organisation confidence that items and processes will fulfil quality specifications. Quality assurance systems attempt to identify the potential of a process for producing defective items *before* such items have in fact been produced.

Quality assurance programmes (and resulting certification) may build quality measures and controls into:

- **Product design** to minimise potential design defects and production difficulties
- **Specifications and contracts**, to set tight tolerances for quality variance of materials and services supplied
- The selection, management and development of quality-capable and improvement-seeking **suppliers**, who may be asked to guarantee the quality of goods or services supplied, or to demonstrate their own quality assurance systems.
- The **continuous monitoring** of operating processes, to identify unacceptable variations in output as soon as they occur: **corrective action** is then taken immediately, preventing further defects from the process variance. (This is the basis of systems like Statistical Process Control or SPC, for example.)

In his classic work *Quality is Free,* Crosby (1979) argued that a prudent company makes certain that its products and services are delivered to the customer by a management system that does not condone rework, repair, waste or non-conformance of any sort. These are expensive problems. They must not only be detected and resolved at the earliest moment, they must be prevented from occurring at all.

2.2.3 Quality management as a business philosophy

In recent decades, and following the one-time competitive success of Japanese management techniques, quality management has come to represent not just a managerial function, but a managerial orientation – affecting all areas of the organisation's structures and processes. Tom Peters (1989) describes this as a 'quality revolution', characterised by the adoption of quality as a guiding system or ideology for an organisation's culture and systems – and the integration and involvement of the whole (internal and external) value chain on on-going continuous improvement. Perhaps the key embodiment of this orientation is Total Quality Management (TQM): we will discuss this in section 3 of this chapter.

2.3 Quality management systems (QMS)

KEY CONCEPT

concept

A **Quality Management System** (QMS) can be defined as a set of co-ordinated activities which will direct and control an organisation in order to continually improve the effectiveness and efficiency of its process and performance.

The main thrust of a QMS is defining and managing the **processes** which will result in the production of quality products and services (a quality assurance strategy) – rather than in detecting defective products or services (a quality control strategy).

A fully documented, systematic QMS is designed to ensure that:

- Customers' requirements are met, and they have confidence in the ability of the organisation consistently to deliver products and services which meet their needs and expectations.
- Organisational performance objectives are consistently achieved, through improved process control and reduced wastage, with the efficient use of available resources (materials, human, technology and information).
- Staff competence, training and morale are enhanced, through clear expectations and process requirements.
- Quality gains are maintained once achieved: learning and good practices do not 'slip' for lack of documentation, adoption and consistency.
- We will look at the international standard for measuring and certifying Quality Management Systems in section 4 of this chapter.

3 Total Quality Management (TQM)

KEY CONCEPT

concept

Total Quality Management (TQM) is an orientation to quality in which quality values and aspirations are applied to the management of all resources and relationships within the firm and throughout the value chain, in order to seek continuous improvement and excellence in all aspects of performance.

3.1 Philosophy and values of TQM

Mullins (1999) synthesises various writers' definitions of TQM as expressing: 'a *way of life for an organisation as a whole, committed to total customer satisfaction through a continuous process of improvement, and the contribution and involvement of people*'.

Some of the key principles and values of TQM can be summarised as follows.

- **Get it right first time**: quality should be **designed** into products, services and processes, with the aim of achieving **zero defects**. The traditional approach to quality management argued that there is an optimal level of quality effort which minimises total quality costs: there is a point beyond which spending more on quality yields a benefit that is less than the additional cost incurred. TQM, however, argues that:
  - Failure and poor quality are simply unacceptable: the inevitability of error is not something that an organisation should accept, as a cultural value. The target should be zero defects.
  - Taking into account the 'wider' costs of poor quality – the potential to lose customers, the taking up of managerial time on non-value adding problem-solving, the loss of morale and trust among staff – *no* amount of defects can be considered 'optimal'.
  - Quality can and should be continually improved, and this need not incur high costs or diminishing returns.
- **Quality chains**. The quality chain extends from suppliers through to consumers, via the 'internal supply chain' (supplier and customer units representing the flow of work within the organisation). The work of each link in this chain impacts on the next one, and will eventually affect the quality provided to the consumer. The chain may be broken at any point where people or processes fail to fulfil the quality requirements of their immediate (internal or external) customer. Clear customer relationships and accountabilities (including service level agreements, where required) need to be established throughout the chain.
- **Quality culture and total involvement.** Quality is a 'way of life': a key cultural value in the organisation. Every person within an organisation potentially has an impact on quality, and it is the responsibility of everyone to get quality right. This needs to be consistently and compellingly expressed and modelled by senior management, and supported and reinforced by recruitment, training, team building, appraisal and reward systems.
- **Quality through people.** Commitment, communication, awareness and problem-solving are more important in securing quality than mere systems. Team-based management and empowerment are key elements of TQM. Teams must be empowered and equipped to take action necessary to correct problems, propose and implement improvements, and respond flexibly and fast to customer needs (particularly in service contexts). There must be high-quality, multi-directional communication. Strict control systems (and associated 'blaming') should be replaced by a culture of learning, in which people are not afraid to try new things or take the initiative to make small improvements.
- **Process alignment**. Business processes should be deliberately designed and modified so that every activity is geared to the same end: meeting the customer's wants and needs. Where this is not the case, there may be the need for radical change programmes such as Business Process Re-engineering (BPR).

- **Quality management**. All processes and operations are monitored and controlled according to clear, specific, measurable performance criteria. Attention is focused on getting the process right – and only secondarily on outputs. Refusal to focus on short-term effects ensures a more proactive commitment to long-term improvement. Quality systems should be thoroughly documented in:
  - A company quality manual, summarising the quality management policy and system
  - A procedures manual setting out the functions, structures and responsibilities for quality in each department
  - Detailed work instructions and specifications for how work should be carried out in order to achieve the desired quality standards. These will have to be continually updated as improvements and adjustments are made.
- **Continuous improvement**. Quality is not a 'one-off' exercise. By seeking to improve continually, organisations remain sensitive to new opportunities and approaches, and encourage learning and flexibility at all levels. In contrast to radical, 'discontinuous' or 'blank slate' change approaches such as BPR, continuous improvement may operate by small-step or incremental changes. Such evolutionary change is less traumatic, less risky, less costly, and can be driven from the bottom up by empowered employees.

3.2 Continuous improvement

Quality management involves the on-going and continual examination and improvement of existing processes: 'getting it more right, next time'. This process is sometimes referred by its Japanese name of 'kaizen': 'a Japanese concept of a total quality approach based on continual evolutionary change with considerable responsibility given to employees within certain fixed boundaries' (Mullins, 1999).

Kaizen looks for uninterrupted, ongoing incremental change: there is always room for improvement and continuously trying to become better, for example through:

- Elimination of wastes (non value-adding activities)
- Immediately accessible improvements to equipment, materials or team behaviour.

It is essentially a **cyclical approach to change**, because it incorporates reflection or evaluation for future learning and improvement. It is also essentially a **bottom-up or empowerment-based** approach to quality, because it utilises the feedback, ideas and initiatives of those closet to quality issues: operational staff and customers.

A basic cyclical approach to kaizen involves:

- Identifying potential areas for improvement, by monitoring performance and gathering feedback from employees and other stakeholders
- Analysing the data to identify possible causes of performance shortfalls common factors or 'hidden messages' in the results
- Plan and implement action to improve performance in the identified area
- Assess the effects of the action, and identify any further problems (in a continuous cycle).

3.3 Quality circles

Japanese quality guru Ishikawa (1991) stressed the importance of people and participation in the process of solving quality problems. He devised the idea of **quality circles** to achieve participation, harness the expertise and commitment of staff, share best practice, and overcome resistance to quality management.

KEY CONCEPT

concept

A **quality circle** is a team of workers from different levels and functions of an organisation which meets regularly to discuss issues relating to quality, and to recommend improvements.

A quality circle typically consists of a **voluntary-participation group** of about eight employees, from different functions, which meets regularly (during working hours) to discuss problems of **quality and quality control** in their areas of work, and to suggest quality improvements. The circle is facilitated by a leader who directs the discussion and helps to orient and develop members of the circle (if required) in quality management and problem-solving techniques.

Management should not impose agendas on the meetings, in order to permit openness about problems and conflicts, and to encourage thinking 'outside the box'. Feedback on suggestions offered and problems raised should, however, be swift and constructive, in order to demonstrate that the quality circle is taken seriously as a participation and quality tool.

3.3.1 Benefits of quality circles

In practice, quality circles may or may not have significant responsibility for making, implementing or monitoring the progress of their recommendations. Even as discussion groups, however, they may have significant benefits, especially if members return to their departments as 'ambassadors' for quality, having been involved in the circle: this may be seen as a tool of internal marketing.

Benefits claimed for quality circles include:

- Greater **motivation**, satisfaction and commitment of employees, through involvement in key organisational values and processes
- Improved **productivity and quality** of output, through involving operational staff, generating new ideas and sharing best practice
- More multi-directional **communication** and the establishment of informal (but work-focused) information-sharing networks
- **Development** of employees in team working, project management and problem-solving skills
- Greater awareness of quality and service issues, and customer focus, supporting a 'culture of quality'.

Drawbacks may include: – **wasted time** and cost (if the meetings do not result in applied improvements) – **perceived powerlessness** causing resentment and resistance to other attempts at participation – possible **empire building** by the quality circle – the risk that business requirements (eg cost control) may not be fully understood by the group in making recommendations.

However, quality circles are generally considered constructive, and have expanded to include quality groups drawn from a wider range of stakeholders in the value network (eg including suppliers, distributors and customers) – and best practice sharing groups or networks, which may include a wide range of organisations with a common interest in quality issues.

3.4 Limitations and criticisms of TQM

TQM is susceptible to various **adverse perceptions**.

- In practice, TQM initiatives may not be introduced or implemented effectively, and the job is 'botched' by management
- After obtaining short-term benefits from introducing TQM, the benefits wear off over time, due to 'quality disillusionment'
- The introductory phase may be resisted as a temporary 'management fad'
- The implementation phase may give rise to the perception that TQM is driven and owned by a particular group, rather than a total involvement concept (unless staff can be involved in implementation from the vision stage).

TQM programmes can also suffer from:

- A **'blitz' approach** to implementation: introducing TQM rapidly, with mass education and communication programmes. This can lead to problems of not knowing what to do or what to do next, and can disrupt and damage business continuity. (A more gradual approach, gaining stakeholder buy-in and collaboration at each stage, and integrating progressive measures into strategic and functional plans may be easier to implement.)

- **Time, cost and difficulty** of introducing, implementing and imbedding the approach (particularly in large, bureaucratic organisations). The impact of TQM cannot be underestimated, as it represents a major strategic and cultural change.
- A lack of long-term, cohesive and visionary **top-management commitment**
- A failure to understand the full range of **quality issues and quality costs** that should be embraced by quality management systems
- **Vested interests and organisation politics**, resisting change attempts. Individuals need to understand the TQM process, its purpose and why it is important for the organisation. They also need to be empowered – and this may cause resistance from managers who fear a loss of control.
- Embedded **cultural cynicism** about quality and fulfilling customer needs: TQM is difficult to do if the organisation merely wants to pay 'lip service' to the concept.

ACTIVITY 1

Application/evaluation

The UK Government Department for Trade and Enterprise promotes the adoption of a TQM approach by British companies. To compete successfully, British companies must start by eliminating the following weaknesses.

1 Doing what has always been done.
2 Not understanding competitive positioning.
3 Compartmentalising of functions.
4 Trying to control people through systems.
5 Confusing quality with grade, or grade with quality.
6 Having an acceptable quality level (AQL).
7 Fire fighting is regarded as macho.
8 The 'not my problem' syndrome.

Explain each of these weaknesses and briefly state how a TQM approach would attempt to address each one.

4 Quality management standards

4.1 EFQM

The European Foundation for Quality Management's *Excellence Model ®* - promoted in the UK as Business Excellence by the British Quality Foundation (BQF) – is a total quality model, used as a world-class benchmark for quality management.

As a conceptual framework, the Excellence Model recognises that processes are the means by which an organisation harnesses the talents of its people to produce results.

Leadership drives **policy and strategy**, **people**, **partnerships and resources** – which in turn shape **processes** – which lead to excellence in **key performance results** (**people**, **customer** and **society**). The model attaches criteria and weightings to each of these nine elements, as the basis of organisational self-assessments and third-party awards. The criteria are summarised as follows.

<table>
<tr><th>ENABLER CRITERIA</th><th>What is the approach in this area and is it appropriate?
Does the approach support the organisation's overall aims?
How widely used is the approach?
How is the approach reviewed?
What improvements are undertaken following review?</th></tr>
<tr><td>Leadership
How the behaviour and actions of leaders support a culture of excellence</td><td>• Leaders develop the mission, vision and values and are role models of a culture of excellence
• Leaders are personally involved in ensuring the organisation's management system is developed, implemented and continuously improved
• Leaders are involved with customers, partners and representatives of society (stakeholders)
• Leaders motivate, support and recognise the organisation's people</td></tr>
<tr><td>Policy and strategy
How effectively these are formulated and deployed into plans and action</td><td>• Policy and strategy are based on the present and future needs and expectations of stakeholders
• Policy and strategy are based on information from performance measurement, research, learning and creativity related activities
• Policy and strategy area developed, reviewed and updated
• Policy and strategy are deployed through a framework of key processes
• Policy and strategy are communicated and implemented</td></tr>
<tr><td>People
How the organisation develops and realises the potential of its human resources</td><td>• People resources are planned, managed and improved
• People's knowledge and competencies are identified, developed and sustained
• People are involved and empowered
• People and the organisation have a dialogue
• People are rewarded, recognised and cared for</td></tr>
<tr><td>Partnerships and resources
How effectively and efficiently the organisation manages its resources</td><td>• External partnerships are managed
• Finances are managed
• Buildings, equipment and materials are managed
• Technology is managed
• Information and knowledge are managed</td></tr>
<tr><td>Processes
How the organisation manages and improves its processes</td><td>• Processes are systematically designed and managed
• Processes are improved, as needed, using innovation in order to fully satisfy and generate increasing value for customers and other stakeholders
• Products and services are designed and developed based on customer needs and expectations
• Products and services are produced, delivered and serviced
• Customer relationships are managed and enhanced</td></tr>
</table>

RESULTS CRITERIA	What has the performance been over a period of time? How does performance compare against internal targets and other organisations? Were the results caused by the approaches described in the enabler criteria? To what extent to the measures cover the range of the organisation's or business area's activities?
Customer results	• Perception measures: what is the customers' perception of the organisation? • Performance indicators: how good are the drivers of (key factors in bringing about) customer satisfaction?
People results	• Perception measures: what are employees' perceptions of the organisation? • Performance indicators: how good are the drivers of employee satisfaction?
Society results	• Perception measures: how does society and the local community perceive the organisation • Performance indicators: what results have been achieved relating to community and environmental concerns?
Key performance results	• What is the organisation achieving in relation to its planned performance?

Organisations can carry out self-assessments against the criteria using a range of methods: discussion groups and workshops; surveys, questionnaires and interviews of key stakeholders; activity or process audits and so on. Such an assessment may be conducted as preparation for a major improvement programme (possibly together with a 'cost of quality' measurement exercise) and/or periodically to steer and monitor improvement progress.

In addition, an organisation may apply for a quality award: examples include the Deming Prize, the EFQM Quality Award (based on the Excellence model), the UK Business Excellence Award and regional Excellence Awards. This is a highly effective way of gaining detailed feedback and benchmarking your performance against best practice and other organisations, including competitors: detailed feedback is given to applicants. However, the organisation opens itself to a rigorous, onerous and lengthy assessment process, involving submissions and site visits.

British Telecommunications (BT) is a founding member of the European Foundation for Quality Management (EFQM) and the British Quality Foundation (BQF). It is committed to the principles of Total Quality, has been the winner of many excellence awards and is certified under ISO 9001 (Quality Management Systems) and ISO 14001 (Environmental Management Systems).

For more information, and to access some useful tools: check out http://www.bt.com/quality

ACTIVITY 2

application/evaluation

Make a very general informal assessment of your work organisation using some of the criteria listed in the EFQM table above.

- What immediate areas for improvement (if any) might you highlight for later follow-up?
- What areas strike you as most relevant to, or dependent upon, marketing input and activity?

4.2 ISO 9001

ISO 9000 was launched in 1987 and comprises a group of quality management standards laid down by the International Organisation for Standardisation (ISO): a worldwide federation of national standards bodies. ISO 9000 standards are 'built around business processes, with a strong emphasis on improvement and focus on meeting the needs of customers': they are intended to be generic and adaptable to all kinds of organisations. The ISO series includes:

- **ISO 9000 Quality Management Systems: Fundamentals and vocabulary**
- **ISO 9001 Quality Management Systems: Requirements**
- **ISO 9004 Guidelines for Performance Improvements**

Organisations may use the standards framework as a benchmark for planning and improving their own quality management systems, or they may seek certification to demonstrate compliance to customers and clients.

The standard identifies quality management systems as comprising four processes. Note the importance of the customer in the model. Customer requirements determine product/service design and production, and monitoring of customer satisfaction (by the marketing function) is key to evaluate and validate whether customer requirements have been met.

The ISO 9001 conceptual map
Source: www.businessballs.com/dtiresources/quality_management_systems_QMS

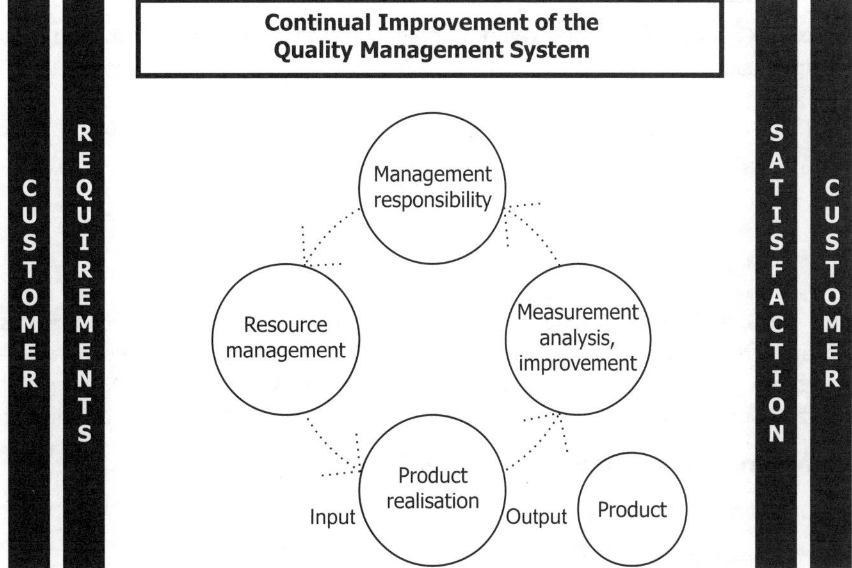

- **Management responsibility** includes aspects such as: management commitment, customer focus, quality policy-setting, planning, responsibility/accountability, communication, and management review
- **Resource management** includes aspects such as: provision of resources, human resources, infrastructure and work environment to support quality
- **Product realisation** includes aspects such as: customer research, product design and/or development, purchasing, production and service operations, and control of measuring and monitoring devices
- **Measurement, analysis and improvement** includes aspects such as: monitoring and measurement of performance, control of non-conforming product, analysis of data, and improvement planning.

System **audits** are carried out to ensure that actual methods are adhering to the documented procedures, and system **reviews** are carried out periodically (eg once a year) to ensure that the system is achieving its desired effect. Reviews should cover issues such as: the results of the audits; customer feedback; process and product conformance; the status of preventative and corrective action plans; the status of follow-up actions from previous management reviews; any forthcoming changes that could affect the QMS; and recommendations for improvements. Most organisations which adopt the ISO 9000/9001 route also get their systems **assessed** by an independent accredited certification body, resulting in certification or registration.

ISO 9000 contains eight **quality management principles** designed to support an efficient, effective and adaptable QMS. (You should recognise some of these from our earlier discussion of TQM.)

- **Customer focus**. Product and service requirements must be based on customer needs and expectations
- **Leadership**. Quality management requires direction and unity of purpose. Leaders must formulate quality policy and ensure that clear, measurable objectives are set.
- **Involvement of people.** Management must act as enablers for employee involvement in quality, which both harnesses their abilities in the interests of the organisation – and enhances their role and satisfaction.
- **Process approach.** Quality management systems must be seen as a business process, transforming one or more inputs to create an output of value to the customer. This is an efficient approach to managing resources and activities.
- **Systems approach to management.** Quality is a complex system of inter-related processes, which need to by identified, understood and managed.
- **Continual improvement**, as a permanent and on-going objective, requiring proactive customer research and feedback monitoring, as well as measuring and monitoring of performance.
- **Factual approach to decision-making**, requiring systems in place to provide timely, relevant data and information to managers.
- **Mutually beneficial supplier relationships**, enhancing the ability of both partners to create value, as links in the quality chain.

You might like to check out the International Standards Organisation website for more detailed information on the standards, if required for your assignment: www.iso.org

4.3 ISO 14001

Launched in 1996, the ISO 14000 series is an equivalent series of international standards focusing specifically on **Environmental Management Systems (EMS)**. An EMS gives an organisation a systematic approach for assessing and managing its impact on the environment: the environmental consequences of its operations. The standard is designed to provide a framework for developing such a system, as well as a supporting audit and review programme.

The major **requirement for an EMS** under ISO 14001 include:

- An **environmental policy statement** which includes commitments to:
  - Prevention of pollution
  - Continual improvement of the EMS leading to improvements in overall environmental performance
  - Compliance with all relevant legal and regulatory requirements
- **Identification** of all aspects of the organisation's activities, products and services that could have a significant impact on the environment (whether or not regulated): focusing on environmental aspects that are within the organisation's control or ability to influence
- Establishing **performance objectives and targets** for the EMS, taking into account legal requirements and organisational policy commitments and information about significant environmental protection issues
- **Implementing** an EMS to meet these objectives and targets, including: training of employees, establishing work instructions and practices, establishing performance metrics and so on
- Establishing a programme for **periodic auditing and review** of environmental performance against the environmental policy and legal/regulatory framework
- Taking **corrective and preventive actions** when deviations from the EMS are identified
- Undertaking periodic **reviews of the EMS** by top management to ensure its continuing performance and adequacy in the face of changing environmental information

An organisation can make a self-assessment and self-declaration, or, if it wishes, it can be audited and certified by a third party, to demonstrate compliance to customers, clients and regulatory bodies.

Benefits claimed for an EMS based on ISO 14001 by various Environmental Protection Agencies include:

- Improvements in compliance and reduced costs of non-compliance
- Improvements in overall environmental performance
- Enhanced predictability and consistency in managing environmental obligations
- Increased efficiency and potential cost savings when managing environmental obligations, through a systematic and informed approach: more effective targeting of limited resources for environmental management
- Enhanced reputation and relationship with internal and external stakeholders (eg employer brand, issues management, potential for 'green' branding/marketing, causal marketing and affinity marketing with 'green' pressure groups and so on)

For more information about ISO 14001 and environmental management in general, check out:

www.environment-agency.gov.uk	***The UK Environment Agency***
www.eea.europa.eu	***The European Environment Agency***

4.4 PAS 2050

Publicly Available Specification (PAS) 2050 was launched in 2008 by the British Standards Institution (BSI). It builds on existing methods established through ISO 14040/14044, by specifying requirements for the **assessment of greenhouse gas (GHG) emissions** arising from products across their life cycle, from initial sourcing of raw materials through manufacture, transport, use and ultimately recycling or waste. (*www.carbontrust.co.uk/carbon/briefing/pre-measurement.htm*).

It is designed to help organisations and consumers to understand the 'carbon footprint' of goods and services, and may also be used for a variety of processes for analysing, improving, comparing and communicating the emissions carbon footprint performance of products and services. For organisations, PAS 2050:

- Supports internal assessment of the life cycle GHG emissions of their goods and services
- Facilitates the evaluation of alternative product designs, sourcing and manufacturing methods, raw material choices and supplier selection, on the basis of GHG emissions
- Provides a benchmark for programmes aimed at reducing GHG emissions
- Allows for comparison of goods or services on the basis of GHG emissions
- Supports reporting (and promotion) on corporate social and environmental responsibility.

PAS 2050 findings may therefore be of particular interest to marketers, for the planning and promotion of carbon-neutral brands, or the improvement and promotion of the organisation's environmental responsibility credentials in general.

Climate change or 'global warming' is perhaps the most topical issue in environmental politics and marketing, with a number of major research reports raising the profile of the issue. Excess levels of GHGs in the atmosphere, including carbon dioxide, are thought to raise the earth's temperature, causing changes to global climate patterns. GHGs are produced by natural as well as industrial processes, but current levels in the atmosphere appear to be higher than in pre-industrialisation eras, and have been attributed to factors such as transport and energy use.

Individuals, societies and corporations are being urged to reduce GHG emissions, and to reduce their 'carbon footprint': that is, the total impact of their activities on the amount of carbon dioxide (CO_2) in the atmosphere. Organisations can **reduce their carbon footprint** by a range of measure such as:

- Setting policies and targets for monitoring and reducing carbon emissions
- Minimising the use of non-renewable energy, and sourcing or generating 'green' (renewable) power
- Reducing business travel, and planning logistics to minimise fuel use and emissions
- Developing and selling products with a lower carbon impact (eg low-energy use household appliances, clothes which can be washed at lower temperatures)
- Carbon labelling: supporting the work of the Carbon Trust to develop the labelling of consumer products and services with their carbon impact
- Supporting the supply chain in reducing carbon emissions. (This includes customers: Marks & Spencer, for example, are now educating their customers on carbon footprint reduction and are locating retail outlets to encourage the use of public transport and cycling.)
- Carbon offsetting (ideally, where no other method of reducing CO_2 emissions is available). Organisations can purchase financial instruments called 'carbon offsets' (representing the fruits of emissions-reducing projects such as reforestation and renewable energy) to compensate for their own greenhouse gas emissions. (The Kyoto Protocol, an international agreement on climate change, sanctioned offsets as a way for governments and private companies to earn 'carbon credits', which can be traded in a compliance market.)

You can download a free copy of PAS 2050 from the Carbon Trust, DEFRA or the BIS

www.bsigroup.com/en/Standards-and-Publications/Industry-Sectors/Energy/PAS-2050

5 Quality improvement approaches

5.1 Benchmarking

KEY CONCEPT

concept

Benchmarking is the establishment, through data gathering, of targets and comparators, through who use relative levels of performance (and particularly areas of underperformance) can be identified.

Benchmarking essentially involves comparing your operations to somebody else's. Bendell, Boulter & Kelly (1993) distinguish four types of benchmarking.

- **Internal benchmarking**: comparison with high-performing units or functions in the same organisation. One division's marketing function might be benchmarked against another, for example, to lift standards and consistency within the organisation.
- **Functional benchmarking**: comparison with a best-practice external example of a function, regardless of industry. This is also known as operational or process benchmarking. An IT company might benchmark its marketing function against that of Apple Computers or Coca Cola, say, as a way of lifting its processes to best-practice level.
- **Competitor benchmarking**: comparison with a high-performing competitor in key areas which impact on performance: for example, Dell comparing its product reliability, time-to-market for innovation or B2B marketing with Hewlett Packard.
- **Generic benchmarking**: comparison of business processes across functional boundaries and industries. The organisation can benchmark itself against 'excellent' companies or an excellence framework (such as the EFQM), or an organisation with a reputation for learning, innovation, relationship marketing – or whatever the organisation is interested in pursuing.

5.1.1 Benefits of benchmarking

Some of the potential benefits claimed for benchmarking include the following.

- It enables the firm to **assess its existing performance** and position, and particularly its competitive strengths and weaknesses or areas in which it falls short of best practice.
- It focuses on **improvement in key results areas** (critical success factors) and sets targets designed to be realistic (since other organisations have achieved them) yet challenging (since the benchmarking organisation hasn't yet achieved them). This is the most effective combination for motivation.
- It replaces an ad hoc or subjective approach to performance measurement, improvement and competitive advantage-seeking with a set of **objective, systematic criteria**.
- The process is generally carried out by the managers who have to implement and live with the changes: this should help to secure **stakeholder buy-in** for improvement.
- It **stimulates research and feedback-seeking** about the organisation's strengths, weaknesses and core competences.
- It generates **new ideas and insights** 'outside the box' of the organisation's usual ways of thinking and acting. Analysis of competitor products and processes, for example, may give rise to ideas which can be learned from or imitated.

It should be noted that there are also **limitations and drawbacks** to benchmarking as an approach to performance measurement and improvement.

- It may suggest that there is **one best way** of doing business. However, the organisation needs to take a contingency approach to problem-solving, suitable to its own resources, strengths, weaknesses and environment – rather than an 'off-the-shelf' approach drawn from other organisations' experience.
- The benchmark may be **'yesterday's solution to tomorrow's problem'**. For example, a cross-channel ferry company might benchmark its activities against airlines and other ferry companies – however the Channel Tunnel has emerged as the main competitor for cross-channel ferry services.
- It is a reactive, **'catch-up' or 'me too' exercise**, which may not result in the seeking and development of unique, distinctive and hard-to-imitate core competences.
- It depends on **accurate and detailed information** about competitors (which may pose research and ethical challenges), and on appropriate analogies/comparisons in other industries (because of the need to compare like with like).

5.1.2 The process of benchmarking

Oakland (1991) puts forward a 15-step benchmarking process.

Stage	No.	Step
Plan	1	Select the function, unit or process to be benchmarked
	2	Identify the exemplar of best practice, key competitor or successful partner (using industry analysis, customer feedback or a benchmarking consultant)
	3	Identify the criteria to be benchmarked (based on critical success factors)
	4	Establish a benchmarking project team (clear roles, authority and resources)
	5	Plan methods for data collection (surveys, interviews, documents, visits)
	6	Conduct research
	7	Manage direct contacts with the target organisation (interviews, visits etc)
Analyse	8	Collate and analyse benchmark data to compare performance: identify performance 'gaps'
	9	Create a 'competence centre' and knowledge bank: document information
	10	Analyse underlying cultural, structural and managerial factors that enable performance to benchmark standard (ie not just performance measures)
Develop	11	Develop new performance standards, targets and measures to reflect desired improvements
	12	Develop systematic action plans (change management programmes, resource plans etc with time-scales, accountabilities and monitoring/review processes)
Improve	13	Implement the action plans
Review	14	Continuously monitor and/or periodically review progress and results
	15	Review the benchmark process for future learning.

5.2 Six Sigma

Six Sigma is a disciplined application of statistical problem-solving tools to identify and quantify waste and indicate steps for improvement (Brue, 2005). It uses the '**DMAIC**' model for **process improvement.**

- **Define** an opportunity or need for improvement: a project team is formed and given the responsibility and resources for solving the problem.
- **Measure** current performance: gather data that describes accurately how the process is currently working and analyse it to produce some initial ideas about what may be causing the problem
- **Analyse** the opportunity for improvement: generate and test theories as to what might be causing the problem, to identify root causes
- **Improve** performance: remove root causes by designing and implementing changes to the 'offending' process
- **Control** performance by designing and implementing new controls to prevent the original problem from returning.

Six Sigma is designed to help an organisation focus on: understanding and management customer requirements; aligning key business processes to achieve those requirements; utilising rigorous statistical data analysis to minimise variation in those processes; and therefore driving sustainable improvement in business processes.

The methodology can be outlined as follows.

- Identify and prioritise characteristics of the product or service that are **critical to quality** (CTQ) for customers
- Identify and focus on factors and variables in the process that most influence those characteristics ('**vital few factors**')
- Calculate the **variation** in the process, when it is operating normally. Six Sigma uses *standard deviation* (sigma) to measure the variation of values (eg time per unit, or defects per x units produced) from the mean (average). A score of '6 sigma' signifies near perfection: 99.999% of items are within specification (3.4 defects per million opportunities).

- Define detailed performance **standards and tolerances** for the key variables, establishing how much variation is acceptable to the (internal or external) customer of the process. There should be a lower **specification limit** (LSL) and upper specification limit (USL) within which outputs should fall.
- Set **control limits** – a lower control limit (LCL) and upper control limit (UCL) which represent the minimum and maximum inherent limits of the process. If these are within the specification limits, the process is capable of meeting specification. If either or both of the control limits are *outside* the specification limits, the process won't consistently be able to meet specification.
- **Implement process control** to minimise variations in the vital few factors, aiming for 6 sigma performance. Workers know the expected range of variation: if measurements taken from samples of the process are within the specification limits, the process is in control – and if not, it can immediately be halted and problems rectified.
- **Involve management** and staff in the process, to create a quality-focused learning culture.

It is difficult to know how much detail you might need on Six Sigma, as a complex statistical technique. If you are called upon to explain or apply it in your assignment, you will need to do your own reading. We can recommend the very short, systematic coverage in:

Greg Brue, Six Sigma for Managers (2005) McGraw Hill Professional Education.

5.3 The PDCA (Deming) Cycle

The Plan-Do-Check-Act or PDCA cycle is a systematic approach to problem solving. It is known as the Deming cycle, although it was developed by Dr Shewhart, a colleague of Deming. PDCA is designed as a 'universal improvement methodology': an approach to process improvement – but also to problem solving and change management in general. It is about learning and on-going improvement: learning what works and what does not in a systematic way, in a continuous cycle.

- **Plan** what is needed
- **Do** it
- **Check** that it works (or what worked and what didn't) by measuring results and comparing them with the plan
- **Act** to correct any problems or improve the process.

The idea is to run a 'pilot project' for the change prior to full implantation: if it doesn't deliver the desired or expected outcomes, you can adjust accordingly – without damage to your credibility or wasted resources. Essentially you plan, test and incorporate feedback before committing to implementation.

5.4 Ishikawa diagrams

Ishikawa (1991) developed a cause and effect analysis diagram (also known as an Ishikawa or fishbone diagram) that enables quality problems to be analysed and identified. It is basically a mind map of factors contributing to problems, classified into five categories, machinery, manpower, method, maintenance and material. (In non-manufacturing contexts, 4 Ps (policies, procedures, people and plant are used instead.)

The 5M fishbone diagram (manufacturing)

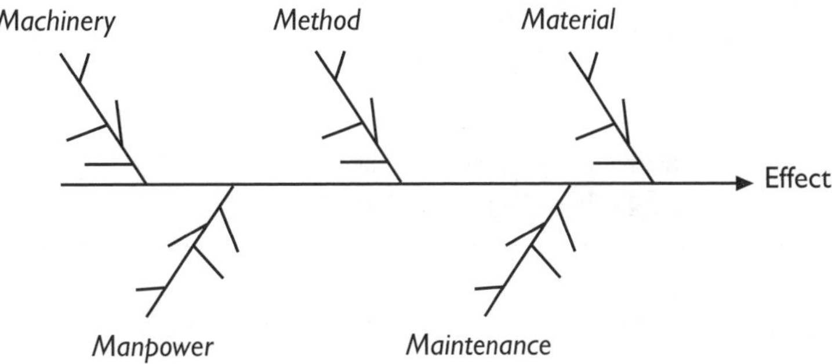

After the basic diagram has been drawn, the main causes of problems can be expanded and treated as separate branches. The map of subcauses is then added to, until all possible root causes have been considered. You might like to try this simple, but powerful technique, to reflect on critical incidents in marketing or quality performance.

5.5 Deming: 14 points for improving quality

Deming's 14 points for quality improvement (Deming, 1986) stressed the need for statistical control methods, participation, education, openness and improvement.

1 Create a constancy of purpose.

2 Adopt a new quality-conscious philosophy.

3 Cease dependence on inspection.

4 Stop awarding business on price.

5 Continuous improvement in the system of production and service.

6 Institute training on the job.

7 Institute leadership.

8 Drive out fear.

9 Break down barriers between departments.

10 Eliminate slogans and exhortations.

11 Eliminate quotas or work standards.

12 Give employees pride in their job.

13 Institute education and a self-improvement programme.

14 Put everyone to work to accomplish it.

You should recognise each of these points from our earlier discussion of TQM.

If you would like to follow up on some of the concepts and techniques discussed in this chapter, there are a number of practical websites with resources on management disciplines and tools.

Mindtools ***www.mindtools.com***

BusinessBalls ***www.businessballs.com/qualitymanagement.htm***

Simply use the search engines and hyperlinks to browse articles and resources on the area you are interested in. ■

6 Service quality

KEY CONCEPT

concept

A **service** may be defined as: an activity or benefit that one party can offer to another that is essentially intangible and does not result in the ownership of anything. Its product may or may not be tied to a physical product.

Egan (2004) notes that in marketing, the term 'service' is used in two main ways.

- To describe businesses where the greater part of the company's central offering is intangible or non-physical: **service industries.** Examples include entertainment, transport, banking, insurance, consultancy, cleaning and hairdressing: the core of the offering is *doing* something for the customer, rather than transferring ownership of a physical product.
- To describe the features of *any* offering or exchange which extend beyond the core product or service, adding value as a result of the contacts between the buyer and the seller: **customer service.**

The following discussion applies equally to either context.

There are particular difficulties associated with measuring and managing the quality of services.

- They are **intangible**, which means that their key attributes are not subject to observation and measurement
- They are **heterogeneous** or variable, due to their dependence on the people delivering them. Individual uniqueness (of provider *and* customer) makes it difficult to compare like with like in measuring quality – and to maintain consistency in service delivery. Indeed, personalisation is regarded as a key service benefit.

Measuring and managing service quality may therefore be a much more subjective and flexible process of gathering feedback from stakeholders, and using feedback to define criteria against which performance can be measured.

6.1 The importance of service encounters

On-going customer relationship (and, by definition, customer retention and loyalty) depends on a supplier's ability consistently to fulfil customer expectations and to create a positive experience of doing business, at every encounter and touch point with the organisation. In many service industries, the service encounter lasts only a few seconds. Services encounters may be seen as **episodes**:' specific interactions between customers and... employees that are especially satisfying or unsatisfying' (Bitner *et al*, cited in Egan, 2004, p 111). Some episodes are merely routine. Others may be 'critical' (or **'moments of truth',** Carlzon, 1989): that is, the continuation of a relationship depends on them, either positively (because they are particularly satisfying) or negatively (because they are particularly dissatisfying).

A single disappointing service encounter – and/or a firm's subsequent poor response to handling the problem – may be sufficient to reduce loyalty and make the customer more amenable to switching brands in response to competitor offers. Customers may tolerate **negative critical incidents** for the time being, but they are taken into account in the long-term evaluation of the supplier's performance. In the worst case scenario, a single disappointment (and related loss of trust) may be sufficient to induce the customer to take her business elsewhere – and to further damage relationship marketing by spreading negative word-of-mouth.

On the positive side of this equation, **positive critical incidents** (unusually satisfying service encounters) are an important source of added value for customers, a part of the package of benefits that helps to attract and retain them, and potentially a key differentiating factor between the supplier and its competitors.

MARKETING AT WORK

application

'Five Star Service Recovery with Thomas Cook

An example of how to handle the dreaded airport delay can be found in the case of Thomas Cook, the UK travel agency and tour operator. An electrical fault on an aircraft... meant that 220 passengers were delayed at Funchal airport for two hours... Towards the end of this period, passengers were directed to the cafeteria to receive a free drink and snack.

When it became clear that the flight would not take place that day, a Thomas Cook representative announced that all passengers would stay the night in a five-star hotel and would receive free dinner with drinks. After 30 minutes, passengers boarded coaches and were seamlessly transferred to the hotel. While at the hotel, passengers were kept fully informed of the situation and given the time to meet the following morning. Representatives were on hand to answer queries...

When passengers met to take the early-morning trip to the airport, they were served coffee and biscuits. Coaches were waiting outside the hotel ready for departure. Despite the inconvenience of arriving a day late, passengers appreciated the smoothness of the service recovery operation. Clearly, Thomas Cook and its airport representative Serviceair had service processes in place.' (Jobber, 2009)

The bottom line of service quality for marketing is that people all over the organisation have direct influence over its image, value proposition and customer retention. It is not possible to exercise direct control over all the 'marketing communications' represented by service encounters, but marketing managers must be aware of them, appreciate their importance and do what they can to control – or at least influence – them indirectly.

This can partly be done through management of the **'extended (service) marketing mix'** elements:

- **Process** (the activities, information flows and supporting procedures and systems which create and deliver the service):
  - Setting up policies, systems and procedures to govern interactions with the customer, to ensure consistency
  - Allowing adaptability and spontaneity, so that adherence to policy and procedure does not create barriers to service (eg dealing with unusual or urgent customer needs)
  - Automating procedures where possible, to ensure consistency (although *not* in areas where customers prefer to deal with human beings!)
  - Constantly monitoring and auditing performance and gathering customer feedback
  - Setting up systems and procedures for service recovery: prompt action to address complaints and re-establish service provision
- **People** (the employees and intermediaries who create and deliver the service):
  - Selecting, training and motivating people to give a high quality of service (and to deal with particular service challenges eg difficult and demanding customers)
  - Using internal marketing to promulgate the culture of service (customer focus, service values) throughout the firm
  - Ensuring conformance with standards of behaviour, dress and appearance, procedures and modes of dealing with the public
- **Physicals** (tangible evidences of purchase/consumption, and physical factors in the purchase/service environment, which influence the service experience of customers):
  - Designing physical expressions of the service that reflect and reinforce its quality goals: evidence of purchase (eg a receipt or voucher, or a bank statement); accessories (eg merchandise or concept programmes)
  - Designing appropriate service brand identifiers (eg staff livery or uniforms, branded vehicles)
  - Designing appropriate service environments (eg showroom or service area décor, furnishing and ambience; website design).

6.2 Perceived service quality

Chris Grönroos introduced the concept of 'perceived service quality' and developed a widely cited model of service quality (Grönroos, 2000).

Perceived service quality

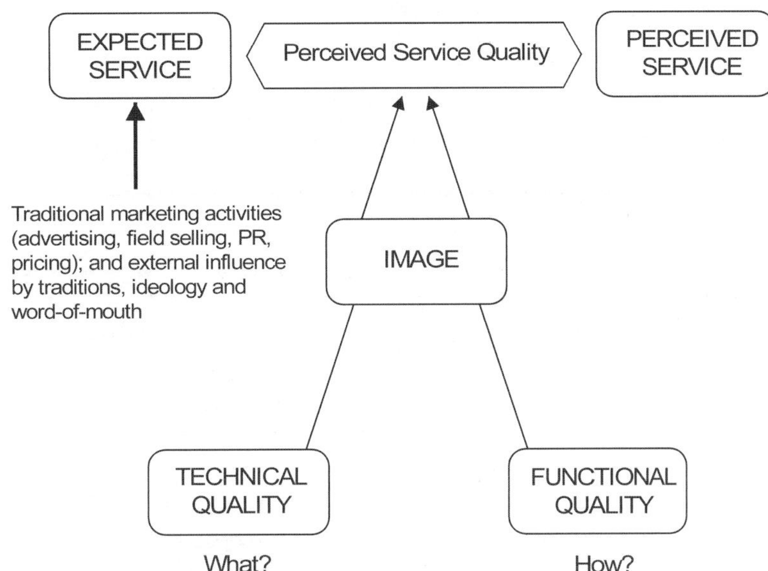

The model suggests that the quality of a given service is the outcome of an evaluation process by which consumers compare what they expected to receive with what they perceive that they have actually received. Their expectations are influenced by factors such as marketing mix activities, external traditions and customs, ideology and word-of-mouth communications – as well as their own previous experience with the service or organisation.

In terms of perceived service quality, Grönroos suggests that there are two principal components of quality – technical and functional – with a third, image, acting as a mediating influence.

- **Technical quality** is what the customer is left with when the service provision has finished. For example, in education this would be the level of attainment and understanding achieved at the end of the course. This can be fairly easy measured by the consumer.
- **Functional quality** is how the consumer receives the technical quality in interactions with the service provider. Service quality is not just dependent on *what* you receive, but on *how* you receive it. This emphasises the importance of service interactions, customer-facing employees and the management of the service experience – and is harder to measure than technical quality.

Customers' expectations and perceptions of the service are influenced by their perception of the company: its **image**. If a student has a positive image of a college or lecturer, say, but then has a negative experience (perhaps a particularly disorganised lecture), the student may still perceive the service to be satisfactory because (s)he will find excuses for the problem. Similarly, a negative image may increase perceived problems with service quality.

6.3 Service gaps

Parasuraman, Zeithaml and Berry (1988) developed a widely applied model of service quality, via interviews with 14 executives in four service businesses and 12 customer focus groups. The findings highlighted five potential quality gaps.

Service gaps

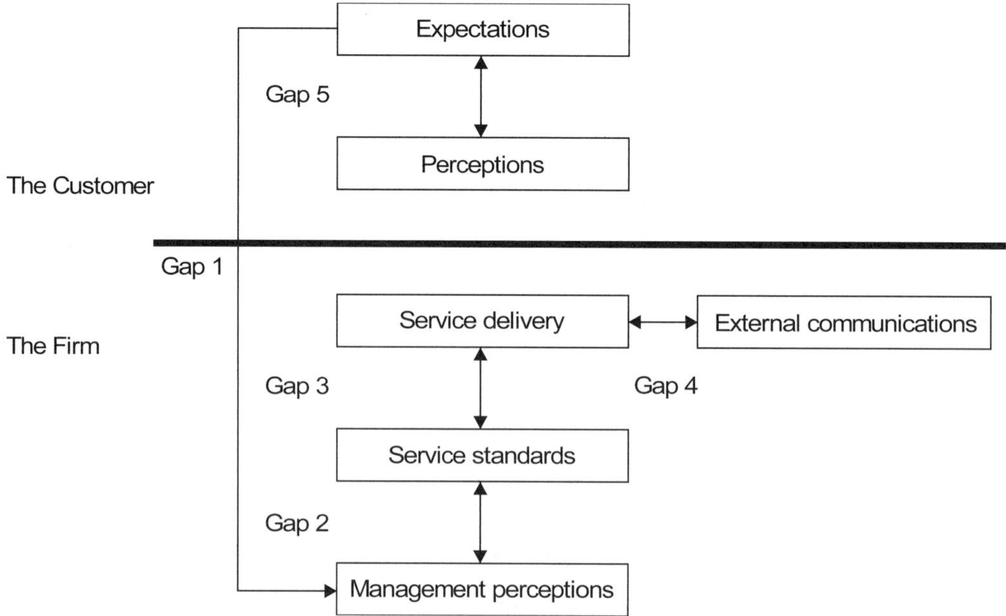

Gap 1 Consumer expectations v management perceptions	Managers' definition of value may not be the same as that of customers. They may not know what features connote high quality for customers, what features a service must have or what levels of performance are required by customers. **Action required:** • Market research programmes • Improvements based on customer comment and complaints • Strategies for service recovery • Improvements based on front line staff experience and suggestion
Gap 2 Management perceptions v service quality specification	Resource constraints, market conditions and/or management indifference may lead to managers' understanding of required service quality *not* being translated into service level agreements or quality specifications **Action required:** • New concepts of service rather than merely improving old ones • Attention to physical evidence of quality • Customer-focused activity goals
Gap 3 Service quality specifications v service delivery	Service level agreements and quality specifications may not translate into actual service levels. Employees may not be willing or able to perform to the specified standard, work may be poorly organised, supervised or resourced. **Action required:** • Define job roles and priorities clearly • Provide proper training • Build teams and team working • Empower frontline service staff • Improve technology • Recruit, train and reward for policy improvements

Gap 4 Service delivery v external communications	External communications may create exaggerated or uninformed expectations of service quality – setting customers up for disappointment. **Action required:** • Improve communications between internal staff • Educate customers as to what to expect from the service • Develop service rules – but do not over-promote to customers • Use marketing communications to emphasise what is actually delivered
Gap 5 Expected service v perceived service	What customers perceive they have received may fall short of what they expected: ie there is a shortfall in perceived service quality. **Action required:** • Research customer expectations • Measure service performance against expectations • Specify service quality/levels according to expectations • Manage and continuously improve service levels to match expectations

6.4 Dimensions of service quality

Parasuraman *et al* (1998) developed the SERVQUAL questionnaire, which claims to be a global measure of service quality across all service organisations. It measures five generic criteria that consumers use in evaluating service quality.

- **Tangibles**: physical facilities, equipment, appearance of personnel
- **Reliability**: ability to perform the promised service dependably and accurately
- **Responsiveness**: willingness to help customers and provide prompt service
- **Assurance**: knowledge and courtesy of employees and their ability to convey trust and confidence
- **Empathy**: caring, individualised attention.

Respondents are asked first to give their expectations of the service on a seven point scale, then to give their evaluation of the actual service on the same scale. Service quality is then calculated as the *difference* between perception and expectation, weighted for the importance of each item.

MARKETING AT WORK

application

Quality in stockbroking

The following table shows the type of factors on which judgements are based in stockbroking.

Dimension and definition	Examples of specific questions raised by stock brokerage customers
Tangibles. Appearance of physical facilities, equipment, personnel and communication materials.	• Is my stockbroker dressed appropriately?
Reliability. Ability to perform the promised service dependably and accurately.	• Does the stockbroker follow exact instructions to buy or sell?
Responsiveness. Willingness to help customers and provide prompt service.	• Is my stockbroker willing to answer my questions?
Competence. Possession of the required skills and knowledge to perform the service.	• Does my brokerage firm have the research capabilities accurately to track market developments?
Courtesy. Politeness, respect, consideration, and friendliness of contact personnel.	• Does my broker refrain from acting busy or being rude when I ask questions?

Dimension and definition	Examples of specific questions raised by stock brokerage customers
Credibility. Trustworthiness, believability, and honesty of the service provider.	• Does my broker refrain from pressuring me to buy?
Security. Freedom from danger, risk, or doubt.	• Does my brokerage firm know where my stock certificate is?
Access. Approachability and ease of contact.	• Is it easy to get through to my broker over the telephone?
Communication. Keeping customers informed in language they can understand, and listening to them.	• Does my broker avoid using technical jargon?
Understanding the customer. Making the effort to know customers and their needs.	• Does my broker try to determine what my specific financial objectives are?

Zeithaml, Parasuraman and Berry, *Delivering Quality Service*

It is worth noting that customer perception of service quality can vary, even when a firm is getting the five generic dimensions 'right', due to intervening factors such as: product quality (where there is a physical element to service provision); price (ie perceived value for money); situational factors (such as the urgency of the customer's need); and personal factors (such as cultural, age or personality differences).

6.5 Managing service quality

Once a firm knows how it is performing on each of the dimensions of service quality, however, it can use a number of methods improve its performance. There are many dimensions in service delivery, before and after the service encounter itself.

- The creation of a **corporate culture** which expresses and models customer-focused values, and reinforces those values through its selection, appraisal and reward systems, and the messages it sends employees at every level.
- The creation of **service-supporting internal relationships** and **internal marketing**: the recruitment of skills customer-facing people; the supply of appropriate training; the empowerment of staff to take decisions that will satisfy and retain customers; and the reward and recognition of staff who deliver outstanding service.
- Gathering, analysing, communicating and acting on **customer feedback.** Feedback and adjustment (addressing customer concerns and complaints) are crucial in minimising dissatisfaction and demonstrating commitment to customer value. Constructive handling of problems and complaints (sometimes called '**service recovery**') may lead to restored satisfaction – and even strengthened relationship, because of the provider's demonstrated commitment.
- Establishing a **partnership approach** to relationships with customers, suppliers and intermediaries (distributors, retail outlets, call centres) in order to support high levels of service at all links in the value-delivery chain.
- Ensuring **promise fulfilment** (Jobber, 2009): Making realistic promises (to manage customer expectations); enabling staff and service systems to deliver on promises made; and keeping promises during service encounters.
- Offering **support services** (eg warranties, servicing, user training and help-lines) to facilitate customers in using the product safely and satisfyingly, and support them through changes and difficulties
- Establishing **customer-friendly** systems. It is no good expecting staff to give great service to customers if they systems, procedures, technology and information flows do not support their efforts.

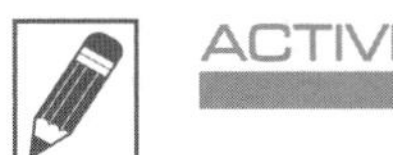

ACTIVITY 3

application

Summarise what you take to be the key roles of the marketing function in the development of service quality and the management of service gaps.

7 Quality and relationship marketing

It is one of the key principles of relationship marketing that customer retention and loyalty is built on the **creation and delivery of superior customer value** (that is, greater than that oared by competitors) on a sustained basis. The shift from transactional marketing to relationship marketing (as you may already be aware from your studies of *Stakeholder Marketing* for the Professional Certificate) reflects a shift in focus (Egan, 2004, p 130) from what you can do *to* customers (persuade, capture, exploit) to what you can do *for* customers (added benefits) and *with* customers (dialogue and co-operation) to ensure customer satisfaction.

Value is effectively 'in the eye of the customer', and organisations must seek to understand exactly what aspects of their offering customers will place value on. However, quality of products/services and customer service (at all touch points, in all activities and throughout the relationship with the customer) is regarded as an essential element of value.

Customers give loyalty in exchange for their expectation that value will flow to them from a relationship with a supplier. Customers are more likely to become repeat customers, loyalty customers and perhaps even active advocates.

"'Marketing is concerned with 'exchange relationships' between the organisation and its customers, and quality and customer service are key linkages in these relationships. At its simplest, the exchange relationship is the customer paying for the benefits they receive. But the relationship marketing view is that the customer gives loyalty in exchange for their expectation that value will flow to them from the relationship. This flow of value includes not just project benefits but a number of less tangible benefits relating to the quality of the experience within a wider customer service context. So the challenge to the organisation is to align marketing, quality and customer service strategies more closely. In the past organisations have tended to treat these as separate and unrelated. Consequently, decisions affecting customer service may have been taken by diverse functions such as distribution, manufacturing or sales. Likewise, quality was seen as the preserve of a specific quality control or assurance function. Under the relationship marketing paradigm, these three areas are merged and given a sharper focus..."

Christopher, Payne & Ballantyne, Relationship Marketing: Creating Stakeholder Value (2002: Elsevier Butterworth-Heinemann) p 9-10.

If you have access to this book, it would be worth reading Chapters 1 (Creating value for the customer) and 5 (Relationship marketing: integrating quality, customer service and marketing) in full ■

Christopher *et al* (2002) argue that:

- **Customer satisfaction** is critical in maintaining relationships and fostering customer loyalty. Traditionally, marketing has focused on customer acquisition, but ***retaining* customers** involves delivering value through fulfilling promises and adding customer value through quality and customer service.
- Quality and customer service are not 'departmental' responsibilities: the ways in which they are delivered and maintained cut **across functional boundaries**. Marketers must build supportive relationships with 'part-time' marketers working in customer-facing roles: providing them with appropriate skills, processes and operational back-

up to meet customer requirements. Quality thinking and know-how has to be **aligned** across all departments – and extend beyond the organisation to embrace the total value network.

- The traditional concept of quality as 'conformance to specifications' (internal quality) must be superseded by concepts of **quality defined by customers** ('customer perceived quality'). 'Because the manufacturing and operations functions have largely led the advances in quality management thinking and practice, the emphasis is on systems and processes, performance reliability and continuous improvement... But without collaborative marketing involvement, quality will never achieve its goals and will fall short of customer defined requirements.' (ibid, p 152)
- Quality assurance alone does not guarantee that customers receive quality as they perceive it. It is marketing's key responsibility to **monitor and interpret customers' perceptions of quality**, providing rigorous market research to support collaborative quality management.

Learning objective review

Learning objectives	Covered
1 Evaluate and assess the relevance of key quality concepts	☑ Definitions of quality ☑ Evaluation of quality requirements for the marketing of products and services
2 Assess what is required to develop effective and efficient quality systems and processes to support compliance	☑ Why quality is important: for brand positioning, pricing, internal marketing, competitive advantage and compliance ☑ Quality control, or defect detection ☑ Quality assurance, or defect prevention ☑ Quality as a managerial philosophy: the principles, values and practices of Total Quality Management (TQM)
3 Outline and evaluate a range of quality management standards	☑ European Foundation of Quality Management ☑ International standards: ISO 9001 and ISO 14001 ☑ PAS 2050
4 Outline and evaluate a range of quality improvement approaches and processes	☑ The nature of process improvement ☑ Benchmarking processes and techniques ☑ The Six Sigma approach to process improvement ☑ The PDCA (Plan, Do, Check, Act) cycle and similar models (such as DMAIC) ☑ Deming's 14 steps for improving quality ☑ Incremental improvement programmes (such as *kaizen)*
5 Appreciate the particular demands of managing service quality	☑ The nature of internal and external service marketing ☑ The nature of service quality, and various models of the dimensions of service quality: eg Grönroos service gaps; SERVQUAL ☑ How service quality can be managed
6 Appreciate the role of quality in relationship marketing	☑ The need to integrate marketing, quality and customer service (Christopher *et al*)

Quick quiz

1 Quality control is based on the concept of zero tolerance in defects. True or false?

2 Total quality managements aims for zero defects. True or false?

3 What is the term used to refer to continuous improvement?

4 What are quality circles?

5 What are the four types of benchmarking as described by Bendell, Boulter and Kelly (1993)?

6 Six Sigma is a qualitative approach to process improvement. True or false?

7 What are the implications of an episode of a negative service experience?

Activity debriefs

1 There is a tendency, when something doesn't work properly, to try doing it again. However, if something hasn't worked properly in the past, there is no reason to suppose that it will work in the future. TQM encourages an attitude that seeks to change how things are done.

Understanding competitive positioning is largely a strategic issue for management, but the Government argues that without a proper understanding of competitive positioning, and the need to have a competitive position in its markets, companies will not survive – particularly in weak or declining industries. A TQM approach includes working out ways of achieving customer satisfaction in order to compete effectively.

In many companies, each department or function in an organisation thinks only about its own needs and doesn't think about the needs and expectations of other departments (that might be its 'internal customers' or 'internal suppliers'). This can create problems for the other department to resolve. For example, a hospital consultant might schedule a number of surgical operations requiring varied and sophisticated nursing support for the patients, without first consulting the ward sister or matron about what support would be required and whether it could be made available. The problem would then be one for the ward sister or matron to try to sort out.

Management have a tendency to treat people like robots. Employees who are treated in this way will tend to act accordingly – with little concern for the work they are doing.

Gold-plated taps in a bath represent a high grade of materials, but if the taps have faulty washers and leak, the quality will be poor. High grade does not ensure good quality. Equally, a low grade product can provide better quality than a high-grade item. For example, uniforms worn by workers might be of a better quality ('fit for the purpose') if they are made from a cheaper, hard-wearing material, than if they are made from more expensive material that is more easily torn or more difficult to clean.

Having an acceptable level of quality implies that some errors are tolerable. A TQM approach is that everything should be done right the first time.

Managers often enjoy dealing with problems (fire-fighting) as it gives them the sense of being 'in charge'. A TQM approach is that managers waste their time if they have to deal with problems that should not have arisen in the first place.

There is a tendency for individuals to be unconcerned about errors they make, so long as the problem does not affect them, but someone else. With a TQM approach, employees are encouraged to think of other departments as internal customers, and accept responsibility for poor service to their customers.

2 The answer to this will depend on your own research.

3 Marketing has a key role in the development of service quality and the management of service gaps, through activities such as:

- Researching, analysing and reporting on customer expectations and perceptions (eg using critical incident analysis, feedback-gathering via complaints systems, customer research via surveys and focus groups), as the basis for service improvement planning
- Establishing systems facilitating customer complaint and feedback
- Internal marketing and communication: informing, motivating, equipping and empowering internal staff to develop and maintain a customer-focused approach to service quality
- Managing customer expectations and perceptions, through marketing communications aimed at: (a) image management; (b) accurate description of services and service levels; and (c) realistic quality promises and pricing
- Specifying expectation-matched and employee-motivating service levels, where customer service (eg in sales) is within the direct control of marketing – and encouraging other managers to do the same
- Developing relationship marketing, in order to enhance customer loyalty, lessening the potential impact of single negative service encounters, and facilitating the restoration of goodwill (eg by emphasising two-way dialogue, maintaining contact, using loyalty rewards and so on).

Quiz answers

1 False. Tolerance levels are determined (these are not always set to zero) and quality control detects defects within these tolerance limits.

2 True. The key principle is to 'get it right the first time'.

3 Kaizen.

4 Teams of workers from different levels and functions within the organisation working together to solve specified problems.

5 Internal benchmarking, functional benchmarking, competitor benchmarking, generic benchmarking.

6 False. It is a quantitative approach using statistical problem solving tools to identify and quantify waste and improve processes.

7 Moments of truth- or service encounters are critical to building strong service relationships with customers. Negative critical incidents will only be tolerated in the short term or in exceptional circumstance.

References

Bendell T., Boulter L. & Kelly J. (1993) Benchmarking for Competitive Advantage, Pitman, London.

Boddy, D. (2005) Management: An Introduction (3rd edition), FT Prentice Hall, Harlow.

Brue, G. (2005) Six Sigma for Managers, McGraw Hill Professional Education, Maidenhead.

Carlzon, J. (1989) Moments of Truth, Collins Business, London.

Christopher M.G., Payne A.F. & Ballantyne D. (2002) Relationship Marketing: Creating Stakeholder Value, Elsevier Butterworth-Heinemann, Oxford.

Crosby, P.B. (1979) Quality is Free, Mentor, London.

Deming, W.E. (1986) Out of the Crisis, Massachusetts Institute of Technology, Boston, MA.

Egan, J. (2004) Relationship Marketing: Exploring Relational Strategies in Marketing, (2nd edition), Pearson Education, Harlow.

Garvin, D.A. (1987) '*Competing in eight dimensions of quality*' in Harvard Business Review, November - December.

Grönroos, C. (2000) Service Management & Marketing, (2nd edition), John Wiley, London.

Huczynski, A. & Buchanan, D. (2001) Organizational Behaviour: An Introductory Text, (4th edition). FT Prentice Hall, Harlow.

Ishikawa, K. (1991) What is Total Quality Control? (The Japanese Way), Prentice Hall, Harlow.

Jobber, D. (2009) Principles and Practice of Marketing, (6th edition), McGraw Hill Higher Education.

Johnson, G., Scholes K. & Whittington R. (2005) Exploring Corporate Strategy, (7th edition), Pearson Education, Harlow.

Juran, J.M., ed. (1988) Juran's Quality Control Handbook, (4th edition), McGraw Hill, Maidenhead.

Mullins, L. (1999) Management & Organisational Behaviour. (5th edition), FT Prentice Hall, Harlow, Essex.

Oakland, J.S. (1991) Total Quality Management: the Route to Improving Performance. Butterworth-Heinemann, Oxford.

Parasuraman, A., Zeithaml V.A. & Berry (1988) '*SERVQUAL: A multiple-item scale for measuring customer perceptions of service quality*' in Journal of Retailing, Spring, pp 12-40.

Peters, T. (1989) Thriving on Chaos, Macmillan, London.

Reichheld, F.F. (1996) The Loyalty Effect, Harvard Business School, Boston.

Slack, N., Chambers S. & Johnson R. (2004) Operations Management, (4th edition), Prentice Hall, New Jersey.

Taguchi, G. (1986) Introduction to Quality Engineering: Designing Quality into Products and Processes, Quality Resources.

Zeithaml, V. Parasuraman, A. & Berry, L. (1990) Delivering quality services, Free Press, New York.

Chapter 3

Measuring marketing performance

Topic list

1 Marketing performance measurement
2 Accounting
3 Productivity measures
4 Customer and Relationship measures
5 Internal measures
6 Innovation and learning measures
7 Analysing performance information

Introduction

Within this chapter we look at the monitoring and control aspects of managing marketing performance. Chapter two took a detailed look at systems and measures of 'quality' whilst our focus here moves to the more business related elements. To ensure that marketing strategies are effective both in the long and short term it is essential to take objective measurements so that plans may be altered and costly mistakes are not repeated in the future. Watkis (2005) outlined the role of measurement succinctly when he wrote an article for Accountancy Age magazine with a summary statement as follows:

"By continuously measuring marketing performance, you will not only keep your chief executives happy but allow marketers to demonstrate the contribution of their function to the business".

The chapter begins by reiterating why it is important to measure marketing before moving to look in sections two and three at different measures and information sources used to assess marketing performance. The final section briefly considers how to analyse measures and integrate recommendations to improve marketing activities.

Syllabus linked learning objectives

By the end of the chapter you will be able to:

Learning objectives	Syllabus link
1 Consider the role of marketing metrics	1.3, 1.4
2 Explore a range of measures used to determine marketing performance	1.3, 1.4

1 Marketing performance measurement

1.1 Why measure?

Data-based marketing where success is assessed through measurable performance and accountability is now a 'given' in business (Farris et al, 2006). The use of 'marketing metrics' is vital for any healthy business as Harvard Business School Associate Dean John Quelch (op cit Farris et al, 2006) discussed in the Wall Street Journal:

"Today's boards want chief marketing officers who can speak the language of productivity and return on investment and are willing to be held accountable. In recent years, manufacturing, procurement, and logistics have all tightened their belts in the cause of improved productivity. As a result, marketing expenditures account for a larger percentage of many corporate cost structures than ever before. Today's boards don't need chief marketing officers who have creative flair but no financial discipline. They need ambidextrous marketers who offer both".

John Quelch has a marketing based blog with useful thoughts on topical marketing issues. It can be found at *http://blogs.harvardbusiness.org/quelch/*

KEY CONCEPT

concept

"*A* ***metric*** *is a measuring system that quantifies a trend, dynamic, or characteristic.*"

Farris et al (2006, pg 1)

Generally the prime reasons for measurement and analysis within marketing are:

- To evaluate success (or failure) of marketing plans
- To rectify and implement corrective actions if an unsuccessful plan is underway and it is possible to change
- To assist future decision making and planning
- To provide a convincing and strong rationale for a marketing plan for the board

Measuring marketing is an essential part of the control system as depicted in the following diagram.

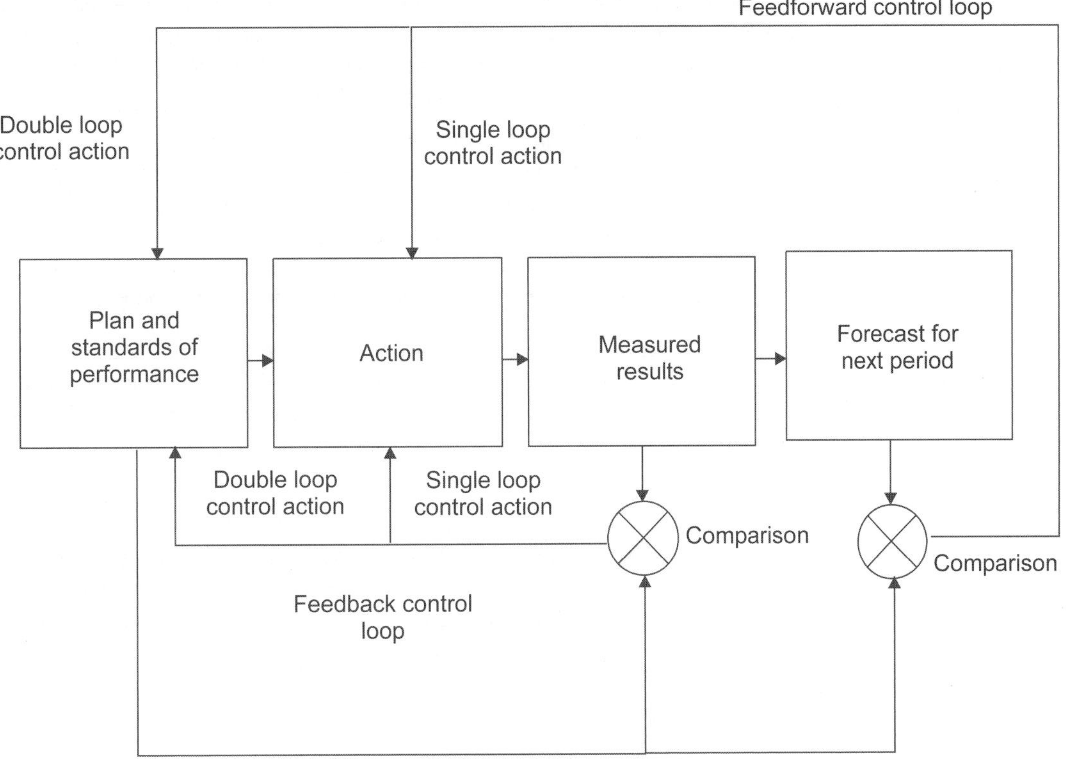

1.2 Basic marketing measures and performance information

There are a number of key measures that can be used by marketers. Later in this chapter we will examine some of the more widely applicable measures of corporate success that are obtained through the processes of financial accounting. First, however, it is worth spending a little while thinking about some of the complications that arise in relation to those *basic* marketing measures.

1.2.1 Market share

Market share is a key indicator of performance found within virtually every marketing plan

KEY CONCEPT

concept

Market share is the percentage of a market accounted for by a specified product or organisation. It is defined in terms of either volume (units) or value (revenue).

Market share enables marketers to identify whether increases in sales are as a result of the market expanding or capturing share from competitors.

There are however a number of issues that make market share a complex measure to use effectively.

Issue with market share	Why?
Defining the market	It may be necessary to define the market in different ways for different purposes. You may be aware that it has been suggested that Coca Cola competes with all other drinks, including water. This illustrates the problem: such a definition of Coca Cola's market might actually be useful for longer-term strategic planning, but a narrower definition would probably be more useful for routine monitoring of performance.
Trends and frequency of measurement	An instantaneous measurement of market share is a snapshot and gives no information about changes that may be taking place in the market. Market share should be measured at suitable intervals so that changes may be noted. Time series analysis will smooth the data to eliminate random fluctuations and enable the diagnosis of seasonal variation and long-term tends. The frequency of measurement will vary from industry to industry; FMCG, for example, may require more frequent measurement than capital goods.
Predictive ability	The past is not necessarily a good guide to the future. A high market share now does not indicate that all will continue to be well indefinitely. PIMS data, indicate that while market pioneers tend to achieve both high profits and high market share, both of these advantages are likely to be eroded over time as new entrants are attracted to the market and gradually catch up.
Volume and value	Volume is measured in units; value is measured in money. It is important to appreciate the difference. Pricing policy is of central importance and, in particular, the offer of large discounts can build volume at the cost of value. Ultimately, discounting can cause a collapse of revenue and can certainly work against other elements of the marketing mix.

1.2.2 Profitability

Profit is quite a tricky concept. It is defined by accounting convention for financial purposes, but we may wish to define it differently for marketing purposes.

A simple example of the complexity of profit is the difference between gross and net profit: gross profit is calculated by deducting the cost of sales and net profit by further deduction of all other expenses. Except for very simple trading operations, even defining 'cost of sales' might be quite contentious, while 'all other expenses' includes depreciation, an expense whose magnitude depends on choice of accounting policy.

There are other issues relating to profit and just what it means, including, in particular, the allocation of fixed overhead costs. This means that you must be prepared to look carefully at profit figures and seek explanations as to how they have been arrived at.

For marketing purposes, we are likely to be particularly interested in making comparisons between products, brands, segments and customers and in assessing the effectiveness of marketing effort expended. It will be necessary to examine very carefully both numerical information and the assumptions that lie behind the processes used to prepare it.

1.2.3 Loyalty

No doubt you are already aware that it is far more expensive to attract a new customer than to do business with an established one.

There are several reasons for this.

- Established customers do not qualify for inducements such as introductory offers and discounts.
- There are communications and other marketing costs associated with obtaining new business.
- There are other benefits to retaining satisfied customers.
- Established customers do not require as much customer service assistance as new ones.
- Established customers are more likely to generate new business through referrals.
- Established customers tend to purchase more as their relationship with the brand or supplier strengthens.

These advantages mean that customer retention is an important factor in successful trading. We therefore need to be able to monitor such matters as the amount of business that comes from new customers, the number of referrals and the proportion of business that comes from established customers. We would also like to monitor the rate at which customers leave us, but this would be more difficult.

We will return to specific relationship measures later in section 2.

As we have previously suggested, there are a number of measures that are used by marketers. In fact Farris et al (2006) have an entire book of over 50 metrics (which the authors state was published because of the need to highlight the most important measures!).

ASSIGNMENT TIP

concept

The CIM have included in the syllabus the categories of business metrics that they require you to pay attention to. They distinguish between accounting, productivity, relationship, internal and innovation and learning measures. The bulk of this chapter will take each in turn and cover their relevance, measures and sources of information.

The CIM have also separated out additional analyses including productivity, comparative, segmental and an innovation audit. These are covered in section 3.

2 Accounting

ASSIGNMENT TIP

concept

The CIM have stipulated that they do not expect you to train as an accountant. It is important however that as a marketer you are familiar with financial terminology in order to participate in business discussions and decisions.

KEY CONCEPT

concept

The **interpretation of financial data** is the key to the understanding of any business, either in a practical application or during your studies.

The **published accounts** are relevant in understanding the basic **financial health** of a company and may provide some insight into fundamental trends and strategies being adopted. This is especially relevant to competitor analysis.

A firm's **management accounting** function can provide valuable information to the marketer.

Perhaps the most important thing for marketers to understand about finance is that by training and personal inclination, accountants tend to be both sceptical and pessimistic. In fact, one of the basic philosophical planks of accountancy theory is known as the **prudence concept**. This dictates that potential losses should be accounted for as soon as they become apparent, while gains may only be recognised when they actually occur. Optimism is not part of an accountant's duties.

Those developing marketing strategy should:

- Understand the impact of their decisions on the finances of the business
- Be able to work effectively with the finance professionals in the business
- Be competent in the use of financial techniques necessary in day-to-day management and planning for their own departments

Financial comparisons can aid decision-making by:

- **Past comparisons and trends**. Looking back at the organisation's financial history and records can identify similar situations and help draw conclusions and trends from the information.
- **Competitor analysis**. Examining published information of other organisations, such as competitors, for financial indicators may aid decision-making.
- **Forecasting** the future is based in part on financial assumptions.
- **Modelling**. Financial data may be used to model the effect of decisions.

2.1 The finance department and marketing

The finance department has three important accounting roles, and produces three different forms of output, all of which are relevant to the marketing department.

- **Financial accounting**. For all limited companies, the financial statements are published in a document called the **annual report and accounts**. This is a legal requirement, to let shareholders know how their business is doing.
    - (i) It will include a **balance sheet** (also referred to as a Statement of Financial Position), a **profit and loss account** (alternatively known as an income statement) and a **cash flow statement** (Statement of Cash Flows). These must follow certain rules laid down by law and by Financial Reporting Standards.
    - (ii) The annual report also includes a **directors' report** and a **chairman's report** which talk about the past and future of the company in general terms.
    - (iii) Financial accounting is **important to marketing activities** because the financial effects of marketing activities must be recorded properly and accurately.
    - (iv) The financial statements are an important communication to outsiders, and thus have a **PR impact**.
- **Management accounting**. While financial accounting is an essentially **historical process**, concerned with describing how the current financial position arose, the role of the management accountant is to look to the **future** by providing data and analysis that support decision-making and the control of continuing operations.
- **Cost** accounting provides inputs into decisions about pricing and the use of resources. It is vital for many of the hard choices that have to be made in budgeting.
- Preparation of **budgets** is essential if progress is to be controlled. (Chapter 9 covers this in detail)
- Special techniques such as **breakeven analysis** are used to aid planning and decisions about products and markets.
- **Corporate finance** is concerned with ensuring that sufficient **funds** are available to the business in order for it to pursue its objectives. For example, a £25m advertising campaign requires the organisation to have these funds to spend.

ACTIVITY 1

application

Obtain some company reports which contain published accounts. These can be obtained from a variety of sources, including the following website where you will find links to reports:

http://www.rba.co.uk/sources/finars.htm

Examine the content of the accounts. Look at the way they are laid out, typical content and consider their role as a piece of communication about the financial health of the organisation.

MARKETING AT WORK

The need for clear financial documents cannot be understated. It is estimated that poor financial management and over complicated systems cost small and medium sized businesses in the UK up to £4.8bn. The key reason for this is that managers spend an unnecessary average of 26 days to complete work on their paper based ledgers.

Based on an article by Business-Inc (2007) which can be found at: http://www.business-inc.co.uk/news/2007/august/poor-financial-management.htm

2.2 Financial statements

One purpose of financial statements is to show whether a business has made a profit or a loss over a period of time from its operations. A statement showing the performance of a business in a given period of time is called a **profit and loss account** (or an **income statement**).

Entities that do not exist to make a profit must nevertheless spend within their means. These organisations produce a **performance statement** disclosing their income and expenditure for a given period, rather than a statement of profit or loss.

2.3 Profit and loss account

Businesses of whatever size or nature exist to make a profit. A financial statement showing the profit or loss earned in a period is the **profit and loss account**. The purpose of a business is to make money for its owners. A business invests money in resources with the intention of making even more money. Profit is the excess of income over expenditure. When expenditure exceeds income, the business is running at a loss.

KEY CONCEPT

concept

A **profit and loss account** measures the operational performance of the company over a period of time.

- **Gross profit** is the profit shown after the purchase or production cost of the goods sold is deducted from the value of sales.
- **Net profit** is the gross profit, plus any other income from sources other than the sale of goods, minus other expenses of the business which are not included in the cost of goods sold.

As an example, let us look at the accounts of ARC Ltd.

ARC LIMITED

PROFIT AND LOSS ACCOUNTS FOR THE YEARS ENDED 31 DECEMBER

	20X0	*20X1*
	£'000	£'000
Turnover (Revenue)	53,470	98,455
Cost of sales	40,653	70,728
Gross profit	12,817	27,727
Distribution costs	2,317	4,911
Administrative expenses	1,100	2,176
Profit on ordinary activities before interest	9,400	20,640
Interest receivable	100	40
Interest payable	–	(280)
Profit for the financial year	9,500	20,400
Taxation for the year	3,200	5,200
Profit	6,300	15,200

The profit and loss account is a statement in which **revenues and expenditure** are compared to arrive at a figure of **profit or loss**.

Most of the **marketing expenses** will appear in these sections:

(a) **Distribution costs**. These are expenses associated with the process of selling and delivering goods to customers and in published accounts they will **include marketing expenses**.

- Salaries of marketing and sales directors and management
- Salaries and commissions of sales staff
- Travelling and entertainment expenses of sales people
- Marketing costs (eg advertising, market research, sales promotion)
- Costs of running and maintaining delivery vans
- Discounts allowed to customers for early payment of their debts
- Bad debts written off

(b) **Administration expenses**

- Salaries of directors, management and office staff
- Rent and rates
- Insurance
- Telephone and postage
- Printing and stationery
- Heating and lighting

2.3.1 Capital and revenue items

Distinction between capital and revenue items

(a) Capital items are related to financing decisions, such as the purchase of a fixed asset and how the purchase is to be financed.

(b) Revenue items are related to trading decisions, that is the sale, purchase and expense, transactions associated with normal trading.

(c) (i) The type of decision-making involved will be very different for revenue and capital items.
(ii) The accounting treatment for capital items is different to that of revenue items.

2.4 Balance sheet

KEY CONCEPT

concept

A **balance sheet** (also known as a **statement of financial position)** is a snapshot of the financial position of a business at a point in time.

- **Assets** are things of value that a business owns or has use of. **Fixed assets** (non-current assets) are assets which are acquired for use within a business with a view to facilitating the generation of revenue (and consequently profits). **Current assets** are assets which are owned by the business which are intended to be turned into cash within one year. **Debtors** are financial obligations **to** us.
- **Liabilities** are financial obligations to someone else. **Creditors** are people to whom the business has a financial obligation. **Capital** is the money put into a business by the owners and it is therefore owed by the business to the owners.

2.4.1 The accounting equation

The **assets** of a business are the things it owns which offer an economic benefit.

A **liability** is money owed by a business, for whatever reason. For example, at any one time, it might owe money to suppliers for goods it has purchased but not yet paid for (trade creditors). It might owe tax.

The **capital** is the amount invested by the owners in the business. Arguably the business 'owes' it to the owners (in a similar way to owing money to creditors).

We can put assets, liabilities and capital together to give us the **accounting equation**:

Capital + Liabilities = Assets

This could equally well be written:

Capital = Assets – Liabilities

Since the second part of this equation is what we call **net assets**, we can write, even more simply:

Capital = Net assets

2.4.2 The balance sheet format

The accounting equation explains why the 'net assets' and the total of 'capital and reserves' are both equal to £16,100,000 in 20X1 in the following balance sheet.

ARC LIMITED

BALANCE SHEET AS AT 31 DECEMBER 20X1

	20X0		*20X1*	
Fixed assets (Non-current assets)	£'000	£'000	£'000	£'000
Intangible assets	100		100	
Tangible assets	7,900		12,950	
Investments	100		100	
		8,100		13,150
Current assets				
Stocks (Inventory)	5,000		15,000	
Debtors (Receivables)	8,900		27,100	
Cash at bank and in hand	600		–	
	14,500		42,100	
Creditors: amounts falling due within one year (current liabilities)				
Bank loans and overdrafts			16,200	
Trade creditors (Payables)	6,000		10,000	
Accruals and deferred income	800		1,000	
Other creditors including taxation	6,200		11,200	
	13,000		38,400	
Net current assets		1,500		3,700
Creditors: amounts falling due after more than one year				
15% debenture stock		600		750
Net assets		9,000		16,100

	20X0	*20X1*
Capital and reserves		
Called up share capital		
Ordinary shares of £1 each	6,000	6,000
Profit and loss account reserve	3,000	10,100
	9,000	16,100

Particular aspects to note about the balance sheets shown above are as follows.

(a) **Date**. The balance sheet is headed up 'as at 31 December 20X1'. This is telling the user that it is a picture of the affairs of the company **at a point in time**. Over time this picture will change.

(b) **Comparative figures** (figures for the previous period) are always given to indicate movement. They should be prepared on a consistent basis and usually refer to the balance sheet one year ago.

(c) **Equation balances**. In the example, capital and reserves (or shareholders' funds) equal net assets.

We will now briefly discuss each heading.

2.4.3 Fixed assets (Non-current assets)

A **fixed asset** is any asset, tangible or intangible, acquired for retention by a **business** to give continuing economic benefits (that is, it must be in use for over one year) by **the business**, and not held for resale in the normal course of trading.

(a) A **tangible** fixed asset is a **physical** asset. A salesman's car is a tangible fixed asset.

(b) An **intangible** fixed asset does not have a physical existence. The expense of acquiring **patent rights** and some new product development costs on occasions would be classified as an intangible fixed asset. The value of a **brand name** also comes under this category although this is a matter of considerable dispute. (We deal with this later in this section.)

(c) **Investments** held for the long term would be classified as fixed assets.

Fixed assets, except freehold land, **wear out or lose their usefulness in the course of time**. The accounts of a business try to recognise this by gradually writing off the asset's cost in the **profit and loss account** (income statement) over several accounting periods to reflect the loss in value in the balance sheet. This is called **depreciation**.

2.4.4 Current assets

Current assets fall into two categories.

(a) **Items owned** by the business (or owed to the business) which will be turned into cash within one year

(b) **Cash**, including money in the bank, owned by the business

These assets are **current** as they are **continually flowing** through the business.

Stock (Inventory)

Stock comprises **goods for use or resale**. They can exist either in their original form (for example, as the component parts which when assembled make up the product), or as **work in progress** or as **finished goods** awaiting resale.

Debtors (Receivables)

A debtor is a person, business or company who **owes money to the business**. When the debt is finally paid, the debtor disappears as an asset, to be replaced by cash at bank and in hand, another asset. **Most debtors are customers who have bought on credit but have not yet paid**.

2.4.5 Current liabilities

A **liability** is owed **by** a business **to** another person or organisation (eg to the bank or government). Here are some examples.

- Loans repayable within one year
- A bank overdraft is normally payable on demand
- A **trade creditor** (owed money for debts incurred in the course of trading)
- Taxation payable
- Accrued charges (expenses incurred, for which no bill has yet been received)

2.4.6 Creditors (Payables)

Creditors are owed money by the business. They represent the **liabilities** part of the accounting equation. It is important to know when their debts fall due for payment. **Trade creditors**, who have supplied goods and services, are usually payable after a very short period. Tax amounts due to the government are usually payable within a few months. Loans to finance the business usually have a **maturity date** which may be imminent or several years away. It is worth noting that bank overdrafts (which many businesses use as a source of working capital) are usually repayable **on demand**, so the bank manager wields a great deal of power.

The arbitrary division on the balance sheet of creditors into those payable within one year and those not payable until at least a year has passed provides a rough division for comparison with fixed and current assets.

This is why many firms have **credit control departments**. They assess the creditworthiness of new customers, and monitor their payments record. They chase any late-payers and employ debt collectors. The purpose of any sale is to make a profit, and offering credit has a cost and a risk.

2.4.7 Long-term liabilities (Non-current liabilities)

Long-term liabilities include:

- Loans which are repayable after one year, such as a bank loan
- A mortgage, which is a loan specifically secured against a freehold property
- Debentures (borrowings at a fixed rate of interest usually repayable by a specified date)

2.4.8 Capital and reserves

The **capital and reserves** figure in the balance sheet represents the **shareholders' funds**.

(a) The original **capital** contributed by the ordinary shareholders (the cost of the shares).

(b) The **profits** the business has **retained** over the years **which** are accumulated in the profit and loss account balance.

2.5 Cash flow

The cash flow statement refers to the flows of monies received and spent by the business. It is a powerful document (Walsh, 2008). The cash flow statement links together the profit and loss account and the opening and closing balance sheets.

A company must maintain sufficient cash resources to pay all legitimate bills as they arise. Walsh (2008) compares cash flowing through an organisation with the flow of blood through a human body. He states:

"*it is crucial to the independent survival of the business that this tank does not run dry*" (Walsh, ibid, pg 100).

When cash runs out, a company's management is no longer in a position to make independent decisions. In this instance the company is no longer 'liquid' and outside agencies such as creditors or a bank may decide it's fate. This could be to file for bankruptcy, restructure or face potential takeover if a buyer emerges.

2.6 Budgetary control

We cover controlling budgets in detail in chapter 9 when we look at managing marketing finances. In chapter 9, we consider the purpose of budgets and the processes used to set and control marketing spend. A budget is a plan for a defined period of time expressed in financial terms to be referred to and used as a **control tool** throughout the budget period. A beautifully laid out budgeted income statement that is rarely referred to is worthless.

3 Productivity measures

Productivity is important to measure because it looks at the effectiveness of the allocation and usage of the organisations resources to turn inputs into outputs.

KEY CONCEPT

concept

Productivity is the ratio of $\frac{\text{Outputs}}{\text{Inputs}}$ or $\frac{\text{Output units}}{\text{Input units}}$.

For example, a measure of productivity might be revenue/profit per employee.

	Revenue	*Profits*	*Employees*
Deutsche Telecom	\$41.8bn	\$2.5bn	179,000
TeleKom Italia	\$27.3bn	\$2.2bn	127,000
BT	\$25.7bn	\$2.8bn	124,000

In this example, BT appears to be most productive generating over \$22,000 profit per employee compared with \$17,000 for TeleKom Italia and \$14,000 for Deutsche Telecom.

Productivity can be targeted to marketing measures too.

Examples of productivity relating to marketing costs

- Increases in customer recognition of a brand name per £ of advertising
- Number of sales leads generated by an exhibition
- Response rate to direct mailshots
- Number of hits on a website converted into purchases per cost of website

MARKETING AT WORK

application

Coca-Cola

Coca-Cola enjoyed volume growth of 7 to 8% pa in the 15 years to 1998, with profits rising 18% pa. However in 1999 it revealed a 13% fall in profits, and a return to shareholders of only 1.4%. The share price fell. Most worrying, unit-case volumes of syrup (the firm's preferred underlying measure of growth) fell by 1% Jan–March 1999, the first fall for a long time. Coca-Cola blamed the world economy.

Coke's previous growth had been due to a unique set of circumstances. It had rationalised its bottling operations and *Pepsi* had not performed well. But in the late 1990s there was market resistance to price increases. Selling expenses were \$6.6bn, compared to net profit of \$3.5bn. In 1997, a 4% rise in selling expenses produced a 10% rise in sales volumes. In 1998 a similar rise only increased volumes by 6%.

Since 1999, Coca-Cola has faced a public relations crisis in Belgium and two changes of chief executive. It is still successful, but is facing yet more changes in direction, and is investing in more brands. In May 2007, Coca-Cola announced its intention to buy *Glaceau*, a maker of energy and vitamin-enhanced drinks for \$4.1 billion.

Dasani, Coca-Cola's bottled water brand, was launched in 1993. Dasani had to be withdrawn in the UK due to contamination with and also for the fact that it turned out to be tap water from the mains. In 2010 Coca Cola announced they would be distributing Dasani water in new packaging comprised of 30% plant based materials. These bottles represent up to a 25% reduction in carbon emissions when compared to standard water bottles (though this still represents 2000 times the energy usage of tap water!).

4 Customer and relationship measures

One of the key influences of relationship marketing theory is the notion of the being able to measure the value of different customer groups. There are a number of commonly used customer measures including:

- **Customer acquisition** – how many new customers attracted, their value and the cost of attracting these customers (eg promotional campaigns, referrals, word of mouth etc.)
- **Customer repeat purchase** – repeat purchase behaviour, frequency and value
- **Customer profitability** – net profit of a customer
- **Customer experience satisfaction** – perceptions, service, compare with other organisation
- **Customer retention** – longevity, lifetime value, costs.
- **Customer loyalty status –** passive or active, good referral, value of loyalty and referral markets
- **Customer segment** – most profitable segments to target and encourage loyalty

4.1 Customer satisfaction

Measuring customer satisfaction is one of the most established marketing metrics. Many agencies specialise in improving satisfaction measures because although it is a commonly used term, it is very difficult to define and therefore measure.

Think for example about an airline passenger. To measure their overall satisfaction with their flight may actually be quite complex for several reasons. As a service, there will be several 'moments of truth' or episodes in the overall service encounter where an opportunity exists for their satisfaction or dissatisfaction. These could include:

- the initial booking
- the check in
- airport security procedures
- airport services and waiting lounge
- transfer to the flight
- the various stages of the flight (eg welcome, take off , baggage reclaim etc.)

Depending on events occurring at these different stages of the overall 'journey experience' the passenger will respond according to whether they are satisfied or dissatisfied (usually only if formal research is conducted). For a large proportion of the journey, the satisfaction of the customer is dependent on the behaviour of third parties such as the airport management and staff, other passengers etc. To directly rate overall satisfaction with a specific airline would provide a false impression.

Other complexities associated with measuring loyalty arise because it is a highly subjective construct which is subject to response bias. One persons rating of 'excellent' may be another's 'good'. Satisfaction is also a function of prior expectations. If expectations are raised before the product or service is experienced, a negative score is more likely.

Where dissatisfaction is seen, marketers can and should use this information to prioritise improvements.

4.2 Customer loyalty

Loyalty is another construct which is not as easy to measure as it initially might appear. The concept of customers using a repertoire of brands at different times in their life and for different usage contexts should not be new to you. For this reason, it would be too simplistic to view a customer who buys more than one brand within the specified sector as 'disloyal' to any specific brand.

Despite this complexity, loyalty is frequently used as an indication of a future revenue stream (Farris et al, 2006). Typical metrics used to measure loyalty include:

- **Willingness to pay a premium**- measured through surveys or observing behaviour patterns
- **Willingness to search** – measured as a percentage of customers willing to delay purchase, change stores, or reduce quantities purchased in order to avoid switching brands
- **Willingness to recommend** – frequently measured through 1-5 scale within surveys

4.3 Customer retention

Relationship marketing theory specifically promotes the notion that it is cheaper (and thus more effective) to retain existing customers than to win new ones. Retention relies on satisfied customers and is not necessarily as simple as reviewing traditional customer loyalty measures. Indeed, some customers may be psychologically loyal to a brand (eg Pampers nappies) but are not retained as customers (babies are now toddlers and therefore do not need nappies!). The value of those loyal customers is still useful to the organisation as a result of positive word of mouth and referrals. Conversely, a customer may be retained because there is a lack of alternative supplier (eg household water). Once competition opens up in the market, however, a customer who is not loyal or is dissatisfied is not likely to be retained (as was the case for BT when telecommunications competition increased).

One approach taken by marketers to measuring the worth of loyal customers is to calculate **customer lifetime value**.

4.3.1 Customer lifetime value

KEY CONCEPT

concept

Customer lifetime value measures the worth of a customer to the firm either as an individual or as part of a segment. (Kumar, 2008).

Customer lifetime value is an important concept because it indicates long term health of the customer relationship along with an upper limit on spending to acquire new customers (Farris et al, 2006).

Customer lifetime value can be calculated using the following formula

$$\text{CLV (£)} = \text{Margin (£)} \times \frac{\text{Retention(\%)}}{1 + \text{Discount(\%)} - \text{Retention(\%)}}$$

The components of the formula are:

- CLV = Customer lifetime value – expressed in £
- Margin = **Constant margin** (contribution after deducting variable costs including retention spending)
- Retention = **Retention rate expressed as a %.** When retention equals 0, the customer will never be retained, when it equals 1, the customer will always be retained.
- Discount = **Discount rate expressed as a %**. A discount rate is used because there is a time and a cost associated with money (eg everyone would rather be paid sooner rather than later). The exact discount factors depend on the discount rate chosen and the number of periods until we receive cash. Money received in ten years will therefore be discounted (eg 50%) more than money received in five years time (eg 25%).

MARKETING AT WORK

concept

An example CLV calculation:

A gym charges £19.95 per month for unlimited swimming in its pool.

Variable costs are £1.50 per member per month

Marketing spend (retention spending) equates to £6 per year

Constant margin is therefore (£19.95 – £1.50 – £6/12) = £17.95

Retention is high so a figure of 0.995 is given.

A monthly discount rate is 1% (expressed as 0.01)

CLV = margin × (retention/ 1+discount – retention)

CVL = £17.95 × (0.995/(1+0.01 – 0.995)

CLV - £17.95 × 66.33

CLV = £1,191

Example adapted from Farris et al (2006)

Kumar (2008), chapter 4, demonstrates in detail how to measure Customer Lifetime Value.

Farris et al (2006) pages 143 – 145 also cover the formula in detail.

Microsoft have a number of business templates available online. They have a simplified version of the CLV calculation available to download at:

http://office.microsoft.com/en-us/templates/TC300019571033.aspx ■

ACTIVITY 2

application

Try to calculate CLV for some of your customers.

4.4 Segmental analysis

"*In a strategic context, segmentation means the identification of customer groups that respond differently from other groups to competitive offerings.*" Aaker & McLoughlin (2007) p.42

Different segments and different customers offer different levels of profit. As you know, one of the most important tools for market analysis is that of **segmentation**.

A company can approach this first by examining what market segments it currently operates in, and how big a contribution each segment is making to total turnover and profit. Finally, it should consider whether each market segment is in growth or decline.

A segmental analysis might look like this.

Market segment	*Turnover*	*Proportion of total turnover*	*Profit*	*Proportion of total profit*
	£k	%	£k	%
A	500	14	50	9
B	1,000	29	200	36
C	1,500	43	150	27
D	500	14	150	27
	3,500		550	

Market segment	*Turnover*	*Profit*	*Profit as a % of turnover*
	£k	£k	%
A	500	50	10
B	1,000	200	20
C	1,500	150	10
D	500	150	30
	3,500	550	

You will note that each segment offers different profit opportunities.

4.5 Evaluating market segments

When evaluating market segments it is necessary to review two issues.

Market attractiveness measures are based upon

- Segment size
- Segment's rate of growth
- Segment's profitability
- Customer price sensitivity
- Stage of industry life cycle
- Predictability
- Demand patterns
- Potential for substitutes
- Five forces analysis
- PEST factors

4.5.1 How to calculate profits on a segmental basis

Identifying total turnover is easy. A segment is a collection of customers, and revenue streams from them are fairly easy to identify. Identifying costs is much harder. Here are some different types of cost.

(a) Fixed or variable

(i) Fixed costs will be incurred however many or however few items are produced or sold. Factory rent is an example. These are also called overheads.

(ii) Variable costs relate directly to the number of units produced. For example, a variable cost item in producing books is paper. These are also called direct costs.

(b) Controllable or uncontrollable

(i) Controllable costs are incurred at management discretion, such as an advertising campaign.

(ii) Uncontrollable costs are those which, in the short-run at least, management are committed to.

(c) Avoidable or unavoidable

(i) Avoidable cost: this cost is affected by a decision.

(ii) Unavoidable cost: this cost will not be affected by a decision.

For example, the cost of the managing director's salary will not be affected by a decision not to serve an individual customer.

Typical marketing costs

Cost	Comment
Direct selling expenses	Personal calls by salesperson
Indirect selling	Sales admin, supervision
Marketing research	Consultancies, primary data collection, analysis
Advertising	Media costs
Sales promotion	Consumer, trade etc
Transport	Carriage costs
Storage	Warehousing
Order processing	Checking, billing, bad debts

These can be allocated, in different ways, to products, customer groups, and sales territories. We are currently interested in segments. The steps involved in segmental analysis are as follows.

Step 1 Identify revenue derived from a segment

Step 2 Identify direct product costs (eg materials)

Step 3 Identify marketing costs

Step 4 Allocate avoidable costs to the segment (ie those costs which would be saved if the segment were not serviced)

4.6 Customer communications

Communications are designed to meet three objectives.

- **Awareness** Increase brand **awareness** and establish brand **recognition**
- **Trial** Stimulate **trial purchase**
- **Reinforcement** Stimulate and **reinforce** brand **loyalty**

To succeed in achieving these goals, communications must:

- Gain attention
- Communicate a message
- Reinforce and improve attitudes to the brand
- Obtain the audience's liking for the message and its execution

There are two elements to the evaluation of the effectiveness of marketing communications campaigns.

(a) **Developing and testing** the messages themselves: **guidance** through **pre-testing**.

(b) Measuring the overall **impact and effect** of the message: **quantitative** evaluation after the campaign (**post testing**).

The difficult part is measuring the effectiveness of the marketing communications process. The following are some possible techniques.

Communication activity	Typical measurement
Personal selling	Sales targets; productivity; costs
Public relations	Editorial coverage; awareness; opinions
Direct marketing	Enquiries generated
Sales promotion	Stock turnover
Exhibitions	Contacts made
Online communications	'Click through' numbers

The following table shows possible advertising effectiveness measures. Generally tests may be conducted in a contrived experimental lab or within a real life context.

Laboratory measures (respondents aware of testing)	Field test measures (respondents unaware of testing)
Pretesting panels • Consumer panels • Portfolio tests • Readability tests • Physiological measure	**Pretesting** • Dummy advertising • Inquiry tests • On air tests
Pretesting labs • Theatre tests • Hall tests • Laboratory scores	**Post testing** • Recognition • Recall tests • Association measures
	Pre and post procedures • Sales tests • Test markets

5 Internal measures

Internal measures of marketing effectiveness will review issues relating to employees and work processes and procedures.

Employee issues include:

- **Team working** (eg supportiveness of each other, collaboration, learning from each other, effectiveness of team task outcomes)
- **Employee morale** (eg willingness/enthusiasm to/for work, absenteeism)
- **Employee productivity** (eg quantity of work, quality of work, speed, accuracy)

5.1 Recruitment

To get a clear idea of how efficient their recruitment and selection practices are, firms can ask themselves these questions.

- Can we identify human resources requirements from the business plans?
- How fast do we respond to demands from line managers for human resources?
- Do we give/receive good advice on labour market trends?
- Do we select the right advertising media to reach the market?
- How effective (and cost effective) is our recruitment advertising?
- How do our recruits actually perform – do we end up employing the right people?
- Do we retain our new recruits?

ACTIVITY 3

Try to answer the questions above for your own work situation. How easy or difficult did you find it to address these questions?

Recruitment and selection practices can be reviewed in various ways.

Review	Comment
Performance indicators	Each stage of the process can be assessed by performance indicators, for example the time it takes to process an application. Data can be collected to check any deviation from standard.
Cost-effectiveness	For example, number of relevant responses per recruitment ad, or cost of various advertising media per application elicited (or person employed).
Monitoring the workforce	High staff turnover, absenteeism and other problems (particularly among new recruits) may reflect poor recruitment and selection. Lack of workforce diversity may highlight discriminatory practices.
Attitude surveys	The firm can ask its recruits what they thought of the process.
Actual individual job performance	A person's actual performance can be compared with what was expected when (s)he was recruited.

5.2 Employee appraisal as a measurement tool

Three basic requirements of a **formal appraisal system** are: defining what is to be appraised, recording assessments, and getting the appraiser and appraisee together for feedback and planning. It can be a key time for employee attitude measurement.

There are three basic requirements for a formal appraisal system.

(a) The **formulation of desired traits and standards** against which individuals can be consistently and objectively assessed.

(b) **Recording assessments**. Managers should be encouraged to utilise a standard framework, but still be allowed to express what they consider important, and without too much form-filling.

(c) **Getting the appraiser and appraisee together**, so that both contribute to the assessment and plans for improvement and/or development.

A systematic appraisal system can be depicted as follows.

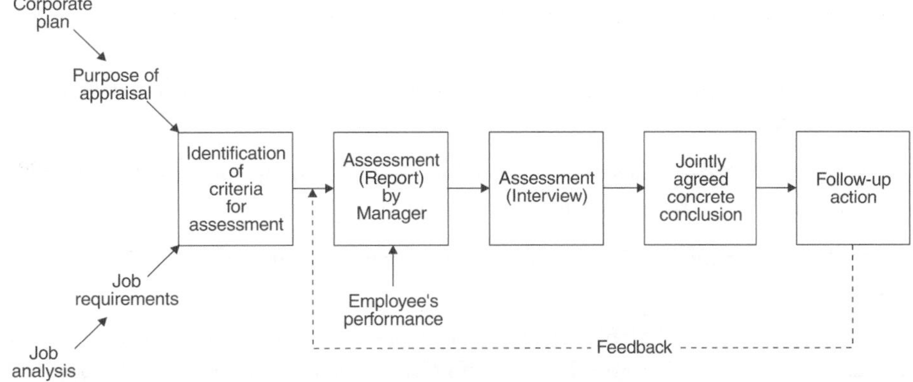

Assessments must be related to a common standard, in order for comparisons to be made between individuals: on the other hand, they should be related to meaningful **performance criteria**, which take account of the critical variables in each job.

5.2.1 Appraisal techniques

A variety of appraisal techniques may be used, measuring different criteria in different ways.

(a) **Overall assessment** The manager writes in narrative form his judgements about the appraisee. There will be no guaranteed consistency of the criteria and areas of assessment, however, and managers may not be able to convey clear, effective judgements in writing.

(b) **Guided assessment**. Assessors are required to comment on a number of specified characteristics and performance elements, with guidelines as to how terms such as 'application', 'integrity' and 'adaptability' are to be interpreted in the work context. This is more precise, but still rather vague.

(c) **Grading**. Grading adds a comparative frame of reference to the general guidelines, whereby managers are asked to select one of a number of levels or degrees to which the individual in question displays the given characteristic. These are also known as **rating scales**.

Numerical values may be added to ratings to give rating scores. Alternatively a less precise **graphic scale** may be used to indicate general position on a plus/minus scale.

Factor: job knowledge

High __✓__ Average ________ Low ________

(d) **Behavioural incident methods**. These concentrate on employee behaviour, which is measured against typical behaviour in each job, as defined by common critical incidents of successful and unsuccessful job behaviour reported by managers.

(e) **Results-orientated schemes**. This reviews performance against specific targets and standards of performance agreed in advance by manager and subordinate together. There are significant advantages to such an approach.

   (i) The subordinate is more involved in appraisal because (s)he is able to evaluate his/her progress in achieving jointly-agreed targets.

   (ii) The manager is relieved of a critic's role, and becomes a coach.

   (iii) Clear and known targets help modify behaviour.

The effectiveness of the scheme will depend on the **targets set** (are they clearly defined? realistic?) and the **commitment** of both parties to make it work.

	Benefits
Individual	• Objectives are established in relation to the whole organisation • Key results and timescales are established • Compares past performance and future activities against standards • Basis for performance related pay schemes
Organisation	• Suitable promotion candidates are identified • Areas of improvement can be seen • Communication is improved • Basis for medium to long term HR planning

Evaluating the appraisal scheme may involve:

(a) Asking appraisers and appraisees how they **felt** about the system (addressing issues of perceived usefulness, fairness and so on)

(b) Checking to see if there have been enhancements in **performance** by the individual and the organisation (as a result of problem solving and improvement planning)

(c) Reviewing other **indicative** factors, such as staff turnover or disciplinary problems, lack of management succession and so on

However, firms should not expect too much of the appraisal scheme. Appraisal systems, because they target the individual's performance, concentrate on the lowest level of performance feedback: they ignore the organisational and systems context of performance.

5.2.2 Staff retention

Whilst researching staff satisfaction as a retention factor, de Bono and Heller (2006) reviewed the American retailer Sears' 70 – question employee satisfaction survey. The researchers identified the following six questions as the most powerful in improving retention and improving customer service related behaviour:

1. Do you like the kind of work you do?
2. Does it give you a sense of accomplishment?
3. Are you proud to say you work for the company?
4. How does the amount of work you are expected to do influence your overall attitude about your job?
5. How do your physical working conditions influence your overall attitude about your job?
6. How does the way you are treated by those who supervise you influence your overall attitude about your job?

de bono and Heller (2006) recommend supplementing these questions with :

7. Do you feel good about the future of the company?
8. Is the company making the changes necessary to compete effectively?
9. Do you understand the company's **business strategy**?
10. Do you see a connection between the work you do and the company's strategic objectives?

5.3 Internal communications

You should already be familiar with the concept of *internal marketing* (the need to actively encourage customer centricity throughout the organisation including treating employees as internal customers).

Varey and Lewis (1990) bring together the core theories of internal marketing if you would like to research them further ■

Effective communications are a key element of internal marketing. Understanding the effect on staff morale, corporate culture, productivity and customer engagement as a result of communication mechanisms used enables future adaptations to assist improved practice.

MARKETING AT WORK

application

In the six months prior to an anticipated Ofsted government inspection, a college principal decided to provide staff with regular updates on:

- required improvements to their working practices
- new procedures to be implemented
- other news relating to the inspection.

The communication mechanisms which existed culturally included formal 'whole college 'briefings at the end of term, staff development days, staff newsletter and widespread email usage.

For Ofsted related briefings however, the principal decided to circulate paper based memos using distinctive bright green paper. The use of green paper was restricted exclusively to these memos.

At no time was the effectiveness of the method of communication (or indeed the content of the message) evaluated. Amongst the staff, the memos were not viewed positively for a number of reasons:

- Paper memos often were lost (and there was no electronic archive system for reviewing past messages)
- Not all staff were based in an office (part time casual lecturers) and so would not receive the communication
- The appearance of a piece of green paper often led to a feeling of resigned dread because it was likely to contain information relating to yet another change in working practice or task to complete by a set time.

Given that the memos were used for such an important aspect of the management of the college, had an evaluation been conducted at an earlier stage, morale, productivity and the overall results from the inspection may have been improved.

As blogging grows in usage (especially by agencies looking to promote their expertise), PR and communications blogs quadruple the number on other related marketing subjects. PR advice for the 'not for profit' section can be found at the blog site below. 'Blogger' Deborah Zanke gives advice for those with no budget to research internal communications:

http://messagecom.wordpress.com/2008/07/15/evaluating-internal-communication/

Typical areas to measure include:

- Effectiveness of the communication medium
- Effectiveness of communicating the 'intended message'
- Informal and formal communication

6 Innovation and learning measures

When assessing the level of innovation within an organisation, the question should be **'Can we continue to improve and create value?'** Whilst the customer and internal process perspectives identify the **current** parameters for competitive success, the company needs to learn and to innovate to **satisfy future needs**. This might be one of the hardest items to measure. Typical questions to address may be:

- How long does it take to develop new products?
- How quickly does the firm climb the experience curve to manufacture new products?
- What percentage of revenue comes from new products?
- How many suggestions are made by staff and are acted upon?
- What are staff attitudes? Some firms believe that employee motivation and successful communication are necessary for organisational learning.

Depending on circumstances, the company can identify measures for training and long-term investment.

6.1 Innovation audit

The chief object of being innovative is to ensure organisational success in a changing world. It can also have the following advantages.

(a) Improvements in quality of **products** and **service**
(b) A **leaner structure** – layers of management or administration may be done away with
(c) Prompt and imaginative **solutions to problems**
(d) **Less formality** in structure and style, leading to better communication
(e) **Greater confidence** inside and outside the organisation in its ability to cope with change

Innovation and new product development (NPD) is therefore essential for many firms to survive and prosper. It is an increasingly important area.

A firm needs to assess how well it is able to deliver the level and type of innovation necessary to continue to meet customer needs and expectations. **Four key areas** for the innovation audit have been identified.

- The current **organisational climate**
- Measures of the organisation's **current performance** with regard to innovation
- Review of **policies and practices** supporting innovation and facilitating it
- The balance of **styles** of the management team

6.2 Barriers to innovation in marketing

Resistance to change

Any new method of management thinking can experience some resistance from established managers. This resistance may be due to concern to protect the *status quo*.

Old planning systems

Old planning systems have sometimes downgraded marketing decisions to the tactical level. Advertising expenditure is decided on the basis of what the company can afford rather than what is strategically required. Promotion is seen as a series of short-term actions rather than as a long-term investment.

Old structures/functional specialists

Complementing traditional planning systems are traditional organisation structures. These structures freeze out new thinking on integrated marketing strategy. Individuals have limited specific responsibilities – just for advertising, say, or just for public relations – and this inhibits new thinking on integration.

Centralised control

If the chief executive keeps tight control of the organisation and of its planning and is unconvinced of the benefits of innovation then it will not happen.

Cost considerations

Innovation usually requires investment which rarely comes without considerable cost.

MARKETING AT WORK

application

Disney and Pixar

Organisational culture is an extremely important influence on innovation. A *Financial Times* report on *Disney's* purchase of *Pixar* in 2006 contrasted their distinct organisational styles.

'Disney has become a pathologically dysfunctional organisation. Like IBM of the 1970s or AT&T in the 1980s, Disney grew fat and bureaucratic in the 1990s, long after cementing its lucrative entertainment franchise. Some of Disney's problems are endemic to large corporations. When a company has 133,000 employees, it cannot be governed by human beings. Instead, it must rely on a culture to preserve its earlier entrepreneurialism, while focusing workers on the continuing mission.

Unfortunately, Disney's culture, like that of IBM and AT&T, encouraged inefficiency and stifled creativity. Over the past five years, Disney's shares have lost a third of their value and the company has become a corporate governance pariah. Many thought the low point was the fiasco surrounding Michael Ovitz, who left Disney with $140m after just 14 months. But more troubling was the release of the abysmal Treasure Planet, a film that cost about as much as Mr Ovitz and avoided universal ignominy only because so few people saw it.

To survive and prosper, large organisations must be divided into manageable pods, whose workers have independence and incentive. In contrast to Disney, Pixar was just such a free-standing, freespirited group with a relaxed, open-plan office and no signs of managerial hierarchy. John Lasseter, Pixar's creative leader, wore Hawaiian shirts and rode a scooter inside. When Pixar won Oscars, employees displayed the statues proudly but dressed them in Barbie doll clothing. Whereas Disney executives micromanaged films, including those with Pixar, Mr Lasseter let his crew run free and encouraged ideas'.

Methods of overcoming these barriers

Overcoming barrier	
Top management commitment	The most effective way of overcoming these barriers to change is through the commitment of top management. The chief executive in particular needs to be convinced of the appropriateness of the new thinking and be enthusiastic about its implementation throughout the organisation.
Marketing reorganisation	One way in which the chief executive can take advice is through a reorganisation of the marketing function in the organisation.
Training and development	It is one thing to change attitudes. It is another thing to be in a position to know exactly what to do. It needs the services of individuals trained in strategic thinking. The individuals chosen to implement any new programme must be enthusiasts capable of overcoming resistance to change.
Marketing as a competitive advantage	Those with responsibility for implementing an integrated marketing programme must do so with the objective of developing it as a sustainable, long-term competitive advantage.
Producing the results	Nothing succeeds like success. Producing the business results as a consequence of effective marketing communications will boost confidence and gain management converts to the new thinking on an integrated approach.

Stages of an innovation audit

Innovation **audits** work best when they are well planned. Here is a possible approach.

Step 1. **Benchmark with leading competitors**. For example, many motor firms regard the rate and speed of NPD as something they must emulate.

Step 2. Assess reactivity: identify performance indicators for innovation and compare with previous years.

Typical performance indicators include:

- Rate of NPD
- Number of innovations
- Success rate (more important than quantity)
- Percentage of revenue derived from innovations (3M has a target for this)
- Incremental sales resulting from innovation
- Average annual sales per new product/service
- Customer satisfaction ratings
- Staff turnover, if this affects climate of innovation

7 Analysing performance information

7.1 Comparative analysis

Making comparisons over time or against standards (or benchmarks) is essential to encourage a culture of continuous improvement.

KEY CONCEPT

concept

A **time series** is a series of figures or values recorded over time. A graph of a time series is called a **histogram**.

There are four components of a time series: **trend**, **seasonal variations**, **cyclical variations** and **random variations**.

The **trend** is the underlying long-term movement over time in the values of the data recorded. **Seasonal variations** are short-term fluctuations due to different circumstances which affect results at different points in time. **Cyclical variations** are medium-term changes in results caused by circumstances which repeat in cycles.

The following are examples of time series.

- Competitor prices for the last three months
- Total annual costs for the last two years
- Employee performance over the last ten years
- Advertising spend over the last five years

The main features to consider within time series data sets are as follows.

- A trend (eg a steadily growing market share over a five year period)
- Seasonal variations (eg porridge sales increase in winter)
- Cycles or cyclical variations (eg popularity of package holidays fluctuation according to fashion)
- Non-recurring random variations (eg a sudden fall in sales due to a competitor promotion)

7.2 Benchmarking

We covered benchmarking in Chapter 2. To recap:

KEY CONCEPT

concept

Benchmark: an external target of performance against which a firm measures its activities.

Benchmarks can be set on a variety of key performance indicators as an objective form of control. Marketing research and competitor intelligence would be needed to establish benchmarks and to monitor progress.

The practice of benchmarking is becoming increasingly popular. There are two principal approaches.

(a) **Process benchmarking**, where data is exchanged between companies with similar administrative and manufacturing processes. For example, one of the factors affecting aircraft turnaround away from the home is the availability of spare parts required for routine maintenance. This process is very similar to the provision of field maintenance for office systems such as photocopiers and computers.

(b) **Competitor benchmarking** focuses on the performance and relative strengths of direct competitors using information from customer and supplier interviews and published data from any source available. A firm tries to be as good as its competitors.

In reality it is difficult to benchmark against competitors because it is often impossible to gain access to key measures. Belonging to relevant trade associations may be one way of overcoming this problem as competitors look to improve standards throughout the industry via the association which may promote more shared information. Typically areas where information may be shared relate to issues of social importance such as environmental awareness and health related issues.

MARKETING AT WORK

application

Several organisations in the processed foods industry benchmark against industry norms with regards to levels of salt, fat and sugars found within foodstuffs.

7.2.1 Types of benchmarking

Benchmark type	Description
Internal benchmarking	comparing one operating unit or function with another within the same organisation.
Functional benchmarking	compares functions with those of the best external practitioners of those functions, regardless of the industry they are in (also known as operational, process or generic benchmarking).
Competitor benchmarking	gathers information about direct competitors, through techniques such as reverse engineering.
Strategic benchmarking	is a type of competitor benchmarking aimed at strategic action and organisational change.

MARKETING AT WORK

application

Land Rover

Land Rover vehicles came last in J D Power's 2007 US Initial Quality Survey. Land Rover is now benchmarking the quality levels of Jaguar, its sister brand, and climbing its way back up the league tables. Ford announced the sale of Jaguar and Land Rover to Tata Motors in March 2008, so presumably the benchmarking programme can continue.

A hair and beauty chain is benchmarked against a lawn mower manufacturer because they are located in the same town and so have similar local external environment conditions.

7.2.2 Advantages of benchmarking

A number of reasons to benchmark exist.

(a) **Position audit**. Benchmarking can assess a firm's existing position.

(b) The comparisons are carried out by **the managers who have to live with any changes** implemented as a result of the exercise.

(c) Benchmarking **focuses on improvement in key areas** and sets targets which are challenging but **achievable**. What is really achievable can be discovered by examining what others have achieved: managers are thus able to accept that they are not being asked to perform miracles.

(d) If **all firms provide the same standard of quality**, it **ceases to be a source of competitive advantage**.

7.2.3 Dangers of benchmarking

(a) It **implies there is one best way** of doing business – arguably this boils down to the difference between efficiency and effectiveness. A process can be efficient but its output may not be useful. Other measures such as developing the value chain may be a better way of securing competitive advantage.

(b) The benchmark may be **yesterday's solution to tomorrow's problem**. For example, a cross channel ferry company might benchmark its activities (eg speed of turnaround at Dover and Calais, cleanliness on ship) against another ferry company, whereas the real competitor is the Channel Tunnel. In any case, it is a **catching-up exercise** rather than the development of anything distinctive. After the benchmarking exercise, the competitor might improve performance in a different way.

(c) It **depends on accurate information** about competitors, in the case of competitor benchmarking, or on **appropriate analogies** in other industries, in the case of functional benchmarking.

(d) It is not focused on the **customer**.

Learning objective review

Learning objectives	Covered
1 Consider the role of marketing metrics	☑ To measure and control marketing ☑ Plan corrective action ☑ Guide future planning
2 Explore a range of measures used to determine marketing performance	☑ Basic marketing measures- market share, loyalty, profitability ☑ Accounting measures- profit and loss accounts, balance sheets, cash flow, budget control ☑ Productivity measures- inputs versus outputs ☑ Relationship and customer measures – retention (loyalty, CLV), satisfaction, communications ☑ Internal measures – recruitment, retention, performance, communications ☑ Innovation- learning, innovation audit ☑ Comparative analysis – time series, benchmarking

Quick quiz

1 What is Customer Lifetime Value?

2 Why is loyalty difficult to measure?

3 Fill in the blank. ___________: an external target of performance against which a firm measures its activities.

4 What is the alternative name for a profit and loss account?

5 The CIM require you to reach the standard of an accountant when evaluating marketing using accountancy measures. True of false?

6 What are the three objectives that customer communications are designed to achieve?

7 Internal measures only refer to marketing procedures. True or false?

8 What measures can be used within comparative analysis?

Activity debriefs

1. This will depend on the company reports you select.
2. Attempt to use the formula to calculate CLV. You may find it easier to use the Microsoft pro forma first.
3. This will depend on your own research. Try discussing the issues with a colleague.

Quiz answers

1. The financial value of a customer relationship over the time of the relationship.
2. Customers have repertoire of brands, different products may be useful at different stages of their life time etc.
3. Benchmarking: an external target of performance against which a firm measures its activities.
4. Income Statement.
5. False. You are to be aware and able to understand the figures but not to the level of detail expected of an accountant who will have trained for many years.
6. Increasing awareness, stimulating trial purchase, and reinforcing loyalty.
7. False. Innovation and staff attitude, behaviour and performance are also important.
8. Time series (eg trends, seasonal variations etc), benchmarking.

References

Aaker, D. & McLoughlin, D. (2007) Strategic Market Management, European Edition, John Wiley & sons, Chichester.

de Bono, E. and Heller, R '*Employees and customers: In the quest for customer satisfaction the link between employees and customers is key*', Thinking Managers available online at http://www.thinkingmanagers.com/management/employees-customers.php, [accessed 1stMay 2009].

Drummond G, Ensor J, and Ashford, R (2001) Strategic Marketing: Planning and control, (2nd edition).

Farris, P., Bendle, N., Pfeifer, P and Reibstein, D (2006), Key Marketing Metrics: The 50+ metrics every manager needs to know, Wharton School Publishing, Harlow.

Kumar, V (2008) Customer Lifetime Value: The Path to Profitability, Now Publishers Inc, New York.

Varey, R. and Lewis, B. (2000) Internal Marketing: Directions for Management, Routledge, London.

Walsh, C. (2008) Key Management Ratios: The 100+ ratios every manager needs to know, Prentice Hall, Harlow.

Watkis N.C. (2005) "*Do you believe the hype*?" Accountancy Age, 12th May 2005, London.

Watkis, N.C. (2009) "*Benchmarking, Balanced Scorecard and Marketing Performance*" Telegraph Business Club, available online at http://www.telegraphbusinessclub.co.uk/default.asp?p_id=search&showresults=1&showarticle=2810 [accessed 15th May 2009].

Chapter 4
Management and leadership

Topic list

1 Management
2 Leadership
3 Leadership theories and models
4 Leadership styles
5 Contingency models
6 Personal development planning

Introduction

The first section of the *Managing Marketing* syllabus is about managerial *infrastructure*: the organisational structures and processes within which the management of people and performance takes place. The third section of the syllabus is about the management of *financial resources* for marketing. In these next five chapters, however, we focus on the management of *people.*

We start by exploring the fundamental concepts of management and leadership. We attempt to get an overview of the manager's task. What is management? How should people be managed? What do managers actually do? What is the role of an operational marketing manager?

We then go on to consider the nature and scope of leadership, and whether it can usefully be distinguished as a separate function (and skill-set) of management. In today's organisations, managers are often called upon to be leaders – and *vice versa,* and it will be worth considering to what extent this is true in your own work context.

We explore a range of key models which seek to explain what makes a 'good' manager or leader. This should provide a framework for you to analyse your own strengths and weaknesses, and to diagnose leadership problems in your work context. We will discuss a range of more specific management (or leadership) *skills and techniques* in later chapters of this Text, in the context of managing marketing teams.

Finally, we set up a framework to help you reflect on your own approach to management and leadership, and prepare a personal development plan.

Syllabus linked learning objectives

By the end of the chapter you will be able to:

	Learning objectives	Syllabus link
1	Describe the scope and role of management and leadership, and critically evaluate the differences between them	2.1
2	Identify the role of an 'operational marketing manager'	2.1
3	Outline and apply a range of leadership models (trait, style and contingency) to identify and evaluate your leadership style	2.1
4	Reflect on your personal approach to management and leadership and produce a personal development plan	2.1

1 Management

1.1 What is management?

KEY CONCEPT

concept

Management may be defined, most simply, as 'getting things done through other people'.

An **organisation** has been defined as '*a social arrangement for the controlled performance of collective goals*' (Huczynski & Buchanan, 2001). This immediately suggests the need for management, because:

- The activity of the organisation, and its roles and relationships, have to be structured and co-ordinated (as we saw in Chapter 1).
- Goals or objectives have to be set for the organisation, at all levels.
- Progress and results have to be monitored to ensure that objectives are met.
- Corporate values, ethics and operating principles have to be communicated and sustained.
- Somebody has to look after the interests of the organisation's owners (shareholders) and other stakeholders.

Management is such a universal feature of the business landscape, that you may not have thought much about what 'management' means – or might mean. For hundreds of years, people have been doing management in organisations. Yet every year there is new research and new ideas about why management is necessary; what managers actually do; and how they can do it better.

There are many different definitions of management. For example:

- The key purpose of management (and leadership) is to 'provide direction, facilitate change and achieve results through the efficient, creative and responsible use of resources' (Management Standards Centre).
- Management is 'a social process entailing responsibility for the effective and economical planning and regulation of the operations of an enterprise, in fulfilment of given purposes or tasks, such responsibility entailing: (a) judgement and decision in determining plans and in using data to control performance and progress against plans; and (b) the guidance, integration, motivation and supervision of the personnel composing the enterprise and carrying out its operations.' (Brech, 1965).

1.2 Functions and focus of management

Classical writers on management and organisation were largely concerned with the manager's role in ensuring *efficiency:* controlling resources and processes rather than people. An awareness of management as first of all an *interpersonal* process, involving communication and influence, only developed later. Let's look briefly at the evolution of thinking on the functions and focus of management.

1.2.1 Henri Fayol

Fayol (1841 – 1925) was a French industrialist who put forward and popularised the concept of the 'universality of management principles': in other words, the idea that all organisations could be structured and managed according to the same rational principles. Fayol himself recognised that applying such principles in practice was not simple: 'Seldom do we have to apply the same principles twice in identical conditions; allowance must be made for different and changing circumstances.'

However, Fayol classified five **functions of management** which apply to any organisation.

Function	Comment
Planning	Determining priorities and objectives, and strategies, policies, programmes and procedures for achieving those objectives, for the organisation and its sub-units.
Organising	Establishing a structure of tasks which need to be performed to achieve the goals of the organisation; grouping these tasks into jobs for individuals or teams; allocating jobs to sections and departments; delegating authority to carry out the jobs; and providing systems of information and communication, for the co-ordination of activities.
Commanding	Giving instructions to subordinates to carry out tasks, for which the manager has authority (to make decisions) and responsibility (for performance).
Co-ordinating	Harmonising the goals and activities of individuals and groups within the organisation. Management must reconcile differences in approach, effort, interest and timing, in favour of overall (or 'super-ordinate') shared goals.
Controlling	Measuring and correcting the activities of individuals and groups, to ensure that their performance is in accordance with plans. Deviations from plans are identified and corrected.

ACTIVITY 1

concept

Group the activities of a manager in your organisation into Fayol's five functions. What do you think is left out from Fayol's list? What do you think is wrong with it – or inadequate about it?

1.2.2 Scientific management

Frederick W Taylor (1856-1915) pioneered the scientific management movement in the USA. An industrial engineer, he was among the first to argue that management should be based on *'well-recognised, clearly defined and fixed principles, instead of depending on more or less hazy ideas'* (Taylor, 1911). The focus of management was on maximising efficiency and productivity.

Scientific management techniques (or 'Taylorism') included the following key elements.

- **Work study techniques** were used to analyse tasks and establish the most efficient methods to use. No variation was permitted in the way work was done, since the aim was to use the 'one best way'.
- **Planning and doing were separated**. It was assumed that the persons who were intellectually equipped to do a particular type of work were probably unlikely to be able to plan it to the best advantage: this was the manager's job.
- Jobs were **micro-designed**: divided into single, simple task components which formed a whole specialised 'job' for an individual, rather than permitting an individual to perform whole or part-task processes. (Task 'meaning' and 'significance', now considered essential to job satisfaction, had not yet emerged as important values.)
- Workers were **paid incentives** on the basis of acceptance of the new methods and output norms; the new methods greatly increased productivity and profits. Pay was assumed to be the only important motivating force.

Scientific management as practised by Taylor and contemporaries such as Gilbreth and Gantt was very much about **manual work**. However, elements of scientific management are still practised today, whenever there is a concern for productivity and efficiency.

Persistent Taylorism?

It has been argued that elements of Taylorism – maximising managerial control through the micro-design of jobs, automation and close supervision – can be seen in the management of junior staff in businesses such as:

(a) Large fast-food franchises (such as McDonalds).

(b) Call-centres, where calls are scripted, timed and monitored – and (in some reported cases) staff must ask permission to leave the 'floor' to go to the toilet.

1.2.3 Human relations

In the 1920s, research began to show that managers needed to consider the complexity of **human behaviour**. It was recognised that an exclusive focus on technical competence (under scientific management) had resulted in social incompetence: managers were not taught how to manage people. At the same time, it emerged that being a 'small cog in the machine' was experienced as alienating and demoralising by workers – whatever the financial incentives offered. A more complex picture of human motivation began to emerge.

Elton Mayo, of Harvard Business School, conducted a series of large scale studies at the Western Electric Company's Hawthorne works in Chicago between 1924 and 1932. These studies were originally firmly set in the context of scientific management, in that they began with an experiment into the effect of lighting on work output. However, it rapidly became apparent that worker **attitudes** and **group relationships** were of greater importance in determining the levels of production achieved than the lighting itself. It was concluded that people are motivated at work by a variety of psychological needs, including social or 'belonging' needs (Mayo, 1933). This became the basis of the **human relations school** of management theory.

Later writers (such as Abraham Maslow and Frederick Herzberg) focused on a wider variety of workers' **'higher-order' needs**, including the need for challenge, responsibility and personal development in the job. This became known as the **neo-human relations school**, which proposed important theories of motivation and job satisfaction (as we will see in Chapter 6).

The human relations approaches contributed an important awareness of the influence of the human factor at work on organisational performance. Most of its theorists attempted to offer guidelines to enable practising managers to satisfy and motivate employees and so (theoretically) to obtain the benefits of improved productivity. However, the approach tends to emphasise the importance of work to the worker, without really addressing the economic issues: there is still no proven link between job satisfaction and motivation, or either of these and productivity (as we will see in Chapter 6).

1.2.4 Management tasks and processes revisited

Drucker (1955) described the basic function of management as comprising five processes.

- **Setting objectives for the organisation.** Managers decide what the objectives of the organisation should be and quantify the targets of achievement for each objective. They must then communicate these targets to other people in the organisation.
- **Organising the work.** The work to be done in the organisation must be divided into manageable activities and manageable jobs. The jobs must be integrated into a formal organisation structure, and people must be selected to do the jobs.
- **Motivating** employees and communicating information to them to enable them to do their work.
- **The job of measurement**. Management must:
  - (i) Establish **objectives** or yardsticks of performance for all personnel
  - (ii) Analyse **actual performance**, appraise it against the objectives or yardsticks which have been set, and analyse the comparison
  - (iii) **Communicate** the findings and explain their significance both to subordinate employees and also to superiors.
- **Developing people**. The manager *'brings out what is in them or he stifles them. He strengthens their integrity or he corrupts them'*.

You may be able to see, in the development of management theory from Fayol to Drucker, a growing focus on the people resource (including managers themselves). 'The manager is the dynamic, life-giving element in every business. Without his leadership, "the sources of production" remain resources and never become production. In a competitive economy, above all the quality and performance of the managers determine the success of a business, indeed they determine its survival' (Drucker, 1955). Management can thus be seen as an **integrating factor** which draws coherence, direction and performance from all the other processes and resources of the organisation.

'One of the cornerstones of the leadership concept is that productivity is not gained solely through programmes and activities, but through people: people **add value** to material, financial, informational and other resources. Why do we need people to work effectively? Why do we need to help them develop their skills and contributions? Because that is the source of competitive advantage and added value in an ever-changing, networked, knowledge-based, customer-focused business environment.' (Profex, 2007).

Personnel practitioners have long argued this viewpoint. Peters & Waterman (1982) argued that 'success through people' was a key characteristic of 'excellent' companies, such as McKinsey and 3M. Employees are increasingly being regarded not as a cost to be controlled, but as human assets to be nurtured, developed and empowered in order to maximise their contribution and commitment to the organisation's objectives.

People are the key resource of businesses in which value is added through knowledge, creativity and interpersonal relations – as in a modern marketing function. Many firms now see themselves as selling not just 'products' but creative solutions to customer 'problems' or needs. Managers are increasingly expected to manage employee's **commitment**, **capability and contribution** as well as processes and finance. This is the focus of the following chapters on managing marketing teams.

The more modern view also emphasises the *interpersonal* and *communication* aspects of managerial functions. The syllabus likewise mentions a range of interpersonal elements (alongside planning, organising, co-ordinating and controlling), including:

- Communication
- Teambuilding
- Coaching
- Networking
- Development

We will discuss these in detail at relevant points in our coverage, focusing on them as managerial skills.

1.3 What do managers actually do?

The classical approach to categorising management functions is simple and useful for management education, but it has been argued that it does not do justice to the complexity of a manager's 'job' in the real world. **Henry Mintzberg (1989)** (1989) did a study of a relatively small sample of US corporations to see how senior managers actually spend their time. He suggests that in their daily working lives, managers fulfil three **types** of managerial role.

Role category	Role	Comment
Interpersonal Based on manager's formal authority or position	**Figurehead (or ceremonial)**	A marketing manager may represent the company at dinners, conferences, awards ceremonies and so on.
	Leader	Selecting, motivating and developing staff, and reconciling individual goals with the objectives of the organisation.
	Liaison	Making contacts outside the vertical chain of command. Marketing managers may spend up to half their meeting time with their peers in other functions, rather than with their teams.

Role category	Role	Comment
Informational Based on managers' access to: • Upward, downward and cross-functional communication channels • External networks	**Monitor**	The marketing manager, in particular, monitors the environment, networks widely, and receives information from a range of internal sources. Much of this information is of an informal nature, derived from network contacts.
	Spokesperson	The manager provides information on behalf of the unit and/or organisation to interested parties.
	Disseminator	The manager disseminates relevant information to team members.
Decisional Based on the manager's formal authority and access to information, which allow him to take decisions relating to the work of the department as a whole.	**Entrepreneur**	A manager initiates projects to improve the department or to help it react to a changing environment.
	Disturbance handler	A manager has to respond to unexpected pressures, taking decisions when there is deviation from plan.
	Resource allocator	A manager takes decisions relating to the mobilisation and distribution of limited resources to achieve objectives.
	Negotiator	Both inside and outside the organisation, negotiation takes up a great deal of management time.

Mintzberg's research challenged the classical view of the manager as separate to, or above, the routine demands of day-to-day work.

- Managers are not always able to be reflective, systematic planners: managerial work is often disjointed and discontinuous.
- Managers do have 'routine' duties to perform, especially of a ceremonial nature (receiving important guests) or related to authority (signing cheques as a signatory) – contrary to the myth that all routine work is done by juniors.
- Managers prefer verbal and informal information to the formal output of management information systems. Verbal information is 'hotter' and probably easier to grasp.
- General management is, in practice, a matter of judgement and intuition, gained from experience in particular situations rather than from abstract principles.

1.4 Challenges of management

Management involves many challenges and trade-offs: between trust and control; between quality, speed and cost; between stability/order/consistency/risk management on one hand and creativity/flexibility/responsiveness/innovation on the other.

Rosabeth Moss Kanter (1992) highlighted some of the incompatible demands placed on managers when seeking improved performance and excellence in flexible, innovative environments – and these may strike a particular chord for marketing managers.

Demands made on managers		
Be entrepreneurial and risk taking	*but*	Don't lose money
Invest in the future	*but*	Keep profitable now
Do everything you're doing now but even better	*but*	Spend more time communicating, on teams and new projects
Lead and direct	*but*	Participate, listen, co-operate
Know everything about your business	*but*	Delegate more
Work all hours	*but*	Keep fit
Be single-minded in your commitment to ideas	*but*	Be flexible and responsive

Demands made on organisations		
Be 'lean and mean'	*but*	Be a good employer
Be creative and innovative	*but*	'Stick to the knitting'
Decentralise to small, simple autonomous units	*but*	Centralise to be efficient and integrative
Have a sense of urgency	*but*	Deliberately plan for the future

ACTIVITY 2

evaluation

Reflect on each of the dilemmas raised by Kanter, in your own experience, or informally interview a manager in your organisation about them.

- Which side of the scale do the culture and approaches of your organisation come down on, in each case?
- Which side of each dilemma *supports* innovation, flexibility and creativity, and which restricts it?
- What suggestions can you come up with for how a manager might resolve these dilemmas, and be supported in doing so by his or her organisation?.

1.5 The role of the operational marketing manager

In addition to all of the above 'standard' functions of a manager, the marketing manager (at an operational level) has three distinct functions identified by the syllabus:

- Information
- Value creation
- Communication

MARKETING AT WORK

application

The following is a job description for a marketing manager (from www.cim.co.uk).

Description

Responsible for the strategic direction of all marketing activity on specific products/services.

Personal specification

- 3 years' experience in marketing or product management
- Able to think strategically and direct delivery
- Works well in multi-disciplinary teams
- Forms close-knit relationships with outside agencies

Suggested Professional Qualifications (CIM)

- CIM Postgraduate Diploma in Marketing (DipM)
- Chartered Marketer

Responsibilities

- Reports to Marketing Director
- Ensures product/service matches brand positioning
- Identifies target markets and works with data manager to provide eternal agencies with relevant data
- Plans communication strategy and liaises with all members of the campaign team to ensure effective and efficient delivery

- Analyses results of all marketing activity and presents findings and recommendations to management
- Builds close knit teams, own and cross-departmental
- Liaises with external agencies to ensure clear understanding of the marketing strategy.

1.5.1 An interface role

The marketing manager also acts as the bridge between the company and its external stakeholder audiences, particularly customers.

- The marketing manager represents and champions the **customer's** needs and interests within the organisation, through customer research, complaint handling, service quality management – and generally seeking to embed customer focus (a marketing orientation) within the organisation, through internal marketing.
- The marketing function generally creates relationships with customers, and controls the firm's **communications** and **interactions** with them (especially through the disciplines of relationship marketing).

The marketing manager as interface

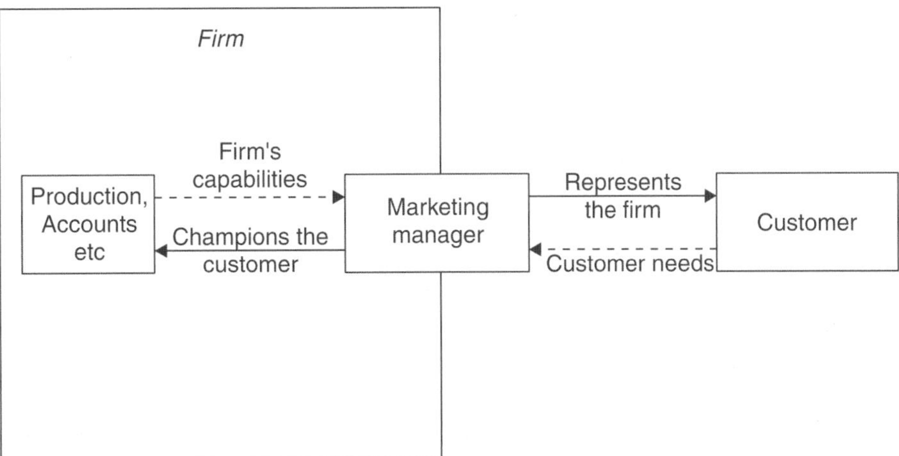

2 Leadership

2.1 What is leadership?

There are as many definitions of leadership as there are writers on the subject. The following are some examples (cited by Hersey & Blanchard, 1988, p86).

- *'Leadership is the activity of **influencing people to strive willingly** for group objectives.'* (Terry, 1960)
- '[Leadership is] ***interpersonal influence*** *exercised in a situation and directed, through the communication process, toward the attainment of a specialised goal or goals.*' (Tannenbaum *et al*, 1959)
- *'Leadership is **influencing people to follow**' in the achievement of a common goal.'* (Koontz and O'Donnell, 1959).

Common to all these definitions is the idea that leadership is an interpersonal process of influencing others to work willingly – and to the best of their capabilities – towards a goal. The essence of leadership is '**followership**': it is the willingness of people to follow that makes a person a leader – rather than merely a manager who has the legitimate authority to enforce compliance with his or her directives.

Leadership comes about in a number of different ways. A manager is **appointed** to a position of authority within the organisation: leadership of subordinates is a function of the position. Some leaders (eg employee representatives and some team leaders) are **elected**. Other leaders simply emerge by popular choice or through their personal drive, as they inspire and influence others.

2.2 Sources of power for leadership

Power is not something a person 'has' in isolation: it is exercised over other individuals or groups, and – to an extent – depends on their *recognising* the person's power over them. French and Raven (1958) identified different types or sources of power and influence in organisations.

Type of power	Description
Coercive power	The power of physical force or punishment. Physical power is rare in business organisations, but intimidation may feature, eg in workplace bullying.
Reward (or resource) power	Based on access to or control over valued resources. For example, marketing managers have access to information, contacts and financial rewards for team members. The amount of resource power a person has depends on the scarcity of the resource, how much the resource is valued by others, and how far the resource is under the manager's control.
Legitimate (or position) power	Associated with a particular position in the organisation. For example, a manager has the power to authorise certain expenses, or issue instructions, because the authority to do so has been formally delegated to her. This type of power is often associated with organisational 'authority'.
Expert power	Based on experience, qualifications or expertise. For example, marketers have expert power because of their knowledge of the market and marketing communications techniques. Expert power depends on others recognising the expertise in an area which they need or value.
Referent (or personal) power	Based on force of personality, or 'charisma', which can attract, influence or inspire other people. This is often regarded as a trait or skill-set of leadership.

Power and influence can be exercised at any level of the organisation, and in any direction – not just 'downwards' (over direct reports and teams), but sideways (over peers and cross-functional colleagues) and even upwards (eg promoting an idea or course of action to senior management). We will look at this aspect of leadership a bit later in this chapter.

2.3 Is leadership different from management?

The terms 'management' and 'leadership' are often used interchangeably. In some cases, management skills and theories have simply been relabelled to reflect the more fashionable term. However, there have been many attempts to distinguish meaningfully between the two concepts.

- Kotter (2001) argues that leadership and management involve two distinct sets of action. Management is about coping with **complexity:** its functions are to do with logic, structure, analysis and control, and are aimed at producing order, consistency and predictability. Leadership, by contrast, is about coping with **change**: its activities include creating a sense of direction, communicating strategy, and energising, inspiring and motivating others to translate the vision into action.
- Yukl (1998) suggests that while management is defined by a prescribed role and position in the structure of the organisation, leaders are given their roles by the perception of others, through election, choice or influence. Leadership is an interpersonal process. In other words, managers have **subordinates**, but leaders have **followers**.
- Zaleznik (1992) suggests that managers are mainly concerned with order and **maintaining the status quo**, exercising their skills in diplomacy and focusing on decision-making processes within the organisation. Leaders, in contrast, direct their energies towards introducing **new approaches and ideas**. They create excitement and vision in order to arouse motivation, and focus with empathy on the meanings of events and actions for people. Leaders search out opportunities for change.
- Katz and Kahn (1974) point out that while management aims to secure compliance with stated organisational objectives, leadership aims to secure willingness, enthusiasm and commitment. Leadership is the **influential increment** over and above mechanical compliance with the routine directives of the organisation.

Management can be exercised over resources, activities, projects and other essentially non-personal things. Leadership can only be exercised over **people**.

2.3.1 Transactional or transformational?

Some of the values used to distinguish between managers and leaders have also been identified as different styles of leadership (Burns, 1978).

- **Transactional leaders** see the relationship with their followers in terms of trading or bargaining: they give followers the rewards they want in exchange for service, loyalty and compliance. A transactional style tends to focus on directive behaviours and carrot-and-stick motivation. The leader's power is based mainly on authority or position in the organisation.

  This style works well in stable organisations (such as bureaucracies) with security-seeking (or authoritarian) cultures, operating in stable, slow-change business environments (including highly regulated industry sectors).

- **Transformational leaders** see their role as an interpersonal process of stimulating interest, generating awareness, inspiring higher achievement, and motivating others to work at levels beyond mere compliance and to think about the big picture. A transformational style is charismatic or inspirational. Only transformational leadership is said to be able to change team/organisation culture and performance: 'transforming' the direction and fortunes of the business.

  This is seen as particularly important in dynamic, fact-changing and competitive environments. It suits lean, flexible organisation structures (such as networks and virtual teams) and innovative, creative and learning cultures (such as, ideally, marketing).

Mullins (2005) notes that 'successful transformational leaders are usually identified in terms of providing a strong vision and sense of mission, arousing strong emotions in followers and a sense of identification with the leader'. When you think of great leaders, they are probably transformational! It is also worth noting that transformational leadership has a lot in common with marketing: arousing strong emotion, identification and commitment in customers...

2.3.2 Is the distinction between management and leadership useful?

Whetten and Cameron (2002) note that management has come to be equated with values such as stability, hierarchy, equilibrium, control and 'doing the right things': leadership has come to be equated with values such as change, dynamism, vibrancy, charisma and 'doing things right'. They argue, however, that such distinctions are no longer useful.

'Managers cannot be successful without being good leaders, and leaders cannot be successful without being good managers. No longer do organisations and individuals have the luxury of holding on to the status quo; worrying about doing things right but failing to do the right things; keeping the system stable instead of leading change and improvement; monitoring current performance instead of formulating a vision of the future; concentrating on equilibrium and control instead of vibrancy and charisma. Effective management and leadership are inseparable. The skills required to do one are also required of the other. No organisation in a post-industrial, hyperturbulent, twenty-first century environment will survive without executives capable of providing both management and leadership.' (Whetten & Cameron, 2002, p16).

ACTIVITY 3

evaluation

It has been suggested that the distinction between management and leadership has become caricatured: leadership is visionary and valuable, while management is old-fashioned, routine and doomed to extinction in the face of turbulent change.

What is your own view on this? Do you find the term 'leader' helpful to describe what you do?

What view of management and leadership is reflected in the terminology and practices of your work organisation?

2.4 Why seek to develop managers as leaders?

Whether or not we make the distinction between management and leadership, attempts to define what makes leadership 'special' (such as those outlined above) have suggested some key points about the benefits effective leadership can bring in a marketing context, and why it is valuable.

- Leaders energise and support **change**, which is essential for survival in highly competitive and fast-changing business environments. By setting visionary goals, and encouraging contribution from teams, leaders create environments that:

  (i) Seek out new information and ideas

  (ii) Allow challenges to existing procedures and ways of thinking

  (iii) Invite innovation and creativity in finding better ways to achieve goals

  (iv) Support and empower people to cope with the turbulence.

- Leaders secure **commitment**, mobilising the ideas, experience and motivation of employees – which contributes to innovation and improved quality and customer service. This is all the more essential in a competitive, customer-focused, knowledge-based business environment and culture such as marketing.
- Leaders set **direction**, helping teams and organisations to understand their purpose, goals and value to the organisation. This facilitates team-working and empowerment (allowing discretion and creativity about how to achieve the desired outcomes) without loss of co-ordination or direction. This may be particularly valuable in a marketing culture, which tends to attract creative, extraverted (and professionally qualified) types.
- Leaders support, challenge and develop **people**, maximising their contribution to the function and organisation. Leaders use an influence-based, facilitate-and-empower style rather than a command-and-control style, and this is better suited to the expectations of empowered, professional teams and the need for information-sharing in modern business environments.

ACTIVITY 4

evaluation

Reflect on your own experience of working under the direction of others. Identify the 'best' leader you have ever 'followed'. Think about how this person behaved and interacted with you and others.

What qualities makes you identify this person as a 'great leader', from your point of view as a follower?

2.5 Leadership in four directions

So far, we have been talking about leadership primarily in a 'downward' sense: that is, leadership of subordinates or team members. However, Boddy (2005) emphasises that leadership is possible – and required – in **four different directions**.

All-directional leadership

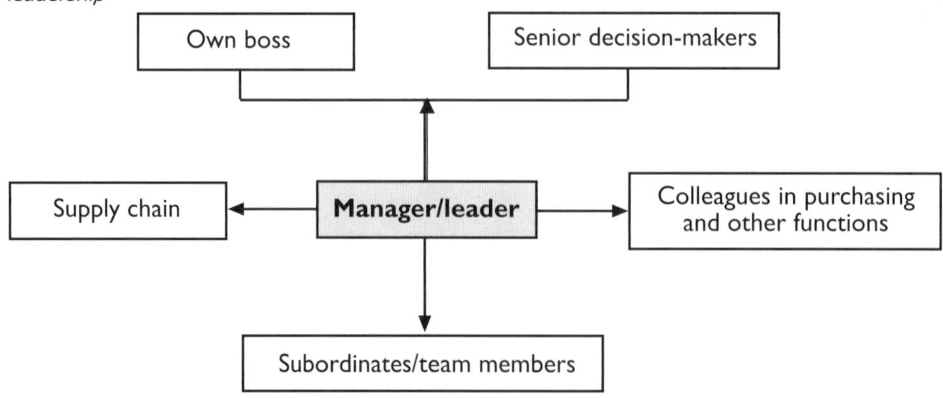

2.5.1 Upward management or leadership

Upward management or leadership is necessary in organisations:

- For lower levels of management to gain access to the decision-making authority, information and resources only available at higher levels
- For people to gain the support (or at least authorisation) required to put their plans into action, and/or to get key influencers to become sponsors or champions of their ideas and initiatives, to get them on the agenda and push for them within the decision-making group
- To manage the expectations of superiors, ensuring that deadlines and success measures are realistic and adequately resourced
- To keep superiors informed, and to habituate them to reporting by exception, in order to avoid micro-management (or 'management by interference')
- To promote the achievements of individuals or teams to superiors, so that their ability and potential will be noticed.

The main issue for managing upwards is that a junior manager lacks positional authority to impose what (s)he wants. Managing upwards requires **assertiveness** (the ability to state clearly, calmly, positively and persistently what you want) and the use of available sources of **influence**, such as personal rapport and rational persuasion (on the basis of expertise and business case).

ACTIVITY 5

evaluation

What can you identify as the beneficial outcomes of effective upward management?

How effectively do you 'manage your managers'?

2.5.2 Leading direct reports or teams

This is in many ways the most straightforward context of leadership, because managers have formally delegated position power 'over' subordinates (or teams of which they are the designated or elected leader). There is a legitimate expectation that requests and instructions will be complied with, and this can be backed up by a disciplinary framework of rewards and sanctions. Leadership is therefore applied to gain commitment over and above mere compliance. We will discuss these aspects in the rest of this chapter and in subsequent chapters on team leadership and motivation.

2.5.3 Leading cross-functional teams and networks

Marketing managers are increasingly called upon to work in cross-functional teams (eg for new product development and marketing planning) or in cross-functional networks: information-sharing and collaboration across functional borders (eg where a marketing manager provides market and customer data, or co-ordinates product launch schedules with the production department, or seeks input into quality management systems).

The key issue for lateral leadership or influencing is that, like upward management, it may not be supported by legitimate positional power: the marketing manager may have expert power and resources to offer, but additional influencing tactics may be required if this is not recognised or valued by others. 'Influencing across' may involve personal rapport, rational persuasion and consultation, exchange or reciprocity (offering something in return for compliance or support) or appeal to shared goals and interests.

- **Networking** (making and cultivating interpersonal contacts) is a key source of cross-functional influence. Other aspects of cross-functional relations were discussed in Chapter 1, as a key component of organisation structure.
- **Internal marketing** is another way in which the marketing function seeks to take a leadership role in the organisation, shaping the focus, values and competences of people in a way that promotes the marketing ethos. This was mentioned in Chapter 1, and will be discussed in detail in Chapter 7.

2.5.4 Managing external stakeholders

Marketing managers operate at the interface with key external stakeholders, publics or target audiences: customers, marketing services providers, investors, the media, pressure groups and society as a whole. You may be able to draw on your studies of *Stakeholder Marketing* or relationship marketing in general to appreciate the importance of developing constructive influence with such groups.

In the case of customers, for example, marketing seeks to exercise leadership influence through the **marketing mix** and **customer communication**, which use a wide range of influencing tactics: rational persuasion (product/price comparisons); inspirational appeal (value-laden branding); consultation (seeking customer feedback); ingratiation (relationship marketing); exchange (sales promotions); and so on.

2.6 Leadership skills

Some of the management skills mentioned in the syllabus are also identifiable as leadership skills, particularly in areas such as motivation and empowerment.

Bass & Avolio (1994) argue that *transformational* leadership is achieved more specifically through a skill set summarised as the '**Four Is' of leadership**.

- **Idealised influence:** identified with 'charisma'. The leader acts as a role model: putting the needs of others before personal interests, taking risks, demonstrating high standards of ethical conduct – and attracting the admiration, respect, trust and imitation of others.
- **Inspirational motivation:** also identified with 'charisma'. The leader articulates the challenge, significance and meaning in work: arouses team spirit; shows enthusiasm and confidence; communicates high expectations and demonstrates commitment.
- **Intellectual stimulation.** The leader encourages free thinking and emphasises rational problem solving, by: questioning assumptions; reinterpreting problems and issues in new ways; encouraging innovation and creativity; and avoiding punishing or publicly criticising mistakes.
- **Individualised consideration.** The leader treats followers on their own merits and seeks to develop them: accepting individual differences; attending to individuals' higher-level needs for growth and challenge; acting as coach/mentor; creating learning opportunities through delegation; and avoiding restrictively close monitoring of performance.

In addition, you might identify a range of business and managerial skills as important to a good leader, including:

- **Entrepreneurship:** the ability to spot business or value-adding opportunities and mobilise resources to capitalise on them
- **Interpersonal skills,** such as networking, rapport-building, influencing, negotiating, conflict resolution, listening, counselling, coaching and communicating assertively. (We will look at a selection of these in section 4 below.)
- **Decision-making and problem-solving** skills, including seeing the big picture (sometimes called 'helicopter ability')
- **Time management and personal organisation**
- **Self-development** skills: the ability to learn continuously from experience, to grow in self-awareness and to exploit learning opportunities (covered in section 6 below).

3 Leadership theories and models

- The picture of leadership that emerges from all that has been written about it is a complex mix of:
- Functional orientations (strategic vision, change management, team building)
- Values (innovation, inspiration, potential)
- Qualities (charisma, dynamism)
- Skills (influencing, persuading, communicating, emotional competence)
- Metaphors and analogies (the military commander; the sports coach; the orchestral conductor).

The more you read about leadership, the more different perspectives and emphases you'll get on it – and the more different terms for discussing it. The important thing to note is that no one approach replaces or invalidates another: they are merely different viewpoints which may (or may not) provide additional insights.

3.1 Schools of leadership theory

It is possible to identify four basic 'schools' of leadership theory.

- **Trait theories** of leadership are based on analysing the personality characteristics or preferences of successful leaders. The old assumption that 'leaders are born, not made' has largely been discredited: the premise that certain leader traits are absolutely necessary for effective leadership has never been substantiated in several decades of traits research (Yukl, 1998).

- **Style theories** of leadership are based on the view that leadership is an interpersonal process whereby different leader behaviours influence people in different ways. More or less effective patterns of behaviour (or 'styles') can therefore be adopted.

- **Contingency theories** of leadership are based on the belief that there is no 'one best way' of leading, but that effective leaders adapt their behaviour to the specific (and changing) variables in the leadership context: the nature of the task, the personalities of the team members, the organisation culture and so on. (We will discuss characteristic behaviours of some basic leadership styles, and how you can select the appropriate style in a given context, below.)

- More recent approaches to leadership have focused specifically on the **interpersonal and emotional competences** of leaders. Examples include transactional and charismatic leadership, and '*resonant leadership*': *'Great leaders move us. They ignite our passion and inspire the best in us. When we try to explain why they are so effective, we speak of strategy, vision, or powerful ideas. But the reality is much more primal: great leadership works through the emotions.*' (Goleman *et al,* 2002, p3)

We haven't got space to review all the leadership theories or the evolution of leadership thinking in detail. We will give a brief survey of some key models, in order to give you a framework for analysis of your own, or others', leadership practices. If you wish to get to grips in more detail with the theoretical concepts, you will find them in most texts on Organisational Behaviour – Huczynski & Buchanan (2001), for example, give an excellent overview.

From the CIM Core Texts, you should look at:

- **Management: Theory & Practice, George Cole (6th ed): Thomson Learning.**
- **Managing Marketing: a practical guide for marketers, Palmer, Cockton & Cooper: Elsevier** ■

3.2 Leadership traits

Early theories suggested that there are certain personality characteristics common to 'great men' or successful leaders. In other words, 'leaders are born, not made'. Various studies attempted to determine exactly *which* traits are essential in a leader. One American study (cited by Stewart, 1963) cites the following fifteen traits.

Judgement	Initiative	Integrity	Foresight	Energy
Drive	Human relations skill	Decisiveness	Dependability	Emotional stability
Fairness	Ambition	Dedication	Objectivity	Co-operation

Trait theory has been more or less discredited, for the following reasons amongst others.

- The premise that certain traits are absolutely necessary for effective leadership has never been substantiated.
- The lists of traits proposed for leaders have been vast, varied and contradictory.
- 'A person does not become a leader by virtue of the possession of some combination of traits, but the pattern of personal characteristics must bear some relevant relationship to the characteristics, activities and goals of the followers' (Stodgill, 1948).
- Personality traits are not a helpful basis for leadership development, because they represent relatively fixed psychological preferences: you can't change your personality. The behaviours arising from personality preferences may be a more helpful focus, however, as behaviours can be learned, adopted or imitated: you *can* change your behaviours.

Perhaps the most useful lesson from trait theory is that it is possible to identify 'great leaders', and by studying and adopting their **successful behaviours** (how they think, talk and act), other managers can develop their leadership performance.

3.2.1 What about charisma?

The idea of an inherent 'gift' for leadership appears to have regained currency in recent decades with the persistent belief in **charismatic** ('gifted') leadership.

Charisma is an aspect of personal or referent power: the ability to inspire followership on the basis of one's personal qualities. However, House (1976) took some of the mystique out of charisma by arguing that it can effectively be acquired or developed as a cluster of purely behavioural competences, including:

- **Role modelling:** setting an example, representing values which are positive for followers
- **Confidence building:** communicating high expectations of, and confidence in, followers
- **Goal articulation**: setting out clear goals in a way that is emotionally resonant, linked to values – and therefore compelling to followers
- **Motivate arousal**: inspiring followers with the desire and confidence to pursue the goals

4 Leadership styles

KEY CONCEPT

concept

Leadership style may be defined (Mullins, 2005) as: 'the way in which the functions of leadership are carried out; the way in which the manager typically behaves towards members of the group.'

It should be obvious from your own experience that not all managers or leaders operate in the same manner! There are various classifications of leadership style. Although the labels and definitions of styles vary, the models are often talking (broadly) about the same thing: a continuum of behaviours from:

- Wholly task-focused, directive leadership behaviours (representing high leader control) at one extreme, and

- Wholly people-focused, supportive/relational leadership behaviours (representing high subordinate discretion) at the other.

4.1 Directive and facilitative leadership behaviours

The dual dimensions just mentioned underpin certain types of leadership behaviour.

- **Directive** leadership behaviours (and styles) involve 'clearly telling people what to do, how to do it, when to do it, and then closely monitoring their performance' (Blanchard et al, 2004). They include: letting subordinates know clearly what the leader expects from them (targets and standards); giving specific guidance and instructions; asking subordinates to follow rules and procedures; scheduling and co-ordinating the work; and monitoring and controlling performance against specific criteria.

  A directive style may be effective when subordinates do not share the leader's objectives, or lack ability or confidence; when time is short and results critical; and when subordinates are willing to accept top-down authority.

- **Facilitative** (or participative or supportive) leadership behaviours involve 'listening to people, providing support and encouragement for their efforts, and then facilitating their involvement in problem-solving and decision-making (ibid). They include: giving team members the opportunity to take responsibility and initiative: jointly agreeing objectives and standards; delegating responsibility to the team for day-to-day planning and organisation, monitoring and control; being available as a resource for guidance, information and mediation, if required; acting as a champion on behalf of the team (accessing information, resources, contacts and influence on its behalf); and performing the role of 'critical friend' to provide constructive/challenging feedback for individual and team development.

  A facilitative style may be effective where subordinates are willing, able and confident enough to participate in decision making; where subordinate input to (and acceptance of) decisions is important; and where the task or problem is relatively unstructured.

4.2 The Ashridge Management College model

The Research Unit at Ashridge Management College in the UK distinguished four different management styles, labelled 'Tells', 'Sells', 'Consults' and 'Joins'. Other style models label similar styles as:

- Telling, Selling, Participating and Delegating (Hersey and Blanchard, 1998)
- Telling, Selling, Consulting and Coaching (Tannenbaum and Schmidt, 1973)

Style	Characteristics	Strengths	Weaknesses
Tells (autocratic)	The leader makes all the decisions, and issues instructions which must be obeyed without question.	(1) Quick decisions can be made when speed is required (eg in crisis) or against team opposition. (2) The most efficient type of leadership for highly–programmed, routine work.	(1) Does not encourage initiative, commitment or contribution from team members. (2) One-way communication between leader and team.
Sells (persuasive)	The leader still makes all the decisions, but believes that team members have to be motivated to accept them and carry them out properly.	(1) Team members are aware of the reasons for decisions, and will be more flexible when unforeseen events arise. (2) Selling decisions to the team might make them more committed.	(1) Communications are still largely one-way. (2) Team members might not accept the decisions. (3) Does not encourage initiative and commitment from subordinates.

Style	Characteristics	Strengths	Weaknesses
Consults	The leader confers with team members and takes their views into account, but retains the final say.	(1) Encourages motivation through greater interest and involvement. (2) An agreed consensus of can be reached, which can be an advantage (eg increasing buy-in and commitment). (3) Team members contribute their knowledge and expertise more effectively.	(1) It might take much longer to reach decisions. (2) Team members might be too inexperienced to formulate mature opinions and give practical advice. (3) Consultation can too easily turn into a façade, concealing a 'sells' style.
Joins (demo-cratic)	Leader and team members make the decision on the basis of consensus.	(1) Can provide high motivation and commitment from employees. (2) Shares the other advantages of 'consults' style (especially where team members have value-adding expertise).	(1) The authority of the leader might be undermined. (2) Shares other disadvantages of the 'consults' style.

The Ashridge studies showed a clear preference among subordinates for the 'consults' style of leadership – although managers were most commonly perceived to be exercising a 'tells' or 'sells' style! Team members also had more positive attitudes to their work under leaders who were perceived to be exercising a 'consults' style. The least favourable attitudes to work, however, were not found among team members under a 'tells' style, but among those who were unable to perceive a **consistent** style in their leader. In order words, subordinates are unsettled by a boss who chops and changes between different styles.

4.3 The managerial (or leadership) grid

Blake and Mouton (1964) carried out research into managerial behaviour and observed two basic dimensions of leadership: **concern for production** (or task performance) and **concern for people**

Along each of these two dimensions, managers could be located at any point on a continuum from very low to very high concern. Blake and Mouton observed that the two concerns did not seem to correlate, positively or negatively: a high concern in one dimension, for example, did not seem to imply a high or low concern in the other dimension. Individual managers could therefore reflect various permutations of task/people concern.

A questionnaire was designed to enable users to analyse and plot the positions of individual respondents on a grid, as a means of analysing individuals' managerial styles and areas of weakness or 'unbalance', for the purposes of management development.

The leadership grid

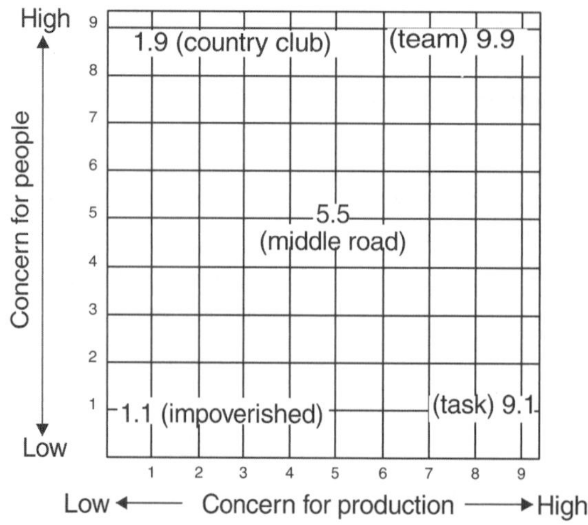

The styles identified on the grid are:

- 1.1 **Impoverished:** the manager exerts (and expects) minimal effort or concern for either staff satisfaction or work targets.
- 1.9 **Country club:** the manager is attentive to staff needs and has developed satisfying relationships and work culture – but with little attention to results. Behaviour is supportive rather than directive.
- 9.1 **Task management:** almost total concentration on achieving results. People's needs are virtually ignored, and work is organised so that human elements interfere to a minimal extent. Behaviour is directive rather than supportive.
- 5.5 **Middle of the road:** adequate performance through balancing the necessity to get work done with maintaining a satisfactory level of team morale. (Alternatively, the manager scores an average of 5.5, as a result of swinging from one extreme to another!)
- 9.9 **Team:** high work accomplishment through 'leading' committed people who identify themselves with organisational goals.

The grid was intended as a tool for management appraisal and development. It recognises that a leader requires a balance between concern for the task and concern for people, and that a high degree of both is possible – and the most effective style of management. It offers a simple and easy-to-use diagnostic tool, showing where the behaviour and assumptions of a manager may exhibit a lack of balance between the dimensions and/or a low degree of concern in either dimension or both.

However, this is a simplified model. For a start, it assumes that 9.9 is the desirable model for effective leadership, while some managerial contexts, this may not be so: a manager may find that a 9.1 approach, for example, is effective in situations of crisis where survival is at stake, or urgent corrective action must be taken to get a project back on track. Moreover, a manager's style of leadership is likely to be influenced by organisational context and culture, technology and wide range of other factors, not just the two dimensions described by the Grid.

ACTIVITY 6

evaluation

The following are some statements about a manager's approach to meetings. Which position on Blake and Mouton's Grid do you think each might represent?

(a) I attend because it is expected. I either go along with the majority position or avoid expressing my views.

(b) I try to come up with good ideas and push for a decision as soon as I can get a majority behind me. I don't mind stepping on people if it helps a sound decision.

(c) I like to be able to support what my boss wants and to recognise the merits of individual effort. When conflict arises, I do a good job of restoring harmony.

4.4 A continuum of leadership styles

Tannenbaum and Schmidt (1973) proposed a continuum of behaviours (and associated styles) which reflected the balance of control exercised in a situation by the leader and the team. The continuum format is a useful reminder that managers do not adopt extreme either/or styles, but select from a wide repertoire of behaviours.

The continuum of leadership styles

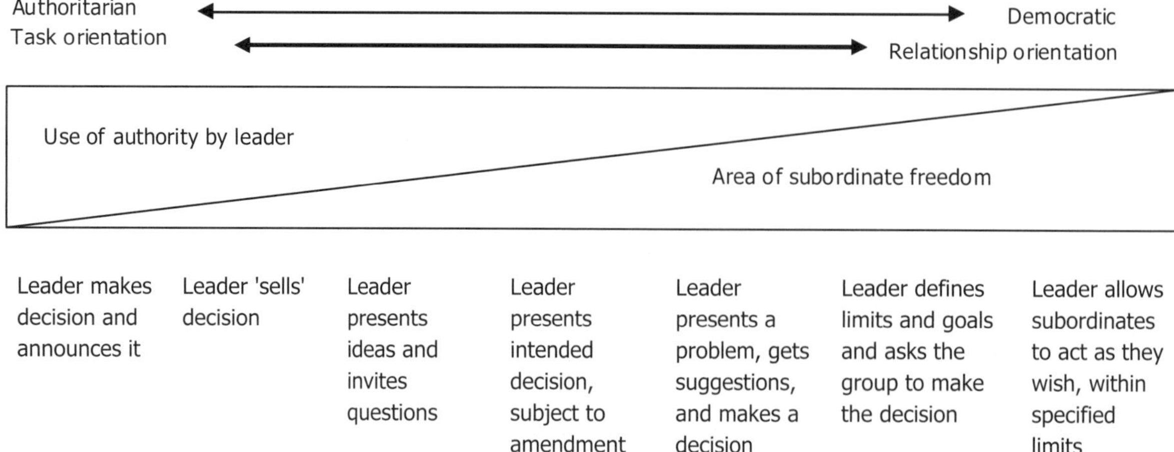

4.5 Evaluating style approaches

Perhaps the most important criticism of the style approach is that it does not consider all the variables that contribute to the practice of effective leadership.

- The manager's personality (or 'acting' ability) may simply not be **flexible** enough to utilise different styles effectively.
- The demands of the task, technology, organisation culture and other managers **constrains** a leader in the range of styles effectively open to her. (If her own boss practices an authoritarian style, and the team is incompetent and requires close supervision, no amount of theorising on the desirability of participative management will make it possible.)
- **Consistency** is important to subordinates. If a manager adapts her style to changing situations, they may simply perceive her to be fickle, or may suffer insecurity and stress.

Huczynski & Buchanan (2001) note that: 'There is therefore no simple recipe which the individual manager can use to decide which style to adopt to be most effective.'

MARKETING AT WORK

evaluation/application

'Optimists assume that management is a linear story of progress – slow perhaps, but we're getting better at it all the time. This is certainly the message you'd take from its public texts (books promising the secrets of success, prospectuses of business schools, the 'solution-speak' of IT firms and consultancies): with more information and research at his/her fingertips than ever, it's the best a manager can be.

Or maybe not. According to the Chartered Management Institute Quality of Working Life report… the most commonly experienced management styles in the UK are bureaucratic (the experience of 40% of respondents), reactive (37%) and authoritarian (30%), while just 17% of the 1,500 managers polled experienced management as innovative, 15% as trusting and 13% as entrepreneurial.

These averages hide huge differences in perception: What directors and senior managers saw as accessible, empowering and consensual, junior ranks judged bureaucratic (half the sample), reactive (38%) and authoritarian (40%).' (Caulkin, 2007)

5 Contingency models

The initial argument of style theories was that there are effective and ineffective leadership styles: that team members prefer some styles to others, and that teams work better under some styles than others (generally a participative style). A manager who naturally uses one style should therefore attempt to develop the skills to use a more effective style.

However, there has been a growing realisation that a range of different styles might be appropriate – depending on the leadership context: the 'right' style is the one that will work best for a particular task, team and situation. Gillen (2002) argues that: *'Using only one leadership style is a bit like a stopped clock: it will be right twice a day, but the rest of the time it will be inaccurate to varying degrees. Leaders need to interact with their team in different ways in different situations. This is what we mean by "leadership style".'*

In essence, contingency theory sees effective leadership as being dependent on a number of variables or contingent factor. There is no one right way to lead that will fit all situations. 'It all depends' on factors such as:

- The manager's **power and influence** in the organisation and with the work group, affecting the extent to which a command-and-control style is possible
- The nature of the **task and technology**, affecting the extent to which workers require close instruction and supervision
- The **skills and motivation** of the work group, affecting the extent to which workers will want or expect autonomy or involvement in decision-making
- The **culture** of the organisation and its management, affecting the style likely to be perceived as acceptable and effective.

5.1 Situational leadership

In their influential Situational Leadership model, Hersey and Blanchard (1988) focus on the **readiness of team members** to perform a given task, in terms of both their *task ability* (experience, knowledge and skills) and *willingness* (whether they have the confidence, commitment and motivation) to complete the task successfully.

- **High-readiness** (R4) teams are able and willing. They do not need directive or supportive leadership: the most appropriate leadership style may be a joins or 'delegating' (S4) style. An example would be any mature and effectively-functioning marketing team which is capable of getting on with performing, only needing to appeal to the leader for guidance in the event of unforeseen problems or new situations.
- **High-moderate readiness** (R3) teams are able, but unwilling or insecure. They are competent, but require supportive behaviour to build morale: the most appropriate leadership style may be a consults or 'participating' (S3) style. An example might be a team member returning from training to apply newly-learned skills for the first time; or a marketing team going through a period of low morale or resistance to organisational changes.
- **Low-moderate readiness** (R2) teams are willing and confident, but lacking ability. They require both directive and supportive behaviour to improve their task performance without damaging morale: the most appropriate leadership style may be a 'selling' (S2) style. An example might be more experienced members of the marketing team taking on new responsibilities for the first time (eg with the emergence of new communications media).
- **Low-readiness** (R1) teams are lacking ability and motivation/confidence. They require more directive behaviours in order to secure an adequate level of task performance: the most appropriate leadership style may be a 'telling' (S1) style. An example might be where staff are new to the marketing department or to particular technology or procedures.

The model can be depicted as follows.

The situational leadership model (Source: Hersey & Blanchard, 1998)

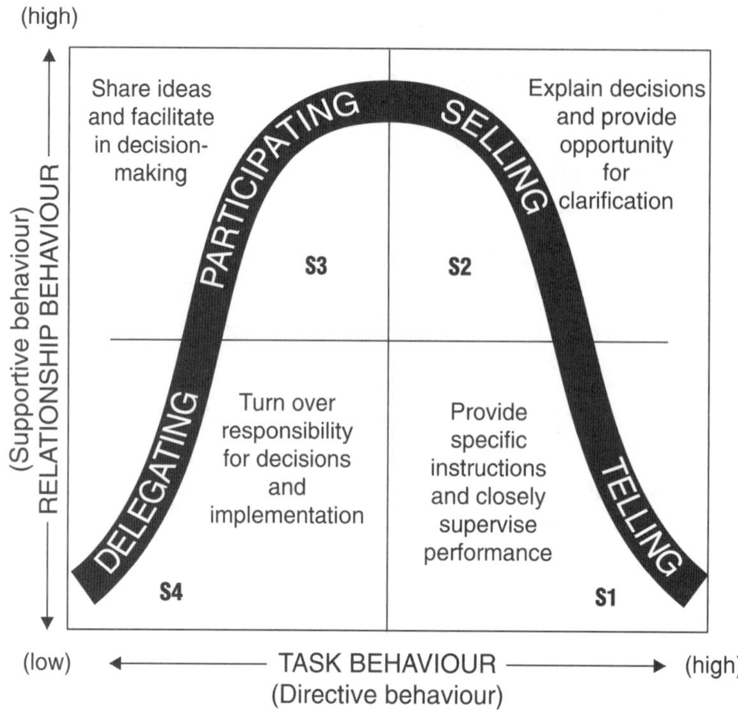

FOLLOWER READINESS

high	moderate		low
R4	**R3**	**R2**	**R1**
Able and willing or confident	Able but unwilling or insecure	Unable but willing or confident	Unable and unwilling or insecure

An effective leader will both adapt his or her style to the current level of readiness of the team *and* help team members to develop maturity or readiness as far as possible (through the process of support and direction that is built into each style).

ACTIVITY 7

application/evaluation

Diagnose the readiness of a work group of which you are a member. What sort of leadership is likely to be most effective, according to Hersey & Blanchard's model? What sort of leadership does the team leader actually exercise? What advice would you give as to the kinds of supportive and/or directive behaviours that he or she might adopt to lead the team more effectively?

If you want to focus further on assessing and improving your leadership style, using the Situational Leadership model, the best (short and accessible) introduction may be:

Leadership and the One Minute Manager, by ***Ken Blanchard, Patricia Zigarmi and Drea Zigarmi (2004) London: Harper Collins***

5.2 Action-centred leadership

John Adair's model (variously called 'action-centred', 'situational' or 'functional') is part of the contingency school of thought, because it sees the leadership process in a context made up of three interrelated variables: **task** needs, the **individual** needs of group members and the needs of the **group** as a whole. These needs must be examined in the light of the **whole situation**, which dictates the relative priority that must be given to each of the three sets of needs. Effective leadership is a process of identifying and acting on that priority, exercising a relevant cluster of roles to meet the various needs (Adair, 1984). This can be depicted as follows.

Action-centred leadership roles

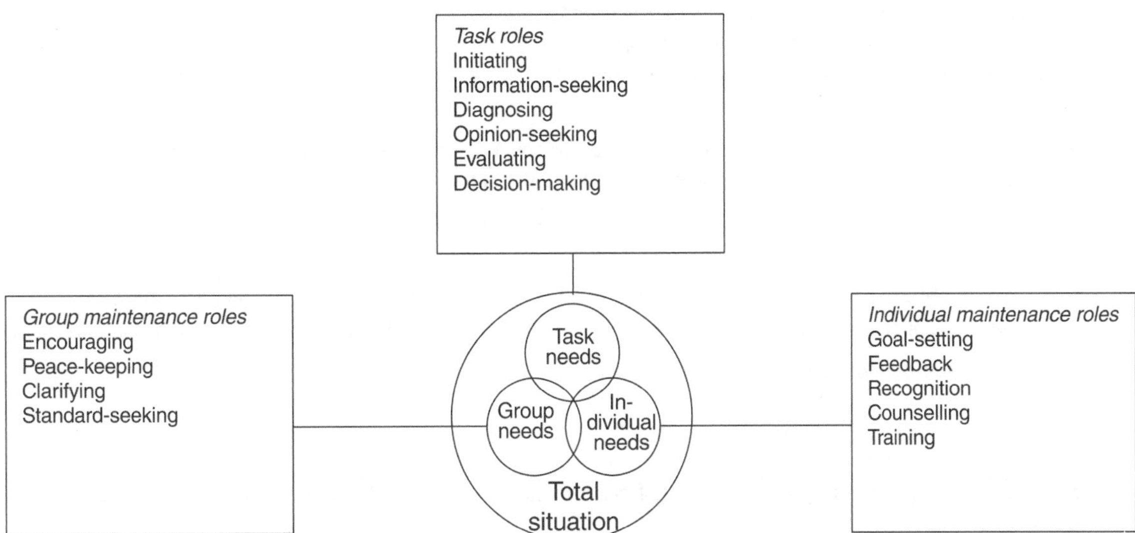

Adair (1984) argued that the common perception of leadership as 'decision-making' was inadequate to describe the range of action required by this complex situation. He developed a scheme of leadership training based on precept and practice in each of eight leadership 'activities' which are applied to task, team and individual: hence, the 'action-centred leadership' model:

- Defining the task
- Planning
- Briefing
- Controlling
- Evaluating
- Motivating
- Organising
- Setting an example

5.3 Evaluating contingency approaches

Contingency theory demonstrates that there is no ideal personality or one best style for a leader. This provides a basis for developing people as leaders: by making them aware of the factors affecting the choice of leadership style, and providing a basis for increased self-awareness, it gives a useful starting point for leadership training.

The full range of variables in a leadership situation may be difficult to identify and analyse in practice, however. The major difficulty for any leader seeking to apply contingency theory, however, is actually to modify his or her behaviour as the situation changes, without inconsistency which may damage team member confidence and security.

6 Personal development planning

Pedler, Burgoyne & Boydell (2001) give the following brief definition of self development.

'Self development is personal development, with the person taking primary responsibility for his or her own learning, and for choosing the means to achieve this.'

One of the key elements of your assignment will be a 'reflective element', requiring you to reflect on your own performance in given areas of management and leadership, and to plan for learning and improvement.

'If asked to think about how we have learned, most of us may think first of when attempts have been made to teach us. If, on the other hand, we are asked about problems we have solved, we think about difficult situations we have faced and managed to overcome. However, in solving problems, we don't just deal with the immediate difficulty, we ***discover a solution which we can use again in some form****, and we may also become better at solving problems generally. Problem solving is, to a large extent, learning'.*

The purpose of the reflective element is to enable you to convert your everyday managerial experience and problem-solving into a **learning opportunity**. The following paragraphs offer a framework for doing this in a systematic way.

- In a '**self awareness**' approach to this task, you start by gathering information about your performance (by observation and feedback gathering), and then select specific areas of interest for reflection and self-evaluation.
- In a '**problem-solving**' approach, you start with identified areas of potential weakness/threat (or strength/opportunity), and plan your information-gathering and reflection specifically to investigate them.

Either may be appropriate, depending on your needs.

6.1 Selecting areas for reflection

When deciding what areas of your management performance to reflect on (if not specified for you in your assignment), you may focus on:

- **Gathered data.** From your periodic observations, notes and feedback, you identify a pattern of behaviour which does or does not appear to be effective in helping you to achieve your aims as a manager or leader.
- **Critical incidents** in which you have participated: specific incidents which highlight a given behaviour – for example, by illustrating it particularly clearly, or by eliciting particularly positive or negative outcomes.
- **Examination of your goals**. You consider a particular desired outcome or objectives which you are or are not (yet) achieving effectively, and identify the strategies you have been using to pursue it: these may represent potential areas for problem-solving and development.
- **Impressions**. You feel generally satisfied or dissatisfied with your performance in a given area.

Note that the highlighted factors may be positive (indicating a possible strength or opportunity) as well as negative (possible weakness, limitation or threat). Learning opportunities may arise from your strengths (how can you build on them? how can you apply them in a wider range of situations?) as well as from your weaknesses (what do you need to do more effectively?)

6.2 Gathering data for reflection

6.2.1 Capturing observation and feedback data

Observations, impressions and intuitions provide valuable data for self reflection, but in order to make them a durable, flexible and practical source of information, you need to capture and record them. Get into the habit of **making notes** – verbal or visual, paper or electronic – during or shortly after any meeting, discussion or managerial action you are involved in. These will probably not be the kind of notes you usually make (content-based minutes of the discussion, decisions reached, action taken and so on), but notes about:

- Repeated patterns of behaviour which you notice in your team (or yourself)
- Thoughts or feelings that come up for you in response to others' behaviours or changes in behaviour: how you 'automatically' react to others' behaviour and what happens; how you make a controlled and intentional response to others' behaviour and what happens
- Other people's responses to your 'usual' behaviours and when you experiment with new behaviours

- What happened in the course of critical incidents and interactions
- Feedback from other people about your actions, decisions or performance.
- Such notes will provide the raw material for reflection and self-evaluation. If you rely solely on your memory, you will probably have insufficiently detailed data to go on.
- Get into the habit of collecting and filing data and feedback on your performance in a **Personal Portfolio**. This may include:
- Any completed self-report questionnaires and feedback forms
- The outputs of activities you do as you work through this Study Text, your wider reading and any other training activities
- Copies of reports from performance appraisals or coaching/mentoring and development planning sessions
- Feedback-bearing messages of all kinds (for example, commendation and thank-you letters; complaints; personal or employment references).

6.2.2 Gathering feedback

Other people are one of the most valuable sources of information about your behaviours, decisions and managerial style – because they are 'on the receiving end'. Other people can tell you how you are *perceived* (and important aspect of leadership) and how, your behaviour *affects* them.

Whetten & Cameron (2002, p48) argued that: *'It is almost impossible to increase skill in self-awareness without interacting with and disclosing ourselves to others. Unless one is willing to open up to others, to discuss aspects of the self that seem ambiguous or unknown, little growth can ever occur.*'

Identify people whom you trust to give you honest and constructive feedback about your performance in a given area. You may be able to take advantage of existing organisational mechanisms for upward appraisal, coaching or mentoring. Otherwise, you may need to co-opt a trusted colleague and *ask* him or her to observe, evaluate and feedback your performance in a specific area: eg how well you run a team meeting, or what style you use to lead your team in routine (and perhaps also stressful) situations.

6.3 Reflecting on your performance

Reflect on the issues raised by your gathered data in your chosen areas. We have already suggested that there is no 'one best way' to manage, communicate, influence, lead, negotiate and so on: it all depends. It depends on what you want to achieve, on the opportunities and constraints inherent in the situation, and on the skills and objectives of the other parties in the process.

In reflecting on your performance, your focus should not be on whether a behaviour or style is more or less 'right', but on whether it is more or less *effective* in achieving your *objectives.* A behaviour may be a strength or a weakness (or both) depending on what you wish to accomplish. An aggressive leadership style, for example, may support your immediate task goals by allowing you to impose your decisions on other people or quell dissent. It may, however, be counterproductive if your goals are to establish and maintain co-operative working relationships, or to encourage the flow of information for problem-solving and creativity.

There is an infinite number of questions you might usefully ask yourself, but as a thought-prompter, you might like to consider:

- The **outcomes** you wanted from your behaviour – and those you actually got
- Your **action tendencies** or patterns of behaviour (how you 'usually' behave or react in a situation) – and perhaps *why* these exist (assumptions, perceptions, past experience, personality factors?)
- Whether you **did anything different** on a particular occasion, and what the results or consequences were
- What you **might do differently**, in order to get a different result
- Any **discrepancies** between feedback from others and your own self-perception or self-evaluation, and what you can learn from them
- What **theoretical models and guidelines** (such as those outlined in this Study Text) might help you to understand what is going on – or what might lead to more effective results.

You may then be able to summarise your **conclusions**: identifying specific behaviours which you perceive to be strengths or limitations in a given context and in light of your goals. This will be the basis of improvement/learning planning.

6.3.1 A Personal Development Journal (PDJ)

A 'journal' is simply a book (or note pad, folder, computer document or whatever) in which you regularly record your experiences and actions – and your reflections on them.

A **PDJ** is a structured approach to recording your experience and reflections, providing you with data which will enable you to learn consciously and intentionally fro your experience, and monitor and track your development over time. Pedler *et al* (2001) suggest the format outlined on the next page: you might like to photocopy this and use it.

6.4 The experiential learning cycle

Research by David Kolb (1984) and its implications for management (Honey & Mumford, 1992) suggests that effective learning is a cyclical process of experimentation and adjustment, which can be applied in any situation. **Experiential learning** is a methodology for 'learning by doing'.

- We perform an action or have an experience
- We reflect on the experience, its results and any feedback we may have obtained from other people
- We formulate a hypothesis about what we might be able to do differently next time to get a better results
- We plan an opportunity to test our hypothesis in action
- We perform the action – and so continue the cycle

PERSONAL DEVELOPMENT JOURNAL

Date:

WHAT HAPPENED:	*[A brief description of events, with the emphasis on objective facts, including what led up to the situation]*
MY EMOTIONS:	*[Be specific about the emotions you experienced and how they changed during the event.]*
MY THOUGHTS/ IDEAS	*[What went through your head during the events]*
MY ACTION TENDENCIES	*[What you usually do in similar circumstances. What you 'wanted' to do. What other factors influenced your action or non-action.]*
MY BEHAVIOUR	*[What you actually said and did, and how]*
IMPLICATIONS FOR MY DEVELOPMENT	*[What you can learn from analysing the event, and how you might change your behaviour for the future.]*

The learning cycle

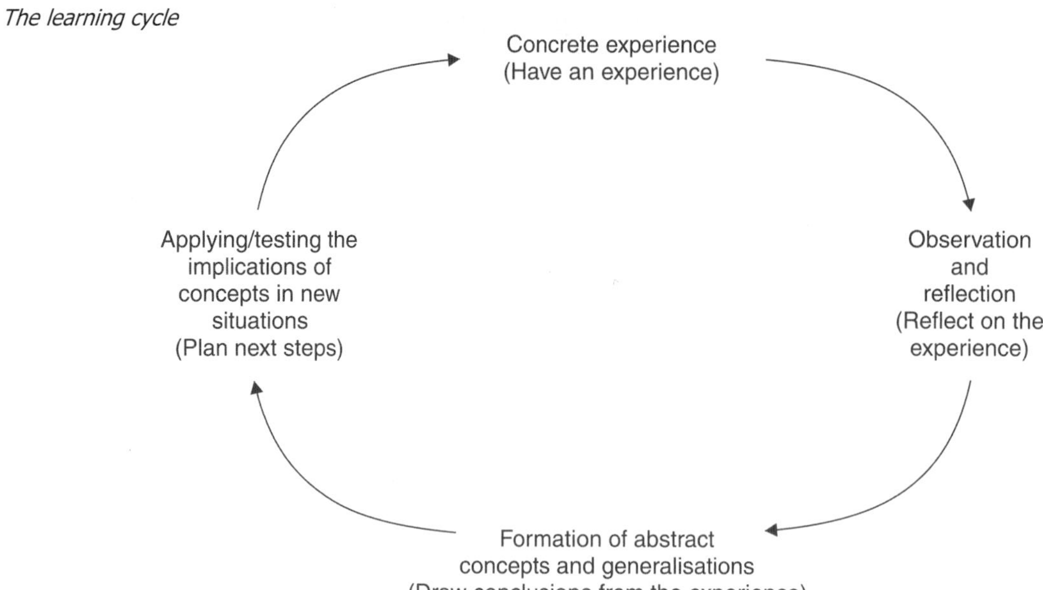

Suppose you are selection interviewing (concrete experience). You observe your own performance and the dynamics of the situation (observation) and afterwards, having noticed that you were unable to pin the candidate down on some crucial points, you think about what you did right and wrong (reflection). You come to the conclusion that perhaps you were too focused on using 'open' questions to encourage the candidate to express herself, and did not use 'probing' questions effectively (generalisation). You decide to try out some 'probing' questions in your next interview, and review some material on questioning styles (application/testing). In your next interview, you intentionally use some probing questions and observe the result – providing you with a new experience with which to start the cycle over again.

Experiential is one approach to self-managed development. You don't necessarily have to seek training in order to learn (although the 'abstraction/generalisation' stage may require some reading or instruction): you can learn on an on-going basis from your own every-day management activities.

6.5 Identifying your learning style preferences

Kolb (1984) recognised that people tend to have a preference for a particular phase of the learning cycle, which he identified as a **preferred learning style.**

Honey & Mumford (1992, p5) also noted that *'people vary not just in their learning skills but also in their learning styles. Why otherwise might two people, matched for age, intelligence and need, exposed to the same learning opportunity, react so differently?*

Honey & Mumford (1992) formulated a popular classification of learning styles.

- **Theorists** seek to understand basic principles and models, and to think problems through systematically and logically, before applying their learning. They prefer training to be:
  - Programmed and structured
  - Based on a system, model or theory
  - Designed to allow time for analysis

  They don't learn well from activities which lack context and theoretical support, involve ambiguity or uncertainty, and require them to act or decide without a basis in principles or concepts.

- **Reflectors** like to stand back and observe and ponder new experiences, preferring to consider all angles and implications, and to analyse all available data, before making any moves. They prefer training to:
  - Allow them to stand back, observe and reflect before acting
  - Allow them to work at their own pace
  - Offer opportunity for painstaking research

They don't learn well from activities which require action without warning or planning, give insufficient data, or impose time pressures (especially if these necessitate short cuts).

- **Activists** involve themselves fully in new experiences – but are easily bored by long-term implementation and consolidation. They prefer training to:
  - Present new experiences/problems and short here-and-now activities
  - Offer excitement, drama, variety and collaboration with other people
  - Allow them to generate ideas without constraints of structure or feasibility (eg brainstorming)
  - Throw them in at the deep end and allow them to 'have a go'

  They don't learn well from activities which are passive, require solitary work, involve precise instructions and 'theoretical' concepts, or require attention to detail and follow-up.

- **Pragmatists** are eager to try out ideas, theories and techniques to see if they work in practice. They are down-to-earth: enjoying practical decisions and problem-solving opportunities. They prefer training which:
  - Offers techniques with obvious practical applications and advantages
  - Relates to real problems, with immediate opportunities to implement learning at work
  - Allows practice with coaching/feedback from a credible expert
  - Focuses on practical issues (plans, tips etc).

  They don't learn well from activities which are too theoretical or distant from reality, offer no practical guidelines, benefits or rewards, or cannot be implemented due to personal or organisational obstacles.

A knowledge of your own learning style will help you to select learning activities and opportunities that are congruent with your preferences and that work to their associated strengths and limitations. Honey & Mumford (1992, p 49) suggest two possible strategies.

- **Seek activities which suit your preferred style**: those which *work* for you.
- **Seek activities which are *not* suited to your preferred style**: those which *stretch* you. This builds a wider range of learning effectiveness. You need all four styles to work through the experiential learning cycle: having an experience (Activist); reviewing the experience (Reflector); concluding from the experience (Theorist); and planning the next steps (Pragmatist).

We will examine a number of learning, training and development options in Chapter 7, when we consider the manager's role in facilitating the training and development of a team.

6.6 Personal development planning

Personal development planning includes the following basic steps.

Step 1 **Analyse the current position**. You could do a personal SWOT (strengths, weaknesses, opportunities, threats) analysis, skills analysis, or summary of the learning needs identified by your reflections.

Step 2 **Set learning and development goals** to cover improved performance in your existing role, preparing for future changes in your current role, preparing for another role, or developing your professional expertise. These should be formulated as SMART objectives (Specific, Measurable, Achievable, Relevant and Time-bounded).

Step 2 **Draw up an action plan** to achieve the goals, including:

- The SMART objective
- Methods you will use to develop the identified skills (including learning experiences, opportunities to try and practise new behaviours and so on)
- Timescales for review of progress
- Methods of monitoring and reviewing progress and achievement of the objective.

You may have your own preferences in regard to formatting and recording action plans. We recommend a simple, systematic format such as the following.

Objective	Methods	Timescale	Monitoring/Review
Statement of SMART learning objective	List of specific methods and activities selected	Target completion date for each listed method/ activity	How, with who and how often will you check your progress?

An example of a completed page from such a plan is included on the next page.

If you want to focus further on assessing and improving your management techniques and skills, in a wide range of areas and contexts, we can thoroughly recommend two 'handbook' style resources:

- **How to Be an Even Better Manager, by Michael Armstrong (6th edition, 2004). London: Kogan Page. A complete (yet short, practical and accessible!) A-Z of management techniques and skills, simply explained.**

- **A Manager's Guide to Self Development, by Mike Pedler, John Burgoyne and Tom Boydell (4th edition, 2001). Maidenhead: McGraw Hill. A practical workbook to help you identify your learning and development needs, set self-development goals, and undertake practical development activities.**

  From the CIM Supplementary Reading List you might also want to target:

- **Effective leadership: how to be a successful leader by John Adair: Pan Books (revised edition, May 2009)**

However, we prefer the more accessible handbook format of:

- **The John Adair Handbook of Management and Leadership, edited by Neil Thomas: Thorogood (2005). See Chapter 6 on 'Leadership and team building', for example** ■

PERSONAL DEVELOPMENT JOURNAL

Date:

WHAT HAPPENED	[A **brief** description of events, with the emphasis on objective facts, and including what led up to the situation.] ***Beware potential pitfall:*** Overly lengthy descriptions including conjections, feelings – not facts.
MY EMOTIONS	[Be **specific** about the emotions you experienced during the event eg: anger, irritation, fear, anxiety, happiness, satisfaction, sadness – and how they changed during the event.] ***Beware potential pitfall:*** expressing thoughts as emotions ('I felt he was wrong' – this is a **thought**).
MY THOUGHTS/ IDEAS	[What was **going through your head** during the events.]
MY ACTION TENDENCIES	[What you **typically do** in these or similar circumstances.] ***Beware potential pitfall:*** Repeating actual behaviour, rather than or 'predisposition' to behave in a certain way.
MY BEHAVIOUR	[What you **actually said and did**, and how: verbal and non-verbal behaviours. How others responded to your behaviours.] ***Beware potential pitfall:*** Generalised statements, lacking in specifics of what was done and said. Include actual words used and body language e.g. eye contact, posture etc
IMPLICATIONS FOR MY DEVELOPMENT	[**What you can learn** about your leadership behaviour from analysing the event. What behaviours were effective/less effective? How you might change your behaviour in similar situations in the future.] ***Beware potential pitfall:*** Not drawing out at least one clear learning point relevant to leadership and not being specific about how you would change your behaviour in the future relating verbal and non verbal behaviours you would change/modify.

Learning objective review

Learning objectives		Covered
1	Describe the scope and role of management and leadership, and critically evaluate the differences between them	☑ The role of management: Fayol's functions of management; Mintzberg's managerial roles ☑ The role and scope of leadership: strategic direction, change management, interpersonal influence and inspiration; Avolio's 'four Is'
2	Identify the role of an 'operational marketing manager'	☑ The role of the operational marketing manager: information, value creation, communication, team leadership
3	Outline and apply a range of leadership models (trait, style and contingency) to identify and evaluate your leadership style	☑ The range and usefulness of trait, style and contingency models of leadership ☑ Trait theories of leadership ☑ Style models of leadership: transactional and transformational leadership (Burns); the leadership grid (Blake & Mouton); a continuum of leadership styles (Tannenbaum & Schmidt; Ashridge studies) ☑ Contingency models of leadership: situational leadership (Hersey & Blanchard); and action-centred leadership (Adair)
4	Reflect on your personal approach to management and leadership and produce a personal development plan	☑ The nature and processes of managerial self-development and personal development planning ☑ Tools of personal development planning: the learning cycle (Kolb); personal development journal (PDJ); feedback gathering ☑ How to identify learning needs ☑ How to identify and access learning opportunities consistent with your learning style preferences (Honey & Mumford)

Quick quiz

1 Work study techniques are applied within

a. Scientific management?

b. Human relations theories?

c. Both schools of management?

2 Match the correct columns within the table below.

Demands made on organisations		
Be 'lean and mean'	*but*	Deliberately plan for the future
Be creative and innovative	*but*	Be a good employer
Decentralise to small, simple autonomous units	*but*	Stick to the knitting
Have a sense of urgency	*but*	Centralise to be efficient and integrative

3 What are French and Raven's sources of power?

4 What are the four schools of leadership theories?

5 Identify as many of the fifteen leadership traits that you can.

6 Reorder the following statements on the spectrum so they are correct where task orientated is at one end and relationship orientated is at the other end.

Task orientated						**Relationship orientated**
Leader allows subordinates to act as they wish, within specified limits	Leader defines limits and goals and asks the group to make the decision	Leader presents a problem, gets suggestions, and makes a decision	Leader 'sells' decision	Leader makes decision and announces it	Leader presents ideas and invites questions	Leader presents intended decision, subject to amendment

7 What is action-centred leadership?

Activity debriefs

1 You may be struck by two key 'omissions' from Fayol's classification, from a more modern viewpoint.

(a) '**Motivating**' is not mentioned. It is assumed that subordinates will carry out tasks when 'commanded' or instructed to do so, regardless of whether or how far they may 'want' to.

(b) '**Communicating**' is not mentioned, although it is implied by the process of commanding (giving instructions), co-ordinating (sharing information) and controlling (giving feedback).

2, 3, 4 Answers will depend on your own research.

5 Effective upward management:

Helps emergent ideas to find shape and direction through the process of communication, evaluation and lobbying for support

Helps secure support and resources, when needed, in order to achieve results

Maximises follow-through on promises of support and resources

Raises the organisational profile/status of a project or department

Minimises managerial interference (by demonstrating competence and/or assertively resisting micro-management)

Models upward communication flow (which may encourage suggestions, ideas and feedback from your own subordinates).

6 (a) 1.1: low task, low people

(b) 9.1: High task, low people

(c) 1.9: high people, low task

7 This will depend on your own research.

Quiz answers

1 a. Scientific Management

2

Demands made on organisations		
Be 'lean and mean'	*but*	Be a good employer
Be creative and innovative	*but*	'Stick to the knitting'
Decentralise to small, simple autonomous units	*but*	Centralise to be efficient and integrative
Have a sense of urgency	*but*	Deliberately plan for the future

3 Coercive, reward, legitimate, expert and referent.

4 Trait, style, contingency, interpersonal theories.

5

Judgement	Initiative	Integrity	Foresight	Energy
Drive	Human relations skill	Decisiveness	Dependability	Emotional stability
Fairness	Ambition	Dedication	Objectivity	Co-operation

6

Task orientated ———————————————— **Relationship orientated**

Leader makes decision and announces it	Leader 'sells' decision	Leader presents ideas and invites questions	Leader presents intended decision, subject to amendment	Leader presents a problem, gets suggestions, and makes a decision	Leader defines limits and goals and asks the group to make the decision	Leader allows subordinates to act as they wish, within specified limits

7 A scheme of leadership training based on precept and practice in each of eight leadership 'activities' which are applied to task, team and individual: hence, the 'action-centred leadership' model.

References

Adair, J. (1984) The Skills of Leadership, Gower, Aldershot.

Armstrong, M. (2009) A Handbook of Human Resource Management Practice, (11th edition), Kogan Page, London.

Bass, B.M. & Avolio, B.J. (1994) Improving Organisational Effectiveness through Transformational Leadership, Sage, Thousand Oaks.

Blake, R. & Mouton, J. (1964) The Managerial Grid, Gulf Publishing, Houston.

Boddy, D. (2005) Management: An Introduction, (3rd edition), FT Prentice Hall, Harlow.

Burns, J.M. (1978) Leadership, Harper & Row, New York.

Drucker, P. (1955) The Practice of Management, Heinemann, London.

Fayol, H. (1949) General and Industrial Management, Pitman, London.

French, J. & Raven, B. (1958) 'The bases of social power' in Studies in Social Power, Cartright D (ed). Institute for Social Research, Ann Arbor, MI.

Gillen, T. (2002) Leadership Skills for Boosting Performance, CIPD, London.

Hersey, P. & Blanchard, K.H. (1988) Management of Organisational Behaviour: Utilising Human Resources, (5th edition), Prentice Hall, New Jersey.

Honey, P. & Mumford, A. (1992) The Manual of Learning Styles, Peter Honey Publications, Maidenhead.

Huczynski, A. & Buchanan, D. (2001) Organizational Behaviour: An Introductory Text, (4th edition), FT Prentice Hall, Harlow.

Jobber, D. (2007) Principles and Practice of Marketing, (5th edition), McGraw Hill Education, Maidenhead.

Johnson, G., Scholes, K. & Whittington, R. (2005) Exploring Corporate Strategy: Text and Cases, (7th edition), Pearson Education, Harlow.

Kanter, R.M. (1992) When Giants Learn to Dance, International Thomson Business Press, London.

Katz, D. & Kahn, R.L. (1974) The Social Psychology of Organisations, (2nd edition), Wiley, New York.

Kolb, D. (1984) Experiential Learning, Prentice Hall, New York.

Kotler, P. (2002) Marketing Management, (11th edition), US Imports and PHIPES, New York.

Kotter, J.P. (1990) A force for Change: How Leadership Differs from Management, Free Press, New York.

Mayo, E. (1933) The Human Problems of an Industrial Civilisation, Macmillan, NY.

Mintzberg, H. (1973) The Nature of Managerial Work, Harper Row, London.

Mullins, L. (2005) Management and Organisational Behaviour, (7th edition), Pearson Education, Harlow, Essex.

Stewart, R. (1963) The Reality of Management, Pan/Heinemann, London.

Stodgill, R.M. (1948) *'Personal factors associated with leadership'* in Journal of Psychology, Vol 25, 1948.

Tannenbaum, R. & Schmidt, W. (1973) *'How to choose a leadership pattern'* in Harvard Business Review, May-June.

Taylor, F.W. (1911) Principles of Scientific Management, Harper, New York.

Whetten, D. & Cameron, K. (2002) Developing Management Skills, (5th edition), Prentice Hall, New Jersey.

Yukl, G. (1998) Leadership in Organisations,(4th edition), Prentice Hall, New Jersey.

Zaleznik, A. (1997) Managers and leaders: are they different?'(4th edition). Prentice Hall, New Jersey.

Zaleznik, A. (1997) *'Managers and leaders: are they different?'*, Harvard Business Review, March.

Chapter 5

Designing and recruiting marketing teams

Topic list

1 Teams in marketing
2 Team structure
3 Team recruitment and selection
4 Development and talent management
5 Structuring team work
6 Outsourcing jobs and projects

Introduction

This chapter explores a range of topics in the formation of marketing staff into high-performing teams. We start by exploring why team working is so popular in modern people management, while also recognising some of the drawbacks of team working (which you might use to diagnose problems in your own work context).

In section 2, we look at some key issues in team structure. What kinds of team structures are best able to deliver different marketing and organisational outcomes? What kinds of resources and competencies are required to form an effectively performing team?

In subsequent sections, we go on to consider how a manager can:

- *Acquire* the human resources required for a team, through a systematic process of team member recruitment and selection
- *Develop* additional skills and competencies within the team, through a systematic process of training and development (although this topic is covered in more detail in Chapter 7)
- *Organise and deploy* the human resources of the team in the most effective and efficient way, through a systematic process of job design.

Note our emphasis on systematic processes. Human resource management is a huge area of study: we can only give you representative best-practice frameworks, which you can use as a foundation for your own more detailed reading, analysis and application, once you know the focus of your assignment.

Finally, we recognise that skills and competencies can also be co-opted from outside the marketing team – as an alternative to recruitment and development – through *outsourcing.*

Syllabus linked learning objectives

By the end of the chapter you will be able to:

	Learning objectives	Syllabus link
1	Determine the need for synergistic and harmonious marketing teams, identifying different types of teams and different applications of team working	2.2
2	Suggest how teams should be structured to deliver organisational and marketing objectives	2.2
3	Propose a range of approaches for the sourcing (recruitment and selection) and induction of team members to provide the right balance of competencies and skills	2.3
4	Propose approaches to manage and co-ordinate the work of teams and individuals, including the structuring of tasks	2.2, 2.3
5	Evaluate the option of outsourcing marketing jobs and processes, as an alternative to recruiting and developing competencies within the marketing team	2.2

1 Teams in marketing

1.1 Groups

Handy (1993) defined a **group** as 'any collection of people who perceive themselves to be a group'. The point of this definition is the distinction it implies between a random collection of individuals (such as a bus stop queue) and a group of individuals (such as a college class) who share a common sense of **identity** and **belonging**, a more or less defined **purpose** or objectives, and some kind of **leadership** to steer them towards those goals.

People are often drawn together into groups by a preference for smaller units where closer relationships can develop; the need to belong and to make a contribution that will be noticed and appreciated; shared space, specialisms, objectives or interests; the attractiveness of a particular group activity or resources; or access to power greater than individuals could wield on their own (one of the reasons for joining a trade union or staff association, say).

(a) **Informal groups** will invariably be present in any organisation: examples include workplace cliques and networks of people who get together to exchange information, groups of friends who socialise outside work and so on. Such groups have a constantly fluctuating membership and structure.

(b) **Formal groups** are intentionally and rationally designed to achieve objectives assigned to them by the organisation, for which they are responsible. They are characterised by: membership and leadership appointed and approved by the organisation; compliance of the members with the group's goals and requirements; and structured relationships of authority, responsibility, task allocation and communication.

It is worth noting that people contribute different skills and attributes to the organisation as group members than they do as individuals, because:

(a) Human behaviour is different in groups than in solo or interpersonal situations: **group dynamics** have an effect on performance.

(b) Groups offer **synergy**: the '2 + 2 = 5' effect whereby the pooling and stimulation of ideas and energies in a group can allow greater contribution than individuals working on their own. ('None of us is as smart as all of us': Blanchard & Bowles, 2001.)

(c) Group dynamics and synergy may also be **negative**: distracting the individual, stifling individual responsibility and flair and so on. Individuals may contribute more and better, in some situations.

1.2 Teams

KEY CONCEPT

concept

A **team** is 'a small number of people with complementary skills who are committed to a common purpose, performance goals and approach for which they hold themselves mutually accountable.' (Katzenbach & Smith).

All teams are groups – but not all groups are, strictly speaking, teams.

1.3 Benefits of using teams

The basic work units of organisations have traditionally been specialised functional departments. In more recent times, organisations have adopted what Peters and Waterman (1982) called 'chunking': the breaking up of the organisation structure into small, flexible units, or teams. From the organisation's standpoint, teams have a number of advantages.

(a) Teams facilitate the performance of tasks which require the **collective skills**, experience or knowledge of more than one person or discipline.

(b) Teams facilitate the **co-ordination** of the work of different individuals or groups, by bringing them together across organisational boundaries (eg departments and functions) with shared goals and structured communication.

(c) Teams facilitate **interactive communication** and interpersonal relationships, and are thus particularly well-adapted for:

- **Testing and ratifying decisions**, because they offer multi-source feedback and may make the decision more acceptable, by taking account of a cross-section of stakeholder views. Teams have been shown to produce better evaluated (though fewer) decisions than individuals working separately.
- **Consultation and negotiation**, because they allow an interactive exchange of views and influence
- **Generating ideas**, because of their potential for 'bouncing' ideas off each other and getting multiple inputs
- **Collecting and disseminating information**, because of the multiple networks in which the various members are involved.

(d) Teams can **motivate** their members, since they offer satisfying relationships, mutual encouragement and support, and the opportunity to share work loads and responsibilities. Peters and Waterman (ibid) argue that teams enable people to make noticeable individual contributions (which bolsters their self-esteem) *and* at the same time to share responsibility and be part of something bigger than themselves (which bolsters their sense of security).

1.4 Drawbacks to using teams

(a) Teams and team working are very much in fashion, but it is important to recognise their potential drawbacks, limitations and challenges.

(b) Team working is **not suitable for all jobs**: it should be introduced because it leads to better performance, not because people feel better or more secure.

(c) Team processes (especially excessive meetings and seeking consensus) can **delay decision making**: groups make fewer decisions than individuals.

(d) Social relationships might be maintained **at the expense of other aspects of performance** or inter-group conflicts may get in the way of effective collaboration.

(e) Group norms may **restrict or inhibit** individual contribution. Mayo's Hawthorne studies, for example, showed that individuals restrict their output in order not to 'show up' the team by producing more or better work than the team average.

(f) Due to a process called **social facilitation**, performance of simple tasks at which people are relatively confident *improves* in the presence of other people – but performance of new, complex tasks is *hindered* by the presence of an audience. (You may be familiar with this 'flustered' feeling ...).

(g) Groups have been found to take **riskier decisions** than individuals on their own. This may occur due to a number of dynamics.

- **Conformity**: group pressures persuade individuals to agree to decisions, suppressing their questions and 'better judgement'.
- **'Group think'** (Janis, 1972): team consensus and cohesion may prevent consideration of alternatives or constructive criticism. The team becomes blinkered to contradictory information, and feels invincible, leading to ill-considered decisions.
- The **'risky-shift phenomenon'**: if a group is broadly like-minded, discussion will tend to strengthen the prevailing attitude, leading to polarised views (group polarisation). Together with the diffusion of individual responsibility, this can support risky decision making.
- The **Abilene paradox**: group members go along with what they *assume* is the group's intention – leading to a situation where the group does what *none* of its individual members really wants to do.

You should also be aware that while 'team working' is regarded as a positive value in itself, there are such things as ineffective, poorly managed and underperforming teams! Team working involves complex dynamics, roles and relationships and it is not easy to get it right. The important thing is not to have teams – but to have *effective* teams mobilised for *appropriate* applications.

1.5 Teams in a marketing context

Teams have steadily become more popular in marketing contexts (as in many other business disciplines), because of their potential to improve cross-functional communication and ideas generation. They may include:

- **Quality or service circles** or customer care task forces: cross-functional teams used to discuss quality and improvement issues
- **Brainstorming groups**, brought together to generate new ideas and suggestions, for problem solving, planning or creativity (eg advertising campaign or new product ideas)
- **Training or study groups**: a cost-effective way of training teams, and an effective way of training people specifically in team working, interpersonal and leadership skills
- **Marketing project teams**. These may be set up to handle specific strategic developments (such as market segmentation, brand identity or pricing); tasks relating to particular processes (such as the computerisation of customer relationship management); investigations of procedures or improvement opportunities (such as a marketing audit, or advertising agency selection and operational marketing projects (such as marketing research, event management or product launch).
- **Specialist marketing teams**: permanent teams responsible for functions or tasks, such as market research, marketing planning, media buying, public relations and so on
- **Key account teams:** taking shared responsibility for all aspects of marketing to, and relationship with, a key client or customer segment
- **Cross-functional teams**: whether permanent (in a matrix structure) or temporary (on a project basis), to co-ordinate collaboration on cross-functional processes such as new product development, marketing mix planning, the setting up of operational systems and so on

More generally, it has become common to think of marketing departments and sub-sections of them, as 'teams', in order to emphasise shared goals and contributions, mutual accountability and the need to manage group processes. You might like to think, for example, to what extent your marketing department or section *really* has the attributes and processes of a team, or whether lip service is paid to this idea, purely as a motivational tool.

2 Team structure

A team may be called together temporarily, to achieve specific task objectives (eg a **project team** or **task force**), or may be more or less permanent, with responsibilities for a particular brand, market segment, or stage of the marketing process (eg a brand or process team).

There are two basic approaches to the organisation of team work which requires a variety of skills and competences: multi-disciplinary working and multi-skilled working.

2.1 Multi-disciplinary or cross-functional teams

Multi-disciplinary or cross-functional teams bring together individuals from **different functional specialisms**, within a matrix structure or on temporary (project) basis, so that their competences can be pooled or exchanged. Such teams are an important tool in situations where technical expertise in a range of different disciplines is required. This used to be regarded as primarily the case in large technical projects, but there has also been an increasing focus (as we saw in Chapter 1) on horizontal business **processes**, and the horizontal (cross-functional) structures required to streamline them.

Multi-disciplinary teams:

- Increase team members' **awareness of the big picture** of their tasks and decisions, by highlighting the dovetailing and interdependency of functional objectives
- Help to generate **solutions to problems**, and suggestions for performance or process improvements, by integrating more pieces of the puzzle
- Aid **co-ordination** across functional boundaries, by increasing the flow of communication, information relationships and co-operation
- Support **stakeholder management and buy-in**, by representing the interests and viewpoints of multiple stakeholders in a project or process

A drawback of multi-functional teams, however, is that their members have dual reporting lines and responsibilities. The team as a whole may represent a wide range of different interests, backgrounds, work cultures, specialist skills and terminology and so on. This creates a particular challenge for the team leader: to build a sense of team identity, role clarity, co-operative working and communication flow. (We will discuss the challenges of diverse teams in Chapter 8.)

2.2 Multi-skilled teams

Multi-skilled teams bring together, in a permanent team structure, a number of **functionally versatile** individuals, each of whom can perform *any* of the group's tasks: work can thus be allocated flexibly, according to who is best placed to do a given job when required. The advantages of multi-skilling may be as follows.

- Performing a whole, meaningful job is more **satisfying** to people than performing only one or two of its component operations (as in the kind of job design favoured by scientific management).
- Allowing team members to see the big picture enables and encourages them to **contribute information and ideas**.
- Empowering team members to take initiative enhances the unit's **responsiveness** to customer demands and environmental changes (particularly in customer-facing units such as sales and customer service).
- A focus on overall task objectives rather than individual job descriptions reduces the need for tight managerial control and supervision.
- Human resources can be allocated more flexibly and efficiently, without potentially disruptive 'demarcation' disputes (about 'whose job' a task is or should be).

Multi-skilled teams are particularly appropriate when a high degree of flexibility is required. They are a cornerstone of team empowerment, since they cut across the barriers of job descriptions to enable teams to respond flexibly to changing demands. However, there is a limit to how versatile most people can be, so multi-skilling is perhaps best suited to relatively limited areas of activity, such as event management or marketing research. (A multi-disciplinary team can be assembled to cover a much wider range of specialist functions and tasks.)

2.3 Virtual teams

Virtual teams bring together individuals working in remote locations, reproducing the social, collaborative and information-sharing aspects of team working mainly – or wholly – using Information and Communication Technology (ICT) links.

A virtual team may comprise members in different offices, branches or worksites; on the road (eg sales force teams); or in different countries. Teleconferencing, video-conferencing, locally networked computers, the Internet, mobile telecommunications and other tools can be used to connect remote and mobile team members for data sharing and task sharing, meetings, joint decision making, performance monitoring and so on.

Localised virtual teams have been used for some time in the form of **teleworking**: working from home, or from a satellite office close to home, with the aid of computers, facsimile machines, modems or other forms of ICT equipment. The main benefits cited for such work include savings on office overheads and the elimination of the costs and stresses of commuting for employees.

More recently, however, the globalisation of business, the need for fast responses to market demands and the increasing sophistication of available technologies has brought about an explosion in **global virtual team working**. More and more organisations are attempting to conduct business 24-7, with people on different continents and in different time zones.

2.4 Self-managed teams

Self-managed teams are the most highly-developed form of team working. They are permanent structures in which team members collaboratively decide all the major issues affecting their work: work processes and schedules, task allocation, the selection and development of team members, the distribution of rewards and the management of group processes (problem solving, conflict management, internal discipline and so on). The team leader is a member of the team, acting in the role of coach and facilitator: leadership roles may be shared or rotated as appropriate.

Self managed teams:

- Contract with management to assume various degrees of **managerial responsibility** (which may increase as the team develops) for planning, organising, directing and monitoring. Teams often report to 'absentee' managers with broad responsibilities for several functions, whose role is to act as integrators/facilitators.
- Perform **day-to-day planning and control** functions: scheduling and co-ordinating the daily and occasional tasks of the team and individuals; setting performance goals and standards; formulating and adopting budgets; collecting performance data and reviewing results
- Perform **internal people management** functions: screening and interviewing candidates to join the team, and contributing to selection/hiring decisions; providing orientation for new members; coaching and providing feedback on member performance; designing and conducting cross-training on all tasks
- Recruit or cross-train members for **multi-skilling**: members rotate or are deployed flexibly from task to task, as required.
- Use weekly **team meetings** to identify, analyse and solve task and relationship problems within the team: reviewing team working and progress; getting team members to research and present team issues and so on.

Self-managed team working is said to have significant advantages in managerial cost savings, and in gains in quality and productivity, through harnessing the commitment and contribution of those who perform the work. However, it obviously presents an additional layer of challenges in developing teams capable of effective self management.

2.5 Team roles and functions

Team membership may be dictated by existing arrangements, organisational appointment or election (eg in the case of a staff representative committee). However, where a manager is able to select team members, a mix of attributes, competencies and resources should be secured to match the needs of the task. Team members should be selected for their potential to contribute to getting things done (**task performance**) and establishing and maintaining good working relationships (**group maintenance**).

Resources required by a given team may include:

- **Specialist skills**. A team might exist to combine expertise from different functions.
- **Power or influence** in the wider organisation (to help mobilise support and resources)
- **Access to resources.** Team members may contribute information or useful network contacts, or be able to access finance, equipment or staff for the task.
- **Personal attributes**, such as commitment, energy or creativity

2.5.1 Belbin's team role model

R Meredith Belbin (1993) researched business game teams at the Henley Management College and drew up a widely-used framework for understanding roles within work teams. Belbin insisted that a distinction needs to be made between:

- **Team (process) role** (a 'tendency to behave, contribute and interrelate with others at work in certain distinctive ways')
- **Functional (task) role** ('the job demands that a person has been engaged to meet by supplying the requisite technical skills and operational knowledge')

Belbin's model of nine roles addresses the mix of team/process roles required for a fully functioning team (Belbin, 1993, p 22).

Belbin's team roles

Role and description	Team-role contribution	Allowable weaknesses
Plant		
Creative, imaginative, unorthodox	Solves difficult problems, presents new ideas	Ignores details. Too preoccupied to communicate effectively
Resource investigator		
Extrovert, enthusiastic, communicative	Explores opportunities, develops contacts	Over-optimistic. Loses interest once initial enthusiasm past.
Co-ordinator (or Chairman)		
Mature, confident, a good chairperson	Clarifies goals, promotes decision making, delegates well	Can be seen as manipulative. Delegates personal work.
Shaper		
Challenging, dynamic, thrives on pressure	Has the drive and courage to overcome obstacles	Can provoke others and hurt people's feelings.
Monitor-Evaluator		
Sober, strategic and discerning	Sees all options, judges accurately	Lacks drive and ability to inspire others. Overly critical.
Team worker		
Co-operative, mild, perceptive and diplomatic	Listens, builds, averts friction, calms the waters	Indecisive in crunch situations. Can be easily influenced.
Implementer (or Company Worker)		
Disciplined, reliable, conservative and efficient	Turns ideas into practical actions	Somewhat inflexible. Slow to respond to new possibilities.
Completer-Finisher		
Painstaking, conscientious, anxious	Searches out errors and omissions, ensures delivery on time	Inclined to worry unduly. Reluctant to delegate. Can be a 'nitpicker'.
Specialist		
Single-minded, self-starting, dedicated	Provides knowledge and skills in rare supply	Contributes only on a narrow front. Dwells on technicalities. Overlooks the 'big picture'.

If you want to look at Belbin's ideas in more detail, including not just the team role model, but also analysis of various team issues and behaviours (including improving unsuccessful teams), the best source might be the title cited in the CIM Supplementary Reading List:

Management Teams: why they succeed or fail, by R Meredith Belbin: Elsevier Butterworth-Heinemann. (Chapter 6 covers the team roles in detail.)

2.5.2 A balanced team

These team roles are not fixed within any given individual. Team members can occupy more than one role, or switch to 'backup' roles if required: hence, there is no requirement for every team to have nine members. However, since role preferences are based on personality, it should be recognised that:

- Individuals will be naturally inclined towards some roles more than others.
- Individuals will tend to adopt one or two team roles more or less consistently.
- Individuals are likely to be more successful in some roles than in others.

The nine roles are complementary, and Belbin suggested that an 'ideal' team should represent a mix or balance of all of them. Effective team working requires a mix and balance of all the roles, which between them support task functions (such as ideas generation, problem solving, implementation and follow-up) and team maintenance functions (support, conflict management, leadership and so on). If managers know employees' team role preferences, they can strategically select, 'cast' and develop team members to fulfil the required roles.

ACTIVITY 1

concept

The following phrases and slogans project certain team roles: identify which. (Examples are drawn from Belbin (1993)).

(a) The small print is always worth reading.

(b) Let's get down to the task in hand.

(c) In this job you never stop learning.

(d) Without continuous innovation, there is no survival.

(e) Surely we can exploit that?

(f) When the going gets tough, the tough get going.

(g) I was very interested in your point of view.

(h) Has anyone else got anything to add to this?

(i) Decisions should not be based purely on enthusiasm.

ASSIGNMENT TIP

concept

Belbin's model is specifically cited in the syllabus, so it is worth focusing on the detail of the model and its application. If you appraise your own work team, and find that it has too many competing leaders, or a lack of an leader/ideas-person/people-person, you should think about using Belbin's model as a framework for rebalancing the team and developing people in the needed roles.

MARKETING AT WORK

application

An 'innovation squad' can be described in terms of personalities:

Mr Blue Skies is the broad thinker who keeps the long-term vision but needs to be kept in touch with reality. His colleague, Mr Margin, gets margins up and thus delivers the all-important profit. However, he cannot see that innovation relies on intangibles such as faith and judgement.

Ms Misery takes her name from her tendency to focus on the negative. But innovation needs her rigorous approach.

Ms Me-Too could bring about a first-to-market situation by keeping a valuable eye on the competition – for instance an innovation abroad. Every innovation needs someone to champion the cause, but Mr Hobby Horse can be in danger of backing the wrong horse. Mr Cavalier is the classic self-confident entrepreneur with high energy levels and a healthy disregard for the established way of doing things; he genuinely cares about a result and is faster at effecting change.

Ms Brands is the player who contributes the strong understanding of the consumer, but unfortunately not everyone shares her passion for her particular brand. Mr Out-of-Depth is unlikely to have that big idea, but he is keen, hard-working and sufficiently junior to do the essential donkey-work.

3 Team recruitment and selection

It will often be necessary to bring new people into the team: to fill an identified skill or competence gap; to replace staff who have left the team; or because the work of the team has expanded, requiring extra people resources. Effective team recruitment is very important. Getting the wrong person can case problems within the existing group, or the need for extensive training before the desired performance level is achieved.

3.1 The recruitment and selection process

The overall aim of the recruitment and selection process in an organisation is to obtain the quantity and quality of employees required to fulfil the objectives of the organisation – and, at the team level, to obtain the mix and balance of skills and competences required to fulfil the team's objectives. This process can be broken down into three main stages:

- **Defining requirements**, including the preparation of job descriptions, job specifications and person specifications (or personnel specifications)
- **Attracting applicants**, including the evaluation and use of various methods for reaching appropriate sources of skills and competences (both within and outside the organisation)
- **Selecting** the appropriate candidates for the job (or the appropriate job for the candidate)

3.1.1 Responsibilities in recruitment and selection

Senior managers and HR specialists will usually be responsible for human resources planning (HRP): identifying the overall skill needs of the organisation, and the types of people it wishes to employee. The HR function will often also have a role in maintaining personnel records; keeping in touch with trends in the labour market; ensuring that the organisation complies with relevant legislation on equal opportunities and diversity; determining recruitment and selection policies; designing standard documentation (such as application forms); and liaising with recruitment consultants (if used).

In many cases, however, recruitment activities will be carried out by (or in partnership with) the recruit's prospective manager. In a small business, the marketing manager may have sole responsibility for recruiting marketing staff. In a larger organisation, (s)he may be responsible for:

- Asking for more staff by notifying vacancies, or issuing a job requisition
- Advising the HR department or recruitment consultant on skills, competences and attributes required
- Selection interviewing (perhaps in collaboration with HR specialists)
- Having a final say in the recruitment decision

ACTIVITY 2

application

Obtain (or look up on the corporate intranet) a copy of the recruitment policy of your organisation.

3.2 Recruitment

A systematic recruitment process can be depicted as follows.

The recruitment process

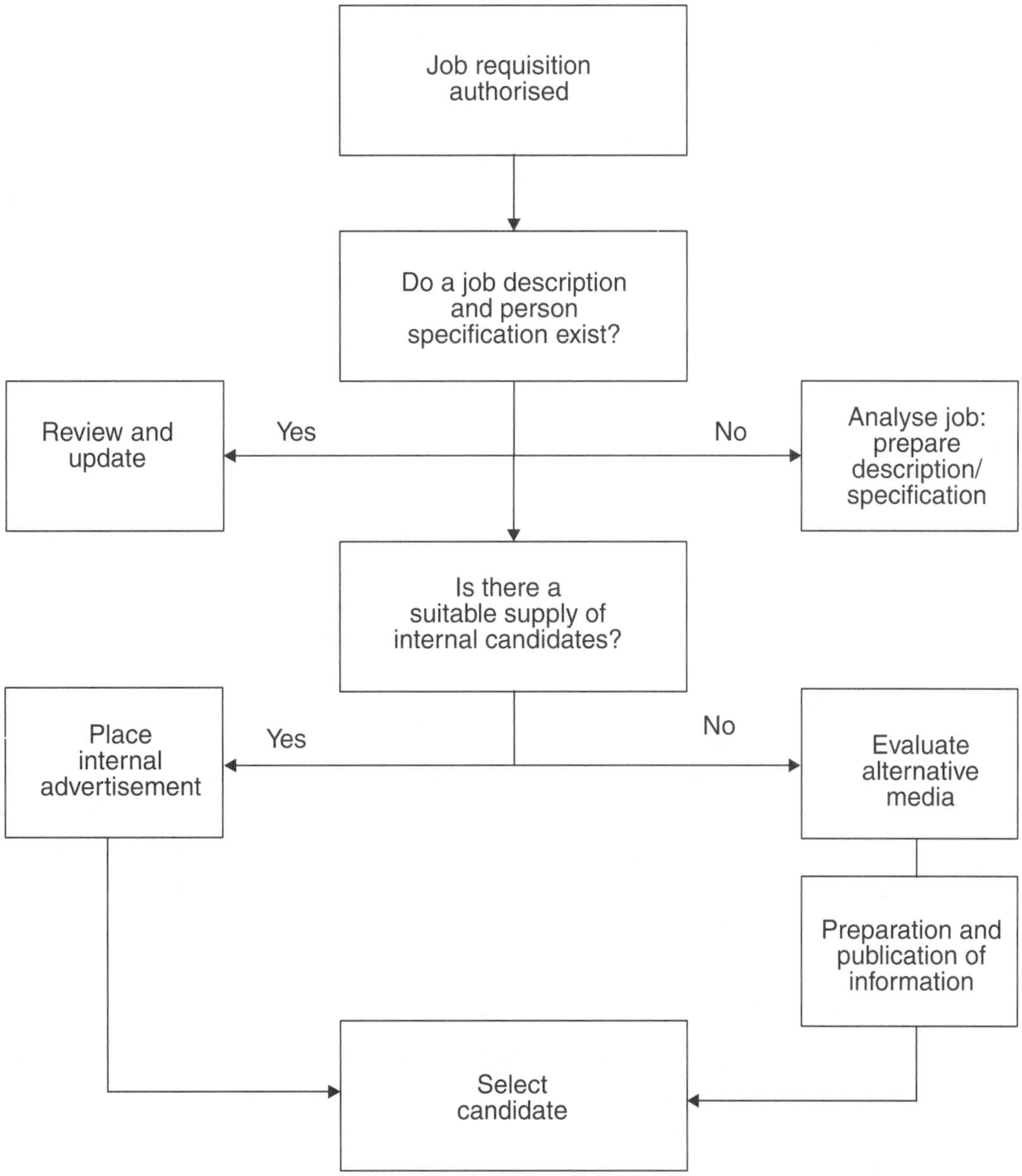

Job requisition authorised

Do a job description and person specification exist?

Yes → Review and update

No → Analyse job: prepare description/ specification

Is there a suitable supply of internal candidates?

Yes → Place internal advertisement

No → Evaluate alternative media

Preparation and publication of information

Select candidate

Note that this process is part of a wider whole.

(a) Detailed **human resource planning** defines what resources the organisation (and marketing department) needs to meet its objectives, and what sources of labour (internal and external) are available. Skill requirements may be met through recruitment – but there may also be plans for *reducing* staff numbers, redeployment, training and development, promotion, retention (to reduce loss of skills through staff turnover) and so on.

(b) **Job analysis** is a process of analysing the content of jobs, which usually produces two outputs.

- A **job description**: a statement of the component tasks, duties, objectives and standards involved in a job.
- A **person specification**: a reworking of the job description in terms of the kind of person needed to perform the job.

(c) Recruitment as such begins with the **identification of vacancies**, either from the requirements of the human resource plan or by a **job requisition** from a department that has a vacancy or need. (A careful review should be undertaken to ensure that an extra full-time post is justified by the contribution the person is expected to make. It should not be assumed that if a team member leaves, a replacement is necessarily appropriate: the role or task may have changed).

(d) The preparation and publication of **recruitment advertising** will have three aims.

- Attracting the attention and interest of potentially suitable candidates.
- Giving a favourable (but accurate) impression of the job and the organisation.
- Equipping those interested to make an appropriate application (how and to whom to apply, desired skills, qualifications and so on).

(e) Recruitment merges into **selection** when processing applications and assessing candidates.

(f) **Notifying applicants** of the results of the selection process is the final stage of the combined recruitment and selection process.

3.2.1 Internal recruitment channels

It is important to recognise that there is an *internal* labour market as well as an external one. Skills and competences required by a marketing team, for example, may be obtained via:

(a) **Training and development** of existing team members (discussed later in this chapter)

(b) **Internal advertising** of the marketing vacancy within the organisation. This may be done formally, via email, or an in-house magazine or corporate notice board, or their intranet equivalents. It may also be done informally, via word-of-mouth among employees, or recommendation by HR or other managers. The organisation might invite formal applications (perhaps ahead of external applications) from employees who would like a transfer or promotion to the vacancy advertised.

(c) The temporary or permanent **transfer, secondment or redeployment** of suitably skilled staff from other units or functions to the marketing team, by negotiation between the relevant managers. Staff with desirable attributes and experience in other functions may be cross-trained in marketing competences, if necessary.

(d) The 'co-opting' of skills to the marketing team in the form of **cross-functional team working** or matrix structures, ensuring that marketing has access to non-marketing competences and resources through collaboration.

3.2.2 External recruitment channels

Depending on the target recruitment market, media for external recruitment advertising include:

- **Professional and specialist journals** and magazines, such as *Marketing Week* or *Marketing Business*
- **National newspapers** (often used for senior management jobs or vacancies for skilled workers, where potential applicants will not necessarily be found through local advertising) or local newspapers (often for lower-skilled jobs, or to support local employment)
- **Job centres** (which mainly advertise unskilled work)
- **School and university careers offices** (particularly for recruitment at school-leaver or graduate level)
- **Recruitment consultancies and employment agencies**, who may be engaged to perform a range of recruitment and selection tasks on the organisation's behalf. The organisation may benefit from the consultant's range of contacts, and from the anonymity of the process in the initial stages.
- **The Internet**. Many business advertise vacancies on their web sites, or register vacancies with on-line databases and job-search directories. The advantages of **e-recruitment** include:
  - A large audience, reached at low cost
  - Interactivity, with links to information, downloadable application forms, e-mail contacts and so on
  - Pre-selection of people with good IT skills.

MARKETING AT WORK

ANZ stadium

MAKING THE GREATEST THINGS HAPPEN

Coordinator, Communications & Media

ANZ Stadium is Australia's premier sports and entertainment venue. The centrepiece of the 2000 Olympic and Paralympic Games and the 2003 Rugby World Cup, the Stadium regularly hosts major sporting events including the Bledisloe Cup, State of Origin, NRL Grand Final, Sydney Swans blockbusters and concerts.

The following opportunity exists to be part of Australia's sporting and entertainment future and join a dynamic, high achieving team which strives to 'Make the Greatest Things Happen'.

Reporting to the General Manager, Marketing & Communications, the successful applicant must have at least 2 years' experience in journalism or public relations and established contacts with a range of media. Experience in a similar role in a sports and entertainment venue is desirable, but not essential.

The key skills and responsibilities of the position are:

- **Strong communication, written and presentation skills**
- **Practical experience in e-communication channels**
- **Competency in Word, Excel, Outlook and Internet applications**
- **Produce written, audio and video content for ANZ Stadium's various communication channels**
- **Manage day to day charity committee relationship**
- **Act as the Stadium's Media Liaison Officer on event and non event days**
- **Assist in management and activation of media and promotional initiatives**

In addition to the above criteria, attention to detail, a customer focus, high levels of energy, willingness to work flexible hours in lieu with the requirements of ANZ Stadium's event schedule (which includes weekend work) and a positive 'can do' attitude, is what is required to successfully undertake this position.

Applications close on Friday 23 May and a more detailed Job Description is available on request. Expressions of interest should be sent to:

Via mail: [Details given]

Or via fax:

Or via email:

AdNews (Australia), 16 May, 2008

ACTIVITY 3

Get hold of (or access via the corporate web site) some examples of job advertisements for your firm, ideally including some for marketing jobs. If none are available, look through *Marketing Business* and national newspapers for marketing job advertisements in general.

What kind of information do they convey to potential candidates?

How effectively do they support potential candidates in (a) deciding whether the job and employer is (or isn't) for them; and (b) making an application?

What is the balance between honesty and attractiveness in the way the organisation and the job are presented?

3.2.3 Recruit or develop/promote?

One of the areas in which an organisation will often formulate a recruitment policy is whether it has a preference for recruiting skills from outside to fill a vacancy, or to develop, promote or transfer someone from within the firm. Some of the factors to be considered in this decision may be as follows.

- **Availability in the current staff** of the skills and attributes required to fill the vacancy. If the lead time to develop current staff to 'fit' the vacancy is too long, there may be no immediate alternative to external recruitment.
- **Availability in the external labour pool** of the skills and attributes required. Where there are skill shortages, it may be necessary to develop them within the organisation.
- **Accuracy of selection decisions**. Management will be familiar with an internal recruit and his or her performance. An outside recruit will be a relatively unknown quantity and the organisation will be taking a risk attempting to predict job performance.
- **Time for induction**. An internal recruit has already worked within the organisation and will be familiar with its culture, structures, systems and procedures, objectives and other personnel. This gives a head start for performance in the new position. An external recruit may have to undergo a period of induction before performing effectively.
- **Staff development**. Internal promotion is evidence of the organisation's willingness to develop people's careers, which may build morale (and avoid resentments). It may also be part of a systematic **succession plan** which maintains managerial continuity and individual performance improvement over time.
- **Fresh blood**. Insiders may be too socialised into the prevailing culture to see faults or be willing to change. Organisations in fast-changing and innovative fields like marketing may require new people with wider views, fresh ideas and perhaps even experience with a competitor.

3.3 Selection tools

3.3.1 Job analysis

KEY CONCEPT

concept

Job analysis is: 'the process of collecting, analysing and setting out information about the content of jobs in order to provide the basis for a job description and data for recruitment, training, job evaluation and performance management. Job analysis concentrates on what job holders are expected to do' (Armstrong, 2009).

The firm has to know what people are doing (or should be doing) in order to recruit effectively. It may want to establish:

- The purpose of the job, set in the context of the function and organisation as a whole
- The detailed duties and responsibilities of the job
- Key results for which the job holder accounts to his or her superior(s)
- The performance criteria used to measure competent performance in the job
- The scope of the job holder's authority, discretion to take decisions, budgetary responsibilities and so on
- Reporting and liaison relationships within the organisation structure
- Opportunities for skill, career and personal development
- Environmental factors (such as working conditions, security and safety issues, equipment utilised and so on).

Various techniques may be used in the analysis process.

- **Interviews** can be conducted with job holders and their supervisors to establish basic facts about the job (main tasks or duties, performance measures used, work conditions and so on) *and* more qualitative information (such as the amount of supervision received, freedom to take decisions, the difficulty and stress of the job, attributes needed to carry out the job and so on).
- **Questionnaires, checklists and inventories** may be designed as a structured and cost-effective way of gathering factual information from multiple job holders.
- **Observation** may be used to analyse physical tasks and processes (tasks undertaken, work conditions etc) although this is more difficult with knowledge-based work.
- **Self-description** may be invited via job diaries and logs (records of what the job holder does over a period of time) or by asking the job holder to compile his or her own job description. Job holders are most familiar with their own work, and can provide qualitative and subjective data.

Workset is a job analysis system developed by Belbin, using colour coding to classify work and working time into seven types.

1. Blue: tasks the job holder carries out in a prescribed manner to an approved standard
2. Yellow: individual responsibility to meet an objective (results, not means)
3. Green: tasks that vary according to the reactions and needs of others
4. Orange: shared rather than individual responsibility for meeting an objective
5. Grey: work incidental to the job, not relevant to the four core categories
6. White: new or creative undertaking outside normal duties
7. Pink: demands the presence of the job holder but leads to no useful results

The manager gives an outline of the proportion of time which the manager expects the jobholder to spend on each 'colour' of work. The job holder then briefs the manager on what has actually been done. This highlights differences: between managers' and job-holders' perceptions of jobs; between the perceptions of different jobholders in the same nominal position, who had widely different ideas as to what they were supposed to do.

ACTIVITY 4

application

Important issues arise when there is a gap in perception. Underperformance in different kinds of work can be identified, and people can be steered to the sort of work which suits them best.

You might like to analyse your own working time according to the Workset classification above. Do the results surprise you?

3.3.2 Competence analysis

A more recent approach to job analysis is the definition and analysis of competences.

KEY CONCEPT

concept

Competence is 'The ability to perform activities in the jobs within an occupation to the standards expected in employment. The concept also embodies the ability to transfer skills and knowledge to new situations within the occupational area and beyond, to related occupations' (Training, Enterprise and Education Directorate in the UK).

Different sorts of competences include:

- **Behavioural/personal competences**: underlying personal characteristics people bring to work (eg interpersonal skills); personal characteristics and behaviour for successful performance, for example 'ability to relate well to others'.
- **Work-based/occupational competences** refer to 'expectations of workplace performance and the outputs and standards people in specific roles are expected to obtain'. This approach is used in the UK's National Vocational Qualification (NVQ) standards.

Competence definitions typically identify the key roles of a given occupation and break them down into areas ('units') of competence. These in turn are formulated as statements describing what a competent person should be able to do at different levels, to what standard, in what contexts, and with what underpinning knowledge and understanding.

3.3.3 Job description

KEY CONCEPT

concept

A **job description** is a detailed statement of the activities (mental and physical) involved in the job, and other relevant factors in the social and physical environment.

Typical contents of a job description include the following.

- **Job title** (eg Marketing Assistant)
- **Reporting to** (eg the Marketing Assistant reports to the Marketing Manager), in other words the person's immediate boss
- **Subordinates** directly reporting to the job holder (if any)
- **Overall purpose** of the job, distinguishing it from other jobs
- **Principal accountabilities or main tasks**: defining each activity as a statement of accountability (what the job holder is expected to achieve)
- **Terms and conditions** of employment, working conditions and special demands (eg hazards)

ACTIVITY 5

format

Get hold of an up-to-date copy of your own job description, or of another marketing job description from your work organisation (or another organisation you might use for your assignment). Start demonstrating your research and contextualisation skills!

(We do provide a simple example of a job description in the debrief to this activity.)

Job descriptions can be used for a number of purposes in human resource management.

- In **recruitment**, to set out the demands of the job and what it offers: a useful basis for advertising vacancies, interviewing candidates, assessing candidates against requirements and so on
- In **reward management**: to set pay rates fair for the job
- In **induction**, giving new recruits a clear guide to job requirements
- In **appraisal** and **training/development**, to suggest areas in which job requirements need to be more effectively met
- In **job design**, to indicate where areas of responsibility are ambiguous, or inflexible; where there could be greater challenge or task variety and so on

However, it has been argued (eg Townsend, 1971) that job descriptions are of limited value, and, at worst, counterproductive. They are able to give an accurate, meaningful description of jobs where the work is largely repetitive and predictable: if a job involves variety, discretion and adaptability (as management and marketing jobs often do), they will be unrealistic and constantly outdated.

Further difficulties arise when job descriptions are taken too literally and cause demarcation disputes and costly over-staffing (because people will only do 'their jobs', rather than what needs doing). Organisational flexibility is a key issue in human resource management: jobs are being redesigned to allow adaptability and responsiveness to changing task requirements, through multi-skilling, cross-functional team working, flexible working hours and so on – as we will see later in this chapter. Commentators such as Bridges (1994) have argued that the 'job' itself is a thing of the past: tasks and teams must be constantly redefined by customer and environmental trends.

It is worth bearing in mind that a job description is only a static 'snapshot' of a job at a given time: it requires flexibility and constant, negotiated revision. It must also be remembered that job descriptions are the 'map' – *not* the 'territory': they are designed as a tool for management, not a constraint. Some organisations have developed alternative approaches such as:

- **Goal or accountability profiles**, setting out the outputs and performance levels expected of individuals and teams
- **Role definitions**, setting out the part played by the job holder in meeting organisational and sub-unit objectives. Role analysis stresses the purpose and contribution of competent performance in the job, rather than its task components (Armstrong, 2009).
- **Competence profiles**, based on key success factors in a given business or sector.

3.3.4 Person specification

KEY CONCEPT

A **person specification** identifies the type of person the organisation wants to recruit for a given job: the education, training, experience, personal attributes and competences a job holder will need, in order to perform the job satisfactorily.

While a job description describes the job, a person specification (or personnel specification) describes the type of **person** required to do the job.

A systematic approach to person specification was formulated by Alec Rodger, a pioneer of recruitment and selection systems in the UK. He argued that 'if matching the demands of the job and the person who is to perform it is to be done satisfactorily, the requirements of an occupation (or job) must be described in the same terms as the aptitudes of the people who are being considered for it' (Rodger, 1970).

Rodger's **Seven Point Plan** draws the selector's attention to seven points about the candidate. It is set out, along with another influential classification, the **Five Point Pattern** by Munro Fraser (1978), in the following table.

Two sets of criteria for person specification

Seven Point Plan	Five Point Pattern
Physical attributes: eg neat appearance, ability to speak clearly	**Impact on others**: physical attributes, force of personality, interpersonal skills
Attainments: including educational and vocational qualifications	**Acquired knowledge** and qualifications
General intelligence: IQ, mental agility, verbal dexterity	**Innate abilities**: numerical/artistic/linguistic aptitudes etc
Special aptitudes: numerical/artistic/ linguistic aptitudes etc	**Motivation**: what sort of goals drive a person and how much effort goes into achieving them
Interests: demonstrating practical abilities and social competence	**Adjustment**: emotional stability, tolerance of stress
Disposition: manner (helpful, calm etc)	
Background circumstances: eg family	

Whichever outline is used, the person specification should classify each feature listed as essential, desirable or contra-indicated (undesirable) for competent performance in the job. For the job of a marketing assistant, for example, organisational ability and interpersonal skills might be considered essential; creativity desirable, given the need to contribute ideas for marketing campaigns; and inability to work under pressure, contra-indicated. An example specification is shown below.

PERSON SPECIFICATION: Public Relations Assistant

	ESSENTIAL	DESIRABLE	CONTRA-INDICATED
Physical attributes	Clear speech Well-groomed	Physical stamina	Chronic ill-health and absence
Attainments	2 'A' levels GCSE English Thorough knowledge of PR methodologies	Degree (any discipline) Marketing/PR training	No experience of marketing or PR disciplines
Intelligence	High verbal intelligence		
Aptitudes	High-level social and networking skills Computer skills	Analytical abilities (problem solving)	
Interests	Social: team activity		Time-consuming hobbies 'Solo' interests only
Disposition	Team player Persuasive Tolerance of pressure and change	Initiative	Anti-social Low tolerance of responsibility
Circumstances	Able to work out of normal office hours when required	Located in area of office	

A wide range of variables may be used in a person specification, including both capacities (what the job holder should be able to do) and inclinations (what the job holder should be willing to do). However, in the same way that a job description must be revised often and used flexibly, a person specification may also lose its relevance if it fails to evolve as job requirements change.

In addition there are some pitfalls when developing person specifications. 'Physical attributes' and 'background circumstances', for example, may suggest criteria which may nowadays be interpreted as potentially discriminatory: to the disabled (in the case of a speech impediment, say) or to women (for example, the contra-indication of family responsibilities) or to workers of a particular age.

MARKETING AT WORK

application

General Electric

In the transformation of General Electric, Jack Welch, the CEO introduced the idea of 'team focus': expecting managers to be team players.

Welch puts forward the example of a multi-functional business consisting of marketing, engineering and components manufacturing. This business has a brilliant marketing manager who is highly numerate and delivers high quality output and meets his deadlines. However, *'this person won't talk with people in engineering and manufacturing. He won't share ideas with them, and won't behave in a boundaryless way with them.*

Now we're replacing that person with someone who may not be quite perfect but who is a good team player and lifts the team's performance. Maybe the predecessor was working at 100% or 120% - but that person didn't talk with team members, didn't swap ideas. As a result, the whole team was operating at 65%. But the new manager is getting 90% or 100% from the total team. That was a discovery'.

3.4 The selection process

A systematic approach to selection may be outlined as follows.

Step 1 Deal with responses to job advertisements. This might involve sending **application forms** or other instructions to candidates, or initial screening of enquiries.

Step 2 Assess each application against **key criteria** in the job advertisement, job specification and person specification. Critical factors may include age, qualifications, experience or whatever.

Step 3 **Sort applications** into 'possible', 'unsuitable' and 'marginal. 'Possibles' will then be more closely scrutinised, and a shortlist for interview drawn up. Ideally, this should be done by both an HR specialist and the prospective manager of the successful candidate.

Step 4 Invite candidates for interview.

Step 5 Reinforce interviews with **selection testing** and other selection techniques, if suitable.

Step 6 **Review** un-interviewed 'possibles', and 'marginals', and put potential future candidates on hold, or in reserve.

Step 7 Send **standard letters** to unsuccessful applicants, and inform them simply that they have not been successful. Reserves will be sent a holding letter: 'We will keep your details on file, and should any suitable vacancy arise in future...'.

Step 8 Make a **provisional offer** to the successful candidate.

3.5 Selection techniques

A wide range of techniques is available for team member selection, including:

- **Interviewing**: individual (one-to-one) or panel (to gain multiple viewpoints)
- **Selection tests**: intelligence, aptitude, personality and proficiency testing
- **Reference checking**: job references and character references
- **Work sampling**: portfolios of previous work outputs, trial employment periods or pilot projects, or work-simulation exercises
- **Group selection methods**: eg assessment centres

Which method is best? Smith and Abrahamsen developed a scale that plots selection methods according to how accurately they predict a candidate's future performance in the job. This is known as a **predictive validity** scale. The scale ranges from 1 (meaning that a method is right every time) to 0 (meaning that a method is not better than chance).

Method	*% use by firms*	*Predictive validity*
Interviews	92	0.17
References	74	0.13
Work sampling	18	0.57
Assessment centres	14	0.40
Personality tests	13	0.40
Cognitive tests	11	0.54
Biodata (biography analysis)	4	0.40
Graphology (handwriting analysis)	3	0.00

The results surprisingly show a pattern of employers relying most heavily on the *least* accurate selection methods. Interviews in particular (for reasons which we will discuss below) seem not much better than tossing a coin! Let's look at some of the most important techniques in a little more detail.

3.6 Interviews

Most firms use interviewing as the main basis for selection decisions. The main purposes of a selection interview are:

- Finding the **best person** for the job, by giving the organisation a chance to assess applicants (and particularly their interpersonal and communication skills) directly
- Making sure that applicants **understand** what the job involves, what career prospects there are, and other aspects of the employment relationship on offer
- Giving the best possible **impression** of the organisation as a prospective employer
- Offering **fair treatment** to all applicants, whether they get the job or not: in the UK, this is covered by anti-discrimination legislation, but it is also part of the organisation's 'employer brand' and reputation in the labour market

3.6.1 Types of interview

Individual or one-to-one interviews are commonly used, as they give:

- Direct face-to-face communication, with opportunities for the interviewer to use both verbal and non-verbal cues to assess the candidate
- Rapport between the candidate and the interviewer: each has to give attention solely to the other, and there is potentially a relaxed atmosphere, if the interviewer is willing to establish an informal style
- Flexibility in the direction and follow-up of questions

However, the candidate may also be able to disguise lack of knowledge in a specialist area of which the interviewer knows little. Moreover, a single interviewer's perceptions and judgements may be biased, and this lack of objectivity may go unnoticed and unchecked. **Panel interviews** are designed to overcome such disadvantages. A panel may consist of two or three people who together interview a single candidate: most commonly, an HR specialist and the departmental manager who will have responsibility for the successful candidate. This saves the firm time – and enables better assessment.

3.6.2 Conducting the interview

The agenda and questions should be at least partly prepared in advance, based on the job description (which sets out the requirements of the job), the person specification (which describes the ideal candidate) and the candidate's application form and/or CV (which outline the candidate's claim to suitability).

Selection interviewing requires highly developed skills. **Questions** should be paced and put carefully, both to encourage candidates to express themselves, and to challenge and probe answers, where required, in order to get to relevant, specific and truthful answers. The interviewer should not be trying to confuse the candidate, plunging immediately into demanding questions or picking on isolated points; neither, however, should the interviewee be allowed to digress or gloss over important points. The interviewer must retain control over the information-gathering process.

Evaluating the response to questions requires another set of interpersonal skills. The interviewer must **listen** carefully to the responses and evaluate them so as to judge what the candidate is wanting to say, trying not to say, having difficulty saying, or saying dishonestly! In addition, the interviewer will have to be self-aware enough to know when his or her own attitudes, perhaps prejudices, are getting in the way of an objective response to the candidate.

Candidates should be given the opportunity to ask questions. The choice of questions might well have some influence on how the interviewers assess a candidate's interest in and understanding of the job. Moreover, there is information that the candidate will need to know about the organisation and the job for the purposes of self-selection.

3.6.3 Advantages of interviews

Interviews in general are by far the most popular selection method used by organisations. They offer some significant advantages.

- They are highly interactive, allowing flexible question and answers. This allows candidates opportunities to ask questions, and allows questions and responses to be adapted to the direction and style of the interview.
- They offer opportunities to use non-verbal communication, which might confirm or undermine spoken answers (eg a candidate looking hesitant or embarrassed when making competence claims). This is particularly helpful to interviewers when challenging or probing in relation to inconsistencies or gaps in a candidate's application or answers.
- They offer opportunities to assess a candidate's personal appearance (relevant in areas such as grooming), interpersonal and communication skills.
- They offer initial opportunities to evaluate rapport between the candidate and his or her potential colleagues/bosses.

3.6.4 Limitations of interviews

Interviews are criticised, however, because **they fail to provide accurate predictions** of how a person will perform in the job, partly because of the nature of interviews, partly because of errors of judgement by interviewers:

Problems with selection interviews

Problem	Comment
Scope	An interview is too **brief** to 'get to know' candidates in the kind of depth required to make an accurate prediction of work performance.
Artificiality	An interview is an **artificial situation**: candidates may be on their best behaviour or, conversely, so nervous that they do not do themselves justice. Neither situation reflects what the person is really like.
The halo effect	A tendency for people to make an **initial general judgement** about a person based on a single obvious attribute, such as being neatly dressed or well-spoken. This single attribute will colour later perceptions, and make an interviewer mark the person up or down on every other factor in their assessment.
Contagious bias	The interviewer changes the behaviour of the applicant by **suggestion**. The applicant might be led by the wording of questions, or non-verbal cues from the interviewer, to change what (s)he is doing or saying in response.
Stereotyping	Stereotyping groups together people who are assumed to share certain characteristics (women, say, or vegetarians), then attributes certain traits to the group as a whole. It then assumes that each individual member of the supposed group will possess that trait.
Incorrect assessment	Qualitative factors such as motivation, honesty or integrity are very difficult to define and assess objectively.
Logical error	For example, an interviewer might decide that a young candidate who has held two or three jobs in the past for only a short time will be unlikely to last long in any job. (This isn't necessarily the case.)
Inexperienced interviewers	Inexperienced or unskilled interviewers may undermine the process through: • Inability to evaluate information about a candidate properly • Failure to compare a candidate against the job description or person specification • Failure to take control of the direction and length of the interview • Using inappropriate question types to elicit data or put candidates at ease • A reluctance to probe into facts or challenge statements where necessary

3.7 Selection testing

There are two basic types of selection test.

(a) **Proficiency** tests measure an individual's demonstrated competence in particular job-related tasks (eg copy-writing, typing or problem-solving tests). **Attainment** (or competence) tests are a similar measurement of the standard an individual has reached at a particular skill. There is a wide range of proficiency testing material available, including 'in-tray' exercises (simulating work tasks).

(b) **Psychometric** tests measure such psychological factors as aptitude, intelligence and personality (eg IQ tests, personality tests). Examples include a variety of IQ and EQ (emotional competence) tests, the 16PF, the Myers-Briggs Type Indicator ™ , and the Minnesota Multiphasic Personality Inventory (MMPI). The validity of such tests has been much debated, but some have been shown by research to be valid predictors of job performance, so long as they are used properly.

Despite current enthusiasm for selection testing, it has its limitations.

(a) There is not always a direct relationship between ability in the test and **ability in the job**: the job situation is very different from artificial test conditions.

(b) The **interpretation of test results** is a skilled task, for which training and experience is essential. It is also highly subjective (particularly in the case of personality tests), which belies the apparent scientific nature of the approach.

(c) Most tests are subject to **coaching and practice effects**: that is, with repeated use, candidates know which answers will be regarded most favourably.

(d) It is difficult to exclude **bias** from tests, and to devise tests which give a fair chance to people from different cultures and social groups.

3.8 Group selection methods (assessment centres)

Group selection assessments (sometimes called assessment centres) tend to be used for posts requiring leadership, communication or team working skills: advertising agencies often use the method for selecting account executives, for example.

Assessment centres consist of a series of tests, interviews and group situations over a period of two days, involving a small number of candidates for a job. After an introductory session to make the candidates feel at ease, they will be given one or two tests, one or two individual interviews, and several group scenarios in which the candidates are invited to discuss problems together and arrive at solutions as a management team.

A variety of tools and techniques are used in group selection, including:

(a) **Group role-play exercises**, in which candidates can explore (and hopefully display) interpersonal skills and/or work through simulated managerial tasks

(b) **Case studies**, where candidates' analytical and problem-solving abilities are tested in working through described situations/problems, as well as their interpersonal skills, in taking part in (or leading) group discussion of the case study

These group sessions might be useful for the following reasons.

(a) They give the organisation's selectors a longer opportunity to study the candidates.

(b) They reveal more than application forms, interviews and tests alone about the ability of candidates to persuade others, negotiate with others, explain ideas to others, investigate problems efficiently and so on. These are typically managerial (and marketing) skills.

(c) They reveal more about how the candidate's personality and skills will affect the work team and his or her own performance in the job.

3.9 Legal considerations when recruiting

Guidance from the CIM indicates that you 'are not expected to have a detailed knowledge of employment law, but should consider the impact of legislation throughout the recruitment process.' Let's start with a brief survey of the issues.

3.9.1 Equal opportunities

KEY CONCEPT

concept

Equal opportunities is an approach to the management of people at work based on equal access and fair treatment, irrespective of gender, race, ethnicity, age, disability, sexual orientation, religious belief or other differences not directly related to job performance.

Equal opportunity employers seek to redress inequalities (eg of access to jobs, training, promotion, pay or benefits) which are based around differences which have no relevance to work performance. Certain aspects of equal opportunities, including discrimination and harassment on the basis of sex, race, age and disability, are enshrined in UK and EU law.

Why is equal opportunity an issue for employers – over and above the humane argument for equity and non-discrimination?

Most organisations have ethical objectives and policies in regard to diversity and equal opportunity, as reflecting principles of decency and fairness.

Equal opportunity reflects good HR policy, and may help to attract and retain talent: the best people for the job (regardless of race or gender) and those who feel strongly about justice issues.

Equal opportunity is in most countries a matter of compliance with relevant legislation and Codes of Practice, which are used by Employment Tribunals in arbitrating employee grievances and discrimination claims.

(a) Equal opportunity widens the recruitment and promotion pool, and aids employee retention, in times of skill shortages (which may exist in certain locations or skill areas, despite high general unemployment).

(b) Equal opportunity practices contribute to a positive employer brand, and a positive corporate image to consumers (and business partners) who benefit from or support equality principles.

3.9.2 The UK legal framework

In Britain, several main Acts have been passed to deal with inequality of opportunity and discrimination at work.

(a) The Sex Discrimination Act 1986 and subsequent amendments outlaw certain types of discrimination on the grounds of **sex**, **marital status and sex change**. The Employment Equality (Sexual Orientation) Regulations 2003 extends the protection to **sexual orientation**.

(b) **Equal pay** legislation is specifically intended to prevent discrimination as regards terms and conditions of employment between men and women and provides that women have the right to equal pay for 'work of equal value' to that of a man in the same establishment (as defined by a job evaluation scheme): Equal Pay Act 1970 and Equal Pay (Amendment) Regulations 1984.

(c) The Race Relations Act 1996 (amended in 2000 and 2003 – which gives you some idea of the need to keep up to date!) outlaws certain types of discrimination on grounds of **race, colour, nationality, ethnic or national origin**. The Race Relations (Amendment) Act 2000 adds the requirement that larger public organisations (more than 150 employees) must draw up detailed plans for achieving racial equality in all employment practices.

(d) The Disability Discrimination Acts 1995 and 2000 outlaw discrimination on the basis of **disability**. A disabled person is defined as a person who has a physical or mental impairment that has a substantial and long-term (more than 12 months) adverse effect on his or her ability to carry out normal day-to-day activities. This may include impairment of hearing, sight, memory, mobility, co-ordination or speech, and serious conditions such as HIV, cancer and multiple sclerosis.

(e) The Employment Equality (Religion or Belief) Regulations 2003 outlaw discrimination and harassment on the basis of **religion or beliefs**.

(f) The Employment Equality (Age) Regulations 2006 prohibit unjustified **age** discrimination in employment and vocational training; support later retirement and retirement planning; and remove upper age limits for unfair dismissal and redundancy rights.

There are four basic **types of discrimination** under the UK legislation (although the various provisions have not yet been fully harmonised).

(a) **Direct discrimination** is where one group is treated less favourably than others, in regard to the decision of whom to interview or employ; the terms of employment and opportunities for promotion, transfer, training or other benefits; and in decisions relating to redundancy and dismissal. Obvious examples would include paying one 'type' of person less than another for the same work, or stating or implying a preference in recruitment advertising. In the new age discrimination, it might include not providing medical insurance to employees aged 50 or older. (There are certain specifically exempted cases, such as 'genuine occupational qualifications' for recruiting a person of a certain gender or race: for example, having a woman employed in women's changing rooms, or requiring a certain race or age for a dramatic role.)

(b) **Indirect discrimination** is where an employer applies a provision, criterion or practice to all groups equally, but in such a way as to put one group at a disadvantage, without a reasonable justification (Employment Equality [Sex Discrimination] Regulations 2006). An example might be changing shift patterns to include early morning starts, as this would disadvantage women responsible for child care, or requiring all new recruits to take a health and fitness test, which would disadvantage older candidates.

(c) **Harassment** is defined (in the 2006 regulations, bringing sex into line with existing race, disability, sexual orientation and religion/belief protection) as unwanted conduct which violates a person's dignity, or creates an intimidating, hostile, degrading, humiliating or offensive environment for a person. It includes verbal, non-verbal or physical conduct: examples might include racial jokes, offensive comments about a woman's appearance or dress, or putting objects on high shelves where disabled employees are unable to reach.

(d) **Victimisation** occurs when a person is penalised for giving information or taking action in pursuit of a claim of discrimination.

The obligation not to discriminate applies to all aspects of employment including job advertising, recruitment and selection procedures, access to training and promotion, terms and conditions of work, access to benefits, the application of disciplinary procedures, selection for redundancy, and compulsory retirement ages.

ASSIGNMENT TIP

concept

Bear in mind that the above provisions apply in the UK. Other countries, for reasons of social policy, may have different legislative measures in place. Be ready to cite legislation in your own country – where relevant – in your assignment. (Bear in mind, however, that the *principles* of UK law may represent good practice anywhere.)

3.9.3 Equal opportunity in practice

Team member recruitment and selection should be made (and *seen* to be made) on the basis of who can best perform the role: other issues should not play a part in the decision, unless (as in 'genuine occupational qualifications') they can be proved to be relevant to job performance.

Practical steps to discrimination-proof the recruitment and selection process include:

(a) **Recruitment advertising**. Any wording that suggests preference for a particular group should be avoided (except for genuine occupational qualifications): the same applies to instructions to recruitment agencies. The placing of advertisements where the target audience is predominantly of one race or sex is construed as indirect discrimination: this may include internal recruitment, if the workforce is not yet broadly representative of the wider population.

(b) **Application forms** and **interviews.** Any non-work-related questions should be asked of all subjects, if at all, and even then, some types of question may be construed as discriminatory (eg only asking women about plans to have a family or care of dependents). A representative of all groups should, where possible, be interviewed. Some organisations protect themselves by having a witness at interviews, or by taking details notes, in the event that a claim of discrimination is made.

(c) **Positive action** to encourage people from disadvantaged groups to apply for jobs and training, and to compete for vacancies. Examples might be: using various languages in job advertisements, or implementing training for women in assertiveness and management skills. (Note that this is not the same as positive discrimination: actively choosing in favour of a disadvantaged group, which is not permitted, other than in regard to training.)

(d) **Awareness training** for personnel involved in recruitment and selection, as part of a wider policy of training, counselling and disciplinary measures to manage sexual, racial and religious discrimination and harassment

(e) Ensuring that women are offered **equal pay for work of equal value** to the organisation, as measured by job evaluation

Wider issues of equal opportunity – and the still wider implications of valuing and managing workforce **diversity** – are discussed in a later chapter, as a particular challenge of team leadership.

MARKETING AT WORK

application

Procter and Gamble

P&G, maker of everything from Pampers nappies to Old Spice deodorant to Pringles crisps, has a huge variety of customers and wants its workforce to reflect that.

'Our success depends entirely on our ability to understand these diverse consumers' needs,' Alan Lafley, the CEO told his company last year'. A diverse organisation will out-think, out-innovate and out-perform a homogenous organisation every single time. I am putting particular importance on increasing the representation of women and minorities in leadership positions at all levels.'

P&G UK has a fairly good record already. Ethnic minority employees make up 6 per cent of P&G's UK workforce, compared with 5.4 per cent of the British population. 'But that is not a reason to be happy with ourselves. We primarily recruit graduates and 17 per cent of the students in this country are from ethnic minorities,' says Neil Harvey-Smith, UK Diversity Manager.

Why is PG not recruiting more of those students? 'It's not the case that people applying aren't getting in. It's that they're not applying.' Why not? 'It's probably fair to say that people perceive that we are a white company or an American company.'

Provided it fits in with their jobs, P&G staff of either sex can share jobs and change their hours. New parents can take up to a year's unpaid leave beyond their statutory maternity or paternity leave entitlements. The result is that the number of women appointed director or associate director in P&G Europe rose to eight last year from its previous rate of one or two a year.

Mr Harvey-Smith says the UK organisation has also made progress in attracting disabled recruits. It designed a computer programme that could read out the questions on a problem-solving test so that a blind applicant could complete it. The technology is now being used by P&G in the US.

Financial Times

3.10 Evaluating recruitment

To get a clear idea of how efficient your recruitment and selection practices are, you might ask yourself the following questions.

- Can we identify our HR requirements from the marketing plan?
- How fast do we respond to a vacancy or recruitment need?
- How good is our awareness of the internal and external labour market (and do we have access to good advice when we need it)?
- Do we select the right advertising media to reach the market?
- How effective (and cost effective) is our recruitment advertising?
- How do our recruits actually perform: do we end up employing the right people?
- Do we retain our new recruits: do they stay with the team and organisation?
- How diverse is our workforce: does it reflect the diversity of the population and customer base, and does it indicate a robust approach to equal opportunity?

Recruitment and selection practices can be reviewed in various ways.

Review	Comment
Performance indicators	Each stage of the process can be assessed by specific performance indicators: eg the time it takes to process job applications. Data can be collected to check any deviation from standard.
Cost-effectiveness	Eg: number of relevant responses per recruitment ad, or cost of various advertising media per application elicited (or person employed).
Monitoring the workforce	High staff turnover, absenteeism and other problems (particularly among new recruits) may reflect poor recruitment and selection. Lack of workforce diversity may highlight discriminatory practices.
Attitude surveys	The firm can ask its recruits what they thought of the process.
Actual individual job performance	A person's actual performance can be compared with what was expected when (s)he was recruited.

3.10.1 Improving recruitment and selection procedures

A systematic model has been proposed in this chapter. If it is considered that recruitment and selection procedures need to be improved, attention may be given to matter such as:

- Improvement of **policies and guidelines** for selectors: eg in equal opportunities and recruit/promote decisions
- Establishment of **systematic procedures** for all stages of the process
- Improved **education and training** of selectors: eg in interviewing skills and testing techniques
- **Auditing of job advertising** content and media, in order to improve the attractiveness and realism of the organisation's offerings and the cost-effectiveness of advertising
- Widening the organisation's **repertoire of selection techniques**, to aim for the highest possible accuracy in predicting job performance and confirming candidate claims
- The possible use of external recruitment and selection **agencies and consultants**.

4 Development and talent management

4.1 What is talent management?

KEY CONCEPT

concept

Talent management (or **human capital management**) is 'the process of ensuring that the organisation attracts, retains, motivates and develops the talented people it needs' (Armstrong, 2009). It refers to the overall process whereby an organisation systematically attracts skilled, high-quality recruits; integrates new workers into the organisation; systematically performance manages, trains and develops current workers, in order to meet current and future competence requirements; and retains skilled workers within the organisation.

The concept of talent management addresses the flow of 'talent' (skills and abilities) into and through the organisation or team at all levels. It should be included in the human resource planning at the strategic level, and implemented in day-to-day people management processes throughout the firm. As the syllabus guidance emphasises: 'it is important to be mindful that [team design and recruitment] is leading towards building the organisation's capacity and capability, and thus it is essential to ensure that the right level of competency, combined with the right balance of individual talent, is achieved to maximise the organisation's potential to achieve competitive advantage'.

Key talent management processes include (Armstrong, ibid):

- Developing the organisation as an 'employer of choice' or 'a great place to work'
- Using selection and recruitment procedures that ensure that good quality people are recruited, who are likely to thrive in the organisation and stay with it for a reasonable length of time
- Designing jobs and developing roles which give people opportunities to apply and grow their skills and provide them with interest and challenge
- Provided talented staff with opportunities for career development and growth
- Developing a positive 'psychological contract' (definition of mutual expectations)
- Recognising those with talent by rewarding excellence, enterprise and achievement
- Succession planning: ensuring that the organisation has suitable people to fill emerging vacancies
- Conducting talent audits to identify individuals with potential

MARKETING AT WORK

application

The Great Place to Work Institute conducts an annual survey identifying the best workplaces in Europe and around the world. The following are the top UK firms in the 2010 survey.

1 Baringa Partners

2 Danone Ltd

3 Impact International

4 Microsoft Ltd

5 Novo Nordisk Ltd

6 NetApp UK Ltd

7 DIAGEO GB

8 General Mills UK

9 Danone Waters (UK & Ire.) Ltd

10 Admiral Group.

You might like to check out **www.greatplacetowork.co.uk**, and follow up on some of the links to learn more about these best-practice organisations.

It cannot be left solely to the HR department to attract, integrate, develop and retain employees – or to track and measure how well the organisation is doing in these areas. Marketing managers, along with other line managers, must take responsibility for these processes within their own teams.

Talent management has to do with the flow of 'talent' (skills and abilities) into and through the organisation or team. We have already discussed the process of talent recruitment and selection. Let's look next at the closely related topic of integrating new talent into the team.

4.2 Team member 'on-boarding'

The handling of new recruits and team members is crucial in ensuring (a) that their integration into both the team and team performance happens as swiftly and effectively as possible and (b) that their experience of employment, in its initial stages, is sufficiently positive to enable them to overcome the difficulties of integration, adjustment and a steep learning curve, so that they stay in the job.

KEY CONCEPT

concept

Induction is the term usually given to the process whereby a new recruit is formally introduced and integrated into an organisation, team or system.

The purposes of induction are:

- To help new recruits to find their bearings
- To begin to socialise new recruits into the culture and norms of the team/organisation
- To support recruits in beginning performance
- To identify on-going training and development needs
- To avoid initial problems at the 'induction crisis' stage of the employment lifecycle, when frustration, disorientation and disappointment may otherwise cause new recruits to leave the organisation prematurely

4.2.1 The process of induction

The immediate superior should commence the **on-going process of induction**.

Step 1 Pinpoint the areas that the recruit will have to learn about in order to start the job. Some things (such as detailed technical knowledge) may be identified as areas for later study or training.

Step 2 Introduce the recruit to the work premises and facilities, so (s)he can get his or her bearings.

Step 3 Briefing by the HR Manager on relevant policies and procedures: conditions of employment, sickness and holiday absences, health and safety and so on.

Step 4 Introduce the recruit to key people in the office: co-workers, health and safety officers, etc. One particular colleague may be assigned to recruits as a **mentor**, to keep an eye on them, answer routine queries, 'show them the ropes'.

Step 5 Introduce work procedures.

- Explain the nature of the job, and the goals of each task.
- Explain hours of work.
- Explain the structure of the department: to whom the recruit will report, to whom (s)he can go with complaints or queries and so on.

Step 6 Plan and implement an appropriate training programme for whatever technical or practical knowledge is required. Again, the programme should have a clear schedule and set of goals so that the recruit has a sense of purpose, and so that the programme can be efficiently organised to fit in with the activities of the department.

Step 7 Monitor initial progress, as demonstrated by performance, as reported by the recruit's mentor, and as perceived by the recruit him or herself. This is the beginning of an on-going cycle of feedback, review, problem-solving and development planning.

Note that induction is an **on-going process**, embracing mentoring, coaching, training, monitoring and so on. It is not just a first day affair! After three months, six months or one year the performance of a new recruit should be formally appraised and discussed. Indeed, when the process of induction has been finished, a recruit should continue to receive periodic appraisals, just like every other employee in the organisation.

4.3 Talent retention

Recruiting and developing team members represents an **investment** for an organisation. It will therefore be important to:

(a) Recruit and develop the right people for the organisation's current and future needs,

(b) Get the best performance out of recruits,

(c) Ensure that they stay with the organisation long enough to give it a return on its investment.

We discuss **motivation** and performance management in later chapters, but it may be worth introducing the concept of employee retention here.

In order to retain and motivate employees, the employer will need to treat them fairly and well – usually, over and above minimum standards set by employment law. ('The law is a floor': it provides for basic standards of ethical and humane treatment, but is not intended to reflect best practice). Responsible employment policies should address matters such as:

- Fair pay for the work and contribution given (and, more aggressively, an approach to defining and maintaining competitive salaries and conditions, to win and retain talent which might otherwise go to other employers – and perhaps, direct competitors)
- Safe and healthy working conditions
- Learning and development opportunities
- Commitment to equal opportunity (non-discrimination) and workforce diversity
- Fair and humane management of disciplinary and grievance situations, dismissals, redundancies and so on
- Willingness to inform and consult employee representatives (unionised or otherwise)
- Support for employee welfare (benefits, compassionate leave, flexible working options, employee counselling and so on, where required).

In addition, it may be necessary to identify causes of **employee turnover** (ie people leaving the team), if this seems abnormally high, it is rising year by year, or it is damaging performance levels and continuity. This may be done by interviewing team members, holding a team meeting, or using employee attitude surveys to gather feedback from remaining team members: what areas of job dissatisfaction or frustration lead people to leave? In addition, **exit interviews** may be held with staff who are leaving or have left, to find out why – and what would have needed to change in order for them to stay. The specific causes of labour turnover can then be addressed, where it is practical and cost-effective to do so: eg by changing leadership style, giving better induction training to new staff, solving problems with working conditions, or reviewing pay levels in the light of competitor rates.

ASSIGNMENT TIP

concept

It is also worth noting that – especially in recessionary periods in the business cycle – there may be an *opposite* need to reduce staff numbers, whether by encouraging **natural wastage** (resignations, transfers and retirements) or by implementing **redundancies** (proactively dismissing staff where the requirement for their work or position no longer exists). This is a complex area, subject to detailed employment protection law: downsizing and redundancy plans will probably be handled, at least initially, by the HR function. These issues are not directly mentioned in the syllabus, but it is worth being aware of them: they may well affect your own work context (and analysis of it) in the current economic climate. At the very least, you should be aware of the potential need to slow or freeze team recruitment, and perhaps encourage natural staff turnover, in order to avoid over-staffing which might later be subject to redundancy.

4.4 Talent development

It is worth noting that talent management means different things to different organisations. For some, it is founded on the assumption that all workers have talent which needs to be identified, maximised and deployed: in other words, it is about managing talent, skills, competences and **employee contribution** in general.

For others, however, it is about identifying, developing and fast-tracking particular 'high-worth' or '**talented' individuals**. The emphasis will be not just on the appraisal of performance (as a standard measure of employee contribution and profitability), but on the measurement of **potential –** or *future* performance, which can only be maximised through retention and development. This philosophy will lead to an approach to talent management focusing on processes such as:

- The identification of talent gaps, as part of human resource planning
- Performance management, including the identification and measurement of potential (which we will discuss in a later chapter)
- Management and leadership development: proactively developing potential leaders, as part of the organisation's succession planning
- External recruitment and accelerated integration (fast tracking) of high-talent individuals, perhaps from competitor organisations (ie 'head hunting')

In either case, **training and development** is a huge topic in its own right: we will explore it in detail in a later chapter, as part of the manager's toolkit for improving team performance.

For more in-depth coverage of these and a wide range of other HRM topics, you can't do better than the title on the CIM Supplementary Reading list:

- **A Handbook of Human Resource Management Practice, Michael Armstrong: Kogan Page. There are helpful chapters on Talent Management, Competency, Recruitment and Selection, Induction and Human Resource Development**

5 Structuring team work

As we saw from our brief discussion of job analysis above, there are many choices to be made about how work is grouped, structured and allocated as 'jobs' or 'roles' for individuals and teams.

Steiner (1972) suggests there are four basic ways in which groups function.

- **Additive.** All members contribute, but no one member depends on others for their performance. Skills and output are simply pooled.
- **Complementary**. The task can be divided into separate parts and allocated to individuals with the skills needed for each. Members effectively work in parallel.
- **Conjunctive** (or **co-ordination**). There is a high degree of dependence between members' contributions, often in a defined, linear sequence (as in assembly lines and office procedures).
- **Disjunctive** (or **collaboration**). Members contribute different skills and abilities, so that solutions are synergistic, reflecting the optimum contribution of each individual. This particularly suits problem-solving groups.

The nature and structure of the task will therefore dictate to a large extent how work is organised and allocated within a team, together with considerations such as time available (parallel working gets the job done faster than a linear sequence of tasks) and the skills and preferences of the team.

In addition to task structure, which may be flexible (determined according to the demand of particular tasks), there is the question of **job design**: how tasks and responsibilities are packaged together into meaningful, efficient jobs or task sets for individuals.

5.1 Job design

KEY CONCEPT

concept

Job design is the way in which tasks are divided or grouped to form the work responsibilities of a given job, and what decisions are made about specialisation, discretion, autonomy, variety and other job elements.

5.1.1 Aims of effective job design

Frederick Taylor (discussed in an earlier chapter) was an early exponent of systematic job design. His aims were improved efficiency and control. Jobs were '**micro-designed**': a complex task was broken down into its most basic component parts, which represented the sole 'job' of a worker or group of workers. Jobs were reduced to single, repetitive, detailed motions (as on assembly lines, packaging or quality inspection), which could be quickly mastered and tightly programmed.

The human relations school of management theory, however, associated job design and **job satisfaction**. Workers would not be satisfied as 'small cogs in large wheels', however well rewarded. In an influential model, Hackman & Oldham (1980) identified **core job dimensions** which were thought to contribute to job satisfaction:

- **Skill variety**: the opportunity to exercise different skills and perform different operations, as opposed to micro-specialisation and repetition
- **Task identity**: the integration of operations into a 'whole' task (or meaningful segment of the task), as opposed to task fragmentation
- **Task significance**: the task has a role, purpose, meaning and worth, according to the values of the organisation and the individual
- **Autonomy**: the opportunity to exercise discretion or self-management in areas such as target-setting and work methods
- **Feedback**: the availability of information by which the individual can assess his progress and performance in relation to expectation and targets and the opportunity to give feedback and have a voice in performance improvement

5.1.2 Approaches to enhancing job design

Motivation researcher **Frederick Herzberg** was among the first to suggest a systematic approach to job satisfaction and its relationship to job design. Herzberg's theory suggested that the job itself can be a source of satisfaction. Huczynski & Buchanan (2001) explain this by pointing out that 'the design of an individual's job determines both the kind of rewards that are available and what the individual has to do to get those rewards'.

The first step in the process of improving job design is **job analysis**, outlined earlier, in order to establish the current scope, tasks and responsibilities of the job. The job can then be assessed according to how far it offers the core job dimensions required for job satisfaction.

Herzberg recommended three basic approaches to increasing worker satisfaction through job design: job rotation, job enlargement and job enrichment.

(a) **Job rotation** is the planned transfer of staff between jobs to give greater task variety. The example documented by Herzberg quotes a warehouse gang of four workers, where the worst job was seen as tying the necks of the sacks at the base of the hopper, and the best job as driving the fork lift truck: job rotation would ensure that individuals spent equal time on all jobs. You should be able to think of equivalents within the work of a marketing team: not just to share the 'liked' and 'disliked' jobs fairly, but to develop functional versatility among the team.

(b) **Job enlargement** is an attempt to 'widen' jobs by increasing the number of tasks in which the worker is involved. This is a 'horizontal' extension of the job, which may reduce repetition and monotony, by giving team members more to do. However, Herzberg himself noted that asking workers to complete three separate tedious, unchallenging tasks is unlikely to motivate them much more than asking them to fulfil one single tedious, unchallenging task!

(c) **Job enrichment** is a planned, deliberate action to build greater responsibility, breadth and challenge of work into a job. This is a 'vertical' extension of the job, which is often equated with empowerment. It involves building in more of the core job dimensions: removing controls over workers' actions; increasing responsibility/accountability; providing more regular feedback on performance; introducing more interesting and challenging tasks; or allocating special assignments.

Job satisfaction is acknowledged as an important factor in staff members' loyalty, commitment and committed performance in a job (Herzberg, 1966). Job enrichment and empowerment programmes are intended to enhance organisational effectiveness by increasing employee's job satisfaction; harnessing their creativity and 'front-line' expertise; and shortening response times at the interface with customers.

However, it is worth getting this in perspective. As Handy (1993) points out: 'Even those who want their jobs enriched will expected to be rewarded with more than job satisfaction. Job enrichment is not a cheaper way to greater productivity. Its pay-off will come in the less visible costs of morale, climate and working relationships.'

Meanwhile, there are acknowledged barriers to empowerment or job enrichment in practice.

- Not all employees desire more challenge or responsibility.
- Not all employees are capable of exercising greater responsibility or undertaking the necessary skill development.
- Managers may struggle to release control and/or to change their role and style.
- Empowerment is not a substitute for other rewards: it must be reinforced by financial rewards for exercising increased responsibility – and this may be costly.

5.2 Flexible working practices

Flexible working is a 'hot topic' in human resource management at the moment, supported by the UK government's commitment to encourage '**work life balance**': that is, a balance between the demands of the job and the demands of home, family and personal life. This in turn reflects the increasing diversity of the workforce, especially the increasing numbers of women in work and single parent families. Despite the desire to increase productivity, many companies are also realising that increasing workloads and working hours is in fact counter-productive, potentially encouraging absenteeism, ill-health, accidents and poor-quality customer service.

A work-life balance programme may include **awareness training and skills training**: in time management, delegation, work organisation or relaxation techniques, say. However, the main thrust of European legislation and social policy in this area has been to introduce **family-friendly policies** on flexible working, designed to give employees options in regard to their hours and/or locations of work.

The UK Employment Act 2002, for example, gives parents of children under the age of six (or disabled children under the age of 18) the right to request flexible working arrangements.

Flexible working arrangements may involve:

- **Part-time working or job sharing**: two people share a single job, working part-time
- **Tele-working, home-working or virtual team working**: working from home, or elsewhere, linked to the office by computers, the Internet, phone and mobile phone
- **Annualised and term-time contracts**: agreeing a number of hours' work per year, rather than per week or month. Intensive hours can be called on during peak periods, but employees can then take time off or work flexible hours in periods of low demand. Term-time contracts allow parents to maximise work hours during school terms, giving them time off during school holidays.
- **Flexi-time systems**: employees are required to be at their job during 'core time', but time at the beginning and end of the day can be scheduled at their discretion. The total working week or month must add up to a set number of hours.
- **Gap years, sabbaticals or long-service leave:** enabling employees to take substantial time off (say, every 10 years) to pursue their own interests, study, attend to family or personal demands – or simply have a refreshing break from work. Such opportunities are often used as a retention tool, as employees need to stay with the organisation in order to earn them.
- **Secondments:** employees may be offered the opportunity to be seconded to other functions, units or locations within the firm (or even with other, allied firms), as a way of broadening their outlook, developing new competences and enhancing their careers. This may also be used as a form of training: for example, giving product managers experience in production or marketing, or giving marketers experience of international branches.

6 Outsourcing jobs and projects

6.1 What is outsourcing?

KEY CONCEPT

concept

Outsourcing is the current term for the practice of contracting external service providers to undertake activities or functions that the organisation would otherwise perform itself, 'in house'.

This is a strategic '**make/do or buy**' or '**boundary of the firm**' 'decision. A firm can perform all its activities in-house, so that the value of the final product or service offered to customers arises almost entirely from its own activity. Increasingly, however, firms seek to reduce or even minimise their in-house activities, buying in products and services from external suppliers or subcontractors, so that they can **focus internal resources** on core, distinctive competences – and reap the benefits of **specialist expertise and economies of scale** available from external suppliers in more 'peripheral' areas.

Thus many firms now **buy in products**, components or assemblies previously produced in-house (often from 'off shore' manufacturers in low labour cost countries), and **outsource a range of support functions** (such as maintenance, catering, warehousing and transport, staff recruitment, training, call centres, data management, 'back-office' administration and so on).

6.2 What can or should be outsourced?

Strategic outsourcing should only be applied to the following:

(a) **Non-core competencies**. Core competences are distinctive value-creating skills, capabilities and resources (Hamel & Prahalad, 1994) which: add value in the eyes of the customer; are scarce and difficult for competitors to imitate; and are flexible for future needs. They offer sustainable competitive advantage: for example, by enabling differentiation, or cost leadership, or putting up barriers to competitor entry into an industry. The organisation will thus need to retain, invest in and develop these competencies, by performing them in-house – or collaborating in partnership with specialist suppliers or service providers.

(b) Non-core competencies which, **if outsourced**:

- Will benefit from the expertise, cost efficiency or synergy of a specialist supplier
- Will enable the firm to focus on and leverage its core competencies
- Will not disadvantage the organisation with loss of in-house capability, or vulnerability to market risks
- Will enable the firm to exploit technology or other operational capabilities which it lacks (and would find too costly to develop) in-house
- Will represent value for money (due to the supplier's cost/profit structure or economies of scale, or potential for the outsourcer to divest itself of its in-house assets), in relation to the service levels that can be obtained

(c) Non-core competencies **for which external contractors have the required competence, capability and capacity**

6.2.1 What jobs or projects might marketing outsource or 'buy in'?

The **marketing function** may choose to outsource a number of jobs and projects to external service providers, including:

- Database development and management, and other information systems tasks (such as record-keeping)
- Call centre operations for customer service and query handling, tele-sales and so on
- Web site development and management
- Marketing research projects (market research, customer research, price research, product research)
- Design services (eg for corporate identity, branding and packaging design)

- Advertising services (concept development, campaign realisation, creative origination and production, media buying and scheduling and so on). Most large marketing departments use advertising agencies, whether on a full-service or single-function basis, for on-going advertising work or single campaigns and projects.
- Other marketing services (which may be provided by a full-service or specialist agency): public relations, direct marketing (direct mail, web marketing), sales promotion, exhibition and event management and so on
- Recruitment, selection or training of marketing staff
- Ancillary functions (probably outsourced by the organisation as a whole): eg catering, car fleet management, security, office/premises management

In addition, marketing should have a role in **make/do or buy decisions at a strategic level**, because of the marketing and branding implications of outsourcing. Marketing will help to:

- Define core competences (from the perspective of the customer)
- Identify and manage risks of brand or reputational damage arising from association with the contractor
- Ensure that the contractor's service levels, brand positioning and marketing messages are consistent and coherent with those of the organisation

6.3 Benefits and challenges of outsourcing

Advantages of outsourcing	Disadvantages of outsourcing
Support for downsizing: reduction in staffing, space and facilities costs	Costs of services and relationship/contract management
Enhanced certainty about costs: eg from long-term fixed price service contracts	Loss of in-house knowledge and competencies (which might be required again for future needs)
Long-term partnership contracts encourage planning for the future	Potential reputational damage if service or ethical issues arise with the supply partner
Allows focused investment of managerial, staff and other resources on core/distinctive competences	Loss of control and difficulties ensuring service standards and coherent/consistent marketing and branding messages
Leverages the specialist expertise, technologies, resources and economies of scale of supply partners, with potential to add more value at less cost than the organisation could achieve itself	Loss of control over confidential information (and possibly also intellectual property: processes, designs etc), particularly if the supplier also serves potential competitors
Flexibility: resources may be scaled up or down depending on demand (without impact on in-house staff and systems)	Ethical, corporate social responsibility and employee relations issues of down sizing and off-shoring
Potential synergy through collaborative supply relationships (eg for co-branding)	Risks of being locked into a long-term, unsatisfactory or incompatible partnership

Recent high-profile examples of outsourcing highlight the risks. British Airways' problems arising from employee strike action at Gate Gourmet, to whom it had outsourced *all* its inflight-catering, illustrate the potential for loss of control, and the risk of problems spreading from the supplier to the outsourcer, with disastrous marketing results.

It should be obvious that marketing managers will not simply be 'saving themselves work' by outsourcing jobs or projects to external suppliers, even at an operational level! There will need to be **rigorous planning and control** effort put into:

- Risk assessment and cost/benefit analysis to ensure the 'buy in' decision is sound
- Selecting and vetting potential suppliers, their financial stability, management, quality/service processes, capabilities and capacities and so on (think about how your organisation goes about selecting an advertising agency, for example).
- Defining requirements, service levels and expectations

- Drawing up contracts with appropriate controls and protections (best done in consultation with legal or purchasing specialists)
- Developing contact/liaison points and communication, data-sharing and reporting systems
- Developing and maintaining a constructive relationship with the supplier-side customer/account manager
- Contract and performance management: monitoring compliance, conformance and performance on an on-going basis, and pushing for adjustment and improvement where required
- Handling risks, problems, conflicts and disputes constructively as they arise.

ACTIVITY 6

application/evaluation

What activities (jobs or projects) does your marketing function outsource to, or 'buy in' from, external service providers? Select one for further analysis.

Who is responsible for managing the relationship and the contract?

What processes or guidelines are in place for managing the relationship and the contract?

Identify two or three key 'points of risk' in the process: how might weaknesses in the process cause the risk of service failure, loss of customer loyalty, poor marketing messages or reputational damage? How could these risks be reduced or managed?

Learning objective review

Learning objectives	Covered
1 Determine the need for synergistic and harmonious marketing teams, identifying different types of teams and different applications of team working	☑ The definition of teams and the nature of effective team-working ☑ Benefits and drawbacks of team working ☑ Different uses of teams in marketing contexts
2 Suggest how teams should be structured to deliver organisational and marketing objectives	☑ Different team structures: multi-disciplinary, cross functional, multi-skilled, self-managed and virtual teams ☑ Different roles and resources required for effective team working: task and maintenance roles; Belbin's team roles model
3 Propose a range of approaches for the sourcing (recruitment and selection) and induction of team members to provide the right balance of competencies and skills	☑ The aims and processes of team recruitment and selection ☑ Recruitment channels: internal and external ☑ Selection tools: describing the requirement using job descriptions and person specifications ☑ Selection techniques: measuring candidates against requirement using work sampling, interviews, assessments centres, references and so on ☑ Legal considerations when recruiting: UK and EU law on equal opportunity ☑ How to evaluate the effectiveness of recruitment and selection processes ☑ Introduction to talent management, team member 'on-boarding' (induction), training and development
4 Propose approaches to manage and co-ordinate the work of teams and individuals, including the structuring of tasks	☑ Job analysis and job design ☑ Flexible working practices, including numerical and functional flexibility
5 Evaluate the option of outsourcing marketing jobs and processes, as an alternative to recruiting and developing competencies within the marketing team	☑ The kinds of activities that can be outsourced ☑ Factors in the outsourcing decision ☑ Benefits and challenges of outsourcing, and how outsourcing should be managed

Quick quiz

1 What is a team?

2 What tests are available to assist selection processes?

3 What questions can be asked to identify how effective recruitment processes are?

4 What does the term 'talent management' refer to?

5 What is the purpose of an induction?

Activity debriefs

1 (a) Completer-finisher

(b) Implementer/company worker

(c) Specialist

(d) Plant

(e) Resource investigator

(f) Shaper

(g) Teamworker

(h) Co-ordinator/Chairman

(i) Monitor-evaluator

2, 3 & 4 These will depend on your own research.

5

ABC Business Machines Ltd: Job description for sales office manager		
1	Job title	Sales Office Manager
2	Branch	Head Office
3	Job summary	To provide effective office support for field sales and an efficient re-ordering system for customers.
4	Job content	Typical duties will include: (a) Ensuring staffing as needed of sales office (b) Providing telesales training to new staff (c) Dealing with customer complaints
5	Reporting to:	Sales Director
6	Responsible for:	4 Telesales staff 1 General assistant
7	Experience/Education	At least 4 years' telesales. Some supervisory experience.
8	Training to be provided	Initial on-the-job training.
9	Hours	38 hours per week
10	Personal characteristics required	Organised, friendly manner and enthusiastic.

11	Objectives and appraisal	Ensure smooth operation of telesales
12	Salary	£18-22K according to experience
13	Job title	Sales Office Manager
14	Branch	Head Office
Job Description prepared by: Sales Director		

6 These will depend on your own research.

Quiz answers

1 'A small number of people with *complementary skills* who are committed to a *common purpose,* performance *goals* and *approach* for which they hold themselves *mutually accountable* .

2 Competence, proficiency and psychometric

3 Can we identify our HR requirements from the marketing plan?

- How fast do we respond to a vacancy or recruitment need?
- How good is our awareness of the internal and external labour market (and do we have access to good advice when we need it)?
- Do we select the right advertising media to reach the market?
- How effective (and cost effective) is our recruitment advertising?
- How do our recruits actually perform: do we end up employing the right people?
- Do we retain our new recruits: do they stay with the team and organisation?
- How diverse is our workforce: does it reflect the diversity of the population and customer base, and does it indicate a robust approach to equal opportunity?

4 'The process of ensuring that the organisation attracts, retains, motivates and develops the talented people it needs'

5
- To help new recruits to find their bearings
- To begin to socialise new recruits into the culture and norms of the team/organisation
- To support recruits in beginning performance
- To identify on-going training and development needs
- To avoid initial problems at the 'induction crisis' stage of the employment lifecycle, when frustration, disorientation and disappointment may otherwise cause new recruits to leave the organisation prematurely

---

References

Armstrong, M. (2009) A Handbook of Human Resource Management Practice, (11th edition), Kogan Page, London.

Belbin, R.M. (1993) Team Roles at Work, Butterworth Heinemann, Oxford.

Blanchard, K. & Bowles, S. (2001) High Five: the magic of working together, Harper Collins Business, London.

Bridges, W. (1994) Jobshift: How to prosper in a workplace without jobs, Allen & Unwin, London.

Fraser, H.M. (1978) Employment Interviewing, (5th edition), Macdonald & Evans, London.

Hackman, J.R. & Oldham, G.R. (1980) Work Re-design, Addison Wesley, Reading, MA.

Hamel, G. & Prahalad, C.K. (1994) Competing for the Future, Harvard Business School Press, Boston.

Handy, C.B. (1993) Understanding Organisations, (4th edition), Penguin, Harmondsworth.

Herzberg, F.W. (1966) Work and the Nature of Man, Staples, New York.

Huczynski, A. & Buchanan, D. (2001) Organizational Behaviour: An Introductory Text, (4th edition), FT Prentice Hall, Harlow, Essex.

Janis, I.L. (1972) Victims of Groupthink, Houghton Mifflin, Boston.

Jobber, D. (2007) Principles and Practice of Marketing, (5th edition) McGraw Hill Education, Maidenhead.

Katzenbach, J.R. & Smith, D.K. (1993) The Wisdom of Teams: creating the high performance organisation, Harvard Business School, Boston.

Peters, T.J. & Waterman, R.H. (1982) In Search of Excellence, Harper Collins, New York.

Rodger, A. (1970) The Seven Point Plan, (3rd edition), National Institute of Industrial Psychology.

Steiner, I. (1972) Group Process and Productivity, Academic Press, New York.

Taylor, F.W. (1911) Principles of Scientific Management, Harper, New York.

Townsend, R. (1971) Up the Organisation: how to stop the corporation stifling people and strangling profits, Michael Joseph, New York.

Chapter 6

Managing team working

Topic list

1 Effective and high-performing teams
2 Managing team processes
3 Motivation
4 Management skills and techniques
5 Interpersonal skills for managers and leaders
6 Personal development planning

Introduction

In Chapter 5, we looked at how a manager can 'put together' a team with the right mix and balance of competences, and the right contribution structure, to provide a foundation for effective team performance and organisational capability.

In this chapter, we start by considering what makes an effective team, and how you might diagnose when a team is ineffective.

We saw, in discussing team roles in Chapter 5, that effective team performance involves two complementary processes: the maintenance of the *team* and team working, and the pursuit of *task* functions and objectives. (You might also connect this to the 'concern for people' and 'concern for task' models of leadership style, discussed in Chapter 4.) In sections 2 – 4 of this chapter, we go on to focus on the manager's role in maintaining team working. In Chapter 7, we will go on to explore the manager's role in securing task performance.

Section 2 of this chapter looks at a number of key *processes* in team working: the development of teams over time; the emergence of team cohesion or solidarity; group decision making; and group communication.

Sections 3 and 4 briefly explore a number of management and leadership skills for team working. Some of these might appear to be task-focused (such as delegation and empowerment), but they are all to do with the management of *people* rather than time or other resources. In Section 4 we focus particularly on the *interpersonal* or people skills, by which a manager or leader can influence the culture, morale and maintenance of the team. Our outline is intended to be a starting point for your own more detailed study in any areas suggested by assignment tasks – or by your own personal development needs analysis.

In Section 5, we return to the key topic of motivation in more detail, examining a range of theoretical models which you might use a framework for diagnosing and solving motivational issues in a team.

Syllabus linked learning objectives

By the end of the chapter you will be able to:

	Learning objectives	Syllabus link
1	Identify the characteristics of effective team working and high performing teams	2.5
2	Propose approaches to manage team processes, including team formation and development, team building, decision-making and communication	2.5
3	Propose approaches to manage and co-ordinate the work of teams and individuals, including the structuring of tasks	2.2, 2.5
4	Outline a range of skills and techniques for the management of team working	2.5
5	Propose approaches to improve and maintain the motivation of team members, assessing and applying a range of management theories in this area	2.5
6	Reflect on your own management skills and approach to team management and produce a personal development plan	2.5

1 Effective and high-performing teams

The task of the marketing manager is to build a 'successful' or 'effective' marketing team. You might immediately think of such a team as one which fulfils its task objectives efficiently and effectively, but there is more to it than that. As we saw in Adair's 'action leadership' model (in Chapter 4), team effectiveness – and management – can be measured by three key criteria:

- **Task performance**: fulfilment of task objectives and marketing/organisational goals
- **Team functioning**: maintenance of consistent and constructive team working, managing the demands of team dynamics, roles and processes, and
- **Team member satisfaction**: fulfilment of individual development and relationship needs.

1.1 Assessing the effectiveness of your team

There are a number of factors, both quantitative and qualitative, that may be assessed to decide whether or how far a team is **functioning effectively** – over and above whether it is meeting its work targets. What does an effectively functioning team 'look like'?

- The team has a clear **mission** and **objectives** which are understood and shared by all members.
- The **mix of personalities and skills** is diverse and complimentary. Members respect each others' differences, and appreciate the synergistic effect of diverse individual contributions.
- Each individual is both **supported** and **challenged** to contribute to his or her best ability.
- There is a sense of **identity and belonging** which encourages loyalty and commitment.
- **Information and ideas** are freely gathered and shared for the use of the team.
- **Constructive conflict** – new ideas, challenges to the status quo, constructive criticism and disagreement – is encouraged, as a way of testing and improving group decisions.
- Each member is encouraged to **participate** and have a voice in the team, so that (s)he 'buys in' to its decisions and activities.
- There is **trust and openness,** so that individual and task problems can be safely aired and addressed.
- There are effective mechanisms for maintaining **communication**, both formal (eg team meetings) and informal (networking and socialising).
- The team accepts and supports the designated **leader**, but continues to function well and maintain discipline in the leader's absence, and is able to share leadership roles when required.

You should be able to think of the opposite signs of an ineffectively functioning team. Some of the characteristics of **effective** and **ineffective** teams, as an aid to assessment, may be summarised as follows. Note that some factors cannot be taken as evidence on their own, but may suggest underlying problems: accident rates may be due to poor safety systems, for example – but may also suggest poor morale and lack of focus due to team problems.

Factor	Effective team	Ineffective team
Quantifiable		
Labour turnover	Low	High
Accident rates	Low	High
Absenteeism	Low	High
Output and productivity	High	Low
Quality of output	High	Low
Individual targets	Achieved	Not achieved
Stoppages and interruptions to the work flow	Low	High (eg due to disagreement or misunderstanding)

Factor	Effective team	Ineffective team
Qualitative		
Commitment to targets and organisational goals	High	Low
Understanding of team's work and why it exists	High	Low
Understanding of individual roles within the team	High	Low
Communication between team members	Free and open	Mistrust
Ideas	Shared for the team's benefit	'Owned' (and hidden) by individuals for their own benefit
Feedback	Constructive criticism	Point scoring, undermining
Problem-solving	Addresses causes	Only looks at symptoms
Interest in work decisions	Active	Passive acceptance
Opinions	Consensus	Imposed solutions
Job satisfaction	High	Low
Motivation/productivity in leader's absence	High	'When the cat's away...'

1.2 High-performance teams

Vaill (1989) identified the characteristics of 'high performance' or extraordinary teams, as follows.

- They perform to a high level against defined external benchmarks or standards, and in comparison to their own previous measured performance (ie they continually improve).
- They perform to a level beyond what is assumed to be their potential best (ie they continually exceed expectations).
- They perform to a level that would enable any informed observer to identify them as better than comparable groups (ie they clearly 'shine').
- They achieve results with fewer resources than would be assumed to be necessary (ie they are efficient).
- They embody the best values of the organisation culture and act as role models (or reference groups) for the culture.

1.3 Barriers to effective team functioning

We will look at some of the potential causes of poor team performance (and how to address them) in Chapter 7. But in terms of team functioning, there are a number of potential barriers.

- Group **norms**, unchallenged by the group or group leader, undermining performance (eg restricting output or resisting leadership)
- **Lack of support**, information or resources from management to fulfil the task (including a lack of genuine decision-making authority and accountability)
- **Lack of communication**, causing un-coordinated effort, the potential for misunderstanding, and a lack of shared identity and sense of collaboration.
- **Unmanaged conflicts** of interest, interpersonal hostility or status barriers blocking team development, co-operation and information-sharing
- **Under-performing or under-motivated individuals** holding back the team, and causing mistrust and resentment
- **Unchecked team cohesion**, diverting attention from the task and causing over-confident decision-making
- **Poor team leadership**, creating power conflicts and imbalances, lack of communication and certainty – or (if too rigid) stifling individual creativity and initiative

- **Corporate culture and reward systems** which value the individual over the group, creating a disincentive to invest energy in team working
- **Powerlessness –** where a team lacks the authority or influence to get its requests met or its recommendations implemented – creating a disincentive to invest energy in the team

You can no doubt think of other factors – perhaps from your own experience...

1.4 Elements in team management

A useful overview of team management was provided by Charles Handy (1993), who took a contingency approach to team effectiveness.

A contingency approach to team effectiveness

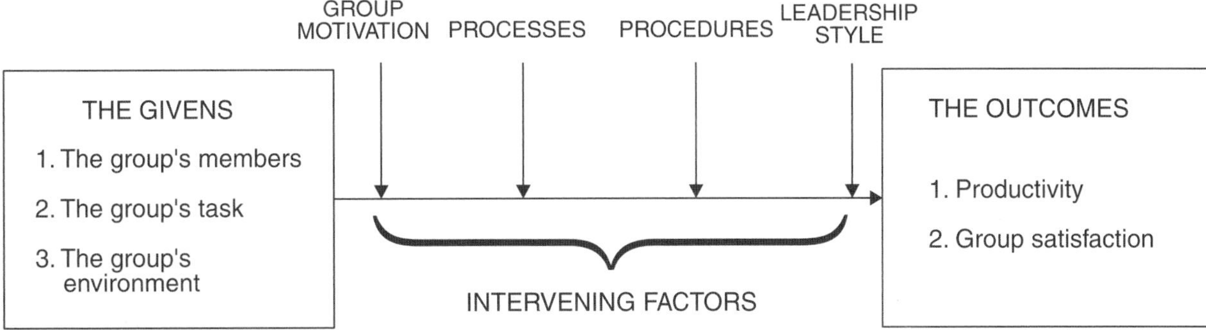

1.4.1 The givens

Some elements of team working may be established by existing arrangements, organisational infrastructure and task structure: they are the raw materials that the manager 'has to work with'.

- There may be an **established team**, providing a mix and balance of skills, competences and personality/role preferences. All these aspects will, as we saw in Chapter 5, shape the personality and functioning of the team.
- The **nature and structure of the task**, as we also saw in Chapter 5, will shape the design and allocation of work for the team, its performance goals and standards, its motivation and culture of work, the type of leadership required (for high-control or high-flexibility, say), the use of technology – and a number of other factors.
- The **environment** includes the physical surroundings and conditions of the team's work, but also the place of the team within overall business processes and structures, the constraint of corporate policies and systems, the influence of organisation culture and so on.

1.4.2 Intervening factors

Intervening factors are the elements which are potentially within the manager's control, and can be manipulated to bring about positive outcomes for and through the team.

- The **motivation** of individuals, and the team as a whole, is a key influence on team effectiveness. The task, and the organisational authority to enforce compliance with task directives, are givens – but motivation is required in order to get team members to comply and perform willingly and to the best of their ability. We will discuss this in detail in section 3 of this chapter.
- **Processes** describe *how* a team performs its functions and maintains steady and constructive team working: how it establishes ways of operating, how it makes decisions, how it structures communication and so on. We will discuss these kinds of processes in detail in Section 2 of this chapter.
- **Procedures** describe the processes laid down by the organisation and team manager for performing tasks: how things should be done in order to achieve outcomes and targets efficiently and effectively. Procedures often take the form of standardised sequences of tasks, and the instructions, tools and guidelines that will support team members in performing them: how to select a venue for a marketing event; how to co-ordinate a promotional campaign; how to establish marketing budgets; and so on. These aspects will be touched on in Chapter 7.

- **Leadership style** is, in effect, the way in which *all* of the intervening factors are mediated to the team: how they are communicated; how influence is used to secure team member 'buy in' and commitment; and so on. We discussed this aspect in Chapter 4 – but do bear in mind, as you work through this chapter, that team processes may be managed, individuals motivated and managerial skills used *in different ways,* according to the style adopted by the team leader.

2 Managing team processes

2.1 Team formation and development

We saw above that the members of the team are a crucial variable in team functioning. Some teams may be set up from scratch, with members who have not worked together before. A team can *change* its character and dynamics as its members change over time. Project teams are constantly being formed, disbanded and re-formed. It is important to realise that effective teams aren't simply 'put together': they have to develop. It can take time for a new or altered group to become a fully functioning and performing team.

2.1.1 Tuckman's stages of team development

Four stages in the process of team development were identified by *Tuckman* (1965).

- **Forming**

  The team is just coming together. Each member wishes to impress his or her personality on the group. The individuals will be trying to find out about each other, and about the aims and methods of the team (as set by organisational traditions and standards). There will at this stage probably be a wariness about introducing new ideas, in order to avoid 'rocking the boat'.

Interpersonal focus		Task focus	
Main concerns:	*Resulting in:*	*Main concerns:*	*Resulting in:*
Inclusion Rejection Acceptance	Cautious behaviour Avoiding conflict	Task orientation	'What are we supposed to do?' 'What are the goals?'

- **Storming**

  This frequently involves more or less open conflict between team members, as individuals seek to assert themselves. There may be challenges to the original objectives, procedures and norms established for the group. If the team is developing successfully, this may be a fruitful phase, as more realistic targets are set, trust between the group members increases.

Interpersonal focus		Task focus	
Main concerns:	*Resulting in:*	*Main concerns:*	*Resulting in:*
Control Status/authority Values and ideas	Conflict Power struggles Challenging ideas	Organisation Rules and agenda	'Do we want to follow these rules?' 'Is this decision right?'

- **Norming**

  A period of settling down as a group. Norms and processes will evolve for group functioning: working sharing, output levels, interactions, decision-making and so on. Group cohesion increases as roles (including leadership) are established.

Interpersonal focus		Task focus	
Main concerns:	*Resulting in:*	*Main concerns:*	*Resulting in:*
Being liked/accepted Open-mindedness Listening	Cohesion Group focus Team spirit	Getting on with the job Information flow	Compromise and collaboration Information sharing

- **Performing**

  The team is functioning well as a group, with each member fulfilling clear roles: focus and energy shifts to task performance. Team processes support performance through genuine collaboration (working together).

Interpersonal focus		Task focus	
Main concerns:	*Resulting in:*	*Main concerns:*	*Resulting in:*
Interdependence Commitment Autonomy	Agreeing to disagree	Creative problem-solving and decision-making	Compromise and collaboration Information sharing

Tuckman and Jensen (1977) later added two stages to Tuckman's model.

- **Dorming**. Once a group has been performing well for some time, it may get complacent, and fall back into self-maintenance and member-satisfaction functions, at the expense of the task.
- **Mourning/adjourning**. The group sees itself as having fulfilled its purpose – or, if it is a temporary project group, is due to physically disband. This is a stage of confusion, sadness and anxiety as the group breaks up. There is evaluation of its achievements, and gradual withdrawal of group members. If the group is to continue, going on to a new task, there will be a re-negotiation of aims and roles: a return to the forming stage.

ACTIVITY 1

application

Read the following descriptions of team behaviour and decide to which category they belong (forming, storming, norming, performing, dorming).

(a) Two of the group are arguing as to whose idea is best

(b) Progress has become static

(c) Desired outputs are being achieved

(d) A shy member of the group is not participating fully

(e) Activities are being allocated by the team

The important thing to note is that Tuckman's model represents an ideal evolutionary lifecycle. Depending on the circumstances and leadership, a team may skip or repeat stages: a very homogenous team, for example, might skip significant storming; a poorly led team may return frequently to storming. A team may also get stuck at any one of the stages, if the issues are not satisfactorily resolved: not all groups develop into mature, high-performing teams.

2.2 Team building

Team building is activity by a manager or leader to support, facilitate and, if necessary, accelerate the process of team development. You might approach this by considering what a manager can do to facilitate each of the stages of group development identified by Tuckman. Some ideas include:

- **Forming**: 'ice breaking' activities; social and 'team bonding' activities, to accelerate familiarity and trust; clear articulation of goals and expectations (where possible, clearly stated as being open to negotiation and question by the team)
- **Storming**: encouraging questioning, challenge and constructive criticism; laying down ground rules to keep conflict/criticism constructive and task focused; managing potentially negative conflict
- **Norming**: team building activity to encourage cohesion and team spirit (discussed further below); providing information and communication mechanisms for decision-making; reinforcing/rewarding positive group norms and challenging negative ones; 'contracting' with the team on agreed ideas, methods and roles

- **Performing**: backing off; reinforcing collaborative behaviours; providing support and information where required; monitoring and managing performance
- **Dorming:** bringing issue into the open; challenging complacency; introducing competition or other incentives to renew motivation
- **Mourning/adjourning:** bringing confusion, sadness into the open for discussion; encouraging positive evaluation of the team's achievements; motivating and encouraging team members to keep performing to the end; planning handover of activity to the new team (if any); generating positive anticipation of new team and tasks

More generally, team-building activity is regarded as focusing on three aspects of team working.

Aspect	Leader activity
Team identity Getting people to see themselves as part of the group and to identify themselves with its objectives.	• Communicating team identity (eg giving the team a title or nickname) • Creating a team 'space' (a personalised meeting area or intranet page, perhaps) • Expressing the team's self-image, eg through shared symbols (a 'badge' or 'mascot'), mottos and value statements, and mythology (sharing stories of the team's successes, heroic failures and funny shared moments)
Team solidarity Encouraging cohesion and mutual loyalty, so that members put in extra effort for the team.	• Expressing solidarity (eg using 'we' language) • Providing opportunities for relationships to develop (eg social interaction time, bonding activities) • Managing conflict within the team: ensuring that disagreements are openly expressed and resolved • Controlling competition within the team (eg by avoiding favouritism) • Injecting an element of competition with *other* teams (eg competitive awards for best results or productivity)
Shared objectives Encouraging the team to commit itself to shared work objectives and to co-operate willingly and effectively in achieving them.	• Clearly articulating team objectives and their place in the big picture of marketing, corporate and value chain activity • Involving the team in setting specific targets and standards and agreeing methods of organising work • Giving regular feedback on progress and results via team briefings • Inviting team self-appraisal, feedback and suggestions, so that they can drive improvement planning • Positively reinforcing behaviour that demonstrates collaboration and commitment to the task (through rewards, recognition etc) • Celebrating the success of the team and championing it to the rest of the organisation

ACTIVITY 2

application/evaluation

Why might the following be effective as team-building exercises?

(a) Sending a project team (involved in the design of electronic systems for racing cars) on a recreational day out go-karting.

(b) Sending two sales teams on a day out playing 'War Games', each being an opposing combat team trying to capture the other's flag, armed with paint guns.

(c) Sending a project team on a conference at a venue away from work, with a brief to review the past year and come up with a vision for the next year.

2.3 Team cohesion

Co-operative groups have been shown to be more effective than competitive groups, where individuals focused on their own contributions rather than the group's shared performance. Team cohesion or solidarity is broadly regarded as desirable in order to create committed, co-operative working, mutual loyalty and accountability, and open information sharing – all of which may help to maximise the potential synergy of team working *and* individual satisfaction.

However, you should be aware that it is possible for groups to become *too* cohesive. Problems may arise in very close-knit groups because:

- The **group's energies** may be focused on its own maintenance and relationships, instead of on the task. Handy (1993) argued that: 'ultra cohesive groups can be dangerous because in the organisational context the group must serve the organisation, not itself.'
- The group may be **suspicious or dismissive of outsiders**, and may reject any contradictory information or criticism they supply; the group will be blinkered and stick to its own views, no matter what; cohesive groups thus often get the impression that they are infallible: they can't be wrong – and therefore can't learn from their mistakes.
- The group may **squash any dissent** or opinions that might rock the boat. Close-knit groups tend to preserve a consensus – falsely, if required – and to take risky decisions, because they have suppressed alternative facts and viewpoints.

Janis (1972) identified this as groupthink: 'the psychological drive for consensus at any cost, that suppresses dissent and appraisal of alternatives in cohesive decision-making groups'.

Since by definition a group suffering from groupthink is highly resistant to criticism, recognition of failure and unpalatable information, it is not easy to break such a group out of its vicious circle. The leader must challenge and encourage the group to:

- Actively seek outside ideas and feedback
- Welcome self-criticism and dissent within the group, and
- Deliberately evaluate conflicting evidence and opinions, looking for useful learning.

We will look at the issue of team **conflict**, and how it can be managed (without increasing the risk of groupthink) in Chapter 8.

2.4 Group decision-making

Decision-making is a key team process, because:

- Pooling skills, information and ideas from different individuals (or functions, specialisms and levels in the organisation) may increase the **quality of the decision.**
- Participation in the decision-making process makes the decision **acceptable to the group**, whether because it represents a compromise or consensus of their views, or merely because they have been consulted and given a sense of influencing the decision.

Team decisions may be arrived at in various ways.

- **Imposition** or application of authority by the leader. This may be most appropriate where the speed or 'rightness' of the decision are more important than team agreement. The manager may involve the team in areas such as problem definition and the formulation of alternative solutions, but will take the final decision herself.
- **Majority rule**: by vote, or the leader's 'getting a sense' of the view supported by the majority of team members. This may be most appropriate where the acceptance of the group is the most important factor, rather than the 'rightness' of the decision.
- **Consensus**: a process by which a range of potentially divergent views is examined and persuasive arguments used until there is broad agreement among all members. This takes longer, but is often more effective at the implementation stage, since all members of the group are able to 'own' the decision.

In less effectively functioning teams, this may be negative process, where decisions are taken without input from team members; by a minority (eg a dominant clique within the team); by default (eg if the leader has abdicated responsibility for decision-making); or not at all (eg the issue is left open until events or higher authority make the decision for the team).

As we mentioned in Chapter 5, group decision-making tends to take longer (especially through consensus-seeking), but decisions are often better evaluated and more representative (owing to the input of different viewpoints) and therefore implemented with more commitment. Perhaps the key tasks of the manager are to:

- **Elicit and utilise team members' views, knowledge and expertise**, without abdicating responsibility for the final decision – but without giving the impression that contribution is a waste of time, or that participation is not genuine
- Encourage **progressively less leader-centred decision-making**, as the group matures (as suggested by the situational leadership model discussed in Chapter 4)
- Providing **information, coaching and other forms of facilitation and support** for group decision-making
- **Avoid the 'risky-shift' phenomenon**, whereby groups tend to take greater risks than the same individuals would on their own. There should be rigorous insistence on hearing divergent viewpoints and evaluating options.

2.5 Team communication

Effectively functioning groups tend to move from a leader-centred, leader-initiated pattern of communication to one where interaction is multi-directional or 'all-channel': any member can communicate directly with any other member. Cliques and isolated individuals become included within this web of interaction over time, facilitating the involvement and contribution of every-member.

Features of **effective group communication**, to be modelled, coached and supported by the leader, include:

- **Open, honest communication** – including the ability to deal with conflicts, issues and criticism openly, directly and fairly (without personal animosity or grudge-holding)
- **Task-relevant information sharing** (no withholding on a 'need to know' or 'knowledge is power' basis)
- **All-member participation** in meetings, discussions and decision-making. Equitable participation does not mean that all members will share *equally*, but that all members can get a fair hearing when they have something to say
- **Absence of artificial status barriers**, so that senior and junior members communicate with ease
- **Positive contributions** (giving/seeking information, suggests and opinions; encouraging and affirming others; being appropriately vulnerable; checking understanding; giving constructive feedback; summarising; explaining and so on) *outweigh* negative contributions (attacking; being defensive; difficulty stating; fault finding; interrupting; overriding others).

Rackham & Morgan (1977) suggest the technique of **contribution profiling**: analysing the number of contributions of different (positive and negative) types made by each member of a team during a meeting or discussion, to identify dysfunctional behaviours which can be fed back to the individual for adjustment, or countered in communication situations by positive leadership intervention.

2.5.1 Team communication tools

You should be aware of a wide range of tools for communicating within and between teams in your own organisation. These may include:

Internal mail systems, carrying messages, letters and memoranda, forms and reports

- E-mail and other forms of electronic communication and data-sharing (eg shared database access)
- The telephone (including mobile phones and their email and SMS messaging capabilities)
- Team meetings, briefings and discussions, whether routine (eg a weekly sales or project team meeting) or required by particular tasks or events
- Individual interviews and discussions
- Electronic equivalents of meetings and discussions eg via teleconferences, video-conferences, web casts and 'virtual' meetings from linked computers
- General 'management by walking around': informal contacts and information sharing in the course of daily activity.

2.6 Team meetings

Teams spend a large proportion of their working week in meetings, particularly with the rise of project working. Meetings are thus both a major cost to organisations, and a major context for decision-making, interpersonal influencing and team collaboration.

Poorly managed meetings can, however, be non-productive or even counter-productive. If meetings are a significant cost, they need to be efficiently utilised – but poorly managed meetings are a waste of time. If meetings are where most decisions are made, they need to facilitate quality decisions – but some group dynamics (as we have seen) result in poor or risky decision-making. If meetings are where teams mainly 'touch base' with each other, they need to facilitate integrative collaboration – but they are often perceived as a waste of time.

Regular team meetings have particular purposes, over and above problem-solving and decision-making on any particular work-related issue.

- They provide an opportunity to review team working processes and appraise (formally or informally) how well they are working. Team members may raise problems of co-ordination or communication, for example.
- They reinforce the team's sense of itself as a team, drawing them together to focus on their shared goals.
- They allow for goal reinforcement, progress feedback and information sharing, to ensure that team members are 'on the same page' with their efforts – especially if they do not directly work together (eg in remote or virtual project teams).
- They allow for all-member involvement and development in team decision-making and information sharing processes. (Discussion leading and research/presentation roles might be rotated, for example, to facilitate this.)
- They allow for informal communication, which is important for working relations, ideas generation and information-sharing. This can be built in at the beginning and end of meeting time.

2.6.1 Managing meetings effectively

Whatever the purpose and level of formality of a given meeting, its effectiveness will broadly depend on the following.

- There is usually a discussion **leader**, chairperson, or at least an organiser, who guides the proceedings of the meeting and aims to maintain order.
- There is often a **sequence of business** or at least a list of items to be covered: topics of discussion or decisions to be reached. It is not essential to formalise this point with an **agenda**, but meetings usually do have one.
- The purpose of the meeting is achieved by reaching some **decision or expression of opinion** at the end of the discussion. In some circumstances this may lead to taking a vote to determine what is the majority view. In other circumstances, the discussion may just be **summarised** by the leader and written confirmation of the decisions reached provided later for perusal by the various parties.

Whetten and Cameron (2002) suggest that the attributes of effective meetings can be classified as Five Ps.

<table>
<tr><td>Purpose</td><td>Meetings should only be convened when there is a defined and adequate reason for doing so; when the cost of meeting is less than the potential benefits; and when face-to-face meeting is more effective than an e-mail or phone call.</td></tr>
<tr><td>Participants</td><td>Meetings can fail because they are too small (insufficient participation) or too large (insufficient information or representation).

Meetings require a balance of skills and competencies – like any team: there may need to be problem identifiers, problem solvers, resource controllers and decision authorisers, for example, in a project meeting.

Key roles and responsibilities in a meeting will include:

• A leader (in formal meetings, called a meeting chair) or facilitator.

Responsible for ensuring that: the meeting follows the agenda; discussion is conducted in a way that permits equitable participation by all members and decisions are reached in appropriate ways.

• A scribe (in formal meetings, called a secretary)

Responsible for taking notes of what is discussed and agreed, what actions will be taken and by what deadlines. Team meetings may or may not require formal minutes, but it will help if someone is concentrating on recording the proceedings.</td></tr>
<tr><td>Planning</td><td>It will be necessary to make arrangements for meeting space, seating layout, equipment and so on.

Notice of the meeting (announcement of and invitation to the meeting): timing and location should be planned to facilitate attendance by those who need to be there.

Agenda: a clear list of the items of business to be discussed at the meeting, ideally circulated in advance to allow preparation. A well-drafted agenda will indicate the meeting's priorities, both in the sequence of the items (so that the meeting focuses its 'best' time on the most important or difficult items) and by allotting target times for the discussion of each item.</td></tr>
<tr><td>Process</td><td>The interpersonal and decision-making processes of the meeting, and the facilitator's efforts to ensure participants contribute appropriately.

Formal meetings have particular rules and conventions covering matters such as how proposals are put forward, how debate is to be managed, how decisions are to be reached (eg by vote) and how resolutions are recorded.

Informal meetings also require structure and leadership, but these will generally come from the facilitator (see below).</td></tr>
<tr><td>Perspective</td><td>Meetings should be reviewed to evaluate their effectiveness, and decide what can be improved next time.</td></tr>
</table>

2.6.2 Leading team meetings

Effective facilitation of a team meeting involves the following.

- Ensuring that all members have the information they require to contribute meaningfully
- Ensuring that all members are able to contribute equitably (eg by encouraging less communicative members, and controlling more dominant members)
- Keeping the discussion 'on track' with the agenda or matter in hand. (Potentially useful but not immediately relevant contributions should be tabled for inclusion at the next meeting.)
- Managing any conflict that emerges in the course of the meeting
- Ensuring that agreed decisions are accurately recorded in the notes or minutes of the meeting, ideally with clearly defined responsibility for action
- Following up on decisions and action points from previous meetings, to ensure that agreed action has been taken

ACTIVITY 3

application

What aspects of the following situations might be a problem for an effective team meeting? What might you, in the role of facilitator, do about it?

(a) One person suggests a revision to the agenda, a complex issue which the rest of the team is unprepared to discuss, and which two members are likely to feel is 'targeted' at them.

(b) The team has more items on its agenda than it can handle in a simple meeting.

(c) A team member has called ahead to say that she will be unavoidably late for a scheduled project team meeting.

3 Motivation

3.1 What is motivation?

The word 'motivation' is used in different contexts to mean:

- The **mental process** of choosing desired outcomes, deciding how to go about them, assessing whether the likelihood of success warrants the amount of effort that will be necessary, and setting in motion the required behaviours. Our 'motivation' to do something will depend on this calculation of the relationship between inputs and rewards.
- The **social process** by which the behaviour of an individual or group is influenced by others. 'Motivation' in this sense usually applies to the attempts of a leader to get team members to put in more effort by offering them certain financial and non-financial rewards if they do so.

For a marketing manager, motivation boils down to questions such as: how can we get people to do more and achieve more? How can we recognise and reward commitment, improvement and achievement?

You may be wondering whether motivation is really so important. It could be argued that if a person is employed to do a job, (s)he will do that job – and no question of how (s)he 'feels' about it really arises. The point at issue, however, is ***how* and *how well* the job is done**. It is suggested that if individuals can be 'motivated', they will work more efficiently (and productivity will rise) or they will produce a better quality of work, or will exercise their creativity and initiative in the service of organisational goals.

'**Job satisfaction**' is an even more controversial concept. It is often said that 'happy bees make more honey' – but this has proved difficult to measure and demonstrate in practice. Job satisfaction is difficult to define: it means different things to different people, and over time, according to their needs and expectations. And, as Huczynski & Buchanan (2001) note, 'there is not so much talk about "the quality of working life" when there is little work to be had'!

On the other hand, it is recognised that low morale, dissatisfaction or demotivation can cause direct and indirect performance problems, through effects such as:

- Higher than usual (or higher than acceptable) labour turnover (resignations and transfers)
- Higher levels of absenteeism (whether through work avoidance or stress-related ill health)
- Deterioration in timekeeping and discipline
- Reduction in upward communication, proactive involvement and other benefits of employee commitment and enthusiasm
- Higher incidence of disputes and grievances
- Restricted output quantity and/or quality

You may gather that motivation is an art, not a science. Managers will attempt to motivate their teams according to their own assumptions about what makes workers 'tick' and what workers want: what will encourage or force them to work better. We will begin by looking at some of these assumptions.

3.1.1 Theory X and Theory Y

Douglas McGregor's Theory X and Theory Y (McGregor, 1960) is an influential model of two extreme sets of managerial assumptions about what makes workers tick, at opposite ends of a continuum. (Note that they are *not* 'types of people'.)

- **Theory X** is the assumption that the average human being has an inherent dislike of work and will avoid it if (s)he can. People must therefore be coerced, controlled, directed and/or bribed or threatened with punishment in order to get them to expend adequate effort towards the achievement of organisational goals. This is quite acceptable to the worker, who prefers to be directed, wishes to avoid responsibility, has relatively little ambition and wants security above all.

- **Theory Y** is the assumption that the expenditure of physical and mental effort in work is as natural as play or rest. The average human being does not inherently dislike work, which can be a source of satisfaction. People can exercise self-direction and self-control to achieve objectives to which they are committed. The average human being learns, under proper conditions, not only to accept but to seek responsibility. The capacity to exercise a relatively high degree of imagination, ingenuity and creativity in the solution of organisational problems is widespread.

McGregor's point is that Theory X and Theory Y assumptions are, in essence, **self-fulfilling prophecies**. If team members are treated as if Theory X were true (using carrot-and-stick motivation, detailed rules and close supervision, low-discretion jobs and so on), they will begin to behave accordingly: it is negative experience at work that fosters lack of ambition, the need for security and intellectual stagnation. If team members are treated as if Theory Y were true (using empowered team working, employee involvement schemes and facilitative managerial styles), they will begin to behave accordingly and rise to the challenge.

3.1.2 Motivation theories

One way of grouping the major theories of motivation is by distinguishing between content and process theories.

- **Content** theories ask the question: '*What* are the *things* that motivate people?' They assume that human beings have a set of innate needs or desired outcomes that they pursue. Maslow's hierarchy of needs, McClelland's motivation needs theory and Herzberg's two-factor theory are the most important approaches of this type.

- **Process** theories ask the question: '*How* can people be motivated?' They explore the conscious or unconscious process of calculation by which individuals choose certain outcomes and the most advantageous or acceptable paths towards them. Vroom's expectancy theory is the best known approach of this type.

ASSIGNMENT TIP

application/evaluation

Theoretical models will be useful to (a) diagnose motivational problems in a team and (b) to support and justify any motivational approaches you propose. Bear in mind, however, that they are only models: they can be challenged, and must be applied only where relevant and appropriate in practice.

3.2 Maslow's hierarchy of needs

Abraham Maslow (1954) described five innate human needs, and put forward certain propositions about the motivating power of each need.

- An individual's needs can be arranged in a **'hierarchy of relative pre-potency'** (as shown).

- Each level of need is **dominant until satisfied**; only then does the next (higher) level of need become a motivating factor.

- A **need which has been satisfied** no longer motivates an individual's behaviour.

- The need for **self-actualisation** (personal growth and the fulfilment of potential) can rarely be fully or permanently satisfied.

The hierarchy of needs (Maslow)

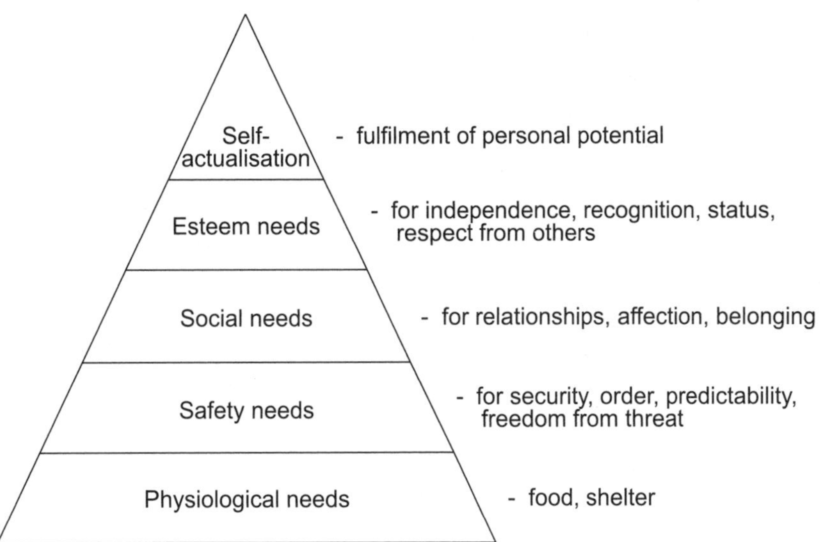

Suggest ways in which rewards or incentives could be offered to team members to satisfy each of the innate needs identified by Maslow.

3.2.1 Evaluating and applying the hierarchy

Maslow's hierarchy is simple and intuitively attractive: you are unlikely to worry about status or respect if you are physically unsafe or about to lose your job. However, it is difficult to use the hierarchy to predict employee behaviour. (Maslow did not intend it to be applied specifically in a work context.)

- The boundaries between the needs are, in practice, indistinct and overlapping: different people emphasise different needs; and the same need may prompt different behaviours in different individuals.
- In some contexts, people are clearly able to suppress even their basic needs for the sake of a perceived 'higher cause' or for the sake of others.
- Maslow's ideas primarily reflected American middle class values and the pursuit of the good life, but these values may not be fundamental universal truths about human psychology.
- The role of pay is problematic, since it arguably acts as a 'stand in' for (or way of obtaining) other rewards.

Nevertheless, the hierarchy is a useful reminder to managers to adopt a contingency approach to team motivation: people may be motivated by different things at different times.

3.2.2 McClelland's motivation needs theory

David McClelland (1988) similarly identified three types of motivating need, which can be identified using various psychometric tests.

The **need for power**. People with a high need for power usually seek positions in which they can influence and control others.

The **need for affiliation**. People who need a sense of belonging and membership of a social group tend to be concerned with maintaining good personal relationships.

The **need for achievement**. People who need to achieve have a strong desire for success and a strong fear of failure.

3.3 Herzberg's two-factor theory

Frederick Herzberg (1966) developed an influential theory of motivation called 'two factor theory', which argued that people have two basic needs at work:

The need to avoid unpleasantness. This need is satisfied by what Herzberg called **'hygiene' factors**: fair pay, fair management, good working conditions and so on. Such factors minimise dissatisfaction and poor job performance, but don't really give positive satisfaction or motivate people to higher-level performance: after a while, they get taken for granted and become a source of dissatisfaction again.

The need for personal growth. These needs are satisfied by what Herzberg called '**motivator' factors**, which can only be found within the job itself: recognition, added responsibility, challenge, interest and achievement. Such factors create positive job satisfaction, and motivate people to higher levels of committed performance.

Herzberg argued that*: 'Dissatisfaction arises from environment factors:* ***satisfaction can only arise from the job'***. We saw in Chapter 5 that Herzberg recommended approaches to job design (job rotation, enrichment and enlargement) that increase the core dimensions of the job thought to create job satisfaction: skill variety, task identity, task significance, autonomy and feedback. **Job enrichment** was the method most highly recommended by Herzberg, as 'the planned process of up-grading the responsibility, challenge and content of the work' to offer greater satisfaction. (Recap our coverage of job design in Chapter 5 if you need to.)

3.3.1 Evaluating and applying the expectancy model

Herzberg's original study focused on 203 Pittsburgh engineers and accountants. Two-factor theory has therefore been criticised as being based on an inadequately small sample size and a limited cultural context. Moreover, the impact of motivator factors on job performance has proved difficult to verify and measure.

Nevertheless, this influential theory has focused managers' attention on motivation through job satisfaction (the intrinsic rewards to be found in work itself), contributing to job redesign and the 'quality of working life' movement – and helping to explain why financial rewards and incentives are frequently less effective than managers hope. It also highlights the two types of reward that can be offered to individuals and teams.

- **Intrinsic** rewards arise from the work itself, and (in a sense) from within the worker: challenge, interest, team identity, pride in the organisation, the satisfaction of achievement and so on.
- **Extrinsic** rewards do not arise from the work itself, but are within the power of others (typically, management) to award or withhold: wages or salary, bonuses, prizes, promotion, improved working conditions and so on.

3.4 Vroom's expectancy theory

Expectancy theory is a process theory of motivation, which basically states that the strength of an individual's motivation to do something will depend on the extent to which he expects the results of his efforts to contribute to his needs or goals.

Victor Vroom (1964) worked out a formula by which human motivation could be assessed and measured. He suggested that the strength of an individual's motivation is the product of two factors:

- The strength of his **preference** for a certain outcome. Vroom called this '**valence'**: it can be represented as a positive or negative number, or zero – since outcomes may be desired, avoided or regarded with indifference.
- His **expectation** that the outcome will in fact result from a given behaviour. Vroom called this 'subjective probability' or **expectancy.** As a probability, it may be represented by any number between 0 (no chance) and 1 (certainty).

In its simplest form, the expectancy equation may be stated as:

$$\mathbf{F = V \times E}$$

where:

F	=	The force or strength of the individual's motivation to behave in a particular way
V	=	Valence: the strength of the individual preference for a given outcome or reward and
E	=	Expectancy: the individual's perception that the behaviour will result in the outcome/reward.

In this equation, the lower the values of valence or expectancy, the less the individual's motivation. A team member may have a high expectation that increased productivity will result in promotion (because of her manager's promises, say), but if she is indifferent or negative towards the idea of promotion (because she dislikes responsibility), she will not be motivated to increase her productivity. Likewise, if promotion is very important to her – but she does not believe higher productivity will get her promoted (because she has been passed over before, perhaps), her motivation will be low.

3.4.1 Evaluating and applying the expectancy model

Expectancy theory can be used to measure the likely strength of a worker's motivation to act in a desired way in response to a range of different rewards, to find the most effective motivational strategy. In particular, it suggests that:

- **Intended results** should be made clear, so that the individual can complete the calculation by knowing what is expected, the reward, and how much effort it will take.
- Immediate and on-going **performance feedback** should be given. Without knowledge of actual results, there is no check that extra effort was justified (or will be justified in future).
- Individuals should be offered **rewards and incentives that they value**: this may require some flexibility (eg a 'cafeteria' approach to rewards and benefits) on the part of the manager.
- If an individual is rewarded for performance tied to **standards**, however, (s)he may set lower standards: the expectancy part of the calculation (likelihood of success and reward) is greater if the standard is lower.
- Managers need to **follow through** with promised rewards for high performance, in order to increase expectancy for future incentives.

Select any one example of how you (or your own manager) approach motivation in your marketing team.

- What approach is being used? What (intrinsic or extrinsic) rewards or incentives are offered? How clear are the attainment targets by which staff will earn those rewards? What kind of feedback on progress/performance is given?
- How *effective* is this approach? Are team members highly motivated? Do they perform up to expectation – or beyond? Are they satisfied in their work?
- Use any one motivation model (eg Herzberg or Vroom) to explain the effect of the approach used on the motivation and performance of the team? If there are motivational problems in the team, what means of improving the manager's approach might be suggested by this model?

3.5 Financial and non-financial performance incentives

3.5.1 The role of pay as a motivator

Pay occupies an ambiguous role in motivation theory. In Maslow's hierarchy, it can 'stand in' for or obtain a wide range of specific need satisfactions. In Herzberg's two-factor theory, it is a hygiene rather than a motivator factor – but it is also the most important of the hygiene factors. It is valuable not only in its power to be converted into a wide range of other satisfactions but also as a consistent measure of worth or value, allowing employees to compare themselves and be compared with other individuals or occupational groups inside and outside the organisation.

Employees need income to live. The size of that income will affect their standard of living, but people tend not to be concerned to maximise their earnings. They may like to earn more, but are probably more concerned to earn *enough* pay – and to know that their pay is *equitable* in relation to others and to the effort they are putting in. Payment systems thus tread the awkward path between equity (an objective rate for the job, preserving pay differentials and so on) and incentive (offering rewards that will stimulate extra effort and attainment by particular individuals and groups).

Goldthorpe, *et al* (1968) researched what they called the **'instrumental' orientation** to work: the attitude that work is not an end in itself, but a means to other ends. In their 'Affluent Worker' research, the researchers found that highly-paid Luton car assembly workers experienced their work as routine and dead-end, and had in fact made a rational decision to enter employment offering high monetary reward rather than intrinsic satisfactions. The Luton researchers did not, however, claim that *all* workers have an instrumental orientation to work, but suggested that people will seek a comfortable balance of:

- The rewards which are important to them and
- The deprivations they feel able to put up with in order to earn those rewards.

Even those with an instrumental orientation to work have limits to their purely financial aspirations and will cease to be motivated by pay if the deprivations – in terms of long working hours, poor conditions, social isolation, boredom or whatever – become too great: in other words, if the price of pay is too high.

3.5.2 Limitations of pay as a motivator

There are a number of difficulties associated with incentive schemes based purely on monetary reward, or performance-related pay.

- Increased earnings may, as we noted above, not be an incentive to all individuals.
- Workers are unlikely to be in complete control of results (especially a company's profitability). The link between effort and reward may be insufficient to act as a meaningful incentive – or may be a cause of frustration to workers, if they put in the effort and are not rewarded to the level of their expectation.
- Drucker (1955) noted that incentives such as pay, once regularly provided, come to be perceived as 'entitlements' and their capacity to create dissatisfaction, to become a deterrent to performance, outstrips their motivational power.
- Even if employees are motivated by money, the effects may not be altogether desirable. An instrumental orientation may encourage self-interested performance at the expense of teamwork. It may encourage attention to output at the expense of quality, or the lowering of standards and targets to make bonuses more easily accessible.

3.5.3 Non-financial rewards and incentives

A range of non-financial rewards and incentives may be offered in addition to monetary incentives. These often include benefits such as: company car, health insurance, above-statutory holiday time; access to facilities (social, sports); a canteen or luncheon vouchers; gift certificates and so on. There has been a trend in recent years towards flexible benefit schemes, allowing employees a choice from a 'menu' of potential benefits: the element of choice increasing the perceived value (valence) of the reward/incentive, and supporting the motivation of an increasingly diverse workforce.

In addition, non-financial motivation approaches (as we have already seen) recognise the motivational value of:

- **Job enrichment**, providing opportunities for job satisfaction
- **Participation and involvement** in goal-setting, values articulation and decision-making
- **Leadership behaviours**, such as: setting clear, challenging and worthwhile goals; giving clear, constructive and where possible immediate performance feedback; and giving praise and recognition
- A **positive corporate culture** which celebrates individual and team achievements.

MARKETING AT WORK

application

Barclays Bank offers its employees a range of charitable benefits. The bank has offered a payroll giving scheme since June 1987, and introduced matching contributions in 2002. In 2009, more than 9,500 employees and pensioners donated through the scheme, provided by Workplace Giving UK.

The bank was also the first employer to run the Pennies from Heaven programme, starting in 2001. Since then, it has raised more than £605,000 from excess pennies.

Barclays also offers a comprehensive range of employee community engagement programmes, called Charity Begins At Work. This involves a global volunteering programme and matched fundraising three times a year. Last year, more than 58,000 Barclays employees in 31 countries used the company's support to become involved in their local communities.

www.employeebenefits.co.uk

For further coverage of motivation and team leadership, if required for your assignment, you might like to look at:

The John Adair Handbook of Management and Leadership, edited by Neil Thomas. Thorogood, Chapters 6 (Leadership and Teambuilding) and 7 (Motivation and People Management) are particularly relevant here

4 Management skills and techniques

4.1 Empowerment

KEY CONCEPT

Empowerment is the current term for initiatives designed to give workers (and particularly work teams) more discretion and responsibility for their work, and for supporting and facilitating them in exercising that responsibility.

Empowerment is regarded as an important support for marketing activity, as a tool of '**internal marketing**': enabling staff to use their discretion, judgement, experience and skills to deliver a better quality of service to customers. There are various levels of empowerment, from the ability to make suggestions (low level of involvement) to the latitude to do whatever is necessary to satisfy the customer in a given set of circumstances (high level of involvement and empowerment).

'Empowerment means that the company must create the right culture and climate for employees to operate in. This includes four empowerment criteria: providing employees with **information** about the organisation's performance; providing **rewards** based on the organisation's performance; providing employees with **knowledge** that enables them to understand and contribute to organisational performance; and giving them **power** to take decisions that influence organisational direction and performance'. (Bowen & Lawler, 1992, cited Peck *et al*, 1999, p322).

The changes in organisation structure and culture as a result of empowerment can be shown in the following diagrams:

Traditional hierarchical structure: fulfilling management requirements

Senior Managers
Middle Managers
Operational Staff
Customers

Authority
Purpose: securing compliance with managerial directives

Empowerment structure: supporting workers in serving the customer

Customers
Operational Staff
Senior Managers

Purpose: to facilitate and support operational staff in adding customer value
Authority

The **argument for empowerment**, in a nutshell, is that by empowering workers (or 'decentralising' control of business units, devolving/delegating responsibility, or removing levels in hierarchies that restrict freedom), not only will the job be done more effectively, but the people who do the job will get more out of it. Advantages claimed for team empowerment include:

Faster and more flexible response to customers' needs (because staff are better informed and more confident)

- Improved employee job satisfaction, motivation and commitment (because empowerment offers a high degree of challenge, interest, responsibility and trust)
- Improved upward communication (from employees to management), which helps keep the organisation sensitive to stakeholder demands and environmental changes
- Improved ability to learn and adapt to change (because employees are more flexible in their attitudes and behaviours, and more confident in their coping skills).

Of course, these benefits must be balanced with the increased costs of training, development, reward and retention of empowered employees (they will still expect to be paid for the extra contribution they are making!) – and the risk of their sometimes getting it wrong. There is also an issue of ensuring service consistency, as individual discretion may lead to wide variations (which may be perceived and resented by some customers).

MARKETING AT WORK

'**Virgin Atlantic** has long recognised the critical role internal marketing plays in its success. One of the secrets of the airline's success has been enthusiastic empowered, motivated employees. Sir Richard Branson has said: 'I want employees in the airline to feel that it is *they* who can make the difference, and influence what passengers get.'

"We want employees who feel involved and prepared to express dissatisfaction when necessary. In fact, we think that the constructively dissatisfied employee is an asset we should encourage and we need an organisation that allows us to do this – and that encourages employees to take responsibility, since I don't believe it is enough for us simply to give it."

Virgin Atlantic's philosophy has been to stimulate the individual, to encourage staff to take initiatives and to empower them to do so.' (Christopher *et al*, 2002, p 111)

4.2 Involvement

The concept of '**employee voice**' embraces 'a whole variety of processes and structures which enable, and sometimes empower employees, directly and indirectly, to contribute to decision-making in the firm' (Boxall & Purcell, 2003). Armstrong (2009) summarises it as 'the say employees have in matters of concern to them in their organisation'. The term has come to embrace a wide range of mechanisms for:

- **Employee involvement:** informing and consulting employees about aspects of decision-making. This is sometimes called 'upward problem-solving': two way communication; the use of staff feedback, suggestion schemes and employee intranet discussion groups; or project teams, which bring staff and management together to solve problems, discuss issues or generate ideas (eg quality circles or customer care task forces).
- **Employee participation:** involving employees (often via their elected representatives) in the decision-making machinery of the organisation. This is sometimes called 'representative participation': collective negotiations and conflict resolution via trade unions, formal consultative meetings with worker representatives, or formal partnership agreements.

Marchington *et al* (2001) argue that paying attention to employee voice offers:

- The ability for individual employees to express dissatisfaction, solve problems within management and preserve working relationships
- The ability for employees collectively to express their needs and wishes in matters that affect them, providing a counterbalance to managerial power
- The ability for employees to contribute to management decisions, allowing the organisation to harness the expertise and commitment of workers to improve quality, productivity and work organisation
- The ability for employers and employees to demonstrate their intention to focus on shared goals, mutual interests and co-operative working relations, for the long-term benefit of the organisation and its people.

4.3 Task allocation and delegation

KEY CONCEPT

Delegation is the process whereby a superior transfers to a subordinate part of his or her own authority to make decisions.

4.3.1 Why delegate?

Delegation has several key benefits for managers – and other stakeholders in the management process.

- There are **physical and mental limitations** to the work load of any individual or group in authority: managers *must* delegate some work in order to get everything done.
- Managers are freed up to concentrate on **higher-level tasks** (such as marketing strategy and environmental scanning).

- The increasing size and complexity of some organisations calls for **specialisation**, both managerial and technical: managers cannot maintain detailed skills in all areas of marketing work.
- Delegated authority contributes to the **job satisfaction and development** of team members. Taking on progressive levels of responsibility supports training, appraisal and management succession planning.
- Delegation **shortens the chain of decision-making** and brings decisions closer to the situations that require them. This is particularly important in fast-changing business environments which require responsiveness to customer demands.

Nevertheless, the first skill of delegation is *willingness* to delegate! Many managers are reluctant to do so, because: they do not trust their team (perhaps because the team genuinely lacks competence to take on a task); they fear that they will be redundant; the organisation culture does not support or reward effective delegation; or simply because they think that 'if you want something done well, you have to do it yourself' (a sure recipe for micro-managing!).

4.3.2 How to delegate effectively

Successful delegation requires that people have the right skills and the authority to do the job, and are given feedback. It also requires a balance of support and trust from the delegator.

The **process of effective delegation** can be outlined as follows.

Step 1 **Specify performance:** the goals and standards expected of the subordinate, keeping in mind his or her level of expertise.

Step 2 **Formally assign tasks** to the subordinate, who should formally agree to do them.

Step 3 **Allocate resources and authority** to the subordinate to enable him or her to carry out the delegated tasks at the expected level of performance.

Step 4 **Back off** and allow the subordinate to perform the delegated tasks without interference or micro-managing.

Step 5 **Maintain contact,** to review progress made, make constructive criticism and be available to give help and advice if requested.

4.3.3 When to delegate

- The decision of *when* to delegate is equally important.
- Is the acceptance of staff affected by a decision required for morale, relationships or ease of implementation of the decision? (If so, it may be worth involving them in the decision.)
- Is the quality of the decision most important? (Many technical and financial decisions may be of this type, and should be retained by the manager if he or she alone has the knowledge and experience to make them.)
- Is the expertise or experience of team members relevant or necessary to the task, and will it enhance the quality of the decision? (if so, it may be worth involving them in the decision.)
- Can trust be placed in the competence and reliability of the team? (If not, it will be difficult to delegate effectively until competence and reliability have been developed.)

5 Interpersonal skills for managers and leaders

KEY CONCEPT

concept

Interpersonal behaviour is behaviour between people. It includes:

- Interaction between people: a two way process such as communication, delegating, negotiating, resolving conflict, persuading, selling, or influencing
- An individual's behaviour in relationship to other people.

Interpersonal skills are, therefore, skills in dealing with other people. It is possible to see them as two 'tiers' of skill: the basic elements of interpersonal skill (first-order skills) and the skills which *apply* them in specific interaction styles and contexts (second-order skills). Such skills are particularly important for team leaders, to support their ability to:

- Understand and manage the roles, relationships, attitudes and perceptions operating in team situations
- Communicate clearly and influence effectively, in order to achieve their aims from a wide range of interpersonal contacts (ideally, allowing other parties to emerge satisfied as well)
- Model constructive interpersonal relationships within the team
- Motivate and build teams: negotiate solutions to problems, manage conflict, conduct interviews, counsel and coach team members, give constructive feedback and so on
- Network effectively within and beyond the organisation, in order to gather information and influence, and mobilise resources, on behalf of the team.

Interpersonal skills

Second order skills

- Persuading/influencing
- Assertiveness
- Negotiation
- Team working
- Leadership
- Managing conflict
- Counselling
- Coaching

First order skills

- Giving and receiving feedback
- Listening and observing
- Questioning
- Communicating clearly
- Understanding and using body language

We will look at some of the key skills mentioned in the syllabus here. Others (such as counselling, coaching and conflict management) will be covered in context, in later chapters.

5.1 Communication

We will not consider communication skills separately, in detail, as all interpersonal skills (listening, assertiveness, negotiation, feedback giving) are communication skills. However, it may be helpful to use a simple communication process model as a framework for analysing 'critical incident' interactions (to diagnose what went wrong), and for determining areas for improvement and learning.

5.1.1 The communication process

Communication can be depicted as a '**radio signal**' model. The sender encodes a message and transmits it to the receiver who decodes it to 'retrieve' the sender's message. This is a two-way cycle, which can be shown as follows.

The communication process

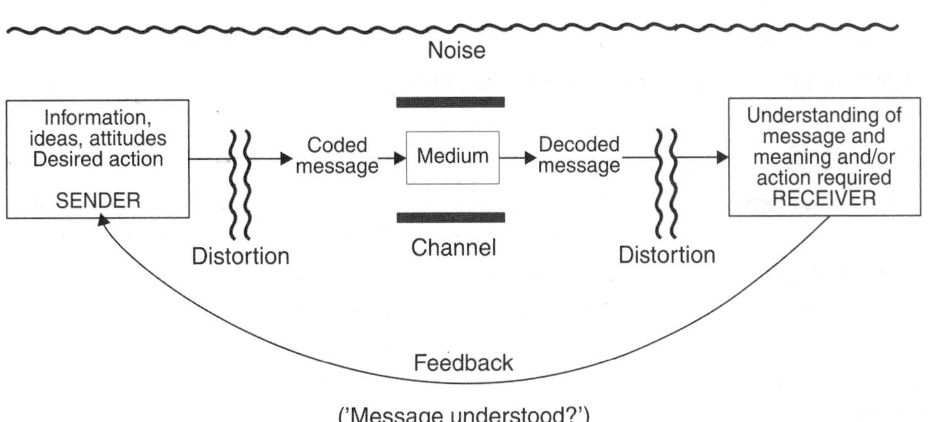

Our diagram raises a number of issues for communication planning and evaluation.

- **Coding and decoding.** The code or 'language' of a message may be verbal (spoken or written) or non-verbal (pictures, diagrams, numbers or body language). The needs and abilities of the target audience must be taken into account: not all codes (eg technical jargon or unlabelled diagrams) will be accessible to others.
- **Media and channels.** The choice of medium (letter, memo, e-mail, report, presentation, telephone call) and channel of delivery (telecom system, notice board, postal system, internet) must be appropriate for the purpose of the communication and its target audience. This may depend on:
  - **Urgency**: the speed of transmission (eg phone or e-mail as opposed to post)
  - **Permanency**: the need for a written record for legal evidence, confirmation of a transaction or future reference
  - **Complexity**: eg the need for graphic illustration to explain concepts
  - **Sensitivity/confidentiality** (eg a private letter)
  - **Ease of dissemination**: wide audience (eg a notice board)
  - **Cost effectiveness** (taking into account all the above)
- **Feedback.** The process by which the sender checks – and recipient signals – that the message has been received and understood. This is a vital skill, as it makes communication a two-way – and much more reliable – process. Feedback may include:
  - Verbal messages ('I'd like to clarify...', 'What does that mean?')
  - Non-verbal cues (eg nodding and making encouraging noises, or looking perplexed)
  - Appropriate action (eg doing as requested by the message)
- **Distortion** is a technical term for processes through which the meaning of a message is lost in the coding or decoding stages. Misunderstandings may arise from technical or ambiguous language, misinterpretation of symbols or tones of voice and so on.
- **Noise** is a technical term for interference in the environment of communication which prevents the message getting through clearly. This may be:
  - Physical noise (eg traffic noise when someone is on a mobile phone)
  - Technical noise (eg a bad Internet connection)
  - Social noise (eg differences in the personalities, status or education of the parties)
  - Psychological noise (eg anger or prejudice distorting what is heard).

5.2 Listening

Listening is about decoding and receiving information and carries much of the burden of communication. Listening is more than just a natural instinct, and listening skills can be taught and developed. **Effective listening** helps:

- Both parties to gather more (and better quality) information
- Reduce the effect of 'noise'
- Resolve problems by encouraging understanding from someone else's viewpoint.

The following are some basic, practical guidelines on being a good listener, to help you evaluate and improve your listening skills.

Guideline	Comment
Be prepared to listen	Put yourself in the right frame of mind (ie a readiness to maintain attention). In meetings, be prepared to grasp the main concepts: familiarise yourself with the agenda.
Maintain interest	Make an effort to analyse the message for its relevance.
Keep an open mind	'Bracket' (put to one side) your own beliefs and prejudices, as they can get in the way of what the other person is actually saying.
Keep an ear open for the main ideas	Learn to distinguish between the 'gist' of the argument and supporting evidence.
Listen critically	Assess what the other person is saying by identifying any assumptions, omissions and biases.
Take notes	Note taking can be distracting at times: give yourself brief reminders – and then re-connect.
Wait before contributing	Don't interrupt (or distract yourself by planning what you will say) while the other person is talking.
Use active listening techniques	'Active listening' means engaging in *dialogue* with the speaker, not just passively soaking up what is said. • Give encouraging feedback (nods, 'uh huh's). • Periodically summarise or 'reflect back' ('You're feeling frustrated by this problem'): a technique which demonstrates empathy and understanding. • Check understanding ('If I've understood you correctly...', 'Are you saying that....?') • Ask questions.

5.3 Non-verbal communication

KEY CONCEPT

concept

Non-verbal communication (often called **body language**) consists of facial expression, posture, proximity, gestures and non-verbal noises (grunts, yawns etc).

We have included non-verbal communication under the heading of listening skills, because – like listening – it involves actively paying attention to the context and process (as well as the content) of communication. Both are used together in face-to-face communication in interviews, discussions, negotiations and team meetings.

Consciously or unconsciously, we send non-verbal messages during every face-to-face encounter. We can use them deliberately to **confirm** our verbal message – for example, by nodding and smiling as we tell someone we are happy to help them – or to **contradict** it, if we want to be ironic or sarcastic (saying 'How interesting!' with a yawn, for example).

More often, however, our body language *contradicts* our verbal message *without* our being aware of it, giving a **'mixed message'** like a team member saying he understands an instruction while looking extremely perplexed. Body language can also **'give away'** messages that we would – for social or business reasons – rather not send, such as lack of interest, hostility or whatever.

Control and use of body language is needed to:

- Provide 'physical' feedback to the sender of a message (eg a nod of understanding)
- Create a desired impression (eg a confident posture)
- Establish a desired atmosphere or conditions (eg a friendly smile)
- Reinforce spoken messages with appropriate indications (eg nodding 'yes').

Reading other people's body language helps a team leader to:

- Receive feedback from listeners and modify his or her message accordingly
- Recognise people's real feelings when their words are constrained by formalities
- Recognise existing or potential personal or interpersonal problems in the team
- 'Read' situations in order to modify his or her communication and response strategy.

5.4 Assertiveness

KEY CONCEPT

concept

Assertiveness may be defined as: 'behaviour based on valuing yourself enough to insist on getting what you want and need by using reasonable and fair means'. (Guirdham, 1996).

Human beings have certain psychological and physical mechanisms which prepare them to 'fight' or 'flee' in response to interpersonal threats or conflicts: by instinct, we fight back (aggression) or give in (passivity). However, we also have a third option: to use rational thinking and language to work our way through a problem in more constructive ways. This is the assertive approach.

According to Back and Back (1999) the differences between assertive, aggressive and passive behaviour can be seen as follows.

	Aggressive behaviour	Passive behaviour	Assertive behaviour
Origins	'Fight' reaction to frustration, conflict or threat	'Flight' reaction to frustration, conflict or threat	'Flow' (rational) response to frustration, conflict or threat
Assumptions	I am more important than others	I am less important than others	I am important, but so are others
Main aim	To 'win' or dominate, if necessary at the expense of others	To please, to be liked and accepted, to avoid conflict	To communicate, maintain relationship and get the needs of *both* parties met
Typical behaviours	• Standing up for your rights in such a way that you violate the rights of others • Ignoring or dismissing the needs, wants, feelings or viewpoints of others • Expressing your own needs, wants and opinions in inappropriate ways	• Failing to stand up for your rights, or doing so in such a way that others can easily disregard them • Expressing your needs, wants, opinions, feelings and beliefs in apologetic, diffident or self-effacing ways • Failing to express honestly your needs, wants, opinions, feelings and beliefs	• Standing up for your own rights in such a way that you do not violate another person's rights • Expressing your needs, wants, opinions, feelings and beliefs in direct, honest and appropriate ways

This is a very important set of distinctions, as being assertive is often misunderstood as being 'aggressive', whereas in fact the two behaviours (and the assumptions underpinning them) are quite different.

5.4.1 Guidelines for assertive behaviour

Assertiveness is a skill that must be learned and practised over time. Some of the key principles of assertive behaviour are as follows.

<table>
<tr><th>Assertive behaviours</th><th>Comment</th></tr>
<tr><td>Respect your feelings, but manage them</td><td><ul><li>If you are angry or anxious, breathe slowly, control your body language and speak calmly.</li><li>Don't use exaggerated language to label your feelings (eg 'angry' when you are only 'mildly annoyed').</li><li>Keep your messages clear: if you've said 'yes' when you wanted to say 'no', don't start giving 'no' signals (eg sulking).</li></ul></td></tr>
<tr><td>Say what you want, feel or think: directly, honestly and without games</td><td><ul><li>Don't assume that others will know, or work out from vague hints, what it is that you really want.</li><li>Don't feel the need to justify or apologise: be simple and direct.</li><li>Don't be pushed into a decision: if you are hesitant about whether to say 'yes' or 'no', say so.</li></ul></td></tr>
<tr><td>Be persistent</td><td>If you don't get a proper response, repeat your statement or request, without raising your voice (the 'broken record' technique). You have the right to be heard – but you must also respect the other person's response.</td></tr>
<tr><td>Focus on the problem, not the person</td><td><ul><li>Use 'I' statements expressing how you perceive and feel about the other person's behaviour, and focus on specifics (not exaggerated generalities). You are focusing on the problem and its impact on you – not attacking the other person.</li><li>It would be aggressive to say: 'You're always so inconsiderate: you make me angry!' It would be assertive to say: 'When you're late, I feel annoyed because it suggests to me that you don't care about my time.'</li></ul>This is particularly important in giving criticism constructively: describe the undesirable behaviour specifically and objectively; specify the change you want; and end on a positive note.</td></tr>
<tr><td>Acknowledge and encourage other points of view</td><td><ul><li>Use 'I' statements to distinguish opinions from facts: 'As I see it...'</li><li>Show that you understand the other person's point of view, by summarising their argument.</li><li>Tackle parts of a view that you specifically disagree with, rather than globally rejecting it: 'I agree that it's a problem, but I don't think it's that damaging'.</li></ul>This is particularly important in receiving criticism constructively. The assertive response is to encourage specific, objective feedback: 'Can you give me an example? How do you think I could do that better?'</td></tr>
<tr><td>Express willingness to look for joint solutions</td><td>Expressions such as 'How can we make this work?' focus attention on shared goals (if only the desire to preserve a co-operative working relationship).</td></tr>
</table>

Assertiveness training is popularly seen as a prime means of remedying underachievement in women, or of helping women to avoid exploitation at work. It is likely to be a part of a 'Women Into Management' or similar training and education programme. The techniques and insights involved are likely to be of benefit to men as well, but it has been recognised that it is primarily women who are disadvantaged in Western society by the failure to distinguish between assertion and aggression, submission and conflict-avoidance.

5.5 Giving feedback

Team leaders have a key role in giving on-going performance feedback to team members, both informally and formally (as part of a performance management approach).

Feedback may be of two broad types:

- **Motivational** feedback (praise, encouragement) is given to acknowledge, reward and encourage positive behaviour or performance by the team member. Its aim is to boost the team member's confidence.
- **Developmental** feedback (constructive criticism, coaching or counselling) is given when an area of the team member's performance requires improvement, helping the individual to identify the problem and plan for change. Its aim is to increase the team member's competence.

5.5.1 Motivational feedback

Praise and recognition should not be underestimated as a reward and incentive: they are highly valued by employees – although they cost the manager nothing to give. Teamworking gurus like Blanchard & Bowles (2001) advocate 'keeping the accent on the positive':

- Looking for (and rewarding) positive behaviours that reflect the purpose and values of the team
- 'Catching people doing things right' (or even 'approximately right') instead of wrong
- Redirecting people towards the goal, when they get things wrong, instead of punishing them
- Linking all recognition ad rewards back to the team's purpose and goals

5.5.2 Developmental feedback

Some guidelines for giving constructive (developmental) feedback are as follows.

Investigate and check your facts before offering criticism: be prepared to coach for improvement

- Choose an appropriate time and place to give feedback; as close as possible after the event being criticised/praised; when the team member will be receptive; and ideally in private, to avoid possible embarrassment
- Clearly explain the positive, development purpose of the feedback
- Start with positives, where possible
- Focus on specific behaviours, actions and results – not generalisations, exaggerations ('you always...') or personality factors: your aim is to facilitate change.
- Gain the team member's cooperation: ask her how effectively she thinks she handled a situation, and invite her to work with you to solve the problem.
- Don't tackle large issues or lots of issues all at once: facilitate 'kaizen' (continuous small-step improvements)
- Close with positive encouragement and support.

5.6 Negotiating

Negotiating is not mentioned in the syllabus, but we thought it worth mentioning here as a key interpersonal skill for leaders. Negotiation gurus Fisher *et al* (1999), among others, have pointed out that:

> 'Negotiation is a fact of life... Everyone negotiates something every day... A person negotiates with his spouse about where to go for dinner and with his child about when the lights go out. Negotiation is a basic means of getting what you want from others. It is a back-and-forth communication designed to reach an agreement when you and the other side have some interests that are shared and others that are opposed.'

Negotiation may be defined as: a process whereby two parties come together to confer, in a situation in which there is some conflict of interests between them, with a view to concluding a jointly acceptable agreement. Gennard & Judge (2003) describe this process as one of:

- **Purposeful persuasion**: whereby each party tries to persuade the other to accept its case or see its viewpoint.
- **Constructive compromise**: whereby both parties accept the need to move closer to each other's position, identifying the areas of common ground where there is room for concessions to be made.

In this broader sense (beyond the context of commercial or sales negotiations), negotiation can be seen as an interpersonal problem-solving technique, enabling managers to meet their objectives (as far as possible) in a conflict of interests with the team or other stakeholders, without damaging on-going relations between them. A team leader may need to negotiate:

- What objectives will be set and given priority (given the potentially differing needs of stakeholders), particularly in the management of strategic change
- Mutually acceptable terms and conditions of work
- Approaches to conflicts and problems that arise in the course of work: differences of values, expectations, interests, priorities or schedules; competition for scarce resources; and so on.

5.7 Influencing

Like negotiation, influencing is not mentioned explicitly in the syllabus, but is a key interpersonal skill for leaders (as we saw in our definitions of leadership in Chapter 4).

KEY CONCEPT

Influencing is the process of applying some form of pressure in order to change other people's attitudes or behaviours: to secure their compliance (with requests), obedience (to orders), conformity (to norms or expectations) or commitment (to a shared vision).

From your own experience (and other marketing studies), you may be aware that there are many forms of pressure that can be used to change people's minds or gain their co-operation: **persuasive arguments** (whether rational or emotional); **compelling goals or ideas** (as when we talk about 'influential' books or movies); the **desire to emulate** a role model; or the **desire to belong** to a group (and therefore to conform to its ideas and behaviours).

Power can also be applied to direct people's behaviour in various ways, because, as we saw in Chapter 4, it implies the right to do so (as in the case of a manager's positional authority), or the ability to offer (or withhold) something that individuals value enough that they are willing to comply.

5.7.1 Ethical influencing

Most modern writers on influencing recognise that influencing skills are 'dangerous', in that they allow people to manipulate or control others: coercing or tricking them into doing something they don't want to do. *Gillen* (1999) distinguishes clearly between what he calls 'manipulative' influencing and 'positive' (or ethical) influencing.

- **Manipulative influencing** uses tactics based on dishonest logic or negative emotion (such as fear or guilt). Such an approach seeks to dismiss or override the influencee's beliefs or interests, using tactics such as bullying, false logic, cajoling, bribing and emotional blackmail.
- **Positive influencing** is defined as 'non-manipulative, persuading behaviours that demonstrate that you are treating people openly, honestly and respectfully' – as befits a leader! A positive influencer seeks to understand the influencee's point of view (through questioning and active listening); allows the influencee to feel heard (through empathy); *then* seeks to help the other person to understand the alternative point of view (through clear, assertive communication); and finally invites or leads the influencee to agree (through rapport-building and persuasion).

Manipulative influencing can be effective in gaining agreement or compliance – in the short term. However, it tends to have negative side-effects such as resentment, unhelpfulness, and lack of ownership of what has been agreed. In contrast, positive influencing 'uses openness and honesty which show respect to the other person, and makes it easy for them to appreciate your point of view. If they accept your invitation to agree with you, their commitment is likely to be sustained into the future'. (Gilles, 1999, p8).

5.7.2 Skills and techniques of leadership influence

Key skills and techniques for influencing include:

- **Rapport-building**: establishing a positive sense of relationship or connection with another person. 'Influencing is easier if the other person feels comfortable with you; if they feel they can trust you; if they feel you understand them' (Gilles, 1999, p 64)
- **Active listening**, to understand the other person's viewpoint and feelings,
- **Using and interpreting body language,** to understand the interpersonal process (rather than merely the content of what is being said)
- **Expressing empathy** with (or understanding of) the other person's viewpoint and feelings
- **Communicating assertively** (as discussed earlier)

Persuasion is the term given to any means of exerting influence over people by means *other* than using authority or power. Persuasion pulls or leads people to change by bringing their beliefs and goals into alignment with those of the leader/influencer.

One key approach to persuasion is **logical argument**, usually supported by relevant and verifiable factual evidence. The demonstration of objectivity or fairness to both sides of an argument or question may also be used to enhance your credibility or 'believability' – since it takes the other party's objections into account. Logical argument is essentially a **facilitative approach**, whereby each step of the argument is clearly explained and linked. 'For someone to be convinced of something, the "penny has to drop" in their mind. That is, it has to make sense to *them*. No matter how obvious something is to you, if you want someone's help, co-operation or agreement, it has to be obvious to them.' (ibid, p 9).

Facilitative techniques include: questions and answers; summarising each section of the argument; asking for feedback (checking understanding); and other forms of **active listening**. Above all, it requires sensitivity and flexibility to respond to signals of resistance, perplexity, readiness to move forward and so on.

A persuasive communication strategy is one which, essentially, appeals to the needs, goals and interests of the person being influenced. Persuasion is a form of motivation: if you can make it look as if aligning themselves with your viewpoint or plans will offer team members something of benefit to them, they will be more amenable to persuasion. This may take the form of positive reinforcement (offering satisfaction of a need or desire, or the solution to a problem) or negative reinforcement (confronting people with the potential negative outcomes of not agreeing or changing).

If you want to focus further on assessing and improving your leadership, interpersonal and influencing skills, we can thoroughly recommend a number of very short, accessible and practical books.

Leadership Skills for Boosting Performance, by Terry Gillen (2002) CIPD: London

Agreed: Improve your powers of influence, by Terry Gillen (1999) CIPD: London

Develop your assertiveness, by Sue Bishop (2nd ed, 2000) Sunday Times/Kogan Page: London

6 Personal development planning

Learning objective 2.5 in the *Managing Marketing* syllabus asks you to 'reflect on your personal approach to team management and produce a personal development plan': a similar requirement to that for Learning objective 2.1 (on approaches to management and leadership, or leadership style).

We have already provided detailed guidance on a systematic approach to **reflection** and **preparing personal development plans** at the end of Chapter 4, and will not repeat that material here: please look back at Chapter 4 if you need to.

We will just note, however, that:

- The 'team management' learning objective presents many more concrete opportunities to evaluate and develop specific managerial, leadership and interpersonal skills. While the nature and effectiveness of your leadership style may prompt reflection and analysis in the light of theoretical models, it is much easier to observe and gather feedback on how well you listen, delegate, communicate and so on.
- There are more manageable opportunities for experiential learning in this area. You can plan to use the experiential learning cycle to incorporate newly-learned techniques of team building, giving feedback, or assertive communication, for example, more easily than you can experiment with changing your leadership style as a whole. There are also many more learning materials and training opportunities in these kinds of skills, should you choose to build them into your development plan.
- The ultimate goal of developing your team management skills is to have an effectively functioning *and* effectively performing marketing team. There may be specific critical incidents or observable issues in team performance and/or in team member satisfaction and team processes – discussed in this chapter – which could act as a stimulus for your self-evaluation.
- This entire section of the syllabus – and chapters 4-8 of this Study Text – come under the heading of 'team management'. Don't segregate your self-evaluation too closely by Learning Objective. You may want to include reflection on your performance in team building, talent management, conflict resolution and change management as well, drawing on material from various areas of the syllabus, as relevant to the assignment and your work context.

Learning objectives	Covered
1 Identify the characteristics of effective team working and high performing teams	☑ Quantitative and qualitative signals of team effectiveness and high performance ☑ Barriers to effective team performance, and how they can be overcome
2 Propose approaches to manage team processes, including team formation and development, team building, decision-making and communication	☑ Stages in team formation: Tuckman's 'forming, storming, norming, performing' model ☑ Team cohesion, team building and conflict management ☑ Team decision-making and the negotiation of solutions ☑ Team communication tools and patterns ☑ Preparing and leading effective team meetings
3 Outline a range of skills and techniques for the management of team working	☑ The nature of management traits, skills and behaviours, and the possibility of change ☑ Skills for management: motivation, empowerment and involvement, delegation and task allocation, and time management ☑ Interpersonal skills for leaders: communication, listening, assertiveness, giving feedback, negotiation and influencing.
4 Propose approaches to improve and maintain the motivation of team members, assessing and applying a range of management theories in this area	☑ Different motivational models ☑ The effect of managerial assumptions on motivational approach (McGregor's Theory X & Theory Y) ☑ Motivational theories: Maslow's hierarchy of needs; McClelland's motivation needs theory; Herzberg's two factor theory; Vroom's expectancy theory ☑ The role of financial and non-financial incentives, and of the team leader, in team motivation
5 Reflect on your own management skills and approach to team management and produce a personal development plan	☑ Recap of personal development planning (from Chapter 4) ☑ Tools for reflecting on your approach to team management

Quick quiz

1 What are the stages of group development in Tuckman's model?

2 What are the features of effective group communication?

3 Match the description with the name:

Name 1 = **Theory Y** / Name 2 = **Theory X**

Description A: ______ is the assumption that the average human being has an inherent dislike of work and will avoid it if (s)he can. People must therefore be coerced, controlled, directed and/or bribed or threatened with punishment in order to get them to expend adequate effort towards the achievement of organisational goals. This is quite acceptable to the worker, who prefers to be directed, wishes to avoid responsibility, has relatively little ambition and wants security above all.

Description B______ is the assumption that the expenditure of physical and mental effort in work is as natural as play or rest. The average human being does not inherently dislike work, which can be a source of satisfaction. People can exercise self-direction and self-control to achieve objectives to which they are committed. The average human being learns, under proper conditions, not only to accept but to seek responsibility. The capacity to exercise a relatively high degree of imagination, ingenuity and creativity in the solution of organisational problems is widespread.

4 According to Maslow's Hierarchy of Needs, when does a 'need' cease to motivate?

5 What are the benefits of paying attention to employees?

Activity debriefs

1 Categorising the behaviour of group members in the situations described results in the following: (a) storming, (b) dorming, (c) performing, (d) forming, (e) norming.

2 (a) Recreation helps the team to build informal relationships: in this case, the chosen activity also reminds them of their tasks, and may make them feel special, as part of the motor racing industry, by giving them a taste of what the end user of their product does.

(b) A team challenge forces the group to consider its strengths and weaknesses, to find its natural leader. This exercise creates an 'us' and 'them' challenge: perceiving the rival team as the enemy heightens the solidarity of the group.

(c) This exercise encourages the group to raise problems and conflicts freely, away from the normal environment of work and also encourages brainstorming and the expression of team members' dreams for what the team can achieve in the future.

3 (a) *Agenda change*: Propose the change to the team, and insist on getting a genuine response. If some members do not want to deal with the item, remind the meeting of the ground rules: consensus is required to put a new item on the agenda. It can be included in the next meeting.

(b) *Leftover items*. The need here is to prevent frustration and loss of focus. You might assign each member an item and ask them to prepare and distribute information before the next meeting. Alternatively, you might keep a legible list of 'other agenda items', so no-one fears they will be forgotten.

(c) *Late attendance*. The meeting should start on time, out of respect for the other team members. When the missing member arrives, this would be a good opportunity to summarise the discussion so far. If people are repeatedly late, however, this may need addressing.

4 Self-actualisation: job challenge, task variety, development opportunities

Esteem needs: merit pay increase, high-status job title, status symbols, recognition from the team leader, weekly/monthly performance awards

Social needs: compatible work group, opportunities for social interaction with workmates, team identity

Safety needs: job security, basic welfare benefits, consistent leadership, maintenance of the status quo (or good management of change).

Basic/physiological needs: basic salary, safe working conditions, stress management.

5 This will be based on your own research.

Quiz answers

1 Forming, storming, norming, performing, dorming and adjourning.

2 Features of **effective group communication**, to be modelled, coached and supported by the leader, include:

- **Open, honest communication** – including the ability to deal with conflicts, issues and criticism openly, directly and fairly (without personal animosity or grudge-holding)
- **Task-relevant information sharing** (no withholding on a 'need to know' or 'knowledge is power' basis)
- **All-member participation** in meetings, discussions and decision-making. Equitable participation does not mean that all members will share *equally*, but that all members can get a fair hearing when they have something to say
- **Absence of artificial status barriers**, so that senior and junior members communicate with ease
- **Positive contributions** (giving/seeking information, suggests and opinions; encouraging and affirming others; being appropriately vulnerable; checking understanding; giving constructive feedback; summarising; explaining and so on) *outweigh* negative contributions (attacking, being defensive, difficulty stating, fault finding, interrupting or overriding others) and so on.

3 **Theory X** is the assumption that the average human being has an inherent dislike of work and will avoid it if (s)he can. People must therefore be coerced, controlled, directed and/nor bribed or threatened with punishment in order to get them to expend adequate effort towards the achievement of organisational goals. This is quite acceptable to the worker, who prefers to be directed, wishes to avoid responsibility, has relatively little ambition and wants security above all.

Theory Y is the assumption that the expenditure of physical and mental effort in work is as natural as play or rest. The average human being does not inherently dislike work, which can be a source of satisfaction. People can exercise self-direction and self-control to achieve objectives to which they are committed. The average human being learns, under proper conditions, not only to accept but to seek responsibility. The capacity to exercise a relatively high degree of imagination, ingenuity and creativity in the solution of organisational problems is widespread.

4 When it has been satisfied.

5 The ability for individual employees to express dissatisfaction, solve problems within management and preserve working relationships

The ability for employees collectively to express their needs and wishes in matters that affect them, providing a counterbalance to managerial power

The ability for employees to contribute to management decisions, allowing the organisation to harness the expertise and commitment of workers to improve quality, productivity and work organisation

The ability for employers and employees to demonstrate their intention to focus on shared goals, mutual interests and co-operative working relations, for the long-term benefit of the organisation and its people

---

References

Adair, J. (1984) The Skills of Leadership, Gower, Aldershot.

Armstrong, M. (2009) A Handbook of Human Resource Management Practice, (11th edition). Kogan Page, London.

Armstrong, M. (2004) How to Be an Even Better Manager, (6th edition), Kogan Page, London.

Blanchard, K. & Bowles, S. (2001) High Five: the magic of working together, Harper Collins Business, London.

Back, K. & Back, K. (1999) Assertiveness at Work, (3rd edition), McGraw Hill, Maidenhead.

Boddy, D. (2005) Management: An Introduction, (3rd edition), FT Prentice Hall, Harlow, Essex.

Boxhall, B.F. & Purcell, J. (2003) Strategy and Human Resource Management, Palgrave Macmillan, Basingstoke.

Christopher, M.G., Payne A.F. & Ballantyne, D. (2002) Relationship Marketing: Creating Stakeholder Value, Butterworth Heinemann, Oxford.

Drucker, P. (1955) The Practice of Management, Heinemann, London.

Fisher, R., Ury, W. & Patton, B. (1999) Getting to Yes: Negotiating an agreement without giving in, (2nd edition), Random House, London.

Gennard, J. & Judge, G. (2003) Employee Relations, (3rd edition), CIPD, London.

Gillen, T. (1999) Agreed: Improve Your Powers of Influence, CIPD, London.

Goldthorp, J.H., Lockwood D.C., Bechofer, F. & Platt, J. (1968) The Affluent Worker: Industrial Attitudes & Behaviour, Cambridge University Press, Cambridge.

Guirdham, M. (1996) Interpersonal Skills at Work, (2nd edition), FT Prentice Hall, Harlow.

Handy, C.B. (1993) Understanding Organisations, (4th edition), Penguin, Harmondsworth.

Herzberg, F.W. (1966) Work and the Nature of Man, Staples, New York.

Huczynski, A. & Buchanan, D. (2001) Organizational Behaviour: An Introductory Text, (4th edition), FT Prentice Hall, Harlow.

Janis, I.L. (1972) Victims of Groupthink, Houghton Mifflin, Boston, MA.

Jobber, D. (2007) Principles and Practice of Marketing, (5th edition), McGraw Hill Education, Maidenhead.

Katzenbach, J.R. & Smith, D.K. (1993) The Wisdom of Teams: creating the high performance organisation, Harvard Business School, Boston.

Kolb, D. (1984) Experiential Learning, Prentice Hall, New York.

Marchington, M., Wilkinson, A., Ackers, P. & Dundon, A (2001) Management Choice and Employee Voice, CIPD, London.

Maslow, A. (1954) Motivation & Personality, Harper & Row, New York.

McGregor, D. (1960) The Human Side of Enterprise, McGraw Hill, New York.

McClelland, D. (1988) Human Motivation, Cambridge University Press, Cambridge.

Peck, H.L., Payne, A., Christopher, M. & Clark, M. (1999) Relationship Marketing: Strategy & Implementation, Butterworth Heinemann, Oxford.

Peters, T.J. & Waterman, R.H. (1982) In Search of Excellence, Harper Collins, New York.

Rackham, N. & Morgan, T. (1977) Behaviour Analysis in Training, McGraw Hill, Maidenhead.

Tuckman, B.W. (1965) *'Developmental sequences in small groups'* in Psychological Bulletin, Vol 63, pp 384-399.

Tuckman, B.W. & Jensen, M.A.C. (1977) *'Stages of small group development revisited'*, in Group & Organisational Studies, Vol 2, No 4, pp 419-427.

Vaill, P. (1989) Managing as a Performing Art, Jossey-Bass, San Francisco.

Vroom, V. (1964) Work & Motivation, Wiley, New York.

Whetten, D. & Cameron, K. (2002) Developing Management Skills, (5th edition), Prentice Hall, New Jersey.

Chapter 7

Managing team performance

Topic list

1 Performance management
2 Individual performance appraisal
3 Training and development
4 Managing poor performance
5 Internal marketing

Introduction

We saw in Chapter 6 that an effective marketing team is one which both functions effectively as a team (maintaining steady and constructive team working) *and* achieves its task objectives and targets. In Chapter 6, we also looked at the manager's role in managing team processes. In this chapter, we now go on to explore a range of issues and techniques in managing team performance and tasks.

We start by giving an overview of the process of performance management within a team, considering what kinds of performance measures can be set, and how performance can be monitored. (This should build on our coverage of performance management at the functional and corporate level, from Chapter 3.) We examine the manager's role in planning the team's work: setting task priorities and objectives that will align the team's performance with marketing and organisational objectives. We look at a range of work targets and how they can be communicated to the team.

In section 2, we focus on the process of individual performance appraisal, as part of an approach to performance management. Since this will ideally be a forum for identifying learning and improvement needs, it leads us, in section 3, to discuss training and development. Training and development may be seen as a proactive approach to maximising human resources, not *just* as a solution to performance shortfalls or improvement needs. (This clearly links back to the topic of talent management, introduced in Chapter 5.)

In section 4, we explore the issue of poor performance and how it can be managed. This can only be an outline, as performance problems will have to be diagnosed and solved in their specific context. However, it should provide you with a framework for analysing your own work context and proposing viable solutions to identified problems.

Finally, we focus on the role of internal marketing, as an important link between people management and external marketing performance.

Syllabus linked learning objectives

By the end of the chapter you will be able to:

	Learning objectives	Syllabus link
1	Plan how the work of the team will be undertaken, establishing priorities, critical activities, objectives and standards which align team performance with marketing and organisational objectives	2.4
2	Explain and implement a process of performance monitoring and measurement within a team, including individual performance appraisal	2.4, 2.8
3	Outline a systematic approach to the training and development of team members to proactively or reactively improve performance	2.3
4	Critically assess team performance, in order to identify poor performance, diagnose reasons for it and make recommendations for how to overcome it	2.8
5	Explain the importance, role and processes of internal marketing in managing marketing performance	2.4, 2.8
6	Plan how the work of the team will be undertaken, establishing priorities, critical activities, objectives and standards which align team performance with marketing and organisational objectives	2.4

1 Performance management

As we saw – at an organisational level – in Chapter 3, performance management is a crucial process of managerial control: defining performance goals and criteria for success, monitoring and measuring performance against those criteria, and planning to adjust or improve performance where required.

At the individual and team level, performance management can be defined as:

'A means of getting better results from the organisation, teams and individuals by understanding and managing performance within an agreed framework of planned goals, standards and competence requirements. It is a process for establishing shared understanding about what is to be achieved, and an approach to managing and developing people in a way that increases the probability that it *will* be achieved in the short and longer term... Performance management is basically concerned with *performance improvement* in order to achieve organisational, team and individual effectiveness.' (Armstrong).

The process of performance management may be outlined as follows.

Step 1 Identify the **contributions and competences** required to carry out the business and functional plans

Step 2 Draw up a **performance agreement**, defining the expectations of the individual or team, covering standards of performance, performance indicators and the skills and competences people need.

Step 3 **Personal development planning**: setting out the development activities necessary for the individual to extend his or her knowledge, skills and competence, or to improve his or her performance in specified areas.

Step 4 **Monitoring and review** of performance against agreed objectives, targets, standards and performance measures, on an on-going basis. This involves a continuous process of providing performance feedback, conducting progress reviews, updating objectives (as milestones are reached) and dealing with any performance problems or shortfalls.

Step 5 **Performance review**: formal evaluation of progress and performance over a given period, with a view to problem solving, improvement and development planning and revising the performance agreement for the following period.

1.1 Marketing strategy and team objectives

One of the key principles of performance management is that it clarifies, translates and cascades **corporate goals** 'down' into divisional, department, team and individual goals. The performance goals of marketing teams, and individual marketers, need to be **integrated** or **aligned** with those of the marketing function and the organisation as a whole.

- **Vertical alignment** is about ensuring that the goal of every activity contributes towards the overall or higher objectives of the business. Corporate plans and objectives should 'cascade down' to the strategic plans of business units and functions, which should in turn influence the objectives set for teams and individuals. Conversely, individuals and teams in marketing should formulate performance goals which *support* the marketing strategy, which in turn should be formulated to support corporate strategic plans. So, for example, an organisation with a vision for innovation may set objectives for new product development. These will flow down to marketing objectives for adding value through market research, relationship development, market penetration, corporate brand positioning and so on.
- **Horizontal alignment** is about ensuring that the plans of every unit in an organisation are co-ordinated or dovetailed, so that they work effectively together. So, for example, marketing plans must be co-ordinated with the requirements of production (operations planning), the availability of resources (eg through HR and financial planning) and so on – just as marketing messages delivered from units across the organisation must be integrated to present a consistent, coherent face to the world.

Taylor argues that the process of mapping unit plans onto each other, and onto corporate strategy, has a range of advantages.

- 'Apart from giving a cohesive view, it helps prevent duplication of effort and resources, encourages everyone to help each other and gives each team a view and feeling of corporate impact – tying everyone's role to the bigger picture. This is hugely motivating for people and teams at every level.'
- 'In addition to improved planning and understanding by all involved in the vision and journey, such contentious issues as ownership, prioritisation and delivery can be more fully explored and explained.'
- 'Adopting this method also leads to improved measurement of your value. It will only be possible to list each and every activity as it is matched to a business justification, rather than being done for its own sake.'

1.2 Establishing priorities, objectives and standards

Prioritisation involves identifying **key results** (objectives which *must* be achieved if the department or section is to fulfil its aims) and **key tasks** (those things that *must* be done on time and to the required standard if the key results are to be achieved). These may be established using various broad approaches.

1.2.1 Role profiling

Role analysis may be carried out to develop a role profile or definition, as a framework for performance management at the individual level. Role analysis defines:

- The **purpose** of the role: what the role holder is expected to do or contribute (in the light of the objectives of the team and department as a whole)
- The **key result areas** or main accountabilities of the role, which define the main output areas for which objectives and performance standards can be agreed
- The **key competencies** of the role: what the role holder has to do in order to perform the role effectively. This may take the form of a separate competence profile, providing the basis for competence assessment and improvement planning.

Armstrong (2009) suggests that information on objectives and priorities can be obtained by asking:

- What do you think are the most important things you do?
- What do you believe you are expected to achieve in each of these areas?
- How will you – or anyone else – know whether or not you have achieved them?

1.2.2 Performance agreements or contracts

Performance agreements may be formulated in collaboration with individuals and teams, to define and agree objectives, standards and expectations of performance. The points to be agreed may cover:

- Objectives, targets and standards of performance to be achieved
- Performance measures and indicators: criteria that will be used to assess how far the objectives, targets and standards have been achieved
- Competence assessment methods (where used): what competences will be required to deliver the expected results, what competence definitions will be used, what evidence of competence will be gathered and so on
- Operational requirements for performance: procedures and standards for health and safety, security (of premises and data) or budgetary control
- Values or principles to be upheld: diversity, ethical codes, and the core values of the organisation (eg quality, customer service, team working and so on).

1.2.3 Individual objectives

Individual objective setting supports not only integration, but motivation and learning. People need to know exactly what their objectives are in order to: plan and direct their effort towards the objectives; monitor their performance against objectives and adjust (or learn) where required; experience the reward of achievement once objectives have been reached; feel that their tasks have meaning and purpose; experience the motivation of a challenge; and avoid the *de*-motivation of vague, unrealistic or unattainable tasks.

Objectives or **goals** describe something that has to be accomplished: a point to aim for. They may be expressed as:

- **Tasks** or projects to be completed (by specified dates and to achieve defined results or deliverables)
- **Targets**: quantified results to be attained – in terms of productivity (output or throughput), sales volume/value, levels of service, cost reduction, learning attainments and so on. Targets may be set for **performance**/output or **improvement** (eg reducing costs or errors).
- **Standing objectives** or **performance standards**: definitions of what competent or 'up to standard' performance consists of. These may be quantified (eg in terms of speed of response or level of output) or qualitative (eg in terms of flexibility, creativity or customer satisfaction). Standing objectives often remain in place unchanged from one review period to the next: that is, they apply more or less continuously (unless the nature or context of the key task changes). One common example is the speed with which telephones are answered, in customer service units.
- **Developmental goals**: how an individual can improve his or her own performance, skills and competence attainment.

Most authors agree that objectives should be 'SMART':

- **Specific:** stated in clear, detailed terms: precisely what the desired outcomes or deliverables are
- **Measurable**: susceptible to monitoring, review and measurement (ideally in quantitative terms) so that you know when or how far progress/success has been attained
- **Attainable**: target outcomes and standards, and the contexts and timescales within which they must be attained, must be realistically achievable, using the capacities, capabilities, readiness and resources available. (We might also add '**Ambitious**': stretching or challenging, in order to motivate development, learning and improvement.)
- **Relevant**: supportive of the strategic objectives of the unit and the business as a whole: leading somewhere meaningful
- **Time-framed**: agreed target timescales and deadlines for completion (or review) must be included in the objective: it is not open ended.

1.2.4 Individual performance measures

The setting of **performance measures** (often called Key Performance Indicators or KPIs) is closely linked with the setting of objectives. Objectives define what is to be achieved: performance measures define how stakeholders will *know* whether or how far it has been achieved, as the basis for performance monitoring and feedback.

The idea of 'SMART' objectives reminds us that performance measures must be results-focused, objective and measurable. However, in order to be motivational, the results must be within the individual's direct control – otherwise they will be measured on something they have no control over, which is very frustrating! As the Balanced Scorecard (which we will look at in more detail in a later chapter) suggests, performance measures may address a wide range of indicators or metrics:

- **Finance:** eg economic value added, cost reductions, rates of return on investment
- **Productivity**: eg number of new accounts, throughput of work
- **Time:** speed of response or task turn-round, achievement of deadlines, lead times for campaign development
- **Response**: internal and external customer satisfaction, enquiry/response/recall rates for marketing campaigns
- **Results**: standard/qualification attainment, changes in internal stakeholder behaviour (eg improved customer focus), changes in external stakeholder behaviour (eg increased sales, order value or customer retention), completion of projects, innovations suggested/adopted
- **Technology leverage**: adoption of new media and technology, transaction costs saved through technology
- **Relationships**: partnership development (eg collaborative promotions); agency relationships; customer retention
- **Ethics and corporate social responsibility:** diversity and equal opportunity; compliance with codes of ethics, law and regulation; stakeholder awareness of CSR initiatives.

ACTIVITY 1

application/evaluation

A senior sales executive has a job which involves: 'building the firm's sales' and maintaining 'a high degree of satisfaction with the company's products and services'. The firm buys sports equipment, running machines and so on, which it sells to gyms and individuals. The firm also charges fees to service the equipment. Service contracts are the sales executive's responsibility, and he has to manage that side of the business.

Here some possible performance indicators to assess the sales executive's performance in the role. What do you think of them? Are they any good?

(a) Number of new customers gained per period

(b) Value of revenue from existing customers per period

(c) Renewal of service contracts

(d) Record of customer complaints about poor quality products

(e) Regular customer satisfaction survey

1.3 Communicating objectives and standards

A wide range of methods is available for communicating performance objectives and standards (standing objectives) to team members. Some will be collaboratively set and agreed and built into individual and team performance agreements. Others may be communicated via:

- The departmental procedures manual, policy documents and notices (or their electronic equivalents on the department intranet)
- Team briefings and periodic performance or project review meetings
- Statements of project deliverables, milestones and targets in project plans and review meetings
- Individual performance appraisals and periodic performance reviews
- Role and competence definitions, used as the basis of performance planning
- Problem-solving meetings such as disciplinary proceedings and employee counselling, at which objectives and standards are re-emphasised as improvement targets
- Training, coaching and mentoring sessions, in which objectives and standards are re-emphasised as learning objectives
- Customer charters and service level agreements (statements of the services and service levels to be delivered to internal and external clients)
- Informal, motivational 'reminders' from the team leader in the course of performance: spoken or emailed re-statement and encouragement, posters in the work space and so on.

1.4 Performance monitoring and measurement

We have stressed that individual performance management is an on-going process of monitoring, measuring and reviewing performance – *not* just a once-a-year formal performance appraisal (which is nevertheless necessary, and is discussed in the following section of this chapter in detail).

Team leaders must take advantage of a range of formal and informal opportunities to monitor, measure and review performance, including:

- **Observation** of individuals at work, both formal (by agreement) and informal (by 'walking around'), giving the leader a chance to observe the processes and approaches of work, not just its results. This may be helpful for complex, creative and relational jobs such as marketing and management, which depend more on *how* things are done than on task outputs.

- **Work sampling**: periodically assessing sample task outputs (eg marketing communications or designs produced, reports, budgets, personal work plans and so on) to check that they are up to standard or specification.
- **Results reporting**: the leader should monitor reports on progress and results, to check that milestones are being met and desired results achieved. Many operational reports are made on an 'exception' basis: that is, only when there is a deviation from the plan or standard, in order to alert the manager to the need for problem solving. However, this represents only negative feedback (requiring corrective action), rather than positive feedback (requiring reinforcing and celebration). Managers should sample a range of reports in order to 'catch people doing something right', as discussed in Chapter 6.
- **Team feedback and review meetings**. Regular team meetings should be used to check in with progress and results, and gather information about potential problems, resource needs and so on. More formal interim reviews may be conducted: say, twice yearly, or at the end of a project stage, or on completion of a 'milestone' in a project or development plan (eg at the end of a training programme).
- **Feedback mechanisms**. Formal feedback on progress and results may be gathered from key stakeholders, for consideration in interim, stage or special reviews: eg internal or external customer satisfaction at the end of a project or project stage; attainment, proficiency or learning assessments obtained from a trainer at the end of a training programme; or feedback provided by a third-party assessor at the close of a certification programme or assessment for an award, say.

  In addition, there should be a continual flow of **informal feedback** which should be monitored: customer complaints or evaluations, commendations, comments from other managers and so on.
- **Discussion with individuals**. The manager may take a coaching or facilitating role in relation to the team, as part of his or her leadership style, and may therefore have the opportunity to sit down with individuals periodically to discuss how they think they are progressing or performing, and what they need to help them perform better.

1.5 Giving feedback

We discussed the giving of feedback in section 5.5 of Chapter 6, as a key interpersonal skill of team management. The important point is that feedback needs to be systematically, positively and periodically given (ideally, immediately following performance, or the results of performance being made clear), in order to have a motivational and developmental effect. Managers should take formal or informal opportunities to:

- Discuss what the individual (or team) has done and achieved
- Recognise and celebrate achievement, improvement and excellence
- Identify (or encourage the individual or team to identify) any shortfalls in achieving objectives or meeting standards, or any performance barriers or problems encountered
- Collaboratively investigate the reasons for shortfalls; agree any changes required to objectives and work plans, in response to changing demands or circumstances; and agree any actions required by the individual or the manager to address problems and improve performance. (We will discuss this further in section 4 of this chapter.)
- Identify (or encourage the individual or team to identify) further learning or improvement opportunities arising form work problems, challenges and successes, to support continuous learning. The experiential learning cycle may be used by a 'coaching' leader to encourage 'on-the-job' learning and development.

2 Individual performance appraisal

We covered appraisals briefly in chapter 3. We will however recap so you are familiar with the concept from a slightly different perspective. The general purpose of any staff appraisal system is to improve the efficiency of the organisation by ensuring that the individuals within it are performing to the best of their ability and developing their potential for improvement and added contribution. Within this overall objective, appraisals have several specific purposes. You should remember from chapter 3 that they are designed with the following in mind:

- To review **performance**: to plan and follow up training and development programmes, to solve performance problems and to set targets for future performance
- To review **potential**: to predict the level and type of work an individual will be capable of in future, and plan learning and development activities to fulfil this potential
- To enhance **motivation** by providing more systematic performance feedback

- To review **rewards**: measuring the extent to which an employee is deserving of performance-related bonuses or pay increases.

You may wonder if formal appraisal systems are necessary to achieve these aims: managers gather performance evaluations, and give feedback, on an on-going basis. However, a formal system ensures that managers make the effort to form a coherent, complete and objective picture of team members' performance (not just random impressions based on their more noticeable successes and failures). It also ensures that managers give adequate feedback, in a positive context of systematic learning, improvement and development planning.

2.1 Overview of the appraisal system

The basic elements of a systematic appraisal system include:

Step 1 **Identification of criteria** for assessment, perhaps based on job analysis, performance standards, person specifications or team KPIs.

Step 2 The preparation by the team leader (and/or stakeholders in the individual's performance) of an **appraisal report**.

Step 3 An **appraisal interview**, for discussion of the appraisal report, targets for improvement, solutions to problems and so on.

Step 4 **Review of the assessment** by the assessor's own superior, so that the appraisee does not feel subject to one person's prejudices. Formal appeals may be allowed, if necessary to establish the fairness of the procedure.

Step 5 The preparation and implementation of **action plans** to achieve improvements and changes agreed.

Step 6 **Follow-up:** monitoring the progress of the action plan.

There may not need to be standard forms for appraisal (and elaborate form-filling procedures should be avoided) as long as managers understand the nature and extent of what is required, and are motivated to take it seriously. Most systems, however, provide for assessments to be recorded, and report forms may be designed for standard use: an example is shown on the next page.

2.2 The assessment report

Assessments must be related to a common standard, in order to compare the performance of different team members, and the performance of individuals over time. They should also be related to meaningful performance-related criteria, taking account of the critical variables of each job.

A range of appraisal techniques may be used, however.

- **Guided assessment**. Assessors are required to comment, in narrative form, on a number of specified characteristics and performance elements, with guidelines as to how terms such as 'application', 'integrity' and 'adaptability' are to be interpreted in the work context. There will be no guaranteed consistency of the criteria and areas of assessment, however, and managers may not be able to convey clear, effective judgements in writing.

- **Grading** adds a comparative frame of reference to the general guidelines, whereby managers are asked to select one of a number of levels or degrees to which the individual in question displays the given characteristic. These are also known as **rating scales**. Numerical values may be added to ratings to give rating scores. Alternatively a less precise **graphic scale** may be used to indicate general position on a plus/minus scale.

  Factor: job knowledge

  High ____✓____ Average __________ Low

- **Behavioural incident methods** concentrate on employee behaviour, which is measured against typical behaviour in each job, as defined by common critical incidents of successful and unsuccessful job behaviour reported by managers.

- **Results-orientated schemes** review performance against specific objectives targets or KPIs and standards of performance agreed in advance by manager and subordinate together.

<table>
<tr><th colspan="7">APPRAISAL REPORT</th></tr>
<tr><td colspan="6">Name:
Position:
Company:</td><td>Time in position:
Period of review:</td></tr>
<tr><td>Overall assessment</td><td>A</td><td>B</td><td>C</td><td>D</td><td>E</td><td>Comment</td></tr>
<tr><td>Job knowledge
Effective output
Co-operation
Initiative
Time-keeping
Other relevant facts (specify)</td><td></td><td></td><td></td><td></td><td></td><td></td></tr>
<tr><td colspan="7">A = Outstanding   B = Above standard   C = To required standard
D = Short of standard in some respects   E = Not up to required standard</td></tr>
<tr><td>Potential</td><td>A</td><td>B</td><td>C</td><td>D</td><td>E</td><td>Comment</td></tr>
<tr><td></td><td></td><td></td><td></td><td></td><td></td><td></td></tr>
<tr><td colspan="7">A = Overdue for promotion   B = Ready for promotion   C = Potential for promotion
D = No evidence of promotion potential at present</td></tr>
<tr><td colspan="7">Training, if any, required:</td></tr>
<tr><td colspan="7"></td></tr>
<tr><td colspan="7"></td></tr>
<tr><td colspan="7"></td></tr>
<tr><td>Assessment discussed with employee?</td><td colspan="5">Yes</td><td>No</td></tr>
<tr><td>Signed</td><td colspan="6">Date</td></tr>
<tr><td>Confirmed</td><td colspan="6">Date</td></tr>
</table>

2.3 Multi-source feedback

An individual's immediate manager may not be the only or best person to give feedback on his or her performance. In recent years, other stakeholders have been involved in appraisal reporting.

2.3.1 Self appraisal

Individuals may carry out their own self-evaluation as a major input into the appraisal process. There are a number of advantages to such an approach: saving managerial time; utilising the individual's insights into his/her own performance issues; and engaging the individual in the process, with greater likelihood of commitment to improvement targets. On the other hand, people are not always the best judges of their own performance, and may deliberately over- (or under-)estimate their performance in order to gain approval or reward (or to conform to team norms).

Many schemes, however, combine self-appraisal with other sources of feedback.

2.3.2 Peer appraisal or rating

An individual may be assessed by workmates or colleagues. This also has advantages: getting feedback from team members who have experienced and observed the individual in action; removing a direct link to reward/promotion planning, and thus removing a potential cause of negative attitudes to the process; and solving performance problems within the context of the work team.

However, peer appraisal requires sensitivity and skill if it is not to cause interpersonal hostility and team conflict - or avoid development feedback altogether, in favour of maintaining working relationships and solidarity. It is often reserved for professionally qualified staff.

2.3.3 Customer appraisal

In some companies, the appraisal process includes feedback from customers, both internal and external. At Rank-Xerox, for example, 30% of a manager's annual bonus is conditional upon satisfactory levels of customer feedback. Customers may be the best judges of the service level and added value provided by team members.

2.3.4 Upward appraisal

- A notable modern trend, adopted in the UK by companies such as BP and British Airways, is upward appraisal, whereby managers are rated by their team members: the followers appraise the leader. This has a number of advantages.
- Subordinates tend to know their superior (particularly in the area of leadership skills) better than anyone.
- As multiple subordinates rate each manager, ratings may be more reliable: instead of the potential bias of a single rating, multiple ratings offer a representative view.
- Subordinates' ratings may have more impact because it is more unusual to receive upward feedback from subordinates.

A major problem with upward feedback is fear of reprisals and vindictiveness: ratings may be made anonymously, but then there is little accountability for their accuracy and truthfulness.

Some bosses in strong positions might refuse to act, even if a consensus of staff suggested that they should change their ways.

2.3.5 360-degree appraisal

Taking downwards, upwards and customer appraisals together, some firms have instituted 360 degree appraisal (or **multi-source feedback**) by collecting feedback on an individual's performance from: her immediate boss; people or groups of people who report to her; peers or co-workers; customers (internal and external) and the individual herself.

Advantages of such an approach include:

- A more rounded picture of performance, within the overall context of the job and its stakeholders
- More relevant to team work and marketing cultures, where there may not be tightly drawn job descriptions
- Multiple ratings, offsetting the subjectivity and bias of any one viewpoint
- Increase in task- and results-related communication in the organisation
- Taking into account the views of best-placed stakeholders: subordinates (eg on leadership skills) and customers (eg on customer service)
- Indicating the seriousness with which appraisal is regarded in the organisation.

Potential disadvantages include:

- The risk that peer appraisal may cause suspicion and hostility, or that upward appraisal will be resisted
- The difficulty of standardising criteria for all feedback sources
- The extra organisation and paperwork required
- The need to educate stakeholders on the purpose of the process, so that it remains development and improvement focused

- The likelihood that not all stakeholders' feedback will result in improvement action, which may disillusion them about the process.

2.4 The appraisal interview

Maier (1966) identifies three types of approach to appraisal interviews.

- The **tell and sell style**. The manager tells the team member how (s)he has been assessed, and then tries to 'sell' (gain acceptance of) the evaluation and the improvement plan. This requires unusual human relations skills in order to convey constructive criticism in an acceptable manner, and to motivate the team member to alter his or her behaviour.
- The **tell and listen style**. The manager tells the team member how (s)he has been assessed, and then invites a response. The manager therefore no longer dominates the interview throughout, and there is greater opportunity for coaching or counselling as opposed to pure direction.
  - The team member is encouraged to participate in the assessment and the working out of improvement targets and methods: it is an accepted tenet of behavioural theory that participation in problem definition and goal setting increases the individual's commitment to behaviour and attitude modification.
  - This method does not assume that a change in the team member will be the sole key to improvement: the manager may receive helpful feedback about how job design, methods, environment or supervision might be improved.
- The **problem-solving style**. The manager abandons the role of critic altogether, and becomes a coach and helper. The discussion is centred not on the assessment, but on the employee's work problems, issues and potential for improvement. The team member is encouraged to think solutions through, and to commit to the recognised need for personal improvement. This approach encourages intrinsic motivation through the element of self-direction, and the perception of the job itself as a problem-solving activity. It may also stimulate creative thinking on the part of team member and manager alike, to the benefit of the organisation's adaptability and methods.

Not unsurprisingly, perhaps, studies showed that most appraisees prefer the more forward-looking, participative and constructive 'problem-solving' style.

Many organisations waste the opportunities for **upward communication** embedded in the appraisal process. In order to get a positive contribution from employees, the appraisal interviewer should ask positive and thought-provoking questions such as:

- What parts of your job do you do best?
- What could we (management, the organisation) do to help you to perform better and contribute more?
- Have you any skills, knowledge or aptitudes which could be made better use of in the organisation?

2.5 Follow up

After the appraisal interview, the manager may complete the report, with an overall assessment, assessment of potential and/or the jointly-reached conclusion of the interview, with recommendations for follow-up action. The manager should then discuss the report with the counter-signing manager (usually his or her own superior), resolving any problems that have arisen in making the appraisal or report, and agreeing on action to be taken. The report form may then go to the development adviser, training officer or other relevant.

Follow-up procedures may include:

- **Carrying out agreed actions** on training, promotion and so on
- Taking necessary steps to **help the team member to attain improvement targets**, by guidance, feedback, upgrading equipment, altering work methods and so on.
- **Monitoring the team member's progress** and checking that (s)he has carried out agreed actions or improvements.

2.6 Problems with appraisal

Lockett (1992) identifies a number of barriers to effective appraisal, depending on how it is perceived by stakeholders in the process.

Appraisal barriers	Comment
Appraisal as confrontation	Many people dread appraisals, or use them 'as a sort of show down, a good sorting out or a clearing of the air'. In this kind of climate: • There is likely to be a lack of agreement on performance levels and improvement needs. • The feedback may be subjective or exaggerated. • The feedback may be negatively delivered. • The appraisal may focus on negative aspects, rather than looking forward to potential for improvement and development.
Appraisal as judgement	The appraisal 'is seen as a one-sided process in which the manager acts as judge, jury and counsel for the prosecution'. This puts the subordinate on the defensive. Instead, the process of performance management 'needs to be jointly operated in order to retain the commitment and develop the self-awareness of the individual.'
Appraisal as chat	The appraisal is conducted as if it were a friendly chat 'without ... purpose or outcome ... Many managers, embarrassed by the need to give feedback and set stretching targets, reduce the appraisal to a few mumbled "well dones!" and leave the interview with a briefcase of unresolved issues.'
Appraisal as bureaucracy	Appraisal is a form-filling exercise, to satisfy the HR department. Its underlying purpose, improving individual and organisational performance, is forgotten – and the process is simply regarded as a 'nuisance' by all concerned.
Appraisal as unfinished business	Appraisal should be part of a continuing future-focused process of performance management, not a way of 'wrapping up' the past year's performance issues.
Appraisal as annual event	Many targets set at annual appraisal meetings become irrelevant or out-of-date. Feedback, goal adjustment and improvement planning should be a continuous process.

Another problem is the extent to which the appraisal system is related to the **pay and reward system**. Many employees consider that positive appraisals should be rewarded, but there are major drawbacks to this approach.

- **Funds available** for pay rises rarely depend on one individual's performance alone – the whole company has to do well.
- **Continuous improvement** should perhaps be expected of employees as part of their work and development, not rewarded as extra.
- Performance management is about a lot more than pay for *past* performance – it is often **forward looking** with regard to future performance.

2.7 Evaluating the appraisal scheme

The appraisal scheme should itself be evaluated (and regularly re-assessed) according to the following general criteria.

Criteria	Comment
Relevance	• Does the system have a useful purpose, relevant to the needs of the organisation and the individual? • Is the purpose clearly expressed and widely understood by all concerned, both appraisers and appraisees? • Are the appraisal criteria relevant to the purposes of the system?
Fairness	• Is there reasonable standardisation of criteria and objectivity throughout the organisation? • Is it reasonably objective?
Serious intent	• Are the managers concerned committed to the system – or is it just something the personnel department thrusts upon them? • Who does the interviewing, and are they properly trained in interviewing and assessment techniques? • Is reasonable time and attention given to the interviews – or is it a question of 'getting them over with'? • Is there a genuine demonstrable link between performance and reward or opportunity for development?

Criteria	Comment
Co-operation	• Is the appraisal a participative, problem-solving activity – or a tool of management control? • Is the appraisee given time and encouragement to prepare for the appraisal, so that he can make a constructive contribution? • Does a jointly-agreed, concrete conclusion emerge from the process? • Are appraisals held regularly?
Efficiency	• Does the system seem overly time-consuming compared to the value of its outcome? • Is it difficult and costly to administer?

Evaluating the appraisal scheme may involve:

- Asking appraisers and appraisees how they **felt** about the system (addressing issues of perceived usefulness, fairness and so on)
- Checking to see if there have been enhancements in **performance** by the individual and the organisation (as a result of problem solving and improvement planning)
- Reviewing other **indicative** factors, such as staff turnover or disciplinary problems; take up (or lack of take up) of training opportunities; lack of management succession etc.

3 Training and development

KEY CONCEPT

Training is 'the planned and systematic modification of behaviour through learning events, programmes and instruction which enable individuals to achieve the level of knowledge, skills and competence to carry out their work effectively'.

(Armstrong, 2009)

Development is a wider process involving the growth or realisation of a person's ability and potential through the provision of learning experiences.

ASSIGNMENT TIP

There is a lot of detail in the study of performance and appraisal systems but a good way to approach it is to put such systems in context and really think about what they are trying to achieve. The overall purpose of employee development is to ensure the firm has the capabilities to meet its current and future performance objectives by:

- Continuous improvement of the performance of individuals and teams, and...
- Maximising people's potential for growth, contribution and promotion.

3.1 The business case for training and development activity

Modern business is increasingly dynamic, with changes in technology, products and processes. An organisation's competitiveness depends increasingly on the proactive and continuous assessment of employees' learning needs, and the provision of planned training interventions to meet those needs – and to develop learning, flexibility and 'talent'.

Training offers some significant benefits for an organisation:

- **Reduced costs** of obtaining the skills the organisation needs (compared to external recruitment or outsourcing)
- Increased **productivity and quality**
- **Less need for close managerial supervision**: reducing supervisory costs; freeing up managers to concentrate on higher roles; and supporting employee empowerment, job enrichment, employee motivation and job satisfaction
- **Greater organisational flexibility** and competitive responsiveness: eg arising from multi-skilling and 'learning to learn'

- **Employer branding and employee retention**: opportunities for development attract quality recruits, support an internal job market (through transfers and promotions) and offer job satisfaction, contributing to employee loyalty. Training may satisfy employees' self-actualisation needs, without the need to change employers for task variety and challenge – and without requiring upward career mobility (where there are few opportunities for promotion).
- **Succession planning**: the organisation identifies and develops managerial and technical talent to meet its future needs and maintain continuity when talented individual leave
- **Change management**: training helps organisations manage change by giving people coping and adjustment skills, and increasing flexibility and willingness to learn
- **Corporate culture**: training programmes can be used to build the corporate culture or direct it in certain ways

Training can contribute to success, but has its limitations.

- It must be the correct intervention for the need: it cannot solve problems caused by poor management, inefficient work organisation or job design, or faulty equipment
- Reasons for neglecting or resisting training must be overcome: these include cost, inconvenience, apathy and disappointed expectations of training in the past.
- Limitations imposed by the intelligence, motivation and learning preferences of trainees must be understood.

3.2 A systematic approach to training

In order to ensure that training meets the real needs of the organisation, best-practice firms adopt a systematic approach.

Step 1 Identify and define (from the HR plan, marketing plan or team performance appraisal) **learning or training needs**. Check that it is a training need: recruitment may be a better solution to skill gaps, for example, or other changes may be a better solution to performance shortfalls.

Step 2 **Define the learning required** – in other words, specify the knowledge, skills or competences that have to be acquired. (For technical training, this is not difficult: for example, all advertising staff will have to become conversant with the buying of new electronic media.)

Step 3 **Define training objectives** – what must be learnt and what trainees must be able to do after the training exercise.

Step 4 **Plan training programmes.** Training and development can be structured and implemented in a number of ways, as we shall discuss a bit later. This covers:

- Who provides the training
- Where the training takes place
- Division of responsibilities between trainers, managers and the individual
- What training approaches, techniques, styles and technologies are used.

Step 5 **Implement the training programme**

Step 6 **Monitor, review and evaluate** training. Has it been successful in achieving the learning objectives? (And if not, go back to Step 1 in a continuous cycle...)

3.3 Training needs analysis

Some training requirements within a marketing team will be obvious and 'automatic'. If a piece of legislation is enacted which affects marketing operations (eg new privacy or permission marketing regulations), training in its provisions will be required. The introduction of new technology (including new marketing media such as 3G mobile phones and hyper-tags) and systems (eg Customer Relationship Management software) similarly implies the need to train marketers in its potential and use.

Other training requirements may emerge from **critical incident analysis**: the analysis of incidents which highlight a potential problem in a key results area. This is usually done in problem-solving meetings with the staff concerned: why did the incident occur and what needs to be done about it? An organisation may, for example, lose a key customer – and the circumstances might be analysed to highlight a need for customer care, key account management or relationship marketing training.

Some form of systematic **training needs analysis** may also be undertaken, at an individual, team or functional level.

3.3.1 Self-assessment by team members

This may be highly informal (eg a list of in-house or sponsored courses is posted on the department intranet page, and interested employees are invited to apply) or more systematic (employees complete surveys on training needs). An example of a self-administered needs survey for managerial staff (suggested by Kramer et al, 1997) is shown on the next page.

3.3.2 Performance appraisal

Performance appraisal, as described in section 2 of this chapter, should be used as an opportunity to identify the learning and training needs raised by performance shortfalls and improvement plans.

3.3.3 Formal training needs analysis

A training need may be identified as: 'required level of competence/achievement *minus* present level of competence/achievement'.

The **required level of competence** may be determined by methods such as:

- Job analysis (identifying the task elements of the job)
- Competence analysis or existing competence frameworks (describing competent performance in a job)
- Role analysis (identifying the contribution made by competent performance in a job)
- Using existing records of job requirements such as job descriptions and KPIs.

The **present level of competence** may be determined by:

- Sampling work outputs
- Formal testing of skills, knowledge, performance or attitudes: eg using proficiency or competence tests, interviews or surveys
- Performance appraisal reports
- A comprehensive human resources audit or skills audit (at the functional level).

Self assessment of training needs

Please indicate in the blanks the extent to which you have a training need in each specific area. Use the following scale

Scale

1 ____________ 2 ____________ 3 ____________ 4 ____________ 5 ____________

(To no extent) (To a very large extent)

To what extent do you need training in the following areas?

Basic management skills (organising, planning, delegating, problem-solving)

________ A Setting goals and objectives

________ B Developing realistic time schedules to meet work requirements

________ C Identifying and weighing alternative solutions

________ D Organising work activities

Interpersonal skills

________ A Resolving interpersonal conflicts

________ B Creating a development plan for employees

________ C Identifying and understanding individual employee needs

________ D Conducting performance appraisal reviews

________ E Conducting a disciplinary interview

Administrative skills

________ A Maintaining equipment, tools and safety controls

________ B Understanding local agreements and shop rules

________ C Preparing work flowcharts

________ D Developing departmental budgets

Quality control

________ A Analysing and interpreting statistical data

________ B Constructing and analysing charts, tables and graphs

________ C Using statistical software on the computer

MARKETING AT WORK

application

People Management reported that a number of *Whitbread* pubs had improved performance as a result of a change in the company's training scheme. Previously the company's training had addressed the service delivery standards of individuals, and there were also discussions with staff on business developments. It was felt, however, that competitors had overtaken Whitbread in these respects. Whitbread therefore introduced an integrated approach to assessment of the performance of pubs.

Assessment is by four criteria; training (a certain percentage of staff have to have achieved a training award), standards (suggested by working parties of staff); team meetings; and customer satisfaction. Managers are trained in training skills so that they can train staff, using a set of structured notes to ensure a consistent training process.

Pubs that fulfill all the criteria win a team hospitality award, consisting of a plaque, a visit from a senior executive, and a party or points-for-goods scheme. To retain the award and achieve further points, pubs have to pass on-going assessments which take place every six months.

The scheme seemed to improve standards. Significantly staff turnover was down and an employee attitude survey suggested that morale had improved, with a greater sense of belonging – particularly by part-time staff.

3.3.4 Individual and team training plans

Once learning needs have been identified, individual and team training plans can be drawn up, setting out:

- **The objectives or outcomes of training**. These should be SMART objectives. Effective learning objectives are precise written statements of what the learner will be able to do as the result of the training: respond to questions or explain concepts; demonstrate the ability to perform a certain task; solve a certain kind of problem and so on. The important point is that you can only assess knowledge, understanding and skill through observable performance.
- **The timescale and schedule for training**, and for periodic review, where required
- **The allocation of responsibilities for training**. These may be shared between:
  - The trainee, especially for self-managed learning
  - The trainee's immediate manager, who may need to authorise training time and resources and monitor results, or who may act as a coach or mentor in the training process
  - The trainee's colleagues, who may act as instructors, coaches or mentors
  - An HR or Employee Development manager, who may be appointed to plan, arrange or deliver training
  - External training providers who may be involved in delivering training.
- **Methods and approaches to be used in training, and resources required**. These may be on-the-job or off-the-job. A wide range of methods is available, and we will some of the main options below.
- **Methods of monitoring and reviewing progress and achievement**: performance appraisal, post-training testing and so on.

3.4 Training methods and media

3.4.1 Off-the-job training methods

Off the job training is formal training conducted outside the context of the job itself in special training rooms or off-site facilities.

- **Courses** may be run by the organisation's training department or may be provided by external suppliers.
- **Computer-based training** involves interactive training via PC. The learn-to-type programme *Mavis Beacon* is a good example.
- **Visits, site tours or secondments** to other organisations may be used to give trainees opportunities to observe other operations and methods.
- **E-learning** is computer-based learning through a network of computers or the Internet (rather than stand-alone CD-Rom or software). Learning support is available from online tutors, moderators and discussion groups. This is a major element of the UK government's Lifelong Learning initiative, through the University for Industry (UfI) and 'learndirect'.
- **Techniques** used for off-the-job training might include lectures and seminars (theory and information) or role plays, case studies and in-tray exercises (to simulate work activities and develop interpersonal skills and problem-solving).
- **Outdoor training** is sometimes used in team-building and leadership training. It involves physical tasks and activities in challenging environments, designed to help trainees learn about themselves and their motivation, leadership skills, group dynamics, co-operation, problem-solving and so on.

The advantages and disadvantages of off-the-job training may be summarised as follows.

Advantages	Disadvantages
Allows exploration/experimentation without the risk of consequences for actual performance	May not be directly relevant or transferable to the job content or context
Allows focus on learning, away from distractions and pressures of work	Immediate, relevant feedback may not be available (eg if assessed by exam)
Suits a variety of learning styles (depending on the method used)	Tends to be more theoretical: does not suit 'hands on' learning styles
May confer status, implying promotability	May be perceived as a waste of working time
Allows standardisation of training	May represent a threat, implying inadequacy

3.4.2 On-the-job training methods

On the job training utilises real work tasks as learning experiences. Methods of on the job training include the following.

- **Demonstration and instruction:** show and tell trainees how to perform the task. The trainee can then attempt to imitate the instructor, with guidance and supervision if necessary.
- **'Sitting with Nellie'**: the trainee sits with a more experienced or skilled colleague ('Nellie') as (s)he performs the task, learning by observing and imitating, with supervision and guidance.
- **Coaching**: a developmental relationship, in which trainees are put under the guidance of an experienced colleague (or perhaps the team leader) who collaboratively helps them to identify their learning needs and set learning targets; plans learning activities; demonstrates and instructs; and gives advice, encouragement and feedback on progress.

  This has become a fashionable aspect of leadership style: many managers take a coaching role in performance improvement.
- **Mentoring:** a longer-term developmental relationship, in which a more experienced person occupies a role as coach/teacher, counsellor, role model, supporter and encourager, in order to foster the individual's personal and career development. Mentoring differs from coaching in two main ways: the mentor is not usually the protégé's immediate manager, and mentoring covers a much wider range of learning and development (not necessarily related to immediate job performance).
- **Switching or shadowing roles:** job rotation (giving the trainee different jobs in succession); temporary promotion or 'assistant to' positions (allowing the trainee to experience or observe more demand roles); project/committee work or assignments.
- **Action learning:** 'Working in small groups, people tackle important organisational issues or problems and learn from their attempts to change things' (Pedler *et al*, 2004). An advisor facilitates, and helps members of the group to identify how their interpersonal and problem-solving skills are effecting the process. This is most often used in management training.
- **Self-development approaches**. As we saw in Chapter 4, any individual can use the experiential learning cycle to turn everyday work events into learning opportunities, through personal development plans (or learning contracts), personal development journals (or learning logs) and self-development groups (which meet to discuss personal development and work issues, give each other feedback etc.).

The advantages and disadvantages of on-the-job training may be summarised as follows.

Advantages	Disadvantages
Takes account of job context: high relevance and transfer of learning	Undesirable aspects of job context (group norms, corner-cutting) also learned
Suits 'hands on' learning styles: offers 'learning by doing'	Doesn't suit 'hands off', theoretical or reflective learning styles
No adjustment barriers (eg anti-climax after training) to application of learning on the job	Trial and error may be threatening (if the organisation has low tolerance of error!)
Develops working relationships as well as skills	Risks of throwing people in at the deep end with real consequences of mistakes
	Distractions and pressures of the workplace may hamper learning focus

3.5 Development

The terms 'training' and 'development' are often used together (or interchangeably) but it may be helpful to distinguish between them. **Training** is, as we have seen, a planned process of using learning experience to achieve effective performance in particular work activities or roles. **Development** is the wider process of growth in people's knowledge and capabilities, and the increasing fulfilment of their potential.

- Development is often linked to systems where (in addition to education and training):
- People gain **experience** of different roles and activities within an organisation, offering opportunities to develop and enhance competence through on-going performance management.

- People are offered increasing **opportunities and challenges**, through upwards or sideways movements in the organisation structure (**career development**). The trend for delayered organisations has reduced opportunities for upward progression: opportunities may be planned for sideways/lateral transfers, secondments to project groups, short external secondments and so on, to offer new opportunities.
- People are encouraged to seek and manage opportunities for their own **self-development**, not necessarily in areas related to the current job, perhaps with the help of mentors (**personal development**). Businesses are increasingly offering employees wider-ranging development opportunities, rather than focusing on skills required in the current job. Personal development creates more rounded, competent employees, who may contribute more innovatively and flexibly to the organisation's future needs. It may also help to foster employee job satisfaction, commitment and loyalty.
- People are encouraged to enhance their **employability**: gathering, maintaining and progressively developing a portfolio of skills that makes them valuable in the wider job market, not just within their current employing organisation (**professional development**). Professional bodies often offer structured programmes of continuing professional development (CPD): the aim is to ensure that professional standards are maintained and enhanced through education, development and training self-managed by the individual. Employability training also represents a recognition that organisations can no longer offer secure (let alone lifetime) employment: despite the need for employee retention, it is realistic and socially responsible to enhance employees' value in the job market.

3.6 Evaluating training programmes and interventions

Validation of training means measuring whether the **training objectives** have been achieved: in other words, 'was training **successful**?'

Evaluation of training means comparing the **costs** of the scheme against the assessed **benefits** which are being obtained: in other words, 'was training **worthwhile**?'

The effectiveness and benefits of a training scheme may be measured at different levels.

Step 1 **Trainees' reactions to the experience**. These are usually measured by post-training feedback forms ('Happy Sheets'), asking whether trainees enjoyed the course, found it relevant etc. This form of monitoring is rather inexact, and it does not allow the training department to measure the results for comparison against the training objective.

Step 2 **Trainee learning** (new skills and knowledge)**:** measuring what the trainees have learned on the course, usually by means of a test at the end of it.

Step 3 **Changes in job behaviour following training**: observing work practices and outputs (products, services, documents) to identify post-training differences. This is possible where the purpose of the course was to learn a particular skill, for example. It measures not just what trainees have learned, but how far they have been able to apply their learning to the job.

Step 4 **Impact of training on organisational goals/results:** seeing whether the training scheme has contributed to the overall objectives of the organisation, in terms of quality, productivity, profitability, employee retention and so on. This is a form of monitoring reserved for senior management, and would perhaps be discussed at board level. It is likely to be the main component of a cost-benefit analysis.

Step 5 **Ultimate value**: the impact of training on the wider 'good' of the organisation in terms of stakeholder benefits, greater social responsibility, corporate growth/survival and so on.

As Armstrong (2009) notes: 'Training produces reactions, which lead to learning, which leads to changes in job behaviour, which lead to results at unit and organisational level. Trainees can *react* favourably to a course... but *learn* little or nothing. They might *learn* something, but be unable or unwilling to *apply* it. They might *apply* it, but it does no *good* within their own areas, or it does some good in their *function*, but does not improve *organisational* effectiveness.'

Evaluating all the way to Level 5 may not be practicable or cost-effective for all training interventions. Many organisations only evaluate at the easiest and least costly Level 1. For trainers, Levels 1-3 represent sufficient feedback for designing or improving training events: obtaining information at higher levels may appear both more costly and less valuable. However, evaluation all the way to Level 4 may be necessary the corporate or functional level to justify training's contribution – particularly in times of recession.

4 Managing poor performance

4.1 A process for managing performance problems

Five basic steps are required to handle performance problems (Armstrong, 2009):

Step 1 **Identify and agree the problem**.

Performance feedback should be analysed, and where possible, the individual should agree on the nature and extent of the shortfall: this is facilitated by having clear, agreed objectives and standards, and immediate, specific feedback. Ideally, the individual should be in a position to assess and regulate his or her own performance *before* significant problems arise.

Step 2 **Establish the reasons for the performance shortfall**

The manager and individual should collaboratively attempt to identify the factors that have contributed to the problem: this is not an exercise in apportioning 'blame', but in problem-solving and improvement planning.

There may be factors outside the individual's (or manager's) control: new pressures and demands, changing circumstances, or wider organisational infrastructure issues (such as inadequate technology or systems, or performance-undermining culture).

However, the focus should be on reasons for the shortfall which can be attributed to:

- A lack of **support, guidance, information or resources** from the manager – suggesting the need for altered input or leadership style (more supportive, coaching, closer supervision) on the part of the manager
- A lack of **clarity about expectations, instructions, objectives or standards** (ie the individual did not fully understand what was required) – suggesting the need for better clarification and perhaps more directive leadership
- A lack of **ability, knowledge, skill or confidence** on the part of the individual (ie he or she could not do, or did not know how to do, what was required) – suggesting the need for induction training, coaching, instruction or other forms of learning, training and development
- A lack of **motivation or willingness** on the part of the individual (ie he or she *would* not do what was required, for various reasons) – suggesting the need for motivation, loyalty building or some other approach to attitude change (including counselling or disciplinary measures).

Step 3 **Decide and agree on the required response**

Depending on the reason for the poor performance, a range of remedial actions may be decided on, as suggested above – and we will discuss some options in more detail in paragraph 4.2 below. Plans (perhaps in the form of learning, improvement or performance contracts or agreements) should be drawn up, including steps to be taken by the individual and/or by the manager. Performance measures, monitoring and feedback arrangements and timescales should be agreed. This might look something like the Personal Development Plan shown at the end of Chapter 4.

Step 4 **Resource and implement the action**

The manager will need to provide or otherwise source the time, facilities, learning resources, coaching, training, guidance – and so on – required to enable the agreed improvement actions.

Step 5 **Monitor and provide feedback**

Performance should be monitored and feedback obtained and shared, in order to check that agreed improvements are being achieved and maintained. Individuals should ideally be empowered to monitor and regulate their own performance – rather than being 'micro-managed' in a way that demonstrates loss of trust, and can damage motivation to learn and improve.

4.2 Handling different types of performance problem

It is worth acknowledging the range of factors which may affect an individual's performance at work.

Profex (2007) suggest that effective performance depends on a mix of:

- **Commitment**: how willingly and energetically people approach their work – a function of motivation and effective leadership, discussed in earlier chapters.
- **Contribution**: the conditions required to support effective working and task fulfilment. Effective contribution needs to be:
  - **Commissioned**: by clear task objectives and delegation of authority to perform them.
  - **Controlled**: by clear values, policies, targets and success criteria – and the feedback to adjust performance.
  - **Championed**: by leadership support, acknowledgement and inspiration
  - **Co-operative:** via mechanisms for co-ordination, information-sharing and team working.
- **Capability**: what people are 'able' to do, as a result of aptitude, education, skills training and competence development.

Factors in individual performance at work

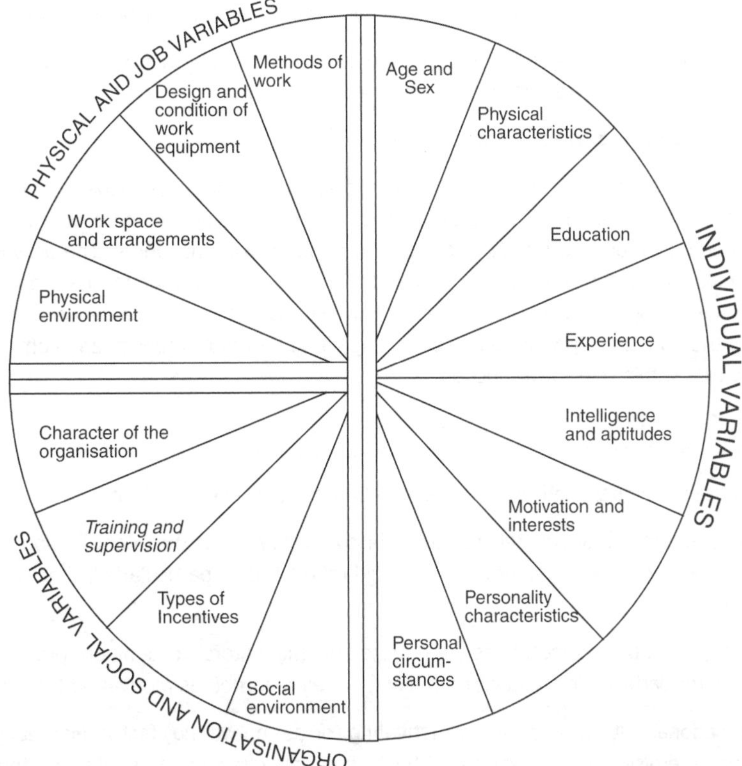

4.2.1 Infrastructure

It may well be that performance problems arise from infrastructure issues, which may or may not be within the individual's or marketing manager's control or sphere of influence. Some examples include:

- **Inadequate technology, procedures or systems**

  These aspects may not be directly within the manager's power to influence, where they reflect lack of resources, organisation-wide systems or organisational inflexibility. Sustained upward leadership may be required to highlight the issue, its negative effects on performance, and the business case for change. Where this is not possible, discussion may be required with the team as to how the dysfunctional elements can be 'worked around'.

- How far can the team 'bend' a procedure to make it more effective?
- What 'tricks' can be learned to make a technology or system work better (perhaps with the help of external experts)?
- How can the negative effect on performance and morale (arising from frustration) be minimised?
- How can the team 'market' its suggestions and improvements to the rest of the organisation?

- **Poor team relations or dysfunctional team dynamics**
  These may be handled in a variety of ways. We discussed team building and team dynamics in Chapter 6, and a range of specific team challenges – managing diverse and remote teams, handling team conflict and managing change – will be covered in Chapter 8.

- **Poor cross-functional relations and co-ordination mechanisms**

  Where formal organisation structures do not support cross-functional co-ordination or horizontal work and information flows (in the ways discussed in Chapter 1):

  - Recommendations for restructuring may be made and marketed to senior management and/or to other functional managers
  - Other functional managers can be co-opted to collaborate in cross-functional meetings (at the managerial and/or team level) for conflict resolution and on-going information-sharing
  - Marketing teams and individuals can unilaterally establish cross-functional networking, to facilitate relationship development and information exchange.

- **Dysfunctional organisation structure or culture**

  Organisation structures and cultures may be dysfunctional in other respects, impacting on marketing performance. Long decision chains may slow responsiveness to customer needs and environmental changes, for example. Artificial status barriers may prevent staff from getting support from managers. The organisation culture may value security over initiative, or may encourage command-and-control rather than facilitate-and-empower management. Again, the individual manager and team members will have to consider whether they can 'drive' change – or investigate 'ways round' the barriers to performance: eg by exploiting informal influence and communication networks, and shaping the culture within their own function.

4.2.2 Motivation, morale and attitude

We discussed team member motivation in detail in Chapter 6. Remember that:

- People expect to be adequately rewarded or compensated for their contribution to the organisation: pay, benefits, recognition and other forms of reward should reflect this – particularly if there are better rewards available elsewhere.
- Monetary rewards and incentives are not the only motivators: recognition, praise, job enrichment, positive leadership and greater participation in decision-making are all regarded as motivating factors.
- Organisational culture is also a key motivating (or de-motivating) factor. Marketing has a key role in promoting positive, energising, shared values, with which people can identify: quality, customer focus, all-member contribution, beating the competition and so on.

Where negative attitudes are the cause of poor performance (ie the individual is unwilling to perform in the required way or to the required standard), **employee counselling** or **disciplinary procedures** may be required: these are discussed separately below.

4.2.3 Learning, skill or competence gaps

One of the most clear-cut causes of poor performance may be a skill, learning or competence gap, where the team member does not know what to do, or is unable to do it well. **Training needs analysis** (covered in section 3 above) should highlight such gaps – and indicate that learning, training or development interventions may be the most effective approach to improving performance.

4.3 Technical and managerial support

Team members must be supported in doing their work effectively, otherwise there will be a mismatch between what they are expected to do and what they are able to do: this is a major source of frustration and stress – as well as under-performance. Staff should be given:

- **Technical support**. That is, they should be equipped with the tools, systems, training and other resources (such as budget, information and help from other staff) needed to perform their work. They should have access to expert instruction, advice and help (eg from an IT support or legal team) when required.
- **Managerial support**. That is, they should be given adequate instruction, guidelines (policies, procedures, goals and standards), encouragement, feedback, supervision (if necessary) and authority/discretion by their managers, so that they can carry out their work and, where possible, grow and develop in the job.
- **Personal support**. Support from managers or colleagues may also be required to help team members who are struggling with their workload, particular work problems, or non-work issues affecting their attitude and performance. This is often the purpose of **coaching** (helping staff to do their jobs better), **mentoring** (helping staff to manage their personal and career development) and workplace **counselling programmes** (helping staff to work through personal problems affecting their work or welfare).
- **Support through change**. Change often causes insecurity, as it brings uncertainty and the loss of competence and confidence, and may be perceived as threatening. Managers should support staff in understanding, accepting and coping with organisational changes, such as the introduction of new systems or work methods. This aspect is discussed in further in Chapter 8.

ACTIVITY 2

application

What forms of technical, managerial and personal support are you given in your work role? What help is available if you have: (a) a work problem or (b) a personal problem affecting your work? How might this support be improved?

What categories of staff in your organisation do you think are most in need of technical, managerial and/or personal support?

4.4 Employee counselling

KEY CONCEPT

concept

Counselling can be defined as 'a purposeful relationship in which one person helps another to help himself. It is a way of relating and responding to another person so that that person is helped to explore his thoughts, feelings and behaviour with the aim of reaching a clearer understanding. The clearer understanding may be of himself or of a problem, or of the one in relation to the other.' (Rees, 1996).

The need for workplace counselling can arise in many different situations.

- During appraisal, to solve work or performance problems
- As part of grievance or disciplinary situations (including cases of sexual, racial or religious harassment or bullying at work, with the need to support the victim and re-educate the perpetrator)
- Following change, such as promotion or relocation – or more traumatic changes such as redundancy or dismissal
- As a result of domestic or personal difficulties affecting work performance.

In some cases, expert input may be required from counselling professionals (eg in the case of trauma or mental illness): Employee Assistance Programmes are often used to provide such services. In other cases, counselling may simply be another approach used by managers and leaders in supporting team members and managing performance.

4.4.1 Benefits of counselling

Effective counselling is not merely a matter of 'pastoral care' for individuals, but is very much in the organisation's interests. Counselling can:

- **Prevent underperformance**, reduce labour turnover and absenteeism and increase commitment from employees
- Demonstrate an organisation's **commitment** to and concern for its employees
- Give employees the **confidence and encouragement** necessary to take responsibility for self and career development
- Recognise that the organisation may be contributing to the **employees' problems** and provide an opportunity to reassess organisational policy and practice
- Support the organisation in **complying with its obligations** (eg in regard to managing harassment in the workplace).

4.4.2 The process of counselling

Managers may be called on to use their expertise to help others make informed decisions or solve problems by:

- **Advising:** offering information and recommendations on the best course of action. This is a relatively *directive* role, and may be called for in areas where you can make a key contribution to the *quality* of the decision: advising an employee about the best available training methods, say, or about behaviours which are considered inappropriate in the workplace.
- **Counselling:** facilitating others through the process of defining and exploring their own problems and coming up with their own solutions. This is a relatively *non-directive* role, and may be called for in areas where you can make a key contribution to the *ownership* of the decision: helping employees to formulate learning goals, for example, or to cope with work (and sometimes non-work) problems.

The counselling process has three broad stages (Egan, 1975).

Step 1 **Reviewing the current scenario**: helping people to identify, explore and clarify their problem situations and unused opportunities. This is done mostly by listening, encouraging them to tell their 'story', and questioning/probing to help them to see things more clearly.

Step 2 **Developing a preferred scenario:** helping people to identify what they want, in terms of clear goals and objectives. This is done mostly by encouraging them to envisage their desired outcome, and what it will mean for them (in order to motivate them to make the necessary changes).

Step 3 **Determining how to get there:** helping people to develop action strategies for accomplishing goals, for getting what they want. This is done mostly by encouraging them to explore options and available resources, select the best option and plan their next steps.

This obviously requires a range of high-quality interpersonal skills in active listening, giving supportive feedback, using questions to encourage problem solving and so on.

4.5 Disciplinary procedures

KEY CONCEPT

Discipline can be considered as: 'a condition in an enterprise in which there is orderliness, in which the members of the enterprise behave sensibly and conduct themselves according to the standards of acceptable behaviour as related to the goals of the organisation'.

The maintenance of discipline has much the same end as motivation: to secure desired behaviour from members of the organisation. **Disciplinary action** may be punitive (punishing an offence), deterrent (warning people not to behave in that way) or reformative (calling attention to the nature of the offence, so that it will not happen again) – but its overriding purpose is to restore appropriate behaviour and performance.

A wide range of situations may require disciplinary intervention. Examples may include: excessive absenteeism or poor timekeeping; persistently inadequate work performance; poor attitudes which influence the work of others or reflect on the image of the firm; violation of rules, regulations and procedures; or refusal to carry out instructions or to implement performance improvements.

4.5.1 Progressive discipline

Many minor cases of poor performance or misconduct are best dealt with by **informal advice, coaching or counselling**. An *informal oral warning* may be issued. None of this forms part of the formal disciplinary procedure, but team members should be informed clearly what is expected and what action will be taken if they fail to improve.

If the matter is not resolved, it may be decided that *formal disciplinary* action is needed. The Code of Practice issued in the UK by the Advisory, Conciliation and Arbitration Service (ACAS) divides this into three stages. These are usually thought of as consecutive, reflecting a *progressive response* – but it may be appropriate to miss out one of the earlier stages in the case of serious infringements.

- **Formal warnings**

  An **oral warning** should include the reason for issuing it, notice that it constitutes the first step of the disciplinary procedure and details of the right of appeal. A note of the warning should be kept on the employee's file for specified period: say, 6 months.

  A **first written warning** is appropriate in more serious cases. It should inform the team member of the improvement required and the consequences of failure to improve. A copy should be kept on file for a specified period: say, 12 months.

  If there is no satisfactory improvement within the timescale set, a *final written warning* may be appropriate.

- **Disciplinary sanctions**

  Various disciplinary sanctions, of increasing severity, may be applied. These may include loss of privileges or discretionary benefits; suspension without pay (or disciplinary lay-off), if this is provided for in the contract of employment; or demotion (setting the team member back to a lower position or salary).

  Dismissal is a drastic form of disciplinary action, and should be reserved as the last resort – or for serious offences. For the organisation, it involves waste of a labour resource, the expense of recruiting a replacement, disruption caused to the work team, and the risk of claims of unfair or wrongful dismissal.

  None of these actions is 'pleasant', and all are potentially damaging to morale and motivation, but they are potentially the only way of imposing compliance with important norms and standards of behaviour. A fully-documented process of progressive discipline may also be the only way to justifiably (and legally) eject a persistently incompetent or disruptive employee from the team.

4.5.2 Relationship management in disciplinary situations

Even if a manager uses sensitivity and judgement, disciplinary proceedings tends to generate **resentment**. The challenge is to apply them as constructively as possible.

- **Immediacy.** Disciplinary action should be taken as speedily as possible after an infringement has come to light, subject to fair investigation – while at the same time avoiding haste and on-the-spot emotions which might lead to unwarranted actions.
- **Advance warning.** Employees should know in advance (eg in a Staff Handbook) what is expected of them and what the rules and regulations are.
- **Consistency.** Appropriate action should be taken each time an infraction occurs, with no favouritism or mixed messages. Inconsistency in application of discipline lowers the morale of employees and diminishes their respect for the manager.
- **Impersonality.** Penalties should be connected with problem – not the person. Once disciplinary action has been taken, no grudges should be borne.
- **Privacy.** As a general rule (unless the manager's authority is challenged directly and in public) disciplinary action should be taken in private, to avoid the spread of conflict and the humiliation or martyrdom of the employee concerned.

Disciplinary action is a sensitive area: interpersonally and legally. If you are involved in such a situation, you should call on the advice of the Human Resource department – or the legal department, in a case where dismissal may be called for.

It is clearly in an organisation's interests to resolve problems before they can develop into major difficulties. Grievances are best dealt with at an early stage, informally, with the immediate line manager. However, organisations should have formal procedures in place to handle cases left unresolved. Pursuing the formal route should be a last resort rather than the first option.

- ***http://www.acas.org.uk***

5 Internal marketing

5.1 What is internal marketing?

KEY CONCEPT

concept

Internal marketing is the use of a marketing approach in the internal environment of an organisation, whose employees are seen as customers who have to be persuaded to 'buy into' management ideas. It also embodies a variety of approaches and techniques by which an organisation acquires, motivates, equips and retains customer-conscious employees (George & Grönroos, 1989), in order to help retain customers through achieving high quality service delivery and increased customer satisfaction.

Gummesson (2002, p 198) suggests that: 'The objective of internal marketing within Relationship Marketing is to **create relationships** between **management and employees**, and between **functions**. The personnel can be viewed as an **internal market**, and this market must be reached efficiently in order to prepare the personnel for external contacts: efficient internal marketing becomes an antecedent to efficient external marketing'.

Peck *et al* (1999) identify the **internal market** as a key component of their Six Markets Model of relationship marketing. It includes employees in all parts of an organisation with potential to contribute towards marketing effectiveness.

'Internal marketing is concerned with creating, developing and maintaining an **internal service culture and orientation**, which in turn assists and supports the organisation in the achievement of its goals. The internal service culture has a vital impact on how service-oriented and customer-oriented employees are, and, thus, how well they perform their tasks... The development and maintenance of a customer-oriented culture is a critical determinant of long-term success in relationship marketing...

The basic premise behind the development of internal marketing is the acknowledgement of the **impact of employee behaviour and attitudes** on the relationship between staff and external customers. This is particularly true where employees occupy boundary-spanning positions in the organisation... The skills and customer orientation of these employees are, therefore, critical to the customers' perception of the organisation and their future loyalty to the organisation.' (ibid, p 313)

In other words, it is through internal marketing that all employees can develop an understanding of how their tasks, and the way they perform them, create and deliver customer value and build relationship.

MARKETING AT WORK

application

LL Bean (US catalogue retailer)

To inspire its employees to practise the marketing concept, LL Bean has for decades displayed posters around its office that proclaim the following:

"What is a customer? A customer is the most important person ever in this company, in person or by mail. A customer is not dependent on us, we are dependent on him. A customer is not an interruption of our work, he is the purpose of it. We are noting doing a favour by serving him, he is doing us a favour by giving us the opportunity to do so. A customer is not someone to argue or match wits with, nobody ever won an argument with a customer. A customer is a person who brings us his wants; it is our job to handle them profitably to him and to ourselves.".

5.2 Aims of internal marketing

5.2.1 Aligning internal and external communications

Internal marketing ensures that internal communications (about everything from focus on the customer, the importance of quality and service, corporate social responsibility and brand values – to details such as when a new product will be available) are aligned with external communications to the customer and other stakeholders, so that the messages given are coherent and consistent.

Kotler (2002) identifies a '**marketing triangle**', which we have adapted as follows.

The marketing triangle

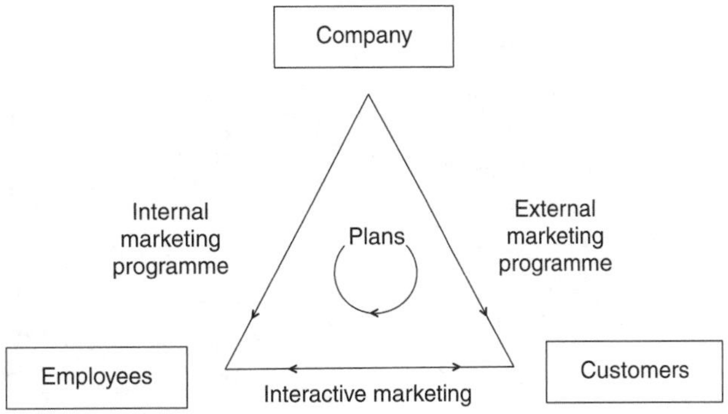

5.2.2 Employee motivation and satisfaction

One of the key principles of internal marketing is that employees throughout an organisation will be motivated, and enjoy enhanced job satisfaction, as a result of:

- A better understanding of their contribution to the objectives, competitive advantage and success of the enterprise
- The linking of their goals and tasks to compelling values such as customer satisfaction, customer value, quality and customer service
- The opportunity to develop new and highly-valued skills and competences (eg in customer care) and to be equipped and empowered to deliver value to customers
- More and better information to support them in doing their jobs, including better cross-functional communication.

Reichheld's loyalty-based cycle of growth (introduced in Chapter 2) traces a clear relationship between employee satisfaction/loyalty and external customer satisfaction/loyalty.

- Investment in employee satisfaction leads to employee retention (improving customer service over time, through familiarity, contacts and learning) and commitment (improving customer service through greater effort, productivity, flexibility and identification with the organisation's customer care values).
- Improved customer service creates more satisfied and loyal customers. This is satisfying for employees (if only because it results in less hassles and complaints!). It also makes marketing more cost-effective, because customer retention is more profitable than customer acquisition – and the resulting profits can partly be reinvested in enhanced employee rewards and retention policies. And so on round the cycle.

A succinct formulation of the argument is provided by Peck *et al (1999)*: 'If management wants its employees to do a great job with customers, then it must be prepared to do a great job with its employees.' Conversely, you should be aware of the potential for unhappy employees to give poor customer service and a poor impression of the organisation!

5.2.3 Customer orientation and satisfaction

Internal marketing implies the promotion of a marketing or customer orientation throughout the organisation – and, in particular, creating customer awareness among staff members who are not designated as marketing staff, nor necessarily directly customer facing, but whose work makes a major contribution to customer satisfaction. (One example would be housekeeping staff in a hotel, or baggage handlers in an airline.)

An article in *Customer Service Management* (July 1996) offered a useful overview of the kind of **corporate integration** required for effective customer care.

Key phases for service delivery

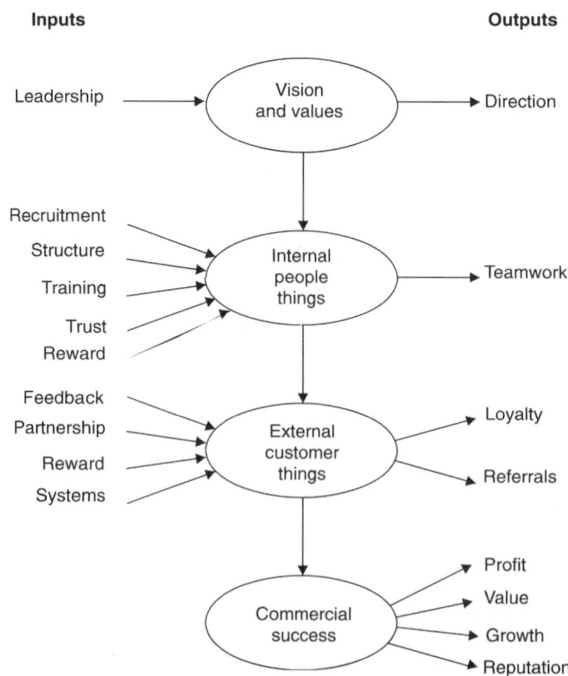

You should recognise many of the elements from earlier chapters, but notice how external customer service is underpinned by:

- **Leadership, vision and values** (organisation culture) which 'sell' the idea of customer focus and organisation-wide marketing responsibility.
- **Internal customer relations**. The satisfaction of *external* customers is the result of a range of satisfying *internal* relationships and transactions between colleagues and departments. Encouraging staff to consider the needs of their internal customers ('the next person to handle your work') helps to foster quality and service at the interface with external customers. Key factors in managing the quality of internal service operations include:
  - The recruitment of skilled customer-facing people
  - The supply of appropriate (and generous) training
  - The empowerment of staff to take decisions that will attract and keep customers
  - The reward and recognition of staff who deliver outstanding service.

As a marketing manager, you should recognise the importance of getting production staff excited about an upcoming launch (which might soften the blow of the production deadlines!), say, or encouraging brand managers and sales staff to feel energised by your marketing support for their efforts.

5.2.4 Inter-functional co-ordination

Internal marketing uses communication to support cross-function co-ordination, through:

- Cultivating an all-employee awareness of their role and contribution to customer value and service
- Integrating the goals and activities of marketing with those of other functions (in the ways discussed in Chapter 1)
- Encouraging information-sharing and cross-functional team-working in the interests of horizontal value-adding processes (eg marketing's input to quality management or new product development)
- Building supportive working relationships: creating a climate of mutual consideration, trust, support and collaboration in pursuit of customer-focused goals.

5.3 Implementing internal marketing

Peck *et al* (1999, p324) identify the following range of inter-related activities thought to be critical in implementing internal marketing.

- **Organisational design**: eg drawing key employees together in cross-functional customer service or quality teams
- **Regular staff surveys**: assessing the internal service culture and attitudes
- **Internal customer segmentation**: adapting the internal marketing mix to different employee groups
- **Personal development and training**: focused on core competencies for internal marketing
- **Empowerment and involvement**: enabling staff, within defined parameters, to use their discretion to deliver better service to customers.
- **Recognition and rewards**: based on employees' contribution to service excellence.
- **Internal communications**: ensuring information flows to support cross-functional co-ordination, and all-employee awareness of their role and contribution to service.
- **Performance measures**: evaluating each individual's and department's contribution to marketing objectives.
- **Building supportive working relationships**: creating a climate of consideration, trust and support, within which internal communications and service delivery can be continuously encouraged and improved.

5.3.1 The internal marketing mix

Jobber (2007, p 864) directly relates the elements of the **marketing mix** to internal customers as follows.

Product	The marketing plan and strategies that are being proposed to employees or other functions, together with the values, attitudes and actions needed to make the plan successful (eg marketing budgets, extra staff).
Price	What internal customers are being asked to pay or sacrifice as a result of accepting the marketing plan (eg lost resources, lower status, new ways of working or harder work).
Promotion (or communications)	The communications media and messages used to inform, persuade and gain the support of internal customers for the marketing plan. The message and language will have to be adapted to the needs, concerns and understanding of the target audience (eg eliminating marketing jargon).
Place	How the product (plan) and communications are delivered to internal customers: eg via meetings, committees, seminars, informal conversations and so on. This may be direct or via intermediaries (eg consultants).
Product	The marketing plan and strategies that are being proposed to employees or other functions, together with the values, attitudes and actions needed to make the plan successful (eg marketing budgets, extra staff).

5.3.2 Segmenting the internal market

The internal marketing mix (like the external marketing mix) will need to be adapted to the needs and drivers of the target audience. The internal market can (like the external market) be **segmented** to allow targeting to the distinctive needs of each group. Jobber (2007) suggests segmentation of internal customers into:

- **Supporters**: those who are likely to gain from the change or plan, or are already committed to it.
- **Neutrals**: those who are likely to experience both gains and losses from the change or plan.
- **Opposers**: those who are likely to lose from the change or plan, or are traditional opponents.

The product (plan) and price may have to be modified to gain acceptance from opponents. Place decisions will be used to reach each group most effectively (eg high-involvement approaches such as consultation meetings for supporters and neutrals). Promotional objectives will also differ according to the target group, because of their different positions on issues.

Christopher *et al* (2002, p 109) suggest an alternative way of segmenting internal customers, according to **how close they are to external customers**:

- **Contactors** have frequent or regular customer contact and are typically heavily involved with conventional marketing activities (eg sales or customer service roles). They need to be well versed in the firm's marketing strategies, and trained, prepared and motivated to service customers on a day-to-day basis in a responsive manner.
- **Modifiers** are not directly involved with conventional marketing activities, but still have frequent contact with customers (eg receptionists, switchboard, the credit department). These people need a clear view of the organisation's marketing strategy and the importance of being responsive to customers' needs.
- **Influencers** are involved with the traditional elements of marketing, but have little or no direct customer contact (eg in product development or market research). Companies must ensure that these people develop a sense of customer responsiveness, as they influence the total value offering to the customer.
- **Isolateds** are support functions that have neither direct customer contact nor marketing input – but whose activities nevertheless affect the organisation's performance (eg purchasing, HR and data processing). Such staff need to be sensitive to the needs of *internal* customers as well as their role in the chain that delivers value to customers. Gummesson (2002) uses the term 'part-time marketers' to describe such employees.

ACTIVITY 3

application

- Draw up Christopher *et al*'s internal market segments as a two-dimensional matrix (like the power/interest matrix, say), using the two dimensions mentioned in our explanations.
- List examples of specific departments or job roles in your own organisation that correspond to each segment, building on the examples we have already given.

Learning objective review

Learning objectives	Covered
1 Plan how the work of the team will be undertaken, establishing priorities, critical activities, objectives and standards which align team performance with marketing and organisational objectives	☑ The hierarchy of objectives in an organisation, and the need for horizontal and vertical alignment ☑ Approaches to prioritising: Critical Success Factors and Key Performance Indicators (KPIs) ☑ The value of setting individual objectives ☑ Different types of objectives and standards and how they can be communicated as policies, standing objectives, competence definitions, learning and development plans
2 Explain and implement a process of performance monitoring and measurement within a team, including individual performance appraisal	☑ Monitoring methods, including observation, work sampling, results reporting and feedback gathering, in a variety of contexts ☑ Individual performance appraisal and competence assessment, using various approaches including peer review and 360-degree feedback
3 Outline a systematic approach to the training and development of team members to proactively or reactively improve performance	☑ A systematic approach to training and development ☑ Learning needs analysis ☑ On- and off-the-job approaches to training ☑ Development opportunities ☑ How to evaluate training and development interventions
4 Critically assess team performance, in order to identify poor performance, diagnose reasons for it and make recommendations for how to overcome it	☑ Reasons for poor performance, and how to diagnose them ☑ How to gain stakeholder co-operation and commitment to improvement ☑ Potential approaches to overcoming a range of performance problems, whether structural, interpersonal, attitudinal/motivational or skill/competence based ☑ Disciplinary procedures
5 Explain the importance, role and processes of internal marketing in managing marketing performance	☑ The nature of internal marketing ☑ The role of internal marketing in communications alignment, employee motivation, customer retention, cross-functional co-ordination and knowledge management.

Quick quiz

1 _____________ is 'the planned and systematic modification of behaviour through learning events, programmes and instruction which enable individuals to achieve the level of knowledge, skills and competence to carry out their work effectively'. Fill in the blank.

2 ____________ is a wider process involving the growth or realisation of a person's ability and potential through the provision of learning experiences. Fill in the blank.

3 Which methods can be used to ascertain level of competence?

4 Why is internal marketing relevant to HR?

5 Disciplinary procedures will always lead to resentment. True or false.

Activity debriefs

1 These measures do not all address the key issues of the job.

(a) *Number of new customers.* This is helpful as far as it goes but omits two crucial issues: how much the customers actually spend and what the potential is. Demand for this service might be expanding rapidly, and the firm might be increasing sales revenue but losing market share.

(b) *Revenue from existing customers* is useful – repeat business is generally cheaper than gaining new customers, and it implies customer satisfaction.

(c) *Renewal of service contracts* is very relevant to the executive's role.

(d) *Customer complaints about poor quality products.* As the company does not make its own products, this is not really under the control of the sales manager. Instead the purchasing manager should be more concerned. Complaints about the service contract are the sales executive's concern.

(e) *Customer satisfaction survey.* This is a tool for the sales manager to use as well as a performance measure, but not everything is under the sales executive's control.

2 Answers will depend on your own research.

3 Answers will depend on your own research.

Quiz answers

1 Training

2 Development

3 Job analysis (identifying the task elements of the job)

Competence analysis or existing competence frameworks (describing competent performance in a job)

Role analysis (identifying the contribution made by competent performance in a job)

Existing records of job requirements such as job descriptions and KPIs.

4 Positive employees will provide a better overall customer experience and help to instil quality.

5 False. If handled sensitively, resentment may be minimised during episodes of disciplinary action.

References

Armstrong, M. (2009), A Handbook of Human Resource Management Practice, (11th edition), Kogan Page, London.

Christopher M., Payne A. & Ballantyne D. (2002), Relationship Marketing: Creating Stakeholder Value, Elsevier Butterworth-Heinemann, Oxford.

Egan, G. (1975), The Skilled Helper: a problem-management approach to helping, (5th edition), Brooks/Cole, Pacific Grove, CA.

George, V. R. & Grönroos, C. (1989), *'Developing customer conscious employees at every level – internal marketing'* in Handbook of Services Marketing, Congram & Friedman (eds). AMACOM, New York.

Gummesson, E. (2002), Total Relationship Marketing, Elsevier Butterworth-Heinemann, Oxford.

Hamblin, A. C. (1972), *'Controlling the Training Process'* in Management Learning Vol 3, no 2 pp 92-97.

Huczynski, A. & Buchanan, D. (2001), Organizational Behaviour: An Introductory Text, (4th edition), FT Prentice Hall, Harlow, Essex.

Jobber, D. (2007), Principles and Practice of Marketing,(5th edition), McGraw Hill Education, Maidenhead.

Johnson G., Scholes, K. & Whittington R. (2005), Exploring Corporate Strategy: Text and Cases, (7th edition), Pearson Education, Harlow, Essex.

Kotler, P. (2002), Marketing Management, (11th edition), US Imports and PHIPES.

Kramer R., McGraw P. & Schuler R. (1997), Human Resource Management in Australia, (3rd edition), Addison Wesley Longman, Melbourne.

Lockett, J. (1992), Effective Performance Management, Kogan Page, London.

Maier, N. R. F. (1966), The Appraisal Interview: objectives, methods and skills, John Wiley & Sons, London.

Peck H. L., Payne A., Christopher M. & Clark M. (1999), Relationship Marketing: Strategy and Implementation, Elsevier Butterworth-Heinemann, Oxford.

Pedler M., Burgoyne, J. & Boydell, T. (2004), A Manager's Guide to Leadership, McGraw Hill, Maidenhead.

Profex (2007), Leading and Influencing in Purchasing, (2nd edition), Profex Publishing, Maidenhead.

Varey, R. J. (2002), Marketing Communications: Principles & Practice, Routledge, Abingdon, Oxon.

Whetten, D. & Cameron, S. (2002), Developing Management Skills,(5th edition), Prentice Hall, New Jersey.

Chapter 8

Managing team challenges

Topic list

1 Managing diverse teams
2 Managing remote teams
3 Managing team conflict
4 Managing change in teams

Introduction

This chapter explores a range of team management 'challenges' raised by the syllabus. As with previous chapters, each one of the aspects mentioned here is the subject of a vast literature in its own right: our coverage offers an orientation to the subject, which you can use to focus your further reading in the light of your own work issues and the topics raised by the assessment tasks.

We start by picking up on some of the issues of team diversity raised in Chapter 5 under the heading of 'equal opportunity' in recruitment. 'Diversity' is a wider concept than equal opportunity, but there is a similar need for managers to avoid and prevent discrimination in order to reap the potential synergies of diverse work teams.

In section 2 we explore the challenges of what the syllabus calls 'remote' (or geographically dispersed) teams: international and virtual teams. Although these aspects may not be directly relevant to your own work context, they are increasingly common in the globalised world of marketing, and it is worth being aware of the opportunities and constraints involved.

In section 3 we cover the issue of team conflict. We explore the causes and effects of conflict within a marketing team, and how conflict can be managed.

Finally, in section 4, we introduce the topic of change management. Change is mentioned only briefly in the indicative content of the syllabus, under the heading of conflict, but it is a major aspect of management in today's turbulent marketing environment. We give you an outline of the issues, so that you can follow them up if you need to.

Syllabus linked learning objectives

By the end of the chapter you will be able to:

	Learning objectives	Syllabus link
1	Plan how to prevent discrimination and value diversity in teams	2.5
2	Propose approaches to manage and co-ordinate the work of remote (virtual and international) teams, and create effective working relations	2.6
3	Identify potential areas of team conflict, identifying causes and making recommendations for conflict management	2.7
4	Propose approaches for managing change in teams	2.7

1 Managing diverse teams

KEY CONCEPT

concept

Diversity may be defined as the 'visible and non-visible differences [between people] which will include sex, age, background, race, disability, personality and work style' (Mullins, 1999).

The concept of '**managing diversity**' is based on the belief that the dimensions of individual difference on which employment legislation currently focuses (under the heading of 'equal opportunity') are not the only, or most work-relevant, ways in which **people meaningfully differ** at work. They may also have different personality traits, preferred working styles, individual needs and goals, educational backgrounds, family circumstances and so on.

As a policy of human resource management, diversity also reflects the belief that the make-up of an organisation's workforce should **broadly reflect that of the external labour market** and society as a whole – and ideally, therefore (from a marketing standpoint), that of the target customer base – in order to be able to meet the challenges posed by those environments.

The UK workforce is becoming **increasingly diverse**, not just in terms of national and ethnic backgrounds, but in: the wider representation of women in the workforce and management; the wider variety of educational experiences and pathways leading to employment; and legislative support for the recognition of workers' rights to equality of opportunity, regardless of sexual orientation, religious affiliation, family structure, age and disability.

1.1 Why value diversity in marketing teams?

The benefits claimed for developing a diverse marketing staff (and workforce in general) include:

- **Widening the recruitment** pool, with access to previously underutilised skill sectors. There may be specific benefits arising from these sectors: older workers, for example, may offer experience and loyalty, and empathy with mature-age customer segments.
- **Improved team performance**, through being able to draw on (and support full contribution from) people with diverse skills, experiences and viewpoints within the team
- **Improved team functioning**. Diverse (and even divergent) viewpoints can, as we saw in Chapter 6, be a positive asset in team working, where their effect is to control the risk of 'group think'; widen the range of information inputs for decision-making and problem-solving; create a climate in which ideas and feelings can be safely expressed; and encouraging questioning and criticism of processes and methods, as a basis for learning and constructive suggestions for improvement.
- Reflecting the **diversity of external stakeholders** (including the market and customer base), allowing marketers to anticipate their needs and concerns.
- Enhanced customer satisfaction and loyalty, both among minority groups (better represented in customer service teams, and more likely to have their needs taken into account in marketing strategies) and among consumers generally (who increasingly demand corporate ethics and social responsibility in such areas)
- Enhanced **employer brand** (as an ethical and diverse employer), supporting the ability to attract and retain quality talent
- **Compliance** with equal opportunities legislation and codes of practice (which are used by Employment Tribunals in arbitrating employee grievances and industrial disputes)
- **Enhanced flexibility and learning**. 'The more open we are to difference, the greater is the learning potential and the greater the ability to embrace change and development. Difference and diversity therefore hold the key to many of the aspirations of leadership.' (*Pedler et al,* 2004).

Conversely, an organisation which does *not* take proactive measures to develop and support diversity may suffer corresponding consequences: inability to empathise with key market segments; reputational damage; reduced staff loyalty and contribution; inability to attract and retain talent; and an impoverished organisation culture (lacking key ethical values, and based on a mono-cultural identity). Not to mention the potential for lawsuits, arbitrations and appeals as a result of claims of discrimination!

1.2 Challenges of team diversity

Potential drawbacks of diversity are based on the idea that difference presents a challenge to management. However, these are management challenges – *not* arguments against diversity!

- Effort and cost of formulating and administering **diversity policies and practices** (policy task forces, diversity monitoring, training, wider recruitment and so on)
- Difficulties of communicating, collaborating and managing in **culturally diverse** teams: differences in language, cultural values and norms, and interpersonal styles (for example, in negotiation or conflict handling) – plus the time and cost of training team leaders to handle them!
- Difficulties and costs of managing a workforce with **diverse family structures and work patterns** (introducing flexible working, equal rights for part-time workers and so on)
- Confronting different levels of **literacy/numeracy** and differences in international **qualification/training schemes** (with implications for recruitment, training and development)
- The need to adapt the work environment and task organisation to support contribution from **disabled and older employees**
- Potential for **misunderstanding, miscommunication and conflict** arising from differences which have not been effectively managed.

Some of these disadvantages may be regarded as costs that must simply be absorbed as an investment in the potential benefits. Others, however, can be minimised by effective management.

1.3 Diversity policy

Ingham (2003) suggests the following key steps in implementing a **diversity policy,** taking into account all relevant equal opportunity requirements.

Step 1 **Analyse your business environment**

- Internally – does the diversity of the organisation reflect the population in its labour market?
- Externally – does the diversity of the workforce mirror that of the customer base?

Step 2 **Define diversity and its business benefits**

- Legal, moral and social benefits
- Business benefits: better understanding of market segments; positive employer brand; attraction and retention of talent
- Employee benefits: more representative workforce; value and respect for people; opportunity to contribute fully; enhanced creativity

Step 3 **Introduce diversity policy into corporate strategy**

Weave diversity into corporate values and mission.

Step 4 **Embed diversity into core HR processes and system**

Review and refocus recruitment and selection, induction, reward and recognition, career management and training and development.

Step 5 **Ensure leaders implement policy**

- Top management needs to provide long-term commitment and resources
- Use diversity as a key factor in coaching, awareness training and development of managers

Step 6 **Involve staff at all levels**

- Educate the workforce through awareness training
- Create a 'diversity handbook'
- Set up diversity working parties and councils
- Establish mentoring schemes

Step 7 **Communicate, communicate, communicate**

- Communicate diversity policy and initiatives clearly
- Internally: updates, briefings, training, intranet pages
- Externally: to boost employer brand and recruitment

Step 8 **Understand your company's needs**

- Match resources to organisation size and the scale of change required
- Consider using diversity consultants or best practice representatives to provide advice, support and training

Step 9 **Evaluate**

- Benchmark progress at regular intervals
- Internally: diversity score cards, employee climate surveys
- Externally: focus groups, customer/supplier surveys

1.4 Equal opportunity and diversity in practice

We outlined the provisions and implications of equal opportunity law in Chapter 5, in relation to recruitment and selection. Wider measures to promote equal opportunity and diversity may include the following.

- **Tolerance and support** of individual differences (beyond merely outlawing discrimination and harassment)
- **Communicating effectively** with diverse work forces, and managing co-operative working in diverse teams
- Taking diversity into account when designing **reward systems** (eg flexible menus of benefits, extending 'spousal' benefits to same-sex partners) and **development programmes** (taking into account education/qualification differences)
- **Adjusting work arrangements and environments** in order to accommodate diverse **family responsibilities** (eg part-time working, term-time or annual hours contracts); **disabilities** (eg wheel-chair access, text-based telecommunications systems or special supervision and support); or **religious beliefs** (eg flexibility for religious holidays, space for prayer, allowances for religious dress requirements which violate company dress codes and so on)

- Managing increasingly diverse **career aspirations and patterns** (eg through flexible and freelance working arrangements, side-ways development opportunities)
- **Positive action** to train disadvantaged groups, or to encourage them to undertake **training** in which they have previously been under-represented (the one area in which positive discrimination is permissible). Examples might be offering training in business English for international workers, or offering women training in management skills.
- **Recruiting internally** for managerial vacancies: giving more opportunities for movement up the ladder for groups currently at lower levels of the organisation.

We will discuss the more general aspects of *cross-cultural* team leadership separately, in the next section.

2 Managing remote teams

2.1 Managing international teams

There has been increasing demand for managerial competence in working with (or within) different cultures in recent decades. Domestic skill shortages have encouraged international recruitment, supported by freedom of labour movement in blocs such as the European Economic Area. There has been a growth in multi-national and global corporations. Meanwhile, Information & Communication Technology (ICT) developments have facilitated virtual organisation and team-working regardless of location.

Marketing managers are increasingly likely to work in organisations that have multinational or multi-ethnic elements; or in another culture (eg via secondment or relocation to an international or regional office); or in 'virtual' teams that include members in other nations.

A number of issues may arise in managing teams whose members are from, or located in, other nations.

- Differences in **educational infrastructure** and opportunities may create wide differences in skills and qualifications, which may need to be harmonised in order to facilitate all-member contribution, and manage differences in expectations
- Differences in **technology infrastructure** between countries may create barriers to effective virtual team working: international offices may need to be supported with hardware or software tools
- **Language** differences may create barriers, where some team members are not equally fluent in the dominant language of the team, organisation or customer base
- **Legal and regulatory** differences (eg on health and safety, quality, intellectual property protection or employment protection) may create issues for people and performance management across national borders
- **Economic differences** between countries in which staff are employed may create issues of equity in team member rewards, in terms of market rates of pay, taxation rates, inflation rates and so on.
- **Distance barriers** have been reduced by ICT developments: instant document transmission and data-sharing (via the e-mail and Internet), virtual meetings and so on. However, there may still be issues of people working in different time zones and different seasons (eg for seasonal products and marketing campaigns).
- **Socio-cultural differences** are a potential source of divergence in work and management practices, values and assumptions, business etiquette, communication styles – and a wide variety of other factors.

The syllabus emphasises cultural aspects, so we will consider them in more detail.

2.2 Cultural differences

Different countries (or world regions) have different cultural norms, values and assumptions which influence how they do business and manage people.

Distinctive cultural features may be a source of competitive advantage in domestic and international markets, because of 'fashions' for the products or management techniques of particular cultures, and because of the synergy that may arise from diverse viewpoints and skills. It has been demonstrated that, in the long term, multi-cultural groups perform as well as

homogeneous (single culture) groups in both their process and overall performance: indeed, diverse groups performed better in some tasks, such as identifying problem perspectives and generating solution alternatives.

However, cultural differences may also be a source of difficulties in cross-cultural management, business relationships and marketing, because of failure to understand underlying needs, meanings and expectations. Underlying cultural assumptions – of which we may not be consciously aware – give rise to:

- Different beliefs and values about the practice of management: about the nature and desirability of employee involvement, say, or the way in which decisions are reached
- Different behaviours by managers and team members
- Differences in the working environment: the design of buildings and offices; codes of dress and address; the way tasks are organised and jobs defined; policies and procedures.

'Before inter-cultural communication can even begin, there needs to be a recognition that we each carry a different mental software because of the way we were brought up, and that others carry a different mental software for equally good reasons. We need to recognise that, if we are to interact with particular other cultures, we have to learn about them... While we may never share their values, we may at least obtain a grasp of where their values differ from ours.' (Guirdham, 1995, p 270.)

Let's look at three influential models of international cultural differences.

2.2.1 The Hofstede model

Geert Hofstede (1996) carried out major cross-cultural research at 66 national offices of IBM and formulated one of the most influential models of work-related cultural differences.

The Hofstede model describes four main dimensions of difference between national cultures, which impact on all aspects of management and organisational behaviour: motivation, team working, leadership style, conflict management and HR policies.

- **Power Distance (PD)**: the extent to which unequal distribution of power is accepted.
  - *High* PD cultures (as in Latin, near Eastern and less developed Asian countries) accept greater centralisation, a top-down chain of command and closer supervision. Subordinates have little expectation of influencing decisions.
  - *Low* PD cultures (as in Germanic, Anglo and Nordic countries) favour less centralisation and flatter organisational structures. Subordinates expect involvement and participation in decision-making. (Japan is a medium PD culture.)
- **Uncertainty Avoidance (UA)**: the extent to which security, order and control are preferred to ambiguity, uncertainty and change.
  - *High* UA cultures (as in Latin, near Eastern and Germanic countries and Japan) value control, certainty and ritual. They prefer task structure, written rules and regulations, and standardisation. Specialists and experts are highly respected. There is a strong need for consensus, with a low tolerance for deviance and dissent, and a strong work ethic.
  - *Low* UA cultures (as in Anglo and Nordic countries) value flexibility and creativity. They prefer less structured tasks, fewer rules, greater variability. Generalists or 'all-rounders' are highly respected. There is more tolerance of risk, dissent, conflict and deviation from norms.
- **Individualism**: the extent to which people prefer to live and work in individualist (focusing on the 'I' identity) or collectivist (focusing on the 'we' identity) ways.
  - *High* Individualist cultures (as in Anglo, more developed Latin and Nordic countries) emphasise autonomy and individual choice and responsibility. They prize individual initiative. The organisation is impersonal and tends to defend business interests: task achievement is more important than relationships. Management is seen in an individual context.
  - *Low* Individualist (or Collectivist) cultures (as in less developed Latin, near Eastern and less developed Asian countries) emphasise interdependence, reciprocal obligation and social acceptability. The organisation is seen as a 'family' and tends to defend employees' interests: relationships are more important than task achievement. Management is seen in a team context. (Japan and Germany are 'medium' cultures on this dimension.)

- **Masculinity**: the extent to which social gender roles are distinct. (Note that this is different from the usual sense in which the terms 'masculine' and 'feminine' are used.)
  - *High* Masculinity cultures (as in Japan and Germanic and Anglo countries) clearly differentiate gender roles. 'Masculine' values of assertiveness, competition, decisiveness and material success are dominant. 'Feminine' values of modesty, tenderness, consensus, focus on relationships and quality of working life are less highly regarded, and confined to women.
  - *Low* Masculinity (or Feminine) cultures (as in Nordic countries) minimise gender roles. Feminine values are dominant – and both men and women are allowed to behave accordingly.

ACTIVITY 1

application

According to the Hofstede model, what issues might arise in the following cases?

(a) The newly-appointed Spanish (more developed Latin) marketing manager of a UK (Anglo) firm asks to see the Rules and Procedures Manual for the department.

(b) A US-trained (Anglo) manager attempts to implement a performance management system in Thailand (less developed Asian).

(c) A Dutch (Nordic) marketing manager of a US (Anglo) subsidiary in the Netherlands is instructed to implement downsizing measures in the function..

2.2.2 Hall's communication model

Edward Hall (1976) suggested that another dimension of cultural difference is the extent to which the content and understanding of communication is influenced by its context: underlying implications, non-verbal aspects, interpersonal factors and so on.

- **Low-context** cultures (eg Germanic, Scandinavian and North American) tend to take the content of communication at face value: words say what they mean. They prefer clear, written, explicit communication.
- **High-context** cultures (eg Japanese, Asian, African, Latin American and Middle-Eastern) interpret and exchange more complex messages. They prefer face-to-face and oral communication, and are good at developing networks and using non-verbal cues and unspoken implications. They tend to divulge less information in official/written forms. (The UK, France, Italy and Spain are classified as only moderately high-context.)

2.2.3 The Trompenaars model

Fons Trompenaars (1997) surveyed 30,000 managers in 55 countries to identify cultural differences that may affect aspects of organisational behaviour. His finds suggested that certain cultures emphasise some values more than others, on seven key dimensions. Cultures do not embody one value *or* another on each dimensions, but differ in the amount of emphasis placed on each.

Focus	Value dimensions	
How individuals relate to other people	**Universalism** Behaviour is governed by the standards rules, and norms of the society or group (eg US, Norway, Sweden)	**Particularism** Behaviour is governed by one's relationship with the individual concerned. (eg Asia, Indonesia)
	Individualism Emphasis is on the individual and individual contribution, the 'I' identity and independence (eg US, E Europe, Austria)	**Collectivism** Emphasis is on the group and team contribution, the 'we' identity (firm, team, family) and interdependence (eg Mexico, Indonesia, Japan, India)

Focus	Value dimensions	
	Affective Issues are dealt with emotionally and emotions are openly expressed and displayed (eg Mid-East, S Europe, US)	**Neutral** Issues are dealt with rationally and unemotionally, with a focus on goal-directed behaviour (eg Japan, Germany, UK, Asia)
	Specific Work and non-work roles and relationships are kept separate, to preserve privacy and autonomy. (eg Netherlands, US, UK)	**Diffuse** Work and non-work roles and relationships are integrated and merged. (eg China, Singapore, Korea)
	Achievement Status is based on personal attainments and abilities (eg US, Norway, Austria)	**Ascription** Status is based on attributes ascribed to age, gender, background etc. (eg Egypt, Korea, S America, Spain)
How people relate to (interpret/ manage) time	**Past-present** The future is seen as growing from the past, history and tradition (eg France, Japan, UK)	**Future** The future is seen as created from a 'zero base' (eg US, Netherlands)
How people relate to the environment	**Internal control** Individuals are presumed to be in control of their own lives: they shape events and create new things. (eg US, UK, Norway, Israel)	**External control** External forces are presumed to control much of life: individuals adapt to events and refine existing things. (eg Korea, China, Indonesia)

2.2.4 Cultural differences in practice

Expressions of the various dimensions and orientations discussed in these models of culture will be very diverse, and specific to particular cultures. However, you should be alert to the possibility of different expectations and norms around practical issues such as:

- The style and formality/casualness of work dress
- Appropriate degrees of formality and deference in different contexts: use of titles, first or last name terms, honorific address (eg variants of 'doctor' are widely used as a courtesy in Europe); deference (to authority, seniority, expertise)
- Social distance or personal space preferred in face-to-face interactions
- The interpretation of body language, gestures, facial expressions and eye contact
- Social behaviours and business etiquette such as bowing, exchange of business cards, greeting styles
- The appropriate balance of task and social communication in business relationships
- The style and pace of decision-making (vote, consensus, autocratic)
- The nature of conflict and the aim and style of conflict management (willingness to challenge, fear of loss of face, reluctance to criticise authority figures)
- The role and status of women in business contexts
- The interpretation of gifts and hospitality as part of business dealings (social facilitation – or bribe?)

And so on. These expectations may have to be brought into the open and negotiated as part of a team 'contract': an agreed framework or strategy for how the team will work together.

2.3 Building and managing a culturally diverse team

Schneider & Barsoux (1997) argue that 'rather than knowing what to do in Country X, or whether national or functional cultures are more important in multi-cultural teams, what is necessary is to know how to **assess the potential impact of culture**, national or otherwise, on performance'.

At the organisational level, there should be a plan to evaluate this potential impact and to implement programmes to encourage: **awareness** of areas of cultural difference and sensitivity; **behavioural flexibility** (being able to use multiple-solution models rather than 'one best way' approaches); and **constructive communication**, conflict resolution and problem-solving.

Building an effective culturally diverse team requires leadership in:

- **Acknowledging cultural conflicts** when they arise (without attributing *all* conflicts to cultural differences)
- Identifying and building on **shared values** and common ground, and gaining commitment to the teams shared goals and objectives.
- Demonstrating **appreciation and respect** for the contributions and strengths of different cultures, and the cultural uniqueness of individuals
- Exploring **culturally appropriate approaches** to team building, rewarding excellence and so on (in the process, potentially developing a distinctive, shared group culture)
- Being sensitive to **power imbalances** (eg English being the second language of some members, or culture-based reluctance to contribute or disagree in public) in order to facilitate all-member contribution.
- **Encouraging team members to learn** about one another's values and culture-based behaviours, developing cultural sensitivity and behavioural flexibility.
- Facilitating **constructive communication and feedback**, so that the team can confront potential conflicts and power imbalances before they become dysfunctional
- **Handling divergent viewpoints**, rather than suppressing them and creating a false consensus (or groupthink) and **negotiating mutually-acceptable decisions**, so that different interests and perspectives have been (and feel) heard and acknowledged.

In many ways, the challenges are not *that* different from those of leading *any* team!

Managers' or leaders' **cross-cultural competence** can be enhanced through:

- Encouraging diversified work experience in international or multi-cultural settings
- Undertaking training exercises (reading, language learning, cultural briefings)
- Networking with managers from other cultures and using them as consultants
- Seeking to learn through all cross-cultural interactions.

ACTIVITY 2

application

Select any one foreign culture that is directly relevant to your work, as a supply or customer market, or as the culture from which a member of your team is drawn, or as a culture you may have an opportunity to work in one day through a foreign posting or secondment.

- Draw up an action plan for gaining a 'cultural briefing': information about the culture. Think as widely about sources of information for such a briefing as you can.
- What opportunities are there in your organisation, or external networks, to develop your cross-cultural competence in the ways listed above?

- **Awareness training** may used to help leaders and staff members to understanding the potential for problems arising from culturally-acquired assumptions: the need to recognise cultural stereotypes and move beyond them through new information and encounters with people; the need to appreciate that 'different' does not necessarily imply 'wrong'; and so on.
- **Intercultural communication** is the only way to bring cultural values and assumptions into the open, in order to limit potential misunderstanding. This cannot be done by single cultural profiles or briefings: it requires ongoing monitoring of messages, interpretations and areas of difference. Mechanisms for this kind of communication may include: cross-cultural teams; cross-cultural discussion, consultation and conflict resolution groups; cultural education and briefings; cross-cultural networking and forums (perhaps on the corporate intranet) and so on.

2.4 Virtual team working

As we saw in Chapter 5, virtual teams bring together individuals working in remote locations, reproducing the social, collaborative and information-sharing aspects of team working mainly – or wholly – using Information and Communications Technology (ICT) links.

2.4.1 Benefits of virtual team working

The benefits of virtual team working include:

- The ability to recruit, co-opt or collaborate with the **best available people** without the constraints of distance or travel. The team can co-opt specialists, consultants or technical support, when required, from a global pool of skills. Members may also (Solomon, 2001) be members of other organisations – supply chain partners, marketing consultancies, clients or competitors – with valuable input from their own stakeholder perspective.
- Enabling the organisation to maintain **close contact** with customers and supply chain partners throughout the world, by having people 'on the spot' and familiar with the local market
- Enabling **24-hour 'follow the sun' working days** (for example, for global customer support) – without having to have UK staff on night shifts
- **Ad hoc, flexible structure**: the team can co-opt members as required for a project or task, and a manager can be a member of a number of teams/projects without relocation
- Improvement in **cross-functional and value-chain communication**, because of the availability of ICT networks and tools developed for virtual meetings and data-sharing
- Reduced time and cost spent in **gathering dispersed individuals** for meetings
- Greater **scheduling flexibility** for people who prefer non-traditional working hours (including the disabled and working parents, for example), and are able to work from home or local satellite offices. This is also said to reduce the stress associated with commuting and with juggling competing demands – and to reduce work time lost to such issues. Home working also offers potential savings on office overheads.

2.4.2 Challenges and constraints of virtual team working

You may be able to come up with a few challenges from your own experience of working (or studying) with others via the Internet. Some challenges and constraints include:

- The complexities and subtleties of dealing with different personalities, cultures and languages – exaggerated by the **impersonality** of electronic communication
- Difficulties of creating a **sense of teamhood** or shared experience and identity, which may be important for knowledge-sharing and creativity
- Lack of **informal team building** and opportunities for informal brainstorming: shared 'down time' or informal getting-to-know-people and information-sharing sessions
- The difficulty of **building trust, confidence and productivity** among team members, in the absence of direct supervision and group competition/accountability. Can the manager trust the team member (and vice versa) to be doing what they say they are going to do, when no one is monitoring?

- Difficulty of **monitoring and measuring work outputs** without direct supervision – which may also raise questions about how team members are rewarded and developed
- Difficulties of ensuring **co-ordination** of effort and information-sharing so that everyone is 'on the same page'
- **Lead-times** in communicating across time zones, requiring regular, clear and accurate communication to avoid misunderstandings that can't immediately be clarified
- The requirement for **training and equipping** to use the technology required
- **Resistance**. Not everyone embraces virtual team working: some managers and employees prefer traditional co-location and may be de-motivated by physical isolation from the team.

The following insights were offered in a journal article by Charlene Marmer Solomon ('Managing Virtual Teams', in Workforce, June 2001).

'Developing a productive virtual team begins with selecting the right people. A successful team member is self-motivated and doesn't need a lot of detailed instructions or structure. Ideally he or she is a strong communicator, a quality that helps counter-balance the anonymous nature of technology. You need people who are adaptable, technically self-sufficient and results-oriented.

'Teams need tools – as well as leaders – to create shared knowledge or shared vision. When a team has a meeting, whether a teleconference, videoconference or face-to-face encounter, the leader must be explicit about goals, and keep the team up-to-date on where the group is at and what the group knows as a whole.

'Managers should set up regular virtual meetings to share expectations and debriefings. It is their task to frame the team's objectives so members clearly understand their roles. They emphasise the consequences of team decisions and provide ongoing monitoring and honest feedback about how the team is doing.

'Virtual teams offer an opportunity to work with the best talent throughout an organisation. But to accomplish this, managers must actively work to create a sense of connectedness and shared space, to use technology effectively and to know when to forgo technology for personal communication.' ■

3 Managing team conflict

One of the key roles of management is to develop and maintain **co-operative working** in the team and wider organisation (and indeed across the whole value chain). This is often a complex, ongoing process of preventing differences and divergent views and interests – which, as we have seen, can contribute positively to the performance and functioning of a team – from becoming dysfunctional.

There are many definitions of conflict. Huczynski and Buchanan (2001) usefully reflect the subjective dimensions of conflict (perceptions and values) in their definition.

KEY CONCEPT

concept

'**Conflict** is a process which begins when one party perceives that another party has negatively affected, or is about to negatively affect, something the first party cares about... Typically, conflicts are based upon differences in interests and values, when the interests of one party come up against the different interests of another.' (Huczynski & Buchanan, 2001, p 770).

3.1 Causes of conflict

Conflict can occur at many different levels: within an individual (eg over two incompatible goals); between two individuals (inter-personal conflict); between groups or teams (eg because of competition for influence or resources, incompatible goals and schedules, or different cultures); and between different levels in the organisation hierarchy (eg workers and their trade unions versus management, or 'turf wars' between levels of management).

3.1.1 Inter-group conflict

It is possible to identify a number of typical sources of conflict between functions and groups in organisations.

- **Goal incompatibility**. Conflict may be caused by differences in the goals of different groups (or individuals), where these have not been adequately aligned or integrated by management. In some cases, this may be institutionalised: for example, the conflict between trade unions and management.
- **Cultural incompatibility.** Different business functions often differ in style or culture. Different goals, attitudes, job roles, technical jargon and work styles create potential for lack of understanding and frustration. (This effect is often worsened as the size of the organisation increases, and informal cross-functional interaction is reduced.)
- **Interdependence and shared resources.** Conflict is more likely to occur when groups are dependent on each other to achieve their goals, and use shared resources in pursuit of these goals: decisions and actions by each group impacts on the work of the other.
- **Competition for limited or scarce resources**, such as budget, staff or space allocations. The reward system, for example, can cause conflict if rewards or incentives are (or are perceived to be) unfairly distributed.
- **Authority, power and status distribution.** Conflict is often caused by disputes about the boundaries of authority (where these are insufficiently clear) or by attempts by one group to enlarge its authority, prestige or status at the expense of another. (This is often described in terms of warfare: 'encroaching on someone else's territory', or 'empire building'.) There is often conflict between line functions and staff/advisory functions like HR, which may be resisted as 'interfering' by line managers – and may seek to bolster their authority by negative means, such as red-tape and rule enforcement.
- **Change and uncertainty**. Conflict can arise in times of change, where new problems arise. There may be conflicting views as to the need for, or approach to, change. Some units' interests may be affected positively and others' negatively. A temporary power vacuum may arise, causing competition.
- **The external environment** may pose threats, through change, competitive pressure, resource scarcity and so on. Again, there may be competing views as to the required response, or conflict arising as groups attempt to protect their own interests.

3.1.2 Conflict within the marketing team

Similar conflict may arise within a team, due to everyday factors such as the following:

- Disagreement about needs, goals, values, priorities and interests. This will be made worse by lack of direction from the leader as to what the team's purpose, values and goals are.
- Poor communication, creating potential negative assumptions, stereotypes and misunderstandings. The perceived withholding of information may also escalate conflict, as a hostile, competitive or 'political' tactic.
- Competition for scarce resources such as influence, office space, a share of rewards, the manager's recognition/attention and so on
- Interpersonal issues :'personality clashes', aggression or domination by strong individuals, argumentative or manipulative communication styles – and, at worst, bullying or harassment, unchecked by the team leader.
- 'Hygiene' issues (in the technical sense used by Herzberg): dissatisfaction with the leadership, working conditions or pay, say, which can cause grievance against the organisation (or leader) and/or spill over into interpersonal conflict in the team (eg if some members feel others are being treated better).

3.2 Symptoms of conflict

How might you diagnose conflict in your team or organisation? Some of the observable signs or symptoms (Handy, 1993) include:

- Stressed individuals (due to intra-personal conflict over incompatible goals or demands, or suffering due to conflict in the team)
- Low morale and frustration
- Interpersonal friction, coldness or hostility
- Inter-group rivalry and jealousy
- Poor communication: upward, downward and lateral. (Information is often withheld or distorted as a tactic of conflict.)
- The proliferation of rules and red-tape (another tactic of conflict)
- Widespread use of arbitration, appeals to higher authority and grievances (conflict handling procedures)
- Inflexible attitudes towards change (often related to protection of interests)
- Poor co-ordination between non-communicating individuals or groups, resulting in work hold-ups, customer complaints and other 'critical incidents'.

ACTIVITY 3

evaluation

Carry out an informal conflict analysis on your own marketing team.

- What signs of conflict (if any) can you observe in the course of a working day?
- To what causes of conflict might your team be particularly prone, given the personalities involved, the nature of the task, and the team's role in the organisation?.

3.3 The impact of conflict

Before we go on to discuss the management of conflict, it is important to realise that there are different views on whether conflict is inevitable or eradicable, subjective or objective – and even positive or negative.

3.3.1 Ideologies of conflict

The interpretation of conflict is often based on ideological or political beliefs about the nature of organisations and management.

- The **happy family (or unitary) view** sees organisations as essentially harmonious, co-operative structures, designed to achieve agreed common objectives, with no necessary conflict of interest: co-operation is both desirable and achievable. Conflicts are therefore exceptional, and arise from aberrations: misunderstandings, incompatible or inflexible individuals, or pressures outside the organisation's control. The theory is that with a strong culture, positive leadership and good communication, conflict can be eliminated.
- The **conflict (or pluralist) view**, on the other hand, sees organisations as natural arenas for individual and group conflict. Members battle for limited resources, status, rewards and professional values. Organisations are political coalitions of stakeholders with their own different, divergent – and often competing - interests. The role of management is to create a workable structure for collaboration: a mutual survival strategy, involving the control of conflict through compromise, can be made acceptable in varying degrees to all concerned.
- The **revolutionary view** (primarily a Marxist perspective) sees conflict as inevitable, positive and necessary – to overthrow the status quo and power structures which exploit workers and appropriate the fruits of their labours for capitalist owners. No mutual survival strategy is possible: the interests of workers is fundamentally at odds with those of management.

- The **evolutionary (or interactionist) view** likewise regards conflict as a positively constructive dynamic, but with the purpose of:
  - **Bringing about evolutionary change**: challenging the status quo while at the same time preserving existing social and organisational arrangements, through the balancing effect of competition
  - **Preventing apathy and complacency**, unresponsiveness, group think and other effects of excessive cohesion and consensus
  - **Stimulating performance**, through encouraging competitive motivation and the generation and testing of ideas.

This constructive view may perhaps be most useful for marketing managers in practice: it neither attempts to dodge the issues of conflict (which is an observable factor of life in most organisations) *nor* assumes that all conflict is negative or destructive.

3.3.2 Conflict: constructive or destructive?

Given that a degree of conflict is inevitable, a number of writers have argued that conflict can be both positive and negative.

As we have suggested, conflict can be **negative or destructive**, where its effect is to:

- Distract attention from the task
- Polarise views, distort judgements and divide the team
- Subvert objectives in favour of secondary goals and agendas
- Encourage defensive, political or 'spoiling' behaviour, damaging co-ordination and co-operation: scapegoating, withdrawal, political game playing, withholding of information, sabotage and so on.
- Disintegrate or split the group, or force individuals to withdraw from the group
- Stimulate emotional, win-lose conflicts or hostility
- Create individual and team stress, low morale and frustration.

You may not have considered, however, that conflict can be **positive or constructive** (Hunt, 1982), where its effect is to:

- Introduce new or different solutions to problems, encouraging creativity and innovation
- Define or re-define power relationships, roles and boundaries of authority more clearly
- Avoid groupthink, by challenging dysfunctional consensus and norms
- Encourage creativity and the testing of ideas (avoiding 'groupthink' effects)
- Highlight previously unrecognised individual contributions to the team (which may in turn contribute to motivation and morale)
- Energise relationships by engaging values and emotions
- Bring differences in values and assumptions out into the open where they can be negotiated
- Provide opportunities for catharsis (the release of hostile feelings that might otherwise be repressed and come out in less overt, more damaging ways)
- Add value, by forcing competing parties to 'enlarge the pie' (rather than just competing for a larger slice).

Robbins (1997) argues that a contemporary approach to conflict:

- Recognises the inevitability (and necessity) of conflict
- Explicitly *encourages* opposition and challenge to ideas and the *status quo*
- Defines conflict management to include stimulation as well as resolution of conflict
- Considers the management of conflict as a major responsibility of all managers.

Eisenhardt, et al (1997) suggest that conflicts can be categorised in terms of whether they focused mainly on **issues** or **people.** Is the conflict over competing ideas, interests or resources – or has it arisen from something that has happened between two people or groups? People-focused conflicts threaten relationships, whereas issue-based conflicts can be turned into negotiation or collaborative problem-solving, which can enhance relationships.

3.4 Managing and resolving conflict

There are many approaches to conflict management, and the suitability of any given approach must be judged according to its relevance to a particular situation. As in other aspects of management, there is no 'right way'.

3.4.1 Conflict handling styles

In an influential conflict management model, Thomas (1976) suggested that individuals' conflict-handling styles can be mapped on two dimensions, according to the **intentions** of the parties involved: *assertiveness* (the extent to which they try to satisfy their own concerns) and *co-operativeness* (the extent to which they try to satisfy the other party's concerns). The five styles identified by this matrix can be shown as follows.

Thomas' conflict handling styles

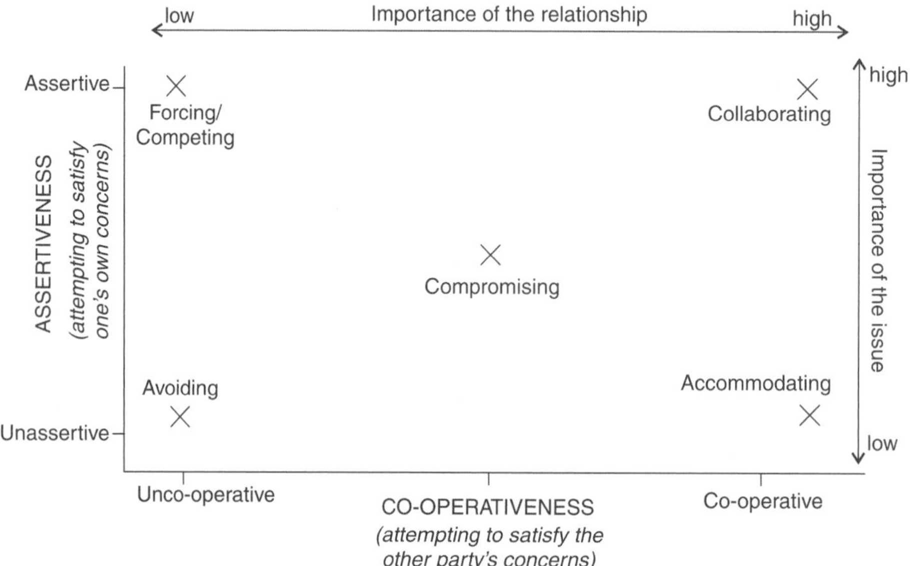

Source: Whetten and Cameron (2002, p. 359)

The five styles can be compared as follows.

- **Avoiding**. You withdraw from the conflict, or deny or conceal the incompatibility ('sweeping it under the carpet'). This may be appropriate where the issue is trivial: it may simply blow over. Withdrawal is also a legitimate short-term response to more serious conflict, allowing tempers to cool and more information to be gathered. However, if underlying causes are not identified and addressed, the conflict may eventually re-emerge or escalate.
- **Accommodating**. You concede the issue, regardless of your own legitimate concerns. This may be appropriate where the relationship is the most important consideration (it avoids upsetting people) – or where you realise you are wrong! It may be the only option where you have relatively low power, especially if time constraints are tight. It may also be appropriate to allow the other person to 'win' the argument even if wrong (eg to allow a team member to learn from his own mistakes). However, your own legitimate interests are not served by accommodating, and your authority may be undermined if you do it repeatedly.
- **Competing/forcing**. You impose your solution on the problem. This may be appropriate where the issue is the most important consideration: where it is necessary to solve ideological disputes, break down the inflexibility of others, implement unpopular measures or establish your authority. In other words, sometimes you just have to 'stick to your guns'. It is useful in emergencies, when quick, decisive action is required. It is facilitated where you have relatively high power. The drawback is that other people may feel defeated and humiliated, which may affect longer term cooperation.

- **Compromising**. You trade concessions through (explicit or implicit) bargaining or negotiation, so that each party makes some concessions in order to obtain some gains. This may be necessary where the power is evenly balanced and there is a genuine conflict of interests. If the issue is complex, compromise may be a temporary resolution while other options are explored: it may also be a 'fall-back' position if collaborating or forcing are unsuccessful. It enables you to reach an agreement that both parties can live with, and enables you to get on with work – but the solution may leave both parties unsatisfied and uncommitted.
- **Collaborating**. You work together to try and find an outcome which meets the clearly stated needs of both parties as far as possible. Conflict-handling is regarded as shared problem-solving, with the potential for a 'win-win' outcome. This may be most appropriate when both the issues and the relationship are highly important to you, and time is not pressing: it is worth seeking an integrative solution because both sets of concerns are recognised as being important. Collaborating encourages communication, facilitates learning and generates more creative options.

3.4.2 Other conflict resolution strategies

Various writers (Robbins, 1997; Hunt, 1982; Handy, 1993) add further strategies for resolving conflict, in addition to those identified in the five conflict-styles model.

- **Super-ordinate goals.** The parties are encouraged to see the bigger picture and identify shared goals that require their co-operation (particularly effective where the parties need to work together in the face of threat or challenge). Research suggests (Sherif, 1966) that this is an effective approach to fostering co-operation even where severe competition and hostility has previously existed.
- **Expansion of resources.** Rather than offering smaller 'slices' of available resources, 'enlarge the pie': resources are freed and mobilised to meet *both* parties' needs, eliminating the need for competition. The potential to expand resources may be limited and costly: nevertheless, it is a win-win-seeking option.
- **Arbitration**. An arbitrator with authority over both parties makes a decisive judgement or applies influence to settle the conflict. This has the benefit of re-establishing working relations in the short term, as long as the arbitrator has sufficient power. However, it may impose compromise or win-lose solutions on the parties: their differences have not been openly or collaboratively addressed and the underlying problems have not been solved.
- **Altering the human variable.** Effort is made to change the attitudes, beliefs and perceptions underlying the conflict. This will underpin any serious attempt at collaborative problem solving. However, some causes of conflict may be 'outside' the perceptions and beliefs of the parties concerned: eg genuine resource scarcity, policy inequity or role ambiguity that need to be addressed.
- **Altering the structural variable.** Effort is made to re-organise work relationships in order to minimise the potential for conflict. Structural variables include: how a situation is set up; role definitions; time constraints; physical proximity of clashing personalities; inequalities of power/authority; and unequal access to, or control of, resources.

3.5 Formal grievance procedures

KEY CONCEPT

concept

A **grievance** occurs when an individual feels that (s)he is being wrongly or unfairly treated by a colleague or manager and wishes to assert his or her rights. **Grievance procedures** embody employees' right to appeal against unfair or otherwise prejudicial conduct or conditions that affect them and their work.

When an individual has a grievance, (s)he should be able to pursue it and ask to have the problem resolved. Some grievances may be capable of solution informally by an individual's manager. However, if an informal solution is not possible, there should be a formal grievance procedure:

- To allow **objective grievance handling** – including 'cooling off' periods and independent case investigation and arbitration
- To **protect employees** from victimisation – particularly where a grievance involves their immediate superiors

- To provide **legal protection** for both parties, in the event of a dispute resulting in claims before an Employment Tribunal
- To **encourage grievance airing** – which is an important source of feedback to management on employee problems and dissatisfactions
- To **require full and fair investigation** of grievances, enabling the employer-employee relationship to be respected and preserved, despite problems.

3.5.1 Elements of formal grievance procedures

A typical progressive procedure for pursuing a grievance includes the following stages:

- **Informal discussion** with a staff/union representative, colleague or manager (subject to confidentiality). This may be sufficient to 'clear the air' or initiate informal conflict resolution or remedial action.
- **Grievance interview** with the immediate manager. If (s)he is the subject of the complaint, this may be referred to the next level up.
- Grievance interview with a **higher authority**. If the first interview fails to satisfy the employee, the matter may be referred upwards.
- **HR department mediation**. Cases referred upwards should also be reported to the HR department: specialist mediation and/or arbitration may be required.

A formal grievance procedure, set out in the company manual, should:

- State the **rights** of the employee for each type of grievance. For example, an employee who is overlooked for promotion might be entitled to a review of his annual appraisal report, or to attend a special appeals promotion/ selection board if he has been in his current grade for at least a certain number of years.
- State what the **procedures** for pursuing a grievance should be.
- Affirm the right of the employee to have the grievance **fairly investigated**.
- Affirm the right of the employee to be **accompanied** to interviews by a colleague or union representative.
- State **time limits** for initiating certain grievance procedures and subsequent stages of them (such as communication of decisions, and appeals).
- Require **written records** of all meetings concerned with the case to be made and distributed to all the participants.

4 Managing change in teams

4.1 Types and levels of change

For some people in some organisations, change is a positive and energising opportunity to make things better, to innovate and to adapt flexibly to changing customer demands and environmental challenges. For others, it means loss of security, loss of competence – perhaps loss of livelihood.

The fact is that in today's fast-moving business environment – with its technological innovation, ever-heightening competition and increasingly fickle consumers – **change is inevitable**. The marketing function, for example, has been affected by change in various ways. Think of the emergence of new disciplines like relationship marketing, web marketing and viral marketing; the impact of new technology on products, media and marketing techniques; the globalisation of markets; and constantly changing consumer preferences and trends.

Some authors make a distinction between '**change**' (meaning incremental change) and '**transformation**' (or fundamental, sweeping, discontinuous change). Others use the terminology 'evolutionary' and 'revolutionary' change.

- **Evolutionary change** is a proactive approach, building on the existing situation or *status quo*, in small steps over a long period of time. This is the basis of business improvement strategies like continuous improvement or *kaizen*, for example. Because it requires only realistic, small operational changes, it can be implemented from the 'bottom up',

involving team members through suggestion schemes, quality circles and consultation. This makes it a particularly effective approach for building up organisational learning and responsiveness to change (such as shifting patterns of customer demand, sector dynamics and cultural change).

- **Revolutionary change** is often a reactive approach, responding to crisis or the need for a completely new way of doing things. It seeks to throw out the *status quo* and introduce radical transformation in a relatively short period of time. This is the basis of business improvement strategies such as Business Process Reengineering, for example: because it requires sweeping change across organisational structures and systems, it can only be implemented from the 'top down'. This makes it particularly effective where the *status quo* has become dysfunctional for organisational survival or growth, or where sudden challenges require a radical response (eg the introduction of a new technology, major competitor initiative or the need for restructuring following a merger).

4.2 The impact of change

Change may affect individuals in different ways: physically (eg different work methods); circumstantially (eg relocations, re-establishing work relationships with a new team); and psychologically (eg the requirement to learn new skills). Change may create feelings of disorientation before new circumstances have been assimilated. Uncertainty may lead to insecurity: especially acute in changes involving work, where there can be very great pressures for continuity and fast acclimatisation.

Individuals and teams often **resist change**, attempting to preserve the existing state of affairs against pressure to alter it. Sources of resistance to change in general may include age and inflexibility, strong needs for security and emotional instability. Sources of resistance to *particular* proposed changes, (eg in location, methods of working or pay structure), may include:

- **Attitudes or beliefs**, perhaps arising from cultural, religious or class influences (for example, resistance to changes in the law on Sunday trading).
- **Loyalty to the team and its norms**, perhaps with an accompanying rejection of other groups, or outsiders (for example, in the case of a relocation so that two departments share office space).
- **Habit, or past norms**. This can be a strong source of clinging to old ways, whether out of security needs, respect for tradition, or the belief that 'you can't teach an old dog new tricks' (for example, resistance to the introduction of new technology).
- **Politics** – in the sense of resisting changes that might weaken the power base of the individual or group or strengthen a rival's position.
- The **way** in which any change is put forward and implemented.

Not all change is resisted, however, and it is important to realise that the aim of change management is to create a **positive energy and impetus for change**. People's reactions to change depend on the type of change, the reason for change, and the way change is handled. Many people long for change at work, and have a wealth of ideas about how it should be achieved.

Four types of **change experience** have been identified (*Torrington and Weightman*,1994).

Type	Comment	Reaction
Imposition	Initiated and driven by someone else	Resistance
Adaptation	A change in attitude or behaviour as a result of changes by others	Uncertainty
Growth	A response to opportunities	Delight
Creativity	The individual instigates and controls the change process	Excitement

More generally, conditions favourable to the acceptance – or even welcoming – of change in an organisation include:

- Adaptable or 'organic' organisation structures: output- or customer-focused, flexible and horizontal (as discussed in Chapter 1).
- Good multi-directional communication systems, and systems for formal and informal negotiation and consultation
- Vision, leadership and support from senior management
- Supportive culture and attitudes: trust between management and staff; receptivity to new ideas, learning and information-sharing; tolerance of mistakes while learning, flexibility and so on.

4.3 Pressures for and against change

Kurt Lewin (1951) developed a technique for visualising the forces for and against change in a particular situation, in order to diagnose some of the change management issues that will need to be addressed, and some of the resources available to support change.

Lewin recognised that in any given situation there exist forces for change (pushing towards a preferred state) and forces for maintaining the status quo (pushing back towards the way things are). The relative strength of these forces determines the current situation (where a balance of forces create a temporary equilibrium) and the pace and direction of change (if one set of forces is stronger than the other).

- **Driving forces** (forces for change) encourage people to give up the old ways of doing things. They may include: the unpleasantness of customer complaints; the frustration of inefficient methods or systems; a focus on customer satisfaction and competitor advantage; new technology becoming available; a new leader in the organisation; or support from a powerful change agent.
- **Restraining forces** (forces against change) support the status quo. They may include: shortage of resources for change; opposition from key influencers; strong cultural values or 'old-fashioned' leadership; already-installed technology and systems; managerial pre-occupation with day-to-day matters; psychological (and/or financial) investment in the current state of things; a low tolerance of risk or high need for security; rigid bureaucratic structures and cultures; and so on.

Force field analysis maps the forces for and against change using directional arrows, the thickness of which represents the strength of each force. Numerical scores can also be added to each arrow (on a scale of 0 for neutral to 4 for strong), giving a total score on each side: the side with the highest score will have the greatest force.

As an example, consider the force field map for a marketing manager seeking to introduce a new system of performance review.

Force field analysis

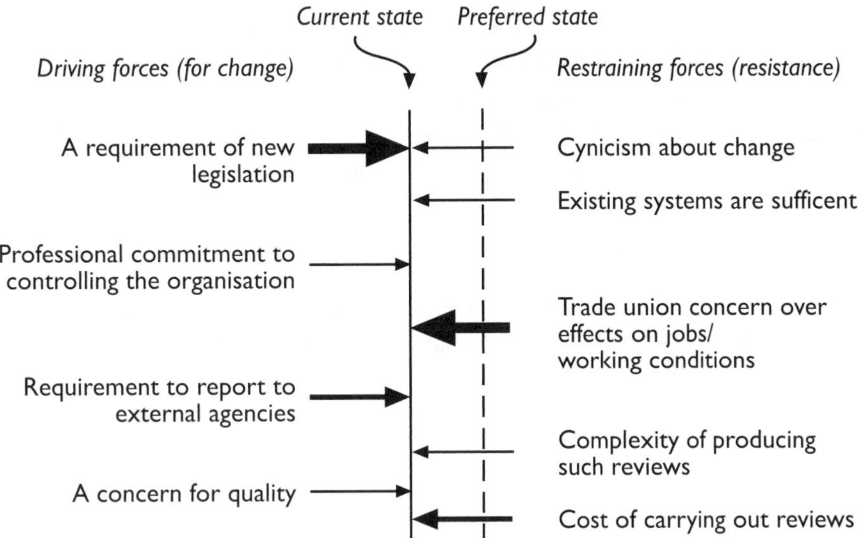

Having identified the forces for and against change, managers can select strategies and styles which focus on:

- Adding and/or strengthening driving forces and/or
- Eliminating and/or weakening restraining forces.

Driving forces can be strengthened by emphasising the needs and benefits of change (for example, threat from competitors or environmental changes); training people to cope with change; co-opting the support of influencers; raising confidence with a positive management style; allocating resources to change; changing the organisation structure to facilitate change; and so on.

Restraining forces can be weakened by participation (involving resistors in solving the problem), education and communication (persuading resistors of the need for change), negotiation (offering concessions to reduce resistance); and so on.

In our example above, for example, we might decide on a programme of negotiation with the trade unions (to weaken one of the stronger restraining forces). This might add to 'cost' – but reduce trade union concern. We could do some internal marketing to strengthen concern for quality. Staff could be shown that performance review gives them more opportunities for development, creating a new driving force. And so on. This should shift the balance towards change.

4.4 The planned change model

Lewin (1951) developed his force field model to draw up a three-step model for changing human behaviour.

The three stage (unfreeze-movement-refreeze) model of change

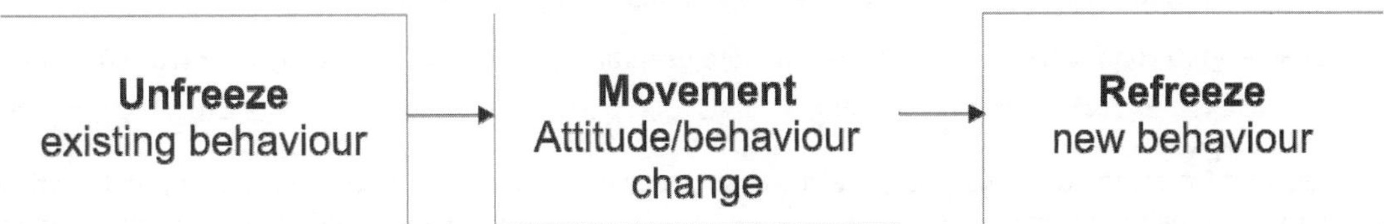

The first stage involves unfreezing or breaking down the existing restraining and driving forces which keep the situation in a state of equilibrium. This is the most difficult stage of the process, concerned mainly with motivating the change, confronting resistance and helping people to *un-learn* what they already know or assume. If the need for change is immediate, clear and critical (eg necessary for the survival of the group or organisation), the unfreeze stage will be greatly accelerated.

The second stage introduces imbalances which allow driving forces to outweigh restraining forces: strengthening driving forces, weakening restraining forces, as discussed earlier.

The third stage is refreezing the driving/restraining forces to hold the new equilibrium in place, by consolidating or reinforcing the new behaviours and attitudes. This may involve the use of rewards for new behaviours, coaching and training, the alteration of policies and procedures to reflect the changes and so on.

It is worth noting that the planned change model was designed for fairly stable environmental conditions. In fast-changing or turbulent business environments, 're-freezing' may be seen as counter-productive, hampering flexibility and responsiveness. Some organisations may need to exist in a constant state of unfreezing and changing, without 're-hardening' a new status quo.

4.5 N-step change models

A number of attempts have been made to describe a process of change based on a phased project management structure: 'n' sequential steps or phases to implement change. A general step-by-step planned model for change at the team level may be as follows.

Step 1 Determine the need or desire for change in a particular area

Step 2 Prepare a draft plan: brainstorming is helpful, as alternative options may be generated

Step 3 Analyse probable reactions and responses to the change

Step 4 Evaluate and select options for change. The decision may be taken either by group problem-solving (participation) or with group input (consultation) or unilaterally by the manager (imposition).

Step 5 Establish a timetable for change, allowing time for consultation and adjustment where possible.

Step 6 Communicate the plan for change and address areas of resistance.

Step 7 Implement the change.

Step 8 Monitor progress and commitment, and adjust as required, in a continuous cycle.

Marketing Success (May 2002) suggested a handy checklist for team leaders and managers.

- **Inform:** let people know what is happening and why
- **Include:** make sure everyone knows their role
- **Investigate feedback:** let people know how well they are doing
- **Identify:** team members may have ideas for improvement
- **Inspire:** lead by example
- **Implement:** try to encourage new ways of implementing useful ideas.

Change guru John Kotter (1995) proposes a more general eight step model for **major or transformational change.**

Why change programmes fail	8-Step model for major change
Allowing too much complexity (not breaking change down into manageable chunks)	Establish a sense of urgency and prioritise change objectives based on market and organisational imperatives
Failing to build a coalition of stakeholder support	Form a guiding coalition of influential stakeholders
Lack of clear vision for the purpose and direction of change	Create a compelling vision for change
Failing to communicate the vision clearly	Communicate the vision as widely and clearly as possible
Allowing resistance and barriers to gather	Empower people to act on the vision by removing cultural, technological and structural obstacles

Why change programmes fail	8-Step model for major change
Lack of short-term wins (to create momentum and confidence)	Plan to create short-term wins (visible performance improvements, recognition and reward for participants) which foster momentum and buy-in
Stopping short (not consolidating change or pushing for on-going improvement)	Consolidate improvements to produce further change, keeping momentum going (eg next steps, developing staff, setting improvement goals)
Failing to embed changes in the corporate culture	Institutionalise new approaches: embed them in culture, procedures, HR systems

4.6 Marketing change

Rosabeth Moss Kanter (1985) advises change agents to define and communicate their projects in ways that make them sound:

- **Try-able** The change should appear capable of being subjected to a pilot before going the whole way
- **Reversible** Convince your team that what you are proposing can be changed back to the status quo if it falls to pieces: irreversible changes are seen as risky
- **Divisible** Where the change has a number of separate dimensions, present these as potentially independent aspects of a broader change programme – so when single issues cause problems, the whole package doesn't have to fold
- **Concrete** Make the changes and their outcomes tangible and avoid expressing what will happen in abstract and general terms which do not convey an accurate feel for the proposal (and may arouse suspicion)
- **Familiar** Make proposals in terms that other people can recognise, because if what you propose is so far over the horizon people can't recognise it, they'll feel out of their comfort zones and start resisting
- **Congruent** Proposals for change should where possible be seen to fit with the rest of the organisation and be consistent with existing policy, practice and values
- **Sexy** Choose projects that have publicity value – in terms of external or media relations, or in terms of internal politics. (What will the local press go for? What will excite the chief executive?)

4.7 Change management styles

The manner in which a change is put across is very important.

- **Confront resistance**. Talking through areas of conflict may lead to useful insights and the adapting of the programme of change to advantage.
- **Keep people informed**. Information should be sensible, clear, consistent and realistic: there is no point issuing information which will be seen as a blatant misrepresentation of the situation.
- **Explain**. The reason for and benefits of change need to be sold to people.
- **Training and support**. Learning programmes for any new skills required by the change will have to be designed.
- **Empathy**. Getting to know the people involved in, and affected by, change enables their reactions to be anticipated – and allows them to feel heard.
- The degree to which **consultation or participation** will be possible (or genuine) will depend on management's attitude towards the potential contribution of the team. Where genuine, employees should be consulted *before* the plan for change has been finalised. Input should be seriously considered and objectively evaluated – and good ideas should be used (and rewarded).
- **Timing**. The more gradual the change, the more time is available for questions to be asked, reassurance/training to be given and so on. Presenting people with a *fait accompli* may short-circuit resistance at the planning and

immediate implementation stage (and may be required in crisis change situations), but may lead to resistance or lack of commitment later.

Johnson, Scholes & Whittington (2008) propose five broad strategies or styles for managing change in order to secure stakeholder buy-in, and for supporting and leading team members through change.

- **Education and communication**: promoting and justifying compelling reasons for the change and the benefits expected to accrue from the change. This process helps to reduce uncertainty, a major cause of resistance to change. Johnson *et al* emphasise that communication is a two-way process: 'feedback on communication is important, particularly if the changes to be introduced are difficult to understand or threatening, or if it is critically important to get the changes right.'
- **Facilitation and support.** Facilitation involves assisting people to change (with training, coaching, resources or extra staffing, say). Support involves helping people to come to terms with the change psychologically (eg through counselling about change issues and help with coping). Although this process can be time-consuming and costly, it reduces fear and uncertainty, and also equips employees to implement change.
- **Participation and involvement.** People are more likely to support changes if they are encouraged to 'own' them through having participated in the decision-making process. Quite apart from the advantages of enhanced commitment to change, participation may allow better quality decision-making by taking advantage of people's expertise and knowledge in relevant areas.
- **Negotiation and agreement.** A negotiation strategy may be required where potential resistance groups have considerable power. It is often practised where a workforce is represented by recognised trade unions, for example. Opposing interest groups bargain towards an agreement based on compromise. The main advantage of a negotiation strategy is that (ideally) it allows conflicts of interest to be acknowledged and taken into account in a systematic fashion.
- **Manipulation and coercion**. It is important to remember that change leaders may have the option of simply applying their power to implement whatever they perceived is required, and to enforce compliance. Although such an approach fails to address resistance, and can cause resentment, it may be effective in a crisis situation (where decisions need to be made and implemented swiftly).

4.8 Change agents

Change agents are individuals or teams who are appointed or empowered to drive a change programme. They may be change programme/project managers, external change management consultants – or marketing managers pursuing change objectives.

Huczynski & Buchanan (2001) point out that change agency is becoming increasingly dispersed, involving change teams whose membership is drawn from all levels of the organisation. They argue further that a change agent can be 'any member of the organisation seeking to promote, further, support, sponsor, initiate, implement or deliver change. Change agents are not necessarily senior managers and do not necessarily hold formal "change management" job titles and positions.'

Crainer (1998) has highlighted seven key skill areas for managing change.

- Managing conflict (while stimulating diversity and expression of concerns)
- Interpersonal skills
- Project management skills (complex planning and control, and stakeholder management)
- Leadership (clear direction) *and* flexibility (being willing to respond to input and contingencies)
- Managing processes (not just the 'content' of change)
- Managing strategy (aligning change objectives to corporate/business goals)
- Managing personal development (own learning and growth for and through change).

It may be argued that marketers are natural change agents, because of:

- Their role and skills in **managing corporate communications** (internal as well as external)
- Their position at the **interface with key stakeholders**, giving them a unique sensitivity to the organisation's environment and changing customer/stakeholder demands (a compelling justification for change)
- Their ability to apply **marketing skills and disciplines** to the marketing of change: communication, persuasion, motive arousal, issues management, relationship development and so on.

Zeus and Skiffington (2002) also argue that **coaches and mentors** (roles which team leaders may already adopt in order to develop team members) are ideally placed to act as change agents, because of their:

- **Communication skills**. Communication is essential to successful change management. Coaching and mentoring provide a trusting, open environment where individuals can share their fears or beliefs about change – and coaches can convey enthusiasm and conviction that the person *can* change and the barriers can be overcome.
- **Orientation**. Change is always more successful when people's needs and goals are taken into account, so that change is seen as a 'win-win' for the individual and the organisation. This is the nature of a coaching/mentoring relationship.
- **Empathy**. Change agents are most successful when they understand (and show that they understand) the difficulties of change for the individual – as well as being challenging and encouraging. These issues can be explored in the course of coaching and mentoring.
- **Credibility**. Coaches and mentors are often in the position of role model, and therefore have the power to influence people to change, or to accept and embrace change.

4.9 Evaluating change management

The effectiveness of change management can be evaluated in a number of ways.

- Has a **sound business case** been made supporting the proposed change?
- Have the **financial** and **non-financial benefits** to be derived from change been fully defined?
- Has a detailed **change plan** been developed?
- Has proper **consultation and consensus-building** been conducted? Are key internal and external stakeholders in the change fully committed to the success of the changes?
- Are the **change objectives** against which success will be measured clearly identified?
- Has the change programme **brought about the planned outcomes**: attitudinal or behavioural change, improved unit or business results and so on?
- What are the **attitudes of key stakeholders** to the change programme and results of change?

ASSIGNMENT TIP

concept

The assignment for December 2009 / March 2010 contained the topic of change management. The examiner noted that the better answers came from candidates who related the differences between management and leadership to innovation and change management. Weaker candidates just described the differences between a manager and leader or offered definitions without applying to the context of innovation and change.

Learning objective review

Learning objectives	Covered
1 Plan how to prevent discrimination and value diversity in teams	☑ The dimensions, benefits and challenges of team diversity ☑ How to foster and leverage team diversity ☑ The UK legal framework on diversity and equal opportunity
2 Propose approaches to manage and co-ordinate the work of remote (virtual and international) teams, and create effective working relations	☑ Challenges of international team working, with particular emphasis on cultural differences ☑ Challenges and benefits of virtual team working ☑ The use of ICT and management/leadership skills in building, controlling and motivating remote teams
3 Identify potential areas of team conflict, identifying causes and making recommendations for conflict management	☑ The sources of conflict in and between teams ☑ The impacts of conflict, both positive and negative, creating the need for flexible conflict management ☑ A range of conflict handling styles: the Thomas model ☑ Approaches to conflict resolution and management ☑ Grievance procedures
4 Propose approaches for managing change in teams	☑ The nature and impact of change ☑ Models of change management, including freeze-unfreeze-refreeze and n-step models ☑ Approaches to supporting team members through change ☑ The role of change agents

Quick quiz

1 Where does conflict in groups often stem from?

2 How can cross cultural competence be enhanced within managers?

3 Fill in the blank. ______________ may be used to help leaders and staff members to understanding the potential for problems arising from culturally-acquired assumptions: the need to recognise cultural stereotypes and move beyond them through new information and encounters with people; the need to appreciate that 'different' does not necessarily imply 'wrong'; and so on.

4 How can change impact individuals?

5 What stage process does Kurt Lewin advocate using when trying to make a positive and maintained change?

Activity debriefs

1 (a) A high-UA manager, expecting to find detailed and generally adhered-to rules for everything, may be horrified by the ad-hocracy of a low-UA organisation: if (s)he attempts to impose a high-UA culture, there may be resistance from employees and management.

(b) A high-individuality manager may implement MbO on the basis of individual performance targets, results and rewards: this may fail to motivate collectivist workers, for whom group processes and performance is more important.

(c) A low-masculinity manager may try to shelter the workforce from the effects of downsizing, taking time for consultation, retraining, voluntary measures and so on: this may seem unacceptably 'soft' to a high-masculinity parent firm.

2 Answer will depend on your own research.

3 Answer will depend on your own research.

Quiz answers

1
- Goal incompatibility
- Cultural incompatibility
- Interdependence and shared resources
- Competition for limited or scarce resources
- Authority, power and status distribution
- Change and uncertainty
- The external environment

2
- Encouraging diversified work experience in international or multi-cultural settings
- Undertaking training exercises (reading, language learning, cultural briefings)
- Networking with managers from other cultures and using them as consultants
- Seeking to learn through all cross-cultural interactions.

3 Awareness training.

4 Change may affect individuals in ways: physically (eg different work methods); circumstantially (eg relocations, re-establishing work relationships with a new team); and psychologically (eg the requirement to learn new skills). Change may create feelings of disorientation before new circumstances have been assimilated. Uncertainty may lead to insecurity: especially acute in changes involving work, where there can be very great pressures for continuity and fast acclimatisation.

5 Unfreeze, change then refreeze.

References

Armstrong, M. (2009), A Handbook of Human Resource Management Practice, (11th edition), Kogan Page London.

Boddy, D. (2005), Management: An Introduction, (3rd edition), FT Prentice Hall, Harlow, Essex.

Cornelius, H. & Faire, S. (1989), Everyone Can Win: How to Resolve Conflict, Simon & Schuster, Sydney.

Eisenhardt, K. M., Kahwajy, J. L. & Bourgeois L. J. (1997), *'Now management teams can have a good fight'* in The Work of Teams, Katzenbach, J. R. (edition), Harvard Business School Press, Boston.

Gardenswartz, L. (2001), *'Cross-cultural awareness'* in HR Magazine, March.

Gardenswartz, L. & Rowe, A. (1993), Managing Diversity: A complete desk reference and planning guide, Irwin, Homewood, Il.

Guirdham, M. (1995), Interpersonal Skills at Work, (2nd edition), Prentice Hall Europe, Harlow.

Hall, E. T. (1976), Beyond Culture, Doubleday, New York.

Handy, C. (1993), Understanding Organisations, (4th edition), Penguin, London.

Hofstede, G. (1996) Cultures and Organisations, McGraw Hill, London.

Huczynski, A. & Buchanan, D. (2001), Organizational Behaviour: An Introductory Text, (4th edition), FT Prentice Hall, Harlow.

Hunt, J. (1982), Managing People in Organisations, McGraw Hill, New York.

Jobber, D. (2007), Principles and Practice of Marketing, (5th edition), McGraw Hill Education, Maidenhead.

Johnson, G., Scholes, K. & Whittington, R. (2008), Exploring Corporate Strategy, (8th edition), Pearson, Harlow.

Mintzberg, H. (1983), Power In and Around Organisations, Prentice Hall, New Jersey.

Mullins, L. (1999), Management & Organisational Behaviour, (5th edition), Pearson Education, Harlow.

Kanter, R. M. (1985), The Change Masters: Corporate Entrepreneurs at Work, Routledge.

Kotter, J. P. (1995), *'Leading Change: Why Transformation Efforts Fail'* in Harvard Business Review, March-April.

Lewin, K. (1951), Field Theory in Social Science, Harper & Row, New York.

Lewin, K. (1974), *'Frontiers in group dynamics: social equilibria and social change'* in Human Relations, June, pp 5-41.

Pedler M, Burgoyne, J. & Boydell, T. (2004), A Manager's Guide to Leadership, McGraw Hill, Maidenhead.

Robbins, S. P. (1997), Managing Organisational Conflict: A Non-traditional Approach, Prentice Hall, New Jersey.

Schneider, S. C. & Barsoux, J-L. (1997), Managing Across Cultures, Prentice Hall, Harlow.

Sherif, M. (1966), In Common Predicament: Social Psychology of Intergroup Conflict and Co-operation, Houghton Mifflin, Boston, MA.

Solomon, C. M. (2001), *'Managing Virtual Teams'* in Workforce, June.

Thomas, K. W. (1976), *'Conflict and conflict management'* in Handbook of Industrial and Organisational Psychology, Dunnette M. D. (edition), Rand McNally, Chicago, pp 889-935.

Trompenaars, F. (1997), Riding the Waves of Culture, (2nd edition), Nicholas Brealey, London.

Whetten, D. & Cameron, K. (2002), Developing Management Skills, (5th edition), Prentice Hall, New Jersey.

Chapter 9

Managing marketing finances

Topic list

1 The marketing manager's role
2 The purpose of budgeting
3 Cost behaviour and budgeting considerations

Introduction

The next four chapters cover Part C of the syllabus, Operational Finances for Marketing. This area of the syllabus is concerned with your understanding of the financial context in which an organisation operates, as well as your ability to effectively control marketing expenditure.

We start this chapter with an overview of the planning and control aspects of the marketing manager's role. Later in the chapter we cover the purpose of budgeting, before looking at different types of cost behaviour and related budgeting considerations.

In the following chapters we examine the budgeting process and its role in the management and control of marketing performance, as well as examining other tools and frameworks that may be utilised to help ensure resources are utilised efficiently.

Syllabus linked learning objectives

By the end of the chapter you will be able to:

	Learning objectives	Syllabus link
1	Assess the marketing manager's role in managing the finances of the marketing function	3.1
2	Explain the purpose of budgeting	3.1
3	Explain the significance of different types of costs (fixed, semi-fixed, variable and semi-variable costs)	3.1

1 The marketing manager's role

Before looking at the financial aspects of the marketing manager's role, let's consider the wider role of the marketing manager and managers in general.

1.1 The role of the manager

KEY CONCEPT

concept

Manager's role:

Managers are responsible for using the organisation's scarce resources efficiently to help the organisation achieve its objectives.

The role of the manager has changed over time, influenced by changes in the environment and the prevalent business culture. Challenges for managers today include the speed of change, customer power and global competition.

Modern managers have many functions and must take responsibility for a range of business activities. The marketing manager is no exception to this. In order to be effective, to contribute to the overall success of the organisation and to be able to make informed decisions, the marketing manager must understand the organisation's overall strategy.

1.1.1 Cross-functional communication

An understanding of other functions and departments (eg production, finance, sales) is required to enable the marketing manager to understand the wider context and organisational priorities. There would be no point planning a marketing communications campaign relating to a particular product if currently production constraints mean supply will be limited.

The marketing manager should therefore communicate with other senior managers, ensuring a coordinated approach to achieving organisational goals. The marketing team should also be kept informed of current organisational priorities and developments.

1.1.2 Planning

KEY CONCEPT

concept

Planning is the process of identifying objectives and formulating strategies to achieve them.

Planning enables the organisation to cope with the uncertainty of the future in a way that will allow its objectives to be achieved. There are three important steps to planning.

Step 1 **Objective setting**. Deciding what the organisation, and units within it, should achieve

Step 2 **Forecasting**. Anticipating, as far as possible, what opportunities and threats are likely to be offered by the future

Step 3 **Detailed planning**. Making decisions about what to do, how and when to do it and who should be responsible for it

Plans provide direction, focus and predictability to the work of the organisation. A planned approach should ensure the organisation is better able to cope with environmental change.

Planning affects all levels of managers tasks, from the determination of overall direction, down to the detail of day-to-day operational tasks. There is a hierarchical structure of plans in which broad, long-term strategies lead to medium-term policies which are supported by short-term operational decisions.

An approach to planning

A systematic approach to planning, based on results and objectives involves:

Step 1 Aims; which dictate

Step 2 Key result areas; for which there should be

Step 3 Standards; and

Step 4 Detailed targets; so that

Step 5 Action plans; can be formulated and implemented, subject to

Step 6 Monitoring; and

Step 7 Control action where required.

ASSIGNMENT TIP

application

Ensure you use an appropriate format for your work based assignment. If your assignment relates to a planning task, the format shown above may be suitable (with an appropriate Appendix). Your assignment must conform to the CIM guidance relating to the format of your Work Based Assignment.

1.1.3 Control

KEY CONCEPT

concept

Control is the process of monitoring the performance of individuals and units, and taking whatever actions may be necessary to bring performance into line with plans, by adjusting performance or, possibly, the plans themselves.

Control is required because unpredictable events occur and actual performance differs from the plan. For example, a powerful new competitor may enter the market. Control systems allow managers to identify deviations from plan and to do something about them.

Robert Anthony (1965) provided a definition of management control that is recognised as a classic and remains valid today. Anthony defined management control as 'the process by which managers assure that resources are obtained and used effectively and efficiently in the accomplishment of the organisation's objectives'.

As Anthony's reference to the organisation's objectives demonstrates, planning is linked very closely with control.

(a) It is necessary to verify whether or not the plan has worked or is working, and whether the objectives of the plan have been/are being achieved. This is where control becomes part of the planning process.

(b) Actual results and performance are therefore compared to the plan. If there are deviations, weaknesses or errors, control measures will be taken – which involves adjusting or setting further plans for ongoing action. Thus planning becomes part of the control process.

Basic control cycle

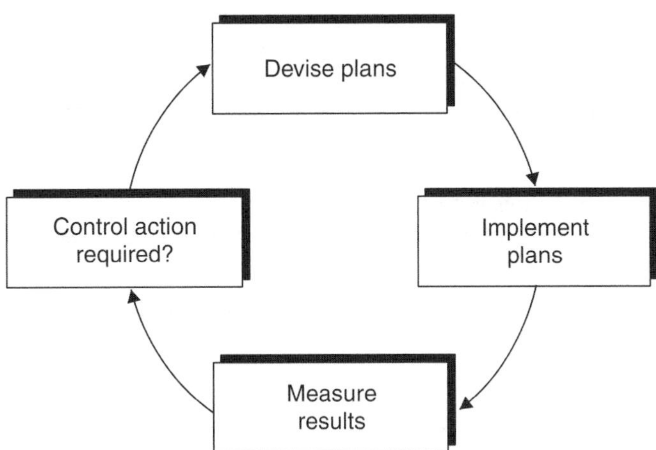

An important aspect of both planning and control activity is the **budget**, which we cover in detail in the next section.

2 The purpose of budgeting

2.1 What is a budget?

KEY CONCEPT

A **budget** is a statement of desired performance expressed in financial terms.

The term 'budget' is often used in a variety of ways. When talking about 'the budget', some people may be referring to any of the following.

Aspect	Comment
Forecast	A budget may be used to forecast expected performance. Forecasting helps managers consider the future. Given conditions of rapid change and uncertainty, however, this function will only be helpful over short periods of time. Budgets or forecasts need to be updated or recast often.
Means of allocating resources	Budgets can be used to decide what resources are needed and how much should be given to each area of the organisation. Budgets often set ceilings on spending, for example on project teams.
Yardstick	Budgets are often used as a yardstick against which to compare actual performance. The budget provides a means of indicating where and when control action may be necessary (and possibly where some managers or employees are open to censure for achieving poor results).

For our purposes in this section, a **budget** is a **quantified plan of action** for a forthcoming accounting period. A budget is a plan of what the organisation is aiming to achieve and what it has set as a target.

A budget is therefore a plan for a defined period of time expressed in financial terms to be referred to and used as a **control tool** throughout the budget period. A beautifully laid out budgeted income statement that is rarely referred to is worthless.

2.2 Objectives of budgeting

Budgets are therefore not prepared in isolation and then filed away but are the fundamental components of what is known as the budgetary planning and control system. A budgetary planning and control system is essentially a system for ensuring communication, coordination and control within an organisation.

KEY CONCEPT

Budgetary control is concerned with ensuring that actual financial results are in line with expected or budgeted targets.

Buckley and McKenna (1972) summed up the budgeting process as '... the influencing of management behaviour by setting agreed performance standards, the evaluation of results and feedback to management in anticipation of corrective action where necessary'.

One way to remember the objectives of a budgetary planning and control system is to use the 'PRIME' acronym.

- **P** – Planning
- **R** – Responsibility
- **I** – Integration and co-ordination
- **M** – Motivation
- **E** – Evaluation and control

Objective	Comment
Planning	Compelling manages to plan is probably the most important feature of a budgetary planning and control system. Planning forces management to look ahead, to set out detailed plans for achieving the targets for each function or department - and to anticipate problems. This ensures management have a plan to work towards. It also helps managers to **foresee potential threats or opportunities**, so that they may take action now to avoid or minimise the effect of the threats and to take full advantage of the opportunities.
Responsibility	Objectives are set for the organisation as a whole, and for individual departments and operations within the organisation. Quantified expressions of these objectives are then drawn up as targets to be achieved within the timescale of the budget plan. Budgetary planning and control systems require that managers of **budget centres** are made responsible for the achievement of budget targets for the operations under their personal control.
Integration and coordination	The activities of different departments or functions of the organisation need to be **coordinated** to ensure **maximum integration of effort** towards common goals. This concept of coordination implies, for example, that the purchasing department should base its budget on production requirements and that the production budget should in turn be based on sales expectations. Coordination can be difficult to achieve, and there is often conflict between departments or functions. This may hinder efforts to achieve a fully integrated combined plan most likely to achieve the company's objectives. Communication is important here to ensure each person, function and department knows their role (and the role of others) in the overall plan.
Motivation	The interest and commitment of employees can be encouraged through **communication** and (later) **feedback** of actual results compared to budget. The identification of controllable reasons for departures from budget, with the managers responsible, provides an **incentive** for improving future performance. Some reward for achieving budget may provide motivation, although care should be taken to ensure this doesn't lead to behaviour that focuses solely on achieving short-term targets to the detriment of other considerations.
Evaluation and control	As well as providing a yardstick for control by comparison, the monitoring of actual results compared with the budget can provide a basis for **evaluating the performance of the budget holder.** As a result of this evaluation the manager might be rewarded, perhaps with a financial bonus or promotion. Alternatively the evaluation process might highlight the need for more investment in staff development and training.

2.3 The marketing budget and the marketing team

The marketing budget plays an important part in the financial management of the marketing function.

- It facilitates **planning** by requiring marketing activity to be planned and costed in advance.
- It ensures the marketing manager is accountable or **responsible** for funds spent.
- As the marketing budget is developed together with other budgets, it helps ensure **integration** and coordination.
- The budget provides **motivation**, particularly to avoid overspend.
- The budget provides control by highlighting possible areas of concern (eg it may be possible to compensate for an overspend in the first quarter later in the year). It is also one of the ways in which the performance of the marketing department will be **evaluated**.

MARKETING AT WORK

application

The Case for Effective Budgeting

With the economy on the ropes, companies need some kind of lifeline. One overlooked strategy is to go back to basics: overhaul fundamentals like financial planning, budgeting and forecasting.

Companies require their financial plans to clearly represent their strategic objectives. Budgeting encompasses all the details for costs and sales across a company. Managers are then able to forecast a number of 'what-if' scenarios based on recent actual performance.

A shrinking economy is reason enough to get a handle on budgets, says William Soward, chief executive of Adaptive Planning. 'If there ever was a good time to manage budgets, it's now'.

Effective budgeting has a big impact on performance. Companies with best-in-class budget processes improved their profitability by 17% over the last 24 months, according to a survey from tech research firm Aberdeen Group. Aberdeen's survey found that best-in-class companies consistently tighten up their internal processes for planning, budgeting and forecasting. They shorten the times between budget cycles and they finalise budgets before the new fiscal year begins.

Aberdeen's survey also found these companies use specialist budgeting software (rather than spreadsheets) to manage their budgets. Spreadsheets are vulnerable to manual errors, whereas budgeting software usually extracts numbers directly from the nominal ledger. That reduces data-entry errors and reduces the likelihood of 'garbage in, garbage out'.

Rather than reforecast every year or quarter, the new aim is to update financial plans monthly or even more closer to real time if possible. Companies are now re-forecasting more often. For example, a company might build models of its best- and worst-case scenarios for a sales slowdown in each geographic region. Specialist budgeting software makes this possible.

J. Bonasia, *Yahoo! Finance*, April 9, 2009

3 Cost behaviour and budgeting considerations

When devising and managing the marketing budget an understanding of how different costs behave is important. If we don't understand how are costs affected by an increase or decrease in activity it is difficult to set a realistic budget.

KEY CONCEPT

concept

Cost behaviour is the way in which a cost changes as the activity level changes.

3.1 Levels of activity

The level of activity refers to the amount of work done, or the number of events that have occurred. Depending on circumstances, the level of activity may refer to measures such as the following:

- The volume of production in a period
- The number of items sold
- The number of invoices issued
- The number of units of electricity consumed

3.2 The basic principle of cost behaviour

The basic principle of cost behaviour is that as the level of activity rises, costs will usually rise. For example we would expect it to cost more to produce 2,000 units of output than it would to produce 1,000. When setting and interpreting budgets, it is important to understand how costs rise as the level of activity increases.

3.3 Cost behaviour patterns

3.3.1 Variable costs

Variable costs increase or decrease with the level of activity.

A **variable cost** is a cost which tends to vary directly with the volume of output. The variable cost **per unit** is the same amount for each unit produced whereas **total** variable cost increases as volume of output increases.

A sketch graph of a variable cost would look like this.

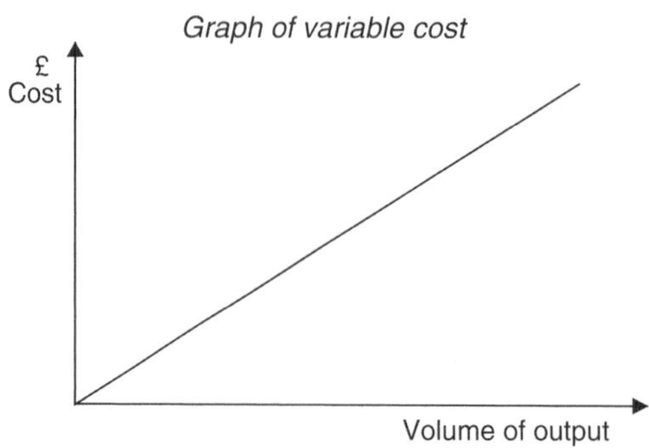

Examples of variable costs

- The cost of raw materials (where there is no discount for bulk purchasing since bulk purchase discounts reduce the unit cost of purchases)
- The cost of agency workers paid by the hour
- Sales commission that varies directly in relation to the value of sales

3.3.2 Non-linear variable costs

Although variable costs are usually assumed to be linear, there are situations where variable costs are **curvilinear**. Have a look at the following graphs.

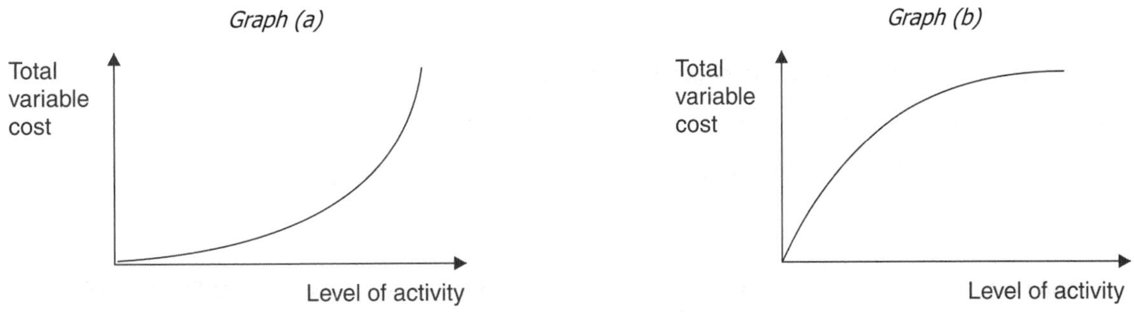

Graph (a) becomes steeper as levels of activity increase. Each additional unit of activity is adding more to total variable cost than the previous unit. Graph (b) becomes less steep as levels of activity increase. Each additional unit is adding less to total variable cost than the previous unit.

ACTIVITY 1

application

The cost of direct labour where employees are paid a bonus which increases as output levels increase might follow the cost behaviour pattern depicted in graph (a) above.

True ☐

False ☐

The cost of direct material where quantity discounts are available might follow the cost behaviour pattern in graph (b) above.

True ☐

False ☐

3.3.3 Fixed costs

Costs which are not affected by the level of activity are **fixed costs**.

A **fixed cost** is a cost which tends to be unaffected by increases or decreases in the volume of output. Fixed costs are a **period charge**, in that they relate to and are charged to a span of time; as the time span increases, so too will the fixed costs.

A sketch graph of a fixed cost would look like this.

Graph of fixed cost

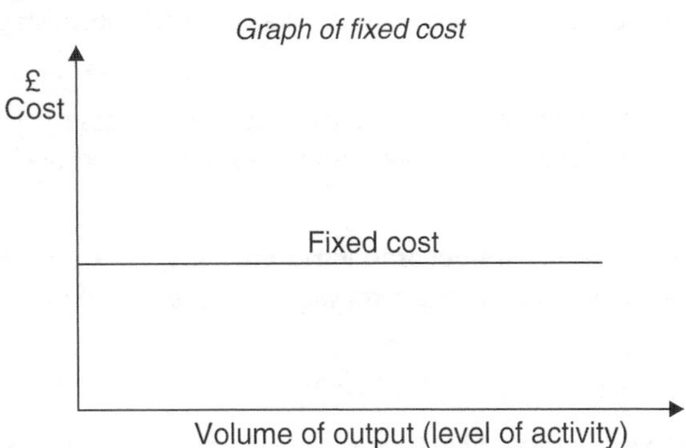

Examples of fixed costs

- The salary of the marketing manager (per month or per annum)
- The rent of a single factory building (per month or per annum)
- Straight line depreciation of a single machine (per month or per annum)

3.3.4 Step costs

A **step cost** is a cost which is fixed in nature but only within certain levels of activity. Depending on the time frame being considered, it may appear as fixed or variable.

Consider a small but growing organisation that currently rents small premises. As the organisation grows (ie activity or output increases) at some point it's likely more space will be required. Larger premises in the same area will be more expensive, so the rental cost would go up a step. This may happen again if the organisation continues to grow.

A sketch graph of a step cost would look like this.

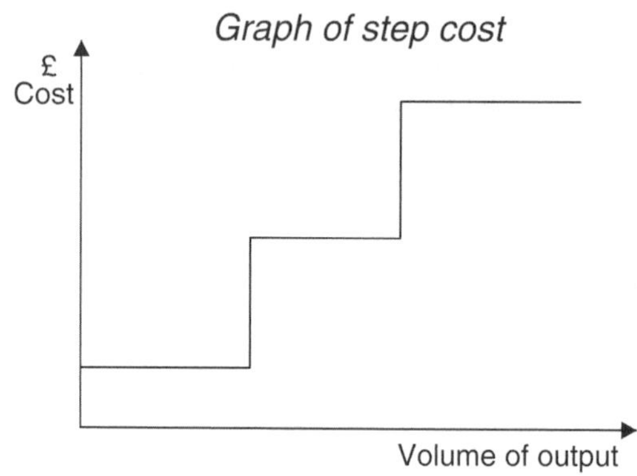

Examples of step costs

- Rent, as explained above
- Salary costs of employees (more employees required as activity increases)

The importance of time scale

The time scale over which we consider the behaviour of what appears to be a step cost can actually result in its classification as a fixed cost or a variable cost.

Over the short to medium term, a cost such as rent will **appear as fixed**, steps in the cost only occurring after a certain length of time.

Over longer periods of time, however, say a number of years, all costs will **tend to vary** in response to large changes in activity level. For this reason, costs traditionally classified as fixed will become step costs as no cost can remain unchanged forever.

As the time span increases, **step costs become variable costs**. For example, when considered over many years, rent will appear as a variable cost, varying in the long term with large changes in the level of activity.

3.3.5 Semi-variable costs (or semi-fixed costs or mixed costs)

Semi-variable, semi-fixed or **mixed costs** are costs which are part-fixed and part-variable and are therefore partly affected by a change in the level of activity.

A sketch graph of a semi-variable cost would look like this.

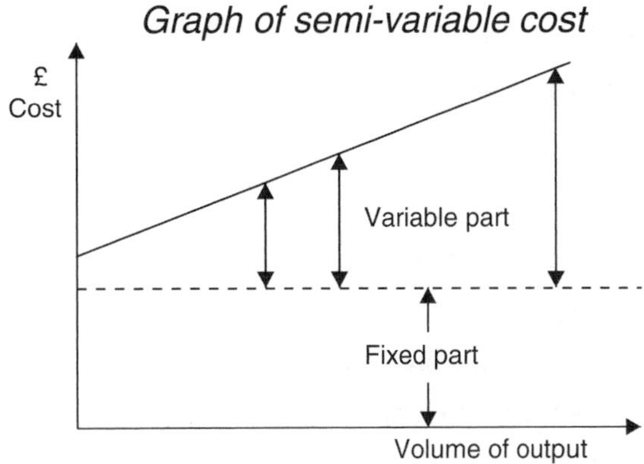

Examples of semi-variable costs

- Electricity and gas bills. There is a basic charge plus a charge per unit of consumption.
- Sales representative's salary. The sales representative may earn a basic monthly amount of, say, £1,000 and then commission of 10% of the value of sales made.

3.4 Cost behaviour – total cost and unit cost

If the variable cost of producing a unit is £5 per unit, this remains true no matter how many units are produced. However, if the business's fixed costs are £5,000 then the **fixed cost per unit** will **decrease** as more units are produced.

If only one unit was produced, fixed costs per unit would be £5,000. If 2,500 units were produced the fixed cost per unit would be £2. If 5,000 were produced the fixed cost per unit would be £1. This demonstrates that as the level of activity increases the **total cost per unit** (fixed cost plus variable cost) decreases.

This is shown in sketch graph form below (remember, these graphs relate to **cost per unit**).

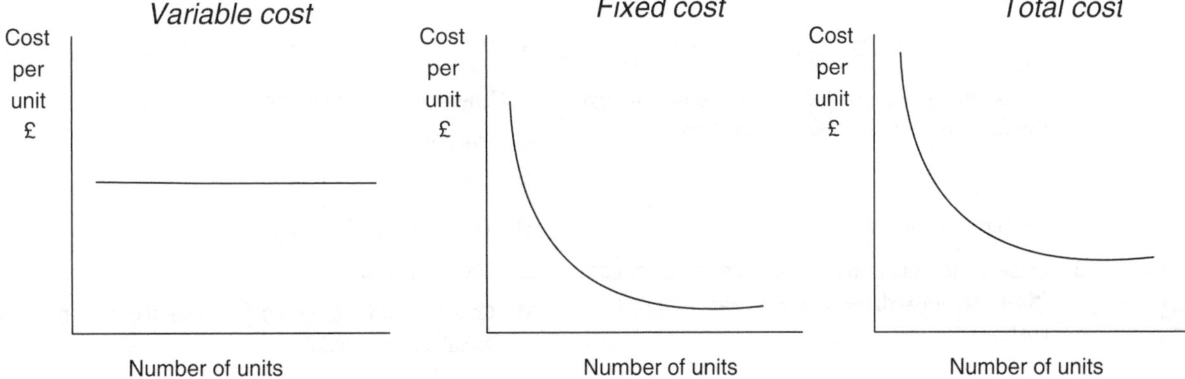

ACTIVITY 2

application

Tick the appropriate box for each cost.

		Fixed	*Variable*	*Mixed*
(a)	Telephone bill	☐	☐	☐
(b)	Annual salary of the marketing director	☐	☐	☐
(c)	The marketing director's annual membership fee to the CIM (paid by the company)	☐	☐	☐
(d)	Cost of packaging materials used to pack one unit of product X into a box	☐	☐	☐

3.5 The relevant range

The **relevant range** refers to the activity levels within which the assumptions made about cost behaviour remain valid.

In practical situations, the relevant range is taken to mean the activity levels at which an organisation has had experience of operating at and for which cost information is available. It can therefore be difficult to predict costs at activity levels which are outside the relevant range.

Chapter 16 'Budgeting' of the core Text 'Accounting for Managers' (Collier) includes a good section 'What is budgeting?'

Learning objective review

Learning objectives	Covered
1 Assess the marketing manager's role in managing the finances of the marketing function	☑ The role of the manager ☑ Planning ☑ Control
2 Explain the purpose of budgeting	☑ The purpose of budgeting
3 Explain the significance of different types of costs (fixed, semi-fixed, variable and semi-variable costs)	☑ Levels of activity ☑ Cost behaviour patterns (variable, fixed, step, semi-variable/semi-fixed) ☑ Total cost and unit cost

Quick quiz

1 List the seven steps in a systematic approach to planning.

2 What is control?

3 Which of the following is not an objective of a system of budgetary planning and control?

A To establish a system of control

B To coordinate activities

C To compel planning

D To motivate employees to maintain current performance levels

4 *Choose the appropriate words from those highlighted.*

A **forecast/budget** is an **estimate/guarantee** of what is **likely to occur in the future/has happened in the past.**

A **forecast/budget** is a **quantified plan/unquantified plan/guess** of what the organisation is aiming to **achieve/spend**.

5 The basic principle of cost behaviour is that as the level of activity rises, costs will usually fall.

True ☐

False ☐

6 Fill in the gaps for each of the graph titles below and on the next page.

(a)

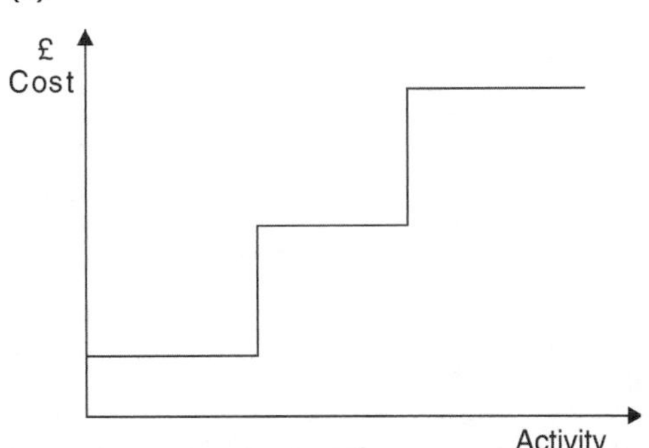

Graph of a .... cost

Example:

(b)

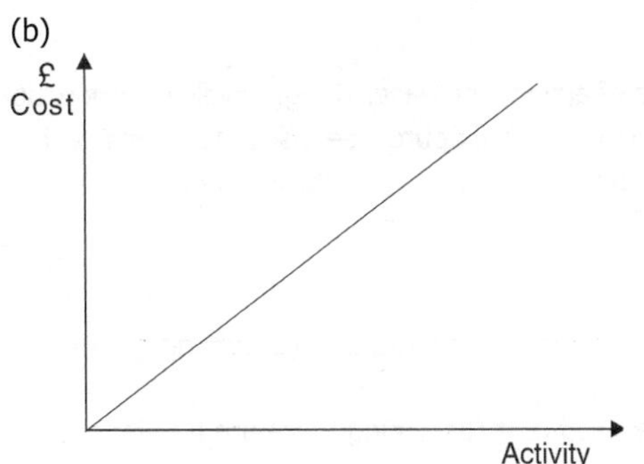

Graph of a .... cost

Example:

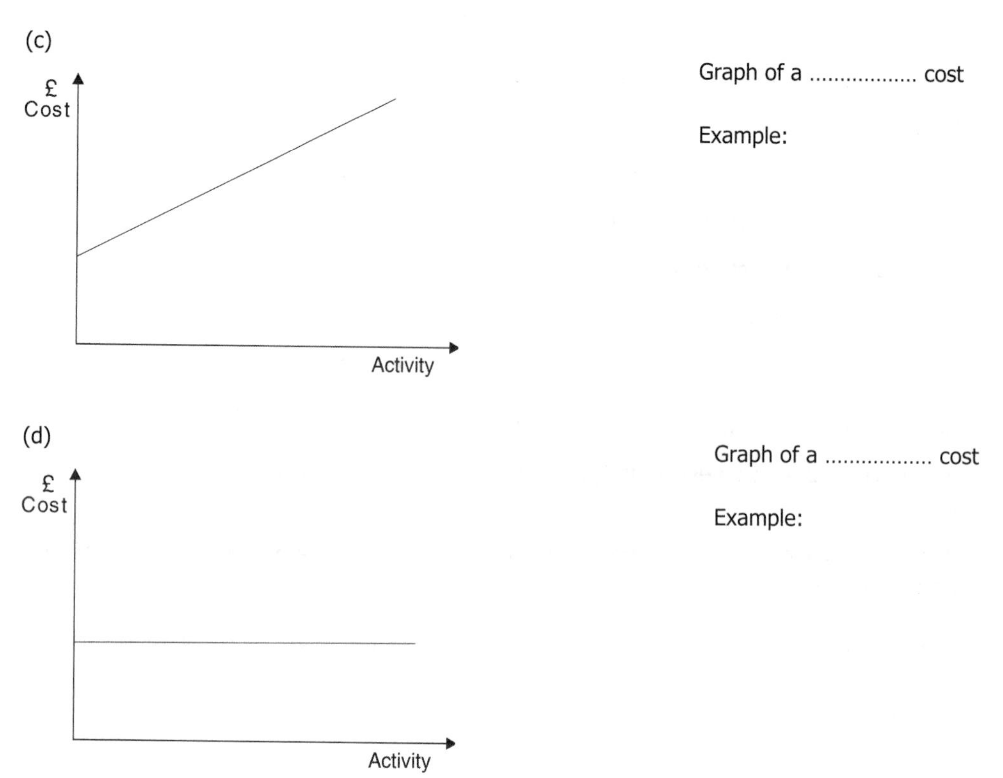

(c) Graph of a .... cost

Example:

(d) Graph of a .... cost

Example:

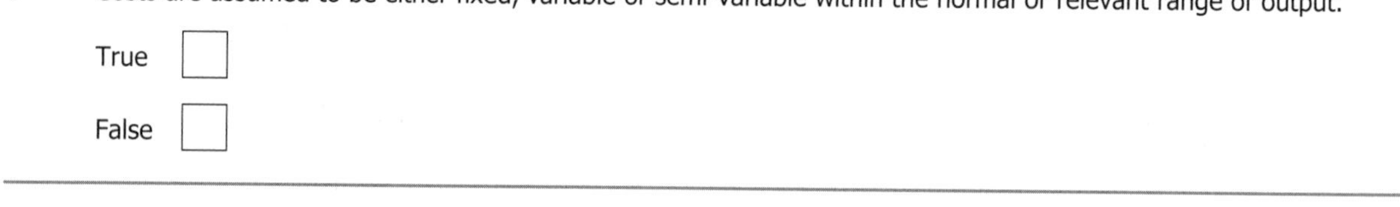

7 Costs are assumed to be either fixed, variable or semi-variable within the normal or relevant range of output.

True ☐

False ☐

Activity debriefs

1 Graph (a) ☑ True

Graph (b) ☑ True

The curve in graph (a) becomes steeper as levels of activity increase. The effect of the employee bonus, rewarding additional production, means each additional unit of production is adding more to total variable cost than the previous unit.

The curve in graph (b) becomes less steep as levels of activity increase. If high levels of production are expected, materials are able to be purchased in bulk. The effect of the bulk purchase discount means each additional unit is adding less to total variable cost than the previous unit.

2 (a) Mixed ☑ Telephone bill

(b) Fixed ☑ Annual salary of the marketing director is a fixed cost (assuming no activity-related bonus)

(c) Fixed ☑ The CIM membership fee is a fixed cost (assuming there are no plans to employ and pay fees for another CIM member)

(d) Variable ☑ The cost of packaging materials required to pack one unit of product X into a box is variable

---

Quiz answers

1 Aims – key results – standards – detailed targets – action plans – monitoring – control action.

2 The process of monitoring performance and taking any action required to maintain it at the desired standard

3 D. The objective is to motivate employees to *improve* their performance.

4 A **forecast** is an **estimate** of what is **likely to occur in the future**.

A **budget** is a **quantified plan** of what the organisation is aiming to achieve (in financial terms).

5 False. They will rise.

6 (a) Step cost. Example: rent, total employees' salaries

(b) Variable cost. Example: raw materials, direct labour

(c) Semi-variable cost. Example: electricity and telephone

(d) Fixed. Example: manager's salary, depreciation (straight-line)

7 True

References

Anthony, R. N. (1965), Planning and Control Systems: A Framework for Analysis, Harvard Business School Press, Boston.

Buckley, A. and McKenna, E. (1972), Budgetary Control and Business Behaviour, Accounting and Business Research (Spring 1972), pp137-150.

Collier, P. (2006), Accounting for Managers, (2nd edition.) John Wiley, Chichester.

Chapter 10

The budgeting process

Topic list

1 Approaches to budget setting
2 Information sources for budgeting
3 Negotiating and agreeing budgets
4 Preparing the budget

Introduction

The previous chapter covered the purpose of budgeting and examined cost-behaviour patterns relevant to the budgeting process. This chapter moves on to look at different approaches to setting the marketing and communications budget.

Marketing has to compete with other organisational functions and demands for funds (or budget). To compete effectively, marketing managers must be able to explain the benefits the marketing spend they are requesting will bring (in financial terms). This isn't possible without some financial and business nous.

The days of senior marketing staff being able to 'leave the numbers to the accountants' are long gone. The marketing budget is your budget. If you understand it, take ownership of it and learn how to negotiate effectively to grow it, you will have a far better chance of securing the resources you need to do an effective marketing job for your organisation.

Syllabus linked learning objectives

By the end of the chapter you will be able to:

	Learning objectives	Syllabus link
1	Evaluate different approaches to setting the marketing and communications budget	3.2
2	Understand the top-down and bottom-up approaches to budgeting	3.2
3	Understand and be able to apply a range of financial approaches to budget setting	3.2
4	Understand and be able to apply marketing approaches to budget setting	3.2
5	Evaluate different information sources required to determine the marketing budget	3.3
6	Explain the role of data, information, intelligence and knowledge in the budget setting process	3.3
7	Evaluate the role of internal data sources (sales figures, headcount, outsourcing costs, consultant costs, Electronic Point of Sale system, Marketing Information System) and external data sources including exchange rates and exchange rate variances	3.3
8	Prepare a budget bid/ business case to obtain a priority budget for marketing activities	3.4
9	Understand that different sources of data are required to monitor and evaluate financial performance	3.8

1 Approaches to budget setting

Marketing budgets (and other resources) are never unlimited. This means choices must be made and priorities set in the budget setting process. There are a range of approaches available when setting budgets.

To be effective, marketing resources should be allocated across a range of tasks and objectives in a co-ordinated manner.

Before we start, let's remind ourselves of what a budget is.

KEY CONCEPT

concept

A **budget** is a statement of desired performance expressed in financial terms.

1.1 Top-down and bottom-up budgets

One way of looking at the budget setting process is to categorise it as either top-down or bottom-up.

- **Top down budgets** are set by senior management and passed down the organisation.
- **Bottom-up budgets** are set by individuals further down the organisation hierarchy, for example 'junior' managers and employees involved in performing the tasks relevant to the budget being set. The figures are usually passed up to senior management for their approval.

Top-down budgets - advantages	
Simplicity and speed	The process can be relatively simple and quick, with figures simply imposed from above.
Authority	Those making the budget have the authority to do so – their figures won't be overruled.
Aware of bigger picture	Senior management aren't focussed on one particular area of the business to the detriment of others - they are aware of the bigger picture and therefore perhaps best placed to decide relative priorities.

Top-down budgets - disadvantages	
May be arbitrary	Senior management may set spending levels simply on the amount they feel the organisation can afford. There may be little analysis of what actually is required if organisational goals are to be achieved.
May cause resentment	Managers often feel they don't have sufficient funds to meet their targets. This can cause resentment and reduce motivation.
Short-term focus	If senior management bonuses are based on annual results (they usually are), the temptation may be to produce a budget that delivers results in the short-term but neglects investment.
Inefficient and divisive	As top management fixes the total budget, lower level managers must compete direct for funds. This does not promote cooperation and can result in a less than optimal allocation of funds.
May be worked-around	Creative accounting may be used to move costs from one area to another. This may happen with any budgeting method, but is more likely if managers feel their actions are justified because the budget is unreasonable.

Bottom-up - advantages	
Empowering / motivation	Involving supervisors and employees in the process recognises their knowledge. If employees are expected to take responsibility for ensuring their roles are performed well, they need the resources to do so.
Encourages acceptance and ownership	Assuming the figures passed up aren't altered too much, employees are more likely to accept the budget and to try to remain within it.

Bottom-up - disadvantages	
Time consuming	Employees may be distracted from their day-to-day tasks by the budget process. Bottom up budgets also tend to go through more reviews and amendments. This process of negotiation takes time.
Funds may not be available	The figures passed up for approval may simply be unrealistic and unaffordable. Then, significant alteration downwards of the budget figures by senior management can cause resentment.
Narrow focus	Employees are unlikely to be aware of competing priorities elsewhere in the organisation.

A hybrid or combination of these two approaches is the 'Goals down, plans up' approach. This involves top management setting overall goals and lower-level employees devising plans and budgets to achieve those goals. This approach is often used in the formulation of marketing communications budgets.

1.2 Approaches to setting marketing communications budgets

Top-down and bottom-up describe two very general approaches to budget setting, from opposite ends of the scale. There are a range of specific approaches used to set budgets. We look at a number of these approaches in this section, in the context of a marketing communications budget.

There are a number of ways of **setting expenditure budgets** for tactical marketing communications activity:

- Arbitrary estimation
- Affordability
- Competitive parity
- Historical basis
- Percentage of sales or profit
- Objective and task
- Share of voice
- Cost-volume-profit (marginal analysis)
- Experiment and testing method
- Modelling and simulation method

We will look at each method in turn.

1.2.1 Arbitrary estimation

This is the least scientific method, an estimation based on the budgeter's experience and knowledge of trends, the industry, the market, organisational profitability and so on. Arbitrary estimation relies more on 'gut feeling' than formal calculations.

Arbitrary estimation has the advantage of being quick and easy: it does not incur any costs of research or the budgeter's time. It may offer a useful 'ballpark' figure for initial brainstorming on a possible communications activity, or for allocating contingency ('just in case') sums as part of a more systematic budgeting exercise.

However, overall this is an unscientific and relatively risky method.

ACTIVITY 1

evaluation

To get you thinking, see if you can identify the disadvantages of arbitrary budgeting in general and from the perspective of *internal marketing*.

1.2.2 Affordability

In this method, communications expenditure is based on what the organisation can afford, in the judgement of the budgeter. In other words: 'How much do we have available to spend?'

Resource availability will inevitably influence the type of communications activities that can be carried out. Some activities, for example, will simply be too expensive, while others may offer better reach and frequency for the same cost. This is likely to be an important factor for micro- and small-medium enterprises and non-profit organisations: resources for marketing may be severely limited.

Affordability therefore certainly needs to be taken into account. However, it has disadvantages as a sole criterion for setting the budget. A balance must be struck between the need to be prudent and the need for investment if the company is to prosper in the future.

- The organisation may not *need* to spend the amount it could afford to meet its objectives. Affordability budgeting creates a temptation and pressure to 'spend to budget' (if only to avoid it being cut next year) - this may be a waste of resources.
- The fact that budget is allocated on an affordability basis reduces the need for justification - so does not encourage the identification of specific marketing communication objectives or encourage an awareness of market opportunities.

MARKETING AT WORK

Tips for writing a marketing plan

It is important for a marketing plan to:

- Set clear, realistic and measurable targets - for example, increasing sales by 10 per cent
- Include deadlines for meeting targets
- **Provide a budget for each marketing activity**
- Specify who is responsible for each activity

Make sure you think through each of your objectives logically. For example, you might set a target for the number of new enquiries. But if you don't provide the resources and training to turn these enquiries into sales, you will have increased costs without any benefits.

www.businesslink.gov.uk Sales and Marketing section, retrieved 13 April 2009

1.2.3 Competitive parity

Competitive parity means setting communications budgets based on matching the spending (or percentage of sales spent, or year-on-year increase in spending) of competitors.

This ensures the organisation matches the activity of competitors so should help maintain its competitive position. It may also be advantageous in preventing potentially costly advertising and promotion wars, as it prevents the organisation from simply trying to outspend the competition.

However, this approach has several disadvantages.

- It assumes that the competitor has made good budgeting decisions or arrived at a 'correct' level of spending, which may not be the case. Competitive parity may be a case of the blind leading the blind!
- It is reactive and lacks direction. It does not take account of specific marketing objectives or opportunities. There may be an opportunity to build market share by additional expenditure, say, or to harvest profits from a declining product by reducing expenditure.
- Like affordability, competitive parity may create pressure to 'spend up' to competitor levels, when the organisation doesn't need to do so – or when, if given the incentive, it could find opportunities to achieve the same marketing effect for less.
- It may also create pressure to 'spend down' to competitor levels, reducing the organisation's ability to exploit opportunities to grow sales and profits by higher-level communications expenditure.

1.2.4 Historical basis

Many budgets are set on the basis of the level spent in previous years. Considerations include:

- The danger of inertia. Spending the same as the previous year (or the same plus an allowance for inflation) ignores possible changes in the environment, in the organisation's objectives and in how the organisation operates. A significantly different approach and budget may be more appropriate.
- For advertising budgets, a media multiplier may be used which reflects changes in media rate cards. However, this may encourage acceptance of cost increases without question or negotiation.

1.2.5 Percentage of sales (or percentage of profit) method

This method bases communication expenditure on a percentage of current or budgeted sales revenue for the year. This may be based on company or industry tradition, or intended as a means of securing a certain level of profit (based on research into the returns that can be expected from different percentage levels of 'typical' expenditure).

Again, this method is quick and easy to apply. It depends less on the subjective judgement of the budgeter than the arbitrary or affordability method. Percentage of sales controls spending levels by ensuring expenditure is tied to revenue.

The appropriate percentage will depend upon the organisation's objectives variables, the type of market they are in (eg consumer or industrial) and how competitive the market is.

The following figures are based on experience of different accounts.

Percentage of sales on total communications budget

State of competition	Consumer markets	Industrial markets
No competition	1%	0.5%
Little competition	2%	1%
Average competition	5%	2%

However, this is still a rule-of-thumb, unscientific method.

- It doesn't take account of specific marketing objectives and opportunities to increase sales or profits by increasing or reducing communications spending.
- It doesn't provide any means of determining the 'correct' percentage to use. There is no reason why communication costs should relate directly to total turnover, since other factors will impact sales levels.
- It may have a detrimental effect on sales. If sales decline, for any reason, this approach means communication budgets also decline – when additional promotion may be required for sales recovery! Reduced promotional spending may only cause further decline in sales, a vicious circle.

1.2.6 Objective and task budgeting

The objective and task method is probably the one which is most logical and appropriate to the complex situation found in planning marketing communications programmes.

The method is based on **three main steps**.

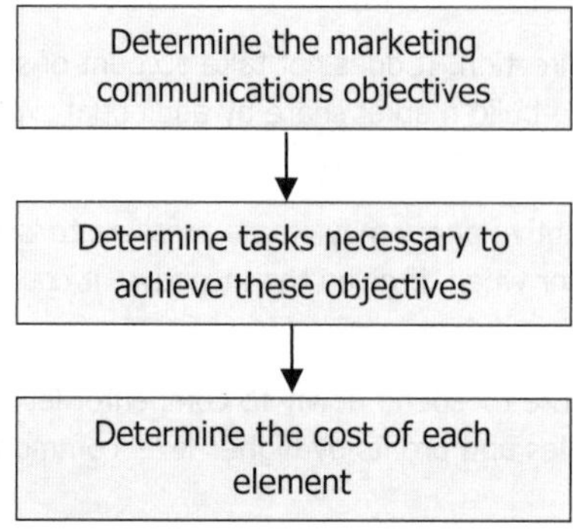

This approach is simple to understand and uses carefully considered and linked objectives and tasks. It is necessary to be realistic about the objectives and accurate in the costing of the tasks. This is an extremely difficult process in reality because of the large number of unknowns.

ACTIVITY 2

application

To demonstrate the logic and difficulty of this method choose a marketing communications problem with which you are familiar.

- Define the precise marketing communication objectives.
- Determine the tasks necessary to achieve these objectives.
- Cost out the problem both in terms of the individual tasks and in total.

The objective and task method is based on a systematic calculation of the expenditure required to fulfil communications objectives and to carry out the specific communications tasks planned to achieve them.

If the objective is to increase awareness of a brand name by 10%, the planned communication campaign will be broken down into its component tasks and elements, and estimated (or known) costs will be allocated to each (eg promotional media, staff time, agency fees, merchandising costs etc).

The total estimated cost of all such campaigns (perhaps with an added contingency sum for emergencies and opportunities) will comprise the communications budget.

Advantages of the objective and task method

This method has several advantages.

- It is relatively scientific and systematic, and can be based fairly closely on known costs (eg media rate cards and known discount rates, agreed agency fees, quoted print costs and so on).
- It can be performed for each communications activity, at a detailed level, building up to the total communications budget.
- It focuses managerial attention on objectives, tasks, opportunities and the effects of expenditure on outcomes (return on communications investment).
- It can be readily justified to internal and external stakeholders, as a sound and results-focused method.

Although it will not necessarily produce perfect results, the objective and task method will lead to disciplined thinking and provide an excellent communication and decision device.

Disadvantages of the objective and task method

Limitations of the method include:

- The amount of effort and activity required to achieve communications objectives is difficult to estimate (particularly if objectives are long-range or qualitative in nature).
- Contingency sums are required to take account of unforeseen tasks (such as crisis communication or countering competitor campaigns).
- The method may reduce the funds available to take advantage of opportunities (such as newly available communication media or reduced-cost media space).

1.2.7 Share of voice

KEY CONCEPT

Share of voice. Within any market, the total advertising expenditure can be analysed in the context of the proportions each player has made to the total.

If one advertiser spends more than any other then more of their messages will be received and therefore stand a better chance of being heard and acted upon. If a brand's **share of market (SOM)** is equal to its **share of voice (SOV)** an equilibrium can be said to have been reached.

It is possible that organisations can use their advertising spending either to maintain **equilibrium (SOV = SOM)** or to create disequilibrium.

The following matrix (*Schroer*, 1990) shows how different spending strategies are appropriate depending on your competitors' share of voice and your own share of market.

SOV/SOM matrix

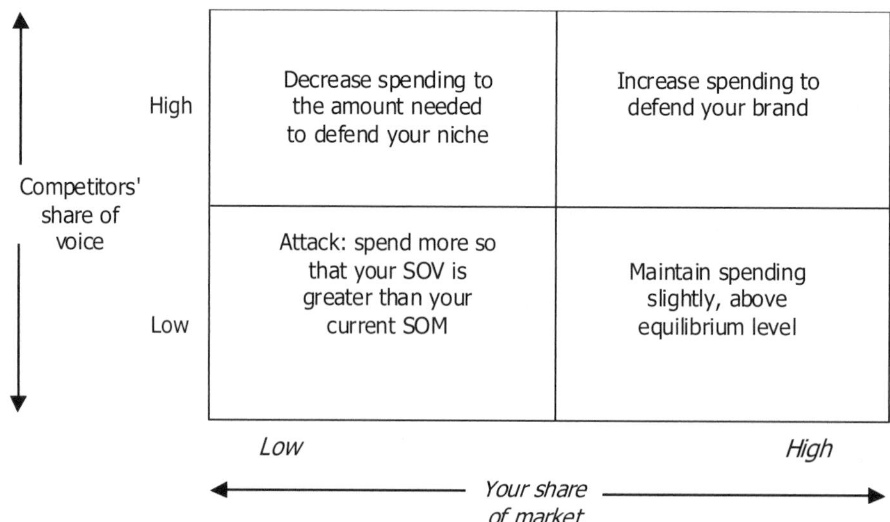

Note that careful monitoring of the fortunes of competitors is needed: if you know that a competitor is spending large sums on restructuring, then they may not be in a position to retaliate to a sudden advertising burst by your company.

1.2.8 Cost-volume-profit analysis (in a budgeting context)

Cost-volume-profit (CVP) analysis involves calculating the impact of additional spend upon results (ie sales and profits).

In the context of budget setting CVP may be used to provide answers to questions such as:

- What benefits are generated by additional or marginal communications expenditure?
- What value of sales can be attributed to marketing expenditure?

These are complex questions, as many variables impact upon sales levels. For example, if a major competitor pulls out of a market at the same time as you run a marketing campaign, it's difficult to know what proportion of additional sales are a result of marketing activities.

Cost-volume-profit analysis may be used as a way of fine-tuning a communications budget to maximise net benefits (total benefits minus total costs).

To carry out this analysis, you would probably use software (such as a spreadsheet) which would enable you to:

- Experiment with different variables in the communications mix (for example the amount of media space bought, or the number of advertisements aired, or the amount of expenditure on communications).
- Establish the optimal level for individual elements of the marketing mix by testing:
  (a) The additional benefit of adding one more unit of the variable (the **marginal benefit** of the unit).
  (b) The additional cost of adding one more unit of the variable (the **marginal cost** of the unit).

As well as computer modelling, marginal analysis may be based on experimentation: that is, changing a variable (eg number of radio spots) and observing the effect on sales/responses.

We look at cost-volume profit analysis and sensitivity analysis, including a worked example, in the context of **breakeven analysis** in a later chapter.

1.2.9 Experiment and testing method

This method of budget setting involves selecting a set of matched markets. Different final promotional budgets can be set for each of these markets and the results carefully monitored. The resulting levels of awareness and sales delivered can be compared. For example, this method can be used to evaluate alternative media schedules. Problems associated with this method include:

- The cost of conducting the experiment
- The time it takes to get results
- The premature informing of competitors
- The fact that markets can never be completely matched

1.2.10 Modelling and simulation method

With advancing use of computer databases and more precise promotional media, it is possible to build models to forecast the likely performance of different media schedules. There are likely to be an increasing number of PC-based modelling programs available which will allow a number of business variables to be examined including:

- Sales levels
- Purchase frequency
- Awareness levels
- Profits achievable

Problems associated with modelling include time and cost and the validity of the chosen model.

ASSIGNMENT TIP

application

What method or methods of budgeting are used in your organisation? Could the budgeting process be improved? Is this a suitable area for your work based assignment?

ACTIVITY 3

application

How are budgets set in your work organisation, or another organisations you are studying?

- Who sets the budget for marketing communications?
- Are there separate budgets for different communications activities or target audiences?
- What expenditure is included in the marketing budget (eg staff salaries, media costs, creative and print costs, agency fees, contingency sums)?

See if you can get hold of a copy of a tactical level marketing budget, just to see what it looks like (if you don't regularly have access to such things).

If confidentiality issues prevent you viewing budget documents (or if you would like further information on practical aspects of budgeting), visit the Business Link website www.businesslink.gov.uk – then: *Finance and grants* > *Financial planning* > *Budgeting and business planning* section.

2 Information sources for budgeting

KEY CONCEPT

concept

Information is required for informed decision making. The **marketing budget** will require information from inside the organisation (eg what products and services will be produced) and from outside the organisation (eg what are competitors doing?, what will our campaign cost?).

2.1 Terminology

The following definitions are relevant when discussing information sources and requirements.

Term	Meaning
Data	Raw facts, for example a customer list.
Information	Data that has been arranged or processed in some way to add meaning. For example a customer list in order based on sales value.
Intelligence	Information that is suitable for a particular purpose, for example reducing risk.
Knowledge	Information within people's minds.
Tacit knowledge	Expertise held by people within the organisation that has not been formally documented.
Explicit knowledge	Knowledge that the company knows that it has, for example facts, transactions and events stored in information systems.
Knowledge management	The process of collecting, storing and using the knowledge held within an organisation.
Environmental scanning	The process of gathering external information, which is available from a wide range of sources.

2.2 Information for budgeting

An organisation is defined as a 'social arrangement for the controlled performance of collective goals' (Huczynski and Buchanan, 2003). The budget is a statement of these goals in financial terms. It is essential therefore that budget decisions are **rational** and **informed**.

If a realistic, logical approach is taken to budget setting, the process will draw upon a wide range of information sources, both internal and external.

2.2.1 The accounting records

The accounting ledgers provide an excellent source of information regarding what has happened in the past. This information may be used as a basis for predicting future events eg budgeting.

Accounting records can provide more than purely financial information. For example a stock control system includes purchase orders, goods received notes and goods returned notes that can be analysed to provide information regarding the speed of delivery or the quality of supplies.

2.2.2 Sales figures

Past sales levels (from the accounting records) and anticipated sales levels (from forecasts) need to be taken into account. If a significant decrease is expected in a product line or range, should marketing spend be reduced accordingly? Or should spend be increased in an attempt to reinvigorate the product line? These decisions can't be taken in isolation – the marketing budget must compliment overall strategy.

2.2.3 Electronic Point of Sale (EPOS)

Electronic Point of Sale (EPOS) devices, which include bar code readers, enable retailers (and those in some other industries) to record and manage stock movements and provide detailed sales figures.

2.2.4 Headcount

Information about staff levels will be relevant to costs. The number of marketing department staff employed throughout the budget period, and the associated salary levels, will obviously impact upon costs.

2.2.5 Consultants and outsourcing costs

Marketing managers need to know about the opinions and buying attitudes of potential customers. To obtain this information, they might carry out market research exercises. This often requires use of an outside agency or consultant.

The budget needs to include these costs. How much is expected to be spent on marketing-related consultancy and outsourcing? For example, will external expertise be required for a specific campaign?

Outsourcing costs also need to be budgeted. Do we expect to employ temporary marketing administration staff at busy times?

2.2.6 Exchange rates

If your organisation operates in more than one country, or sources products or services from other countries, exchange rate movements need to be considered in the budget.

For example, if a UK based organisation plans an advertising campaign in the Republic of Ireland, conducted by an Irish agency, these costs are likely to be quoted in Euros. Any movement of the GBP to Euro exchange rate will change the cost of this campaign.

A **contingency** may be added to the budget to account for any adverse movement, or the organisation could take out a **forward exchange contract** (in effect buying the foreign currency at today's prices) to reduce this element of uncertainty.

MARKETING AT WORK

application

Procter & Gamble have devised a Statement of Business Principles, setting out 10 guiding principles for all their activity. The top three are as follows:

1. *Plan all action in advance.* Always forecast business in relation to expenditure, always check that the business is reaching objectives according to forecast, and always be ready to adjust plans as necessary.
2. *Base all actions on facts.* One fact is worth many judgements. Strive always to find the factual truth as a subject before acting. This applies to all fields of business: product, packaging, advertising, promotions and expenditure.
3. *Always know the objective of your actions.* Know what advertising, individual promotions and sales plans are intended to do and judge their success by whether they achieve objectives.

2.2.7 How much information?

There will always be some element of judgement required when setting budget levels and priorities.

- Most decisions are based on **incomplete information**.
  - All possible information is not available.
  - Beyond a certain point, the gathering of more information would not be worth the extra time and cost of obtaining and analysing it.
- Too much information (**information overload**) makes decision-making harder rather than easier.

2.2.8 Where do we find information?

Information can be sourced:

- **Inside the organisation**. This is information we already have, such as sales figures, reports, price lists, literature, customer information etc. It may be stored electronically in a central database or in forms and files scattered throughout the organisation.
- **Outside the organisation**. Information we don't have, but can get access to, often at a cost – from customers, suppliers, research organisations, publishers, websites and so on.

2.3 The marketing information system (MkIS)

Much of the information relevant to budget decisions will be held in the Marketing Information System (MkIS). This should be familiar to you from earlier studies, but here's a brief recap.

KEY CONCEPT

The **marketing information system** (MkIS) is 'the framework for the day-to-day management and structuring of information gathered regularly from sources both inside and outside an organisation' (Dibb *et al.*, 2001).

A **marketing information system** consists of people, equipment and procedures to gather, sort, analyse, evaluate, and distribute needed, timely and accurate information to marketing decision makers.

A wide range of information is systematically gathered for marketing purposes. Some examples include:

- Prices
- Advertising expenditure
- Sales
- Competitor activity
- Distribution costs
- Stock levels
- Attributes of potential promotional/supply chain partners
- Buyer behaviour (and the social trends affecting it)
- PESTLE (Political, Economic, Socio-cultural, Technological, Legal and Environmental) factors
- Internal audit (and/or SWOT analysis) of the organisation's marketing capabilities

ACTIVITY 4

application

Think about how information is collected, stored and communicated in your organisation. Does the representation of a marketing information system shown below apply (in part if not in full)?

Often, unless it is carefully organised and all stakeholders know where they can access it, the value of the information is lost. Marketing information systems provide a way of centralising the information contained within an organisation and facilitating knowledge through it's careful usage.

The marketing information system

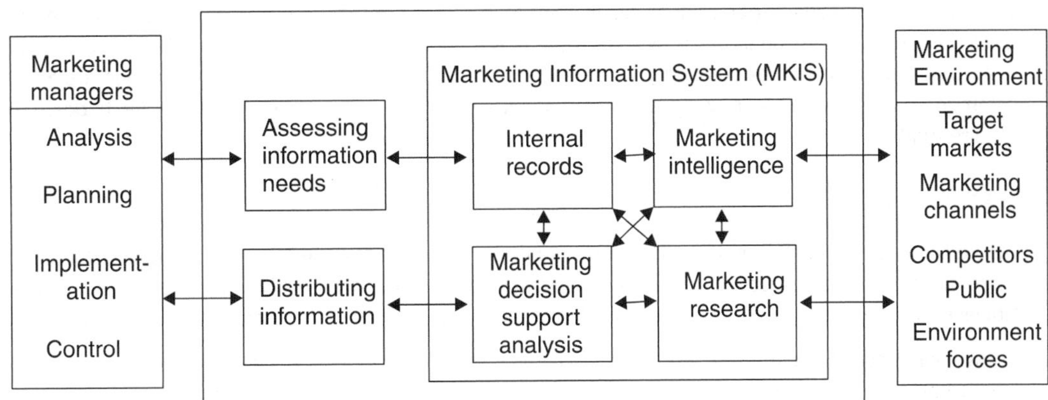

Source: Kotler

(a) **Internal records system**

Internal records includes reports of orders, sales figures, headcount, consultancy costs, accounts payable and receivable etc which provide a store of historical customer data. One aspect of the internal records system is the accounting system.

Marketing staff should utilise the data held here, for example to monitor customer profitability.

The payroll systems and human resource systems should include details of factors such as headcount (ideally including headcount forecasts) that will impact costs.

(b) **Marketing intelligence system**

This is the term used for information gathered on the market place by managers on a day-to-day basis. It is derived from **continual monitoring** of the environment to alert managers to new trends.

(c) **Marketing decision support system**

Firms can use statistical analysis within this level of the system including regression and correlation analysis, sales forecasting, time series analysis, product design and site selection models.

(d) **Marketing research system**

Marketing research aids management decision making by providing specified information in time for it to be of value.

(e) **External data sources**

The MkIS is linked to external sources, perhaps via an Internet link or simply by individuals gathering information from external sources and feeding it into the system. The Internet can be a fast, efficient way to search for and access data that may be required for budget setting (for example competitor activity, advertising agency rate cards).

3 Negotiating and agreeing budgets

3.1 Negotiating the marketing budget

The marketing function or department has to **compete** with other functions and departments for resources. Although you are a marketing professional and likely to be keen to deliver the benefits increased marketing spend could bring, it is important to remember that you and your colleagues are all part of the same organisation and are all working towards common goals. Your role is to use your marketing expertise to help the organisation achieve its goals. To do this, you will require funds!

3.1.1 Pre-negotiation preparation

Before the budget negotiation process starts ensure you know exactly what it is you want to achieve. Some managers bid for more funds than they expect to receive simply because they know there will be a process of negotiation and compromise. However, be careful, you will lose credibility if you can't justify the figure you originally requested.

Know your absolute minimum figure, but don't communicate this (at least not early in the negotiation process). Although ideally you may feel you need and could effectively utilise more, it is worth knowing the absolute minimum amount you feel is required for the marketing department and marketing activities to perform and contribute effectively to the organisation.

3.1.2 Negotiating with other managers

Try and establish what other functions, departments and managers hope to achieve. Their activities and budget will impact the level of funding you require and your ability to secure it. You may be able to present a united front , but be careful not to come across as a clique.

Avoid appearing self-centred and only focussed on your role. Emphasise that the funds you require will help the organisation achieve its goals. Remain professional and always refer to the overall aims of the organisation.

3.1.3 Negotiation techniques

You may be called to attend a budgeting workshop or meeting with other departmental heads, or you may have a one-to-one meeting with the person responsible for the budget (for example the financial controller, finance director or managing director).

Negotiate professionally and with confidence, but not with arrogance. Aim as high as you feel is credible, other parties may bring this down but it is always easier to go down than to gain.

Remain reluctantly flexible! Ensure your preparation included establishing clear concise benefits the organisation will obtain from the marketing budget you are requesting. Unless you are work for a very large corporate, reasons such as 'improved brand awareness' are unlikely to be sufficient! Quantifiable benefits, in monetary terms, are more likely to succeed in securing the budget you require.

3.1.4 Point out the consequences of not spending

If cuts to the budget bid you have submitted are proposed, point out the **consequences** of the cuts. For example, if the organisation has a target to grow sales in the London area by 10%, but you have been asked to reduce radio advertising spend with London radio stations, ensure senior management is aware that this reduction will make the sales increase unlikely.

3.1.5 Know your priorities

Remain positive, and know your priorities. The budgeting process can be frustrating. Just when you think a figure has been agreed you may find an edict is issued that 'all budget figures must be cut by 15%' - an example of top-down, affordability budgeting discussed earlier.

This can be extremely frustrating. Ensure you know your priorities and where any cut-backs would have **least impact**. Remember the enforced cuts though if later in the financial year you are asked to justify perceived shortcomings in marketing activities!

3.2 Delegated and provisional budgets

3.2.1 Delegated budgets

A delegated budget is one that the ultimate budget holder passes-on (delegates) responsibility for. This is relevant from two points of view .

- The marketing budget is delegated to the **Marketing Director** from above (for example from the Managing Director). Responsibility for the marketing spend has been delegated to the Marketing Director, but ultimate responsibility for all aspects of the organisation's performance remains with the Managing Director.
- The Marketing Director may also delegate budget to others, for example part of the marketing staff costs budget may be delegated to the **Marketing Manager**.

Typically, budget requests are passed to senior management annually. Heads of divisions pass this information to departments and sections, who complete and aggregate the relevant parts of the budget, and pass them back up the ladder.

Along with the formal budget request comes supporting information, such as: the percent of wage increases estimated for the year and potential project priorities. As the budget requests are passed up the organisation, they are reviewed against organisational goals and adjusted.

3.2.2 Provisional budgets

Organisations that favour a **participative** approach foster dialog and compromise between management levels. A typical iterative approach starts with top management setting a budget framework for each year of a strategic plan. This framework then directs the selection of new projects and serves as a guideline for managers as they prepare their budgets.

Detailed project budgets are aggregated into provisional functional unit or departmental budgets and finally, into a provisional organisational budget that top management reviews and, usually, modifies.

Depending upon the top management approach, departmental and project managers may then be asked to modify their respective budgets. The process may undergo several iterations until the budget is finally agreed.

This process is based on input from all levels of management and should help ensure coordination between the different budgets (functional versus project and long- term versus short- and mid-term).

4 Preparing the budget

4.1 Preparing budgets

4.1.1 The budget manual

Procedures for preparing the budget should be formalised, ideally in a **budget manual** which indicates:

- People responsible for preparing budgets
- The order in which they must be prepared
- Deadlines for preparation
- Standard forms

4.1.2 The budget committee

The preparation and administration of budgets is usually the responsibility of a **budget committee**. Every part of the organisation should be represented on the committee.

The preparation of a budget may take weeks or months before the master budget is finally agreed. Functional budgets and cost centre budgets prepared in draft may need to be amended many times over as a consequence of discussions between departments, changes in market conditions, reversals of decisions by management and so on during the course of budget preparation.

4.1.3 The budget period

The budget period is the time frame the budget relates to. A budget does not necessarily have to be restricted to a one year planning horizon. The factors which should influence the **budget period** are as follows.

- The 'lead times' of different aspects of the plan or budget. A plan decided upon now might need a considerable time to be put into operation. Many companies expect growth in market share to take a number of years.
- In the short-term, many resources are fixed. The fixed nature of these resources, and the length of time which must elapse before they become variable, might therefore determine the planning horizon for budgeting.
- All budgets involve some element of forecasting and even guesswork, since future events cannot be quantified with accuracy.
- Since unforeseen events cannot be planned for, it isn't realistic to plan in detail too far ahead. Many organisations restrict themselves to a five year planning horizon.
- Most detailed budgets are prepared over a one year period to enable managers to plan and control financial results for the purposes of the annual accounts.

4.1.4 The principal budget factor

The first task in budgeting is to identify the principal (key, limiting) budget factor. This is the factor which is most likely to constrain growth or prevent additional activity. The principal budget factor could be:

- **Sales demand**. This is the 'usual' situation for commercial organisations - a company is restricted from making and selling more of its products because demand (at a profitable price) is limited.
- **Resources**. Capacity, distribution and selling resources, the availability of key raw materials or the availability of cash etc can be a limiting factor. For example, a production plant or a service centre required to increase output of a certain product or service may be running at capacity.

Once this factor is defined the budget can be prepared.

4.1.5 Budgets and forecasts

- A **forecast** is an estimate of what those within an organisation expect to happen, or think might happen, in the future.
- In contrast, a **budget** is a plan of what the organisation would like to happen, and what it has set as a **target**, although it should be realistic and so it will be based to some extent on the forecasts prepared.
- In formulating a budget, management will be trying to establish some control over the conditions that will apply in the future. (For example, in setting a sales budget, management must decide on the prices to be charged and the advertising expenditure budget, even though they might have no control over other market factors.)

Budgets therefore perform a **dual role**.

- They incorporate forecasting and **planning** information.
- They incorporate **control** measures, in that they plan how resources are to be used to achieve the targets, and they can be flexed for corrective action.

4.1.6 Sales budget

Many organisations start the budgeting process by producing a sales budget. This could involve the following steps and considerations.

- Prepare a **preliminary sales estimate** based on a combination of the following
  - Previous period sales
  - Expected growth forecast
  - A forecast of general business conditions
  - A knowledge of potential markets for each product
  - The practical judgement of sales and management staff
  - Production capacity
- **Adjust the preliminary sales estimate** based on a combination of the following
  - Demand and pricing factors
  - Seasonal demand and/or capacity considerations
  - Cashflow considerations
  - Smoothing production loads if required or desirable
  - Profitability
  - The overall strategy of the business
- The overall sales budget should be broken down into suitable **sales categories**. These will differ depending upon the organisation, likely classifications include by product groups, market sectors, geographic territories and major customers.

4.1.7 The expense budgets related to marketing

(a) *Selling expenses budget*

- Salaries and commission
- Materials, literature, samples
- Travelling (car cost, petrol, insurance) and entertaining
- Staff recruitment and selection and training
- Telephones and telegrams, postage
- After-sales service
- Royalties/patents
- Office rent and rates, lighting, heating
- Office equipment
- Credit costs, bad debts

(b) *Advertising budget*

- Trade journal – space
- Prestige media – space
- PR space (costs of releases, entertainment)
- Blocks and artwork
- Advertising agents commission
- Staff salaries, office costs
- Posters
- Cinema
- TV
- Online
- Signs

(c) *Sales promotion budget*

- Exhibitions: space, equipment, staff, transport, hotels, bar
- Literature: leaflets, catalogues
- Samples/working models
- Point of sale display, window or showroom displays
- Special offers
- Direct mail shots – enclosure, postage, design costs

(d) *Research and development budget*

- Market research – design and development and analysis costs
- Packaging and product research – departmental costs, materials, equipment
- Pure research – departmental costs materials, equipment
- Sales analysis and research
- Economic surveys
- Product planning
- Patents

(e) *Distribution budget*

- Warehouse/deposits – rent, rates, lighting, heating
- Transport – capital costs
- Fuel – running costs
- Warehouse/depot and transport staff wages
- Packing (as opposed to packaging)

The Core Text 'Accounting for Managers' (Collier) includes a good section 'The Budgeting Process' within Chapter 16 'Budgeting'.

Collier identifies 9 steps in the budget cycle:

1 **Identify business objectives**
2 **Forecast economic and industry conditions, including competition**
3 **Develop detailed sales budgets**
4 **Prepare production budgets (materials, labour, overheads)**
5 **Prepare non-production budgets (by cost centre)**
6 **Prepare capital expenditure budgets**
7 **Prepare cash forecasts and identify financing requirements**
8 **Prepare the master budget (profit and loss, balance sheet, cash flow)**
9 **Obtain board approval of profitability and financing targets** ■

4.2 The marketing communications budget

An important element of the overall marketing budget is the communications budget. There is no one uniform method of deciding what to spend on marketing communications.

Here are some considerations that can affect the amount of expenditure.

- The number and type of marketing communication tools to be used
- The associated tasks to be undertaken
- Is the market the organisation operates in competitive?
- Does the market the organisation operates in respond to marketing communications?
- How well known is the organisation?
- How competitive is the market for external agency work (can a significant discount be negotiated?)
- Are there any special requirements requiring specialist skills?

4.2.1 The costs to be budgeted

- Air time and broadcast media
- Space and printed media
- Production costs
- Staff salaries
- Overheads and expenses
- Online marketing (see below)

MARKETING AT WORK

Online advertising still growing – but the rate of growth slows

Online advertising growth slowed in the second half of last year as the downturn began to hit even the most resilient part of the media landscape.

Figures from the UK's Internet Advertising Bureau and PricewaterhouseCoopers found that online advertising spending increase to £3.35bn last year, up 17.1% like-for-like on 2007. That compares with 38% growth in 2007. The second half increased less than 1% compared to the first, the worst intra-year performance since 2001.

Online was the only medium to grow last year, apart from cinema spending which increased 0.1%. It increased its share of total marketing budgets to 19.8% in the second half of the year, equivalent to press display, which saw revenues fall 6.7%.

Search engine advertising, which is dominated by Google, continues to be the strongest part of online advertising, up 22% for the year.

Adapted from an article by Tim Bradshaw, *Financial Times*, 1 April 2009

4.3 Business case justification

There are a range of techniques available to evaluate or justify the financial viability of a project or campaign. Some common techniques are outlined in the table below.

Method	Comment
Payback period	Calculates the length of time a project will take to recoup the initial investment; in other words how long a project will take to pay for itself. The method is based on cash flows.
Accounting rate of return (ARR) or **Return on Investment (ROI)**	This method calculates the profits that will be earned by a project and expresses this as a percentage of the funds invested. The higher the rate of return, the higher a project is ranked.
Internal rate of return (IRR)	Internal rate of return (IRR) involves comparing the rate of return expected from the project calculated on a discounted cash flow (NPV) basis with the rate used as the cost of capital. Projects with an IRR higher than the cost of capital are worth undertaking.

Cost-benefit analysis is a key part of a business case justification. Cost-benefit analysis of marketing activities is complicated by the fact that many of the benefits are **subjective** and difficult to measure.

All **costs** and **benefits** (financial, commercial, strategic etc) should be considered. For example, a supermarket chain may find that a national advertising campaign brings few tangible benefits in areas the chain has few stores, but if these areas are targets for future expansion the increased awareness may be beneficial in the longer term.

We look at cost benefit analysis in greater detail in a later chapter.

ACTIVITY 5

application

Before moving on to the next section, note down a brief structure or table of contents for a document to be submitted to senior management requesting allocation of funds for a marketing communications campaign.

4.4 The business case report

The business case or budget bid should be presented to the decision-makers in an appropriate format to enable them to clearly identify the issues made and conclusions found.

The format may be provided, for example many large organisations distribute skeleton 'applications' to various departments for completion.

The report should summarise the findings of the activities carried out under the stages of the general framework.

The report should contain:

- An introduction stating the terms of reference
- An outline of the current position highlighting any problem areas
- The relevant objectives from the organisation's strategy
- A gap analysis showing the current position and the desired position
- Different options explored and a summary of the costs and benefits
- A conclusion, and a recommended course of action

Any detailed analysis should be attached to the report as appendices.

Learning objective review

Learning objectives	Covered
1 Evaluate the different approaches to setting the marketing and communications budget and associated marketing activities	☑ Approaches to budget setting
2 Evaluate the different information sources required to determine the marketing budget for marketing operations and activities	☑ Information sources for budgeting
3 Negotiate delegated budgets with colleagues and agree provisional budgets	☑ Negotiating and agreeing budgets
4 Prepare a budget bid/business case to obtain budget priority for marketing activities	☑ Negotiating and agreeing budgets ☑ Business case justification
5 Understand that different sources of data are required to monitor and evaluate financial performance	☑ Information sources for budgeting

Quick quiz

1 What name is given to the approach to budgeting that involves budgets being set by senior management and passed down the organisation?

2 The approach to budgeting that relies to a significant extent on the actions of competitors is known as:

A Share of voice
B Affordability
C Objective and task
D Competitive parity

3 The approach to budgeting considered the most logical is:

A Share of voice
B Affordability
C Objective and task
D Competitive parity

4 What is the main advantage of affordability as an approach to setting the marketing communications budget?

5 What is the main advantage of competitive parity as an approach to setting the marketing communications budget?

6 Briefly explain the main disadvantage of the percentage of sales approach to budget setting.

7 Briefly explain the main disadvantage of the objective-and-task approach to budget setting.

8 Briefly explain what is meant by the term 'share of voice'.

9 Data is information that is suitable for a particular purpose, for example reducing risk.

True ☐

False ☐

Activity debriefs

1 Arbitrary budgeting presents a crucial disadvantage of bearing no accurate or predictable relation to the levels of expenditure that may be affordable, profitable, or required to fulfil marketing objectives. This will be particularly critical if the budget is under-estimated, allocating inadequate funds to fulfil task objectives or to meet unexpected contingencies – or causing internal customer problems when marketing overspends the budget.

Arbitrary budgeting is poor internal marketing. It conveys the message that the marketing function has no awareness of the organisation's strategic objectives or resource constraints; that it always overestimates its budget needs (and can therefore have less resource allocated to it in future); or that it is careless with its expenditure.

2 This could involve looking at your own organisation or use a past examination paper mini case study.

3 This activity relies upon your own research. It's possible that the budgeting approach taken in your organisation includes elements of a number of approaches or theories explained in this chapter.

4 Some organisations have made tremendous progress in recent years in their use of information and information systems. For example, although centralised call centres have their frustrations, many organisations have improved the information systems used by staff in these centres to ensure complete and up-to-date information is available from all areas of the business. Data warehousing and data mining is also used.

5 Your outline should have had some similarities to that provided in section 4.4 (as reproduced below).

The report should contain:

- An introduction stating the terms of reference
- An outline of the current position highlighting any problem areas
- The relevant objectives from the organisation's strategy
- A gap analysis showing the current position and the desired position
- Different options explored and a summary of the costs and benefits
- A conclusion, and a recommended course of action

Remember, ensure you use an appropriate format for your work based assignment. Your assignment must comply to the assignment guidance issued by the CIM.

Quiz answers

1 Top-down budgeting.

2 D. Competitive parity is dependent upon the actions of competitors.

3 C. The objective and task method is probably the one which is most logical (and the method most appropriate to the complex situation found in planning marketing communications programmes).

4 Affordability is a realistic approach as it takes account of resource availability.

5 Competitive parity ensures matching of competitor activity so may help preserve market share.

6 Percentage of sales doesn't take account of marketing objectives and opportunities. Effective promotion causes sales. The strict implementation of the percentage of sales method means a reduction in sales leads to a reduction in promotion. It could be that increased promotion would reverse the decline in sales.

7 The main disadvantage of objective-and-task budget-setting is the time, effort and difficulty involved in estimating the costs of tasks, particularly unforeseen contingencies.

8 The term 'share of voice' refers to an organisation's or brand's total communications presence or 'advertising weight', measured as a percentage of a defined total market or market segment in a given time period.

9 False. Data is a collection of raw facts. Intelligence is information that is suitable for a particular purpose.

References

Collier, P. (2008), Accounting for Managers, (2nd edition), John Wiley & Sons, Chichester.

Dibb, S., Simkin, L., Pride, W. and Ferrell, O. (2001), Marketing Concepts and Strategies, (4th European edition), Houghton Mifflin, New York.

Hucyznski, A. and Buchanan, D. (2003), Organisational Behaviour: An Introductory Text, Prentice Hall, London.

Kotler, P. (2008), Marketing Management: Analysis, Planning, Implementation and Control, (13th edition), Prentice Hall, London.

Schroer, J. (1990), *'Ad Spending: Growing Market Share'*, Harvard Business Review January/February 1990, pp44-48.

Chapter 11

Cost management

Topic list

1. Cost management: general principles
2. Variance analysis
3. Ratio analysis
4. Monitoring marketing mix effectiveness
5. Activity based costing (ABC)
6. Critical success factors (CSFs) and key performance indicators (KPIs)

Introduction

So far in this Finance section of the syllabus we've focussed on the purpose of budgeting and the budget setting process. In this chapter we extend our study of budgeting to cover the identification and analysis of budget variances (that is, results that differ from budget).

We also consider other aspects of cost management and measuring effectiveness such as ratio analysis, activity based costing and the use of key performance indicators based on critical success factors.

When looking at numbers or ratios, it is important to use your awareness of the operating environment and of general business issues to enable reasonable conclusions to be drawn. If a certain activity is 100% over budget (ie expenditure is double the budgeted level), this may well indicate costs are out of control - but this cannot be stated without further investigation. For example, if it was decided after the budget was issued to double the volume of activity in this area, the actual spend may be justifiable.

Syllabus linked learning objectives

By the end of the chapter you will be able to:

	Learning objectives	Syllabus link
1	Establish effective cost management processes for marketing operations	3.6
2	Understand how activity based costing may be used to identify and manage factors that drive marketing expenditure	3.6
3	Identify and reconcile budget variances	3.7
4	Identify the causes of budget variances (both internal and external) and recommend corrective actions where appropriate	3.7
5	Establish systems to monitor, evaluate and report upon the financial performance of marketing operations and associated activities	3.8
6	Understand the concepts of critical success factors and key performance indicators	3.8
7	Suggest appropriate key performance indicators in a marketing context	3.8

1 Cost management: general principles

KEY CONCEPT

concept

Cost management is a wide, general concept. Any activity intended to ensure expenditure is monitored and achieves value can be considered a cost management activity.

There are a range of cost management tools and techniques available to control and monitor costs and to evaluate performance. Tools that aim to control costs or another aspect of performance often have certain features or principles in common.

Control is vital if management is to ensure that planning targets are achieved. The control process involves three steps (these steps are based on the four aspects of the basic control cycle covered in Chapter 9).

Step 1 Set standards or targets.

Step 2 Measure and evaluate actual performance.

Step 3 Take corrective action.

1.1 Targets

Targets provide a context when managing costs.

The following objectives or targets are relevant to marketing managers.

- The organisation's overall financial objective or target for the year (or the planning period).
- The individual subsidiary financial targets that will help the organisation meet its overall objective.
- The annual budget (including the sales budget and marketing expenditure budget).
- Product-market strategy targets.
- Targets for each element of the marketing mix.

A key tool in cost management is the budget. As we have already discussed, a **budget** is a plan expressed in financial terms. It is also used as the basis for controlling or managing the activities it concerns.

1.1.1 Setting standards or targets

KEY CONCEPT

concept

Standard costs are predetermined estimates of the cost of performing an operation or producing a good or service under normal conditions. Standard costs are used as targets and as a basis for comparison with actual costs.

The organisation's objectives provide the basis for setting targets and standards. Each manager's targets will be directed towards achieving the company objectives. Targets or standards:

- Tell managers what they are required to accomplish, given the authority to make appropriate decisions.
- Indicate to managers how well their actual results measure up against their targets, so that control action can be taken where it is needed.

When setting standards for performance, it is important to distinguish between controllable or manageable variables and uncontrollable ones. Any matters which cannot be controlled by an individual manager should be excluded from their standards for performance.

1.1.2 Quantitative and qualitative targets

Performance can be measured in quantitative or qualitative terms.

- Quantitative measurements are expressed in figures, such as cost levels, units produced per week, delay in delivery time and market penetration per product.
- Qualitative targets, although not directly measurable in quantitative terms, may still be verified by judgement and observation.

Where possible, performance should be measured in quantitative terms because these are less subjective. Qualitative factors such as employee welfare and motivation, protection of the environment against pollution, and product quality might all be gauged by quantitative measures (such as employee pay levels, labour turnover rates, the level of toxicity in industrial waste, reject and scrap rates).

1.2 Measures

The most common measures by which marketing performance is judged are **sales levels**, **costs** and **market share**. Increasingly, organisations are also measuring **ethical** and **social responsibility** performance. As all organisations rely on customers for revenue, many companies seek to measure **customer satisfaction**.

Performance standards could thus be set at sales of £X for the period, Y% market share and Z% profit, all set against a minimum customer satisfaction rating.

ACTIVITY 1

application

List four possible disadvantages of using money (revenue or expenditure) as the sole measure when collecting management control information.

The organisation monitors performance at given time intervals **by comparing actual results with the standards set** to determine whether it is on, above or below these targets.

Costs and targets must always be considered against operating conditions. For example, if activity has unexpectedly dropped by 50% but related costs are only 25% below budget, this could indicate poor cost control. If activity is 75% up on expected levels and related costs are 50% above budget, this may actually indicate effective cost management.

1.2.1 Comparing results against standards or targets

- **Performance measures**. Mechanisms must be put in place for collecting information on actual results, so that comparisons can be made and control action taken. Marketing performance is often judged by analysing two main indicators: sales and market share.
  - **Sales analysis** is based on the comparison of actual with budgeted turnover, but this is only the first stage. It is appropriate to delve deeper and consider the effects of differences in unit sales and selling price. Further analysis by product, region, customer and so on may be required.
  - **Market share analysis**. Market share is important to overall profitability, and the attainment of a given market share is likely to be an important marketing objective. Market share should always be analysed alongside turnover, since the growth or decline of the market as a whole has implications for the achievement of both types of objective.
- **Marketing organisation**. As well as overall responsibility, individual responsibilities within the overall marketing plan should be clearly allocated. One example of a specific responsibility is the preparation of performance reports.

Other roles may include the management of promotional activities and management of marketing research. In some organisations, brand managers may have overall responsibility for a brand.

- **Implementation milestones**. Progress in implementing a programme can be monitored by the establishment of **milestones** and the dates by which they should be achieved.

MARKETING AT WORK

application

Example milestones for the launch of a new car might include:

- First delivery to show rooms
- First thousand sold
- Breakeven sales achieved

- **Contingency planning**. Events in the real world very rarely go according to plan. It is necessary for planners to consider problems that might arise and make appropriate preparations to deal with them. There are several requirements.
  - The organisation must have the capability to adapt to new circumstances. This will almost certainly imply financial reserves, but may require more specific resources, such as management and productive capacity.
  - There is a range of possible responses to any given contingency. The organisation should consider its options in advance of needing to put them into action.
  - A prompt response will normally be appropriate. Achieving this depends to some extent on having the resources and having done the planning mentioned above, but it will also depend on a kind of organisational agility. In particular, decision-making processes need to be rapid and effective.

1.2.2 Taking corrective action

Where performance against the standard or target is below a tolerable level (after considering operating conditions and the attainability of the standard or target) then remedial action needs to be taken.

This may mean invoking contingency plans previously drawn up for this purpose or taking ad hoc actions such as initiating sales promotions.

ACTIVITY 2

application

Give two possible reasons why a target or standard may eventually prove to be unrealistic.

Emmanuel *et al* (1990) describe four necessary conditions that must be satisfied before any process can be said to be controlled.

- **Objectives** for the process being controlled must exist, for without an aim or purpose control has no meaning.
- The **output** of the process must be **measurable** in terms of the dimensions defined by the objectives.
- A **predictive model** of the process being controlled is required so that causes for the non-attainment of objectives can be determined and proposed corrective actions evaluated.
- There must be a capability of **taking action** so that deviations from objectives can be reduced.

It is important to understand that this concept of control involves more than just measuring results and taking corrective action. Control in the broad sense embraces the formulation of **objectives –** deciding what are the things that need to be done – as well as monitoring their attainment by way of feedback. Note two important points.

- As *Drucker* (1954) pointed out many years ago, the most crucial aspect of management performance in a commercial business is **financial success**. If financial performance is consistently poor, a business will eventually cease to exist.
- Targets are only useful if performance can be **measured**.

1.2.3 Examples: feedback, standards and control actions

Feedback	Standards	Control actions
Sales figures	Against budget plus or minus	Stimulate/dampen down demand
Complaints	Number, frequency, seriousness	Corrective action
Competitors	Relative to us	Attack/defence strategies
Market size changes	Market share	Marketing mix manipulation
Costs/profitability	Ratios	Cost cutting exercises
Corporate image	Attribute measures	Internal/external communications
Environmental factors	Variances from norm	Invoke strategic alternatives

2 Variance analysis

KEY CONCEPT

concept

Variance analysis involves comparing actual results against budgeted or expected figures to evaluate performance and as a basis for managerial action.

2.1 Variance analysis

A **variance** is the difference between planned, budgeted, or standard cost (or revenue) and the actual cost (or revenue) incurred (or earned).

Variance analysis involves evaluating performance through variances including an investigation of what has caused the variance.

The budgeting process does not stop once the budgets have been agreed. Actual results should be compared on a regular basis with the budgeted results (at least monthly). Management should receive a report detailing the differences and should investigate the reasons for the differences. For example, if profitability of a particular product line is below budget, is this because fewer units have been sold, or because costs have risen?

The essence of a variance is that it directs attention to a specific area of management responsibility. If the differences are within the control of management, corrective action should be taken.

2.1.1 Example

Assume that, in a month, **budgeted** sales revenue amount to £1m. Actual sales amount to £960,000. The total **sales variance** is thus £40,000 (ie £1m – £960,000). It is **adverse**, as we have brought in less revenue than planned. So far so good. But with a little bit more information we can find out a lot more.

Let us assume that the budgeted £1m sales revenue was to result from selling 100,000 units at £10 each. However the cost of a key component rose suddenly, so to remain profitable we increased the selling price to £12 each.

Only 80,000 units were sold: total sales revenue amounted to £960,000. There is a total negative sales variance of £40,000 as actual sales are less than we anticipated (£1,000,000).

This variance of £40,000 can be analysed into two elements.

- **Price variance**. The part of the variance due to the price rise from £10 to £12.

  (£12 – £10) × 80,000 = £160,000, a positive or **favourable** price variance

- **Volume variance**. We sold fewer, so in volume terms, at the budgeted/standard price of £10 we have a negative or **adverse** volume variance of (100,000 – 80,000) × £10, which equals £200,000.

	£
Budgeted sales revenue	1,000,000
Price variance	160,000
Volume variance	(200,000)
Actual sales revenue	£960,000

Clearly, the two aspects of the total sales variance are linked. The analysis shows us that the additional revenue from the price rise has been 'eliminated' and more, by the resulting drop in sales volume.

Under other circumstances we might find a negative sales variance could be due to excessive discounting - sales volume might be satisfactory but this has only been achieved through significantly lower prices.

Other applications of sales variances include the **sales mix variance**. If a firm sells a higher than expected proportion of a cheaper product in a range and a lower than expected proportion of a more expensive product, this is likely to cause an adverse sales variance.

2.2 Causes of variances

Variances may be caused by anything that impacts upon how and what an organisation does as these changes result in different conditions to those envisaged when the budget was drawn up.

Investigation into variances should reveal the cause(s). Common causes of variances include:

- Volume different (volume)
- Costs or prices different (price)
- Sales mix
- Exchange rate movements
- Customer tastes
- Competitor actions
- Suppliers
- External stakeholders

2.3 Reconciling budget variances

Earlier we covered one method of reconciling a variance – by identifying the price and volume elements of the variance. Taking a wider view, the complete operating statement can be analysed to reconcile the difference between budgeted and actual profit.

An **operating statement/statement of variances** is a report, usually to senior management, at the end of a control period, that shows actual and budgeted costs and revenues, and reconciles budgeted profit for the period to actual profit.

So far, we have considered how variances are calculated without considering how they combine to **reconcile the difference between budgeted profit and actual profit** during a period. This reconciliation is usually presented as a report to senior management at the end of each control period. The report is called an operating statement or statement of variances.

The Core Text 'Accounting for Mangers' (Collier) includes a good section 'Reconciling the Variances' in Chapter 17 'Budgetary Control'.

3 Ratio analysis

KEY CONCEPT

Ratio analysis is simply the use of ratios to measure performance. The term is most often used to refer to the analysis performed on financial statements - but the technique provides a useful tool in many settings.

When considering marketing performance, a mixture of financial and non-financial ratios are relevant. For example:

- **Financial ratio only**
  - Sales revenue or marketing expenditure can be compared: over time, against budget or against competition

	20XX	*20XY*
Revenue	£10m	£15m

Comparing 20XX revenue with 20XY revenue gives an increase of 50%.

  - There may be relationships between different variables. For example:

	20XX	*20XY*
Revenue	£10m	£15m
Bad debts	0.5m	1.2m
Bad debts/revenue	1:20 or 5%	2:25 or 8%

Comparing these over time suggests that while income has increased, the quality of sales (in terms of the credit worthiness of purchasers) has fallen, as bad debts have increased to 8% of revenue from 5%. Perhaps the organisation has been too eager to generate sales without considering credit worthiness.

- **A mixture of financial ratios and non-financial data**

	20XX	*20XY*
Revenue	£10m	£15m
Number of sales personnel	50	60

Revenue has increased by 50% whereas the sales force has increased by 20%.

	20XX	*20XY*
Revenue per sales employee	£0.2m	£0.25m

The sales force was more productive in 20XY than in 20XX (in terms of revenue generated).

- **Non-financial data only**

Non financial data could relate to any aspect of a company's operations.

	20XX	*20XY*
Sales orders	250	300
Sales leads	1,000	1,025
Sales personnel	50	60

In 20XX, 25% of leads turned into orders, whereas in 20XY this has increased to 29%, so the sales force is more effective. The number of orders by sales person has stayed the same.

We look at another key marketing ratio, advertising to sales, later in this chapter.

4 Monitoring marketing mix effectiveness

4.1 Controlling the marketing communications budget

There is no one uniform method of deciding what to spend on marketing communications. This is not so surprising. The following are some of the **considerations that can affect the amount of expenditure**.

- What variety of marketing communications is to be used?
- What tasks are to be undertaken?
- How competitive is the market place?
- How well known is the organisation?
- Are there any special requirements?

Costs to be budgeted

- Air time and broadcast media
- Space and printed media
- Production costs
- Staff salaries
- Overheads and expenses

Marketing communication budgets may be very substantial and have a major effect on profitability (depending upon the organisation and the industry they are in). The effectiveness of this spend may be difficult to measure. It is possible is to use normal budgetary control techniques in marketing expenditure, and to review its effectiveness regularly, even if this is only by means of informed judgement.

Controlling budget expenditure and measuring effectiveness

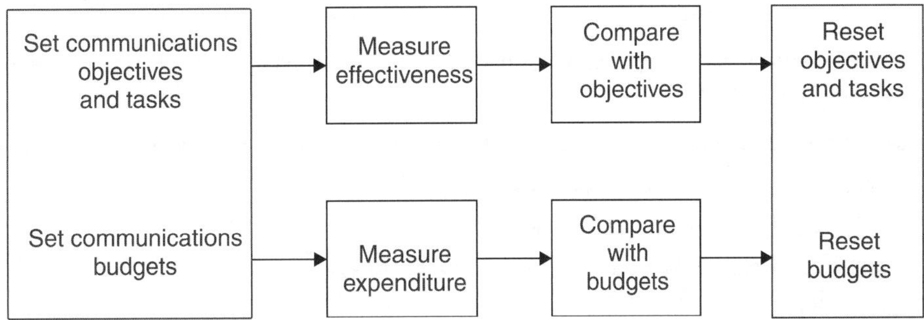

MARKETING AT WORK

application

Media evaluation

Dunnhumby believes the launch of its marketing effectiveness evaluation tool, Marketing Mix Optimisation (MMO), will prove invaluable to sales and marketing directors, finance directors and chief executives.

Based on the actual shopping behaviour of about 13m households (roughly half the population), MMO offers what the firm claims is 'unrivalled statistical robustness'.

Because it uses individual transaction data taken straight from the till, the system produces granular information, down to the level of hourly sales.

The shopper data comes from Tesco, which is such a significant magazine and newspaper retailer that the MMO tool can cross-reference shopper behaviour with their press consumption. But Dunnhumby can also quantify the effect of TV and

outdoor advertising, for example, by analysing the behaviour of customers who have been exposed to such campaigns. The tool also tracks relations between pricing and sales.

Martin Hayward, director of strategy and futures at Dunnhumby, says: 'This is the beginning of a new wave of analysis that is possible as a result of getting better data. It should spell the end of marketers having to allocate budgets based on the analysis of tiny groups.'

It also ushers in a new era of accountability and transparency for marketers and their agencies, who are under pressure to measure return on investment in marketing activities in the short term.

Jane Simms, *Marketing*, 23 October 2007

Marketing managers are responsible for monitoring their progress towards the agreed targets and objectives. To do this it is necessary to evaluate the effectiveness of the marketing mix.

This section will consider ways of controlling the effectiveness of four of the mix elements.

- Personal selling
- Advertising and sales promotions
- Pricing
- Channels of distribution

4.2 Personal selling

The effectiveness of personal selling can be measured for:

- The sales force as a whole
- Each group of the sales force (eg each regional sales team)
- Each individual salesperson

If there are telephone sales staff, their performance should be judged against different criteria than the criteria used to measure sales staff in the field.

Measures of performance would compare **actual** results against a **target** or standard. Possible areas include:

- Sales, in total, by customer, and by product
- Contribution, in total, by customer and by product
- Selling expenses (budget versus actual) in relation to sales
- Customer call frequency
- Average sales value per call
- Average contribution per call
- Average cost per call
- Average trade discount
- Number of new customers obtained
- Percentage increase in sales compared with previous period
- Average number of repeat calls per sale
- Average mileage travelled per £1 sales

It is not an easy task to decide what the standards should be. It is important not to assume that the efficient sales person who makes ten calls a day is doing a better job than the colleague who makes fewer calls but wins more orders.

There can be a big difference between net sales (ie sales after returns and discounts) and eventual profit. The performance of a sales force should be based on productivity and profitability, rather than on sales alone.

4.3 The effectiveness of advertising

4.3.1 Performance measures for advertising

- **Exposure**. Exposure can be measured in terms of frequency (eg the number of times a TV advertisement is screened) and the number of potential customers reached.
- **Awareness**. Awareness of the existence of a product or brand. Awareness could be measured by recall tests or recognition tests.
- **Sales** (volume and/or revenue). Advertising is often intended to increase sales but the effect of advertising on sales is not easy to measure, as many other factors influence buying behaviour.
- **Profits**. The difficulty of measuring the effect of an advertising campaign also apply here. Breakeven analysis might be used to calculate the volume of extra sales required to cover advertising costs. However, advertising might be necessary to build a brand, in which case awareness may be a better measure.
- **Attitudes**. The aim of a campaign might be expressed in terms of 'x% of customers should show a preference for Product A over rival products'.
- **Enquiries**. Advertising might be aimed at generating extra enquiries from potential customers. Where possible, enquiries should be traced to the advertisement.

Post-testing involves finding out how well people can **recall** an advertisement and the product it advertises, and whether (on the basis of a sample of respondents) attitudes to the product have changed since the advertising campaign.

If there is a noticeable increase in sales volume that coincides with an advertising campaign, it should be reasonable to assume the campaign has played a significant part in attracting the extra sales. Then, the extra profit per £1 of advertising could be measured.

MARKETING AT WORK

application

Many companies are slashing their marketing budgets and evaluating how marketing dollars are spent due to the tough economic times. Slashing budgets is a clear sign that 'Lean and Mean' is the current theme for many businesses. On average most research suggests that (while growing) online advertising still only represents less than 10% of where marketing dollars are spent. Yet even online advertising budgets are getting scrutinised.

For advertisers who wish to get the best ROI (Return On Investment) for their online marketing dollar the focus tends to shift to display advertising and whether or not they should keep spending in that category. Display advertising (eg banner ads on websites) is typically the hardest online advertising initiative to measure.

Therefore, when under pressure to justify every marketing dollar spent the inclination is to slash display advertising budgets and increase more accountable marketing channels such as affiliate marketing. At the surface this seems to make sense. However, if you take a holistic approach to looking at this situation you may find that display advertising plays an important role.

Display advertising can boost other online marketing efforts such as paid search and affiliate programs. Spikes and dips in performance driven marketing channels such as search and affiliate can sometimes be directly related to display advertising efforts. When significant display advertising campaigns are running for clients there may be a boost in traffic and conversions in other online marketing channels.

Measuring the impact of display advertising on other media channels and choosing the right allocation of marketing dollars is the tricky part. Companies should evaluate the impact display advertising has on other online campaigns and use that data to determine exactly how much spend to allocate to this channel in order to maximise online marketing ROI.

Peter Figueredo, *NetExponenet.com*, 24 Nov 2008

4.3.2 Advertising to sales ratio (A/S Ratio)

KEY CONCEPT

The **Advertising to sales ratio** or the **A/S ratio** is calculated by dividing the total amount spent on advertising as a proportion of total sales (in that particular market). Therefore, if sales in a market are valued at £150 million per year and the total amount spent on advertising is £14 million then the market or industry A/S ratio is said to be 9.33%.

The A/S ratio can be used to make comparisons with competitors.

An important consideration is the amount spent on communications by competitors. It can be difficult determining the amount spent by competitors, although reasonable estimates can be made based on visible advertisements and using data bought from marketing research agencies.

The A/S ratio for an industry provides a benchmark against which it is possible to determine how much should be spent or stimulate consideration of why certain amounts have been spent.

One important strategic decision is whether an individual company's A/S ratio should be higher, lower or the same as the industry average.

- **Reasons to spend more** than the industry average could include the introduction of a new product to the market requiring greater expenditure to develop product awareness (reach).
- **Reasons to under spend** the industry average could include a desire to simply maintain an established market position (rather than increase market share) or a need to reduce spending in one area to focus on other industries.

4.3.3 The effectiveness of sales promotions

There is often a direct link between sales promotions and short-term sales volume.

- The **consumer sales response** to the following is readily measurable.
  - Price reductions as sales promotions (for example introductory offers)
  - Coupon 'money-off' offers
  - Free send away gifts
  - On-pack free gift offers
  - Combination pack offers
- It might also be possible to measure the link between sales and promotions for industrial goods, for example special discounts, orders taken at trade fairs or exhibitions and the response to trade-in allowances.
- There are other promotions where the effect on sales volume is indirect and not readily measurable, for example sponsorship, free samples, catalogues, point-of-sale material and inducements.
- Promotions may go hand-in-hand with a direct advertising campaign, especially in the case of consumer products, and so the effectiveness of the advertising and the sales promotions should then be considered together.

An organisation can try to control sales promotion costs by:

- Setting a time limit to the campaign (for example money off coupons must be used before a specified date).
- Restricting the campaign to certain areas or outlets.
- Restricting the campaign to specific goods.

4.4 Pricing

4.4.1 Aspects of pricing

- Prices are set with a view to the total sales volume they should attract.
  - New product pricing policy might be to set high skimming prices or low penetration prices.
    - For skimming prices, consider whether they have been too high, because the market has grown faster than anticipated, leaving the organisation with a low market share because of its high prices.
    - For penetration prices, consider whether the price level has succeeded in helping the market to grow quickly and the organisation to grab its target share of the market.
  - Decisions to raise prices or lower prices will be based on assumptions about how much this would affect sales (the elasticity of demand). Did actual increases or decreases in demand exceed or fall short of expectation?
- An aspect of product-market strategy and positioning is the mixture of product quality and price. An organisation might opt for a high price and high quality strategy, or a low price and average quality strategy. Actual price performance can be judged:
  - By comparing the organisation's prices with those of competitors, to establish whether prices were comparatively low, average or high, as planned
  - By judging whether the mix of product quality and price appears to have been effective
- Discounts may be offered as part of pricing strategy. There are two types of discounts.
  - **Bulk purchase discount** that encourage higher sales and are justified by economies of scale.
  - **Settlement discounts**, which are given to encourage prompt payment of accounts, thus reducing the amount of working capital needed.

MARKETING AT WORK

application

Pricing pharmaceuticals in the UK

UK pharmaceuticals companies are introducing new drug pricing models as pressure mounts to offer better value for money.

The National Institute for Health and Clinical Excellence, the government's medicines advisory body that studies clinical and cost effectiveness, has agreed three different experimental approaches to pricing with drug companies in the past year alone.

Manufacturers have also proposed their own money-back offers and discounts as a way to win reimbursement by the National Health Service or boost sales for costly new treatments. The initiatives are important for drug companies' sales and future pricing strategy around the world.

Belen Garijo, senior vice-president for Europe and Canada for Sanofi-Aventis, said: "Pressure to keep costs under control is forcing us more and more to document the value of new products. These are times of unprecedented change. The UK has almost invented pay for performance."

While the UK accounts for about three per cent of global pharmaceutical sales, it has a disproportionately greater influence internationally, reflecting its importance in research and development, relatively high prices and methods of scrutiny.

Andrew Jack, *Financial Times*, 9 April 2008

4.5 Channels of distribution

Attempts should be made to establish the relative profitability of different distribution channels. An organisation may then be in a position to improve profitability by focussing on more profitable channels, or to improve the profitability of other channels (eg through cost improvement programmes or by increasing the minimum order size). The following example illustrates this.

Example: Jazz Ltd

Jazz Ltd sells two consumer products, X and Y, in two markets A and B. In both markets, sales are made through the following outlets.

- Direct sales to supermarkets
- Wholesalers

Sales and costs for the most recent quarter have been analysed by product and market as follows.

	Market A			*Market B*			*Both markets*		
	X	*Y*	*Total*	*X*	*Y*	*Total*	*X*	*Y*	*Total*
	£'000	£'000	£'000	£'000	£'000	£'000	£'000	£'000	£'000
Sales	900	600	1,500	1,000	2,000	3,000	1,900	2,600	4,500
Variable production costs	450	450	900	500	1,500	2,000	950	1,950	2,900
	450	150	600	500	500	1,000	950	650	1,600
Variable sales Costs	90	60	150	100	100	200	190	160	350
Contribution	360	90	450	400	400	800	760	490	1,250
Share of fixed costs (production, sales, distribution, administration)	170	80	250	290	170	460	460	250	710
Net profit	190	10	200	110	230	340	300	240	540

This analysis shows that both products are profitable, and both markets are profitable. But what about the channels of distribution?

Further analysis of market A reveals the following.

		Market A	
	Supermarkets	*Wholesalers*	*Total*
	£'000	£'000	£'000
Sales	1,125	375	1,500
Variable production costs	675	225	900
	450	150	600
Variable selling costs	105	45	150
Contribution	345	105	
Direct distribution costs	10	80	90
	335	25	360
Share of fixed costs	120	40	160
Net profit/(loss)	215	(15)	200

This analysis shows that although sales through wholesalers make a contribution after deducting direct distribution costs, the profitability of this channel of distribution is disappointing, and some attention ought perhaps to be given to improving it.

5 Activity based costing (ABC)

KEY CONCEPT

concept

Activity based costing is an approach to cost management that relates costs to the factors that cause or 'drive' them to be incurred and to change. These factors are called **cost drivers**.

A **cost driver** is a factor influencing the level of cost, for example the number of adverts placed would be a cost driver for advertising costs.

ABC relates overhead/resource costs to the activities that cause or drive them. This is done using resource cost drivers. The costs of activities are related to cost units using activity cost drivers.

A **resource cost driver** is a measure of the quantity of resources consumed by an activity. It is used to assign the cost of a resource to an activity or cost pool.

An **activity cost driver** is a measure of the frequency and intensity of demand placed on activities by cost objects. It is used to assign activity costs to cost objects.

An example of a resource cost driver is floor space, which can be used to assign office occupancy costs to the marketing department, the finance department and so on.

An example of an activity cost driver is number of customer orders, the number of orders measuring the consumption of order entry activities by each customer.

In traditional costing (referred to as absorption costing), overheads are first related to cost centres and then to cost objects (for example, products).

In ABC, overheads are first related to activities or grouped into cost pools (depending on the terminology preferred) and then related to cost objects (for example, products, services, clients or customers).

5.1 The operation of an ABC system

An ABC system operates as follows.

Step 1 Identify an organisation's (or department's) major activities.

Step 2 Identify the factors which determine the size of the costs of an activity/cause the costs of an activity. These are known as cost drivers.

Step 3 Collect the costs associated with each cost driver into what are known as cost pools.

Step 4 Charge the costs of each cost pool to products on the basis of their usage of the activity (measured by the number of the activity's cost driver a product generates) using a cost driver rate (total costs in cost pool/number of cost drivers).

Supporters of ABC claim that it gives a more realistic picture of cost behaviour as costs collected into cost pools tend to behave in the same way (as they have the same cost driver).

Example: ABC

An online computer retailer is considering outsourcing its order fulfilment function. Tenders from suppliers have been received, the lowest quote received being £15 per order. To make an informed decision, management need to know the cost of the function internally, per order.

Step 1 Identify the activities that cause the costs – Order filling, Shipping and Returns.

Step 2 Identify cost drivers for each of these activities (see table below).

Step 3 Calculate the cost driver rates (see table below).

Activities	Cost drivers	Monthly cost	Monthly volume	Cost driver rate
Order taking	Number of orders	£2,500	1,000	£2.50
Order filling	Number of orders	£1,500	1,000	£1.50
Shipping	1: Number of orders	£500	1,000	£0.50
	2: Number of units shipped	£3,000	3,000	£1.00
Returns	Number of units shipped	£5,000	1,000	£5.00
Total cost per order				**£10.50**

The internal cost of £10.50 per unit is significantly lower than the lowest outsourcing quote (£15). Activity based costing has revealed the function should remain in-house.

It has also revealed that returns is a significant cost driver. Efforts should be made to reduced the level of returns (for example improving the product information provided on the website).

ACTIVITY 3

application

Identify two activities and cost drivers for a typical marketing department.

5.2 ABC and CPA

KEY CONCEPT

concept

Customer profitability analysis (CPA) assigns revenues and costs to customers or groups of customers with the aim of focussing effort and resources towards more profitable customers.

Many costs are driven by customers (delivery costs, discounts, marketing costs, after-sales service and so on), but traditional absorption costing systems do not account for this. Organisations may be trading with certain customers at a loss but may not realise it because costs are not analysed in a way that reveals the true situation.

ABC can be used in conjunction with customer profitability analysis (CPA) to determine more accurately the profit earned by servicing particular customers.

Customer profitability analysis involves an analysis of the income and costs associated with specific customers or customer groups.

The use of Activity Based Costing in a marketing context should enable you to establish how much it costs you to acquire and retain each of your customers. This depends initially upon identification of the cost drivers for customer attraction and retention. Many of these costs may be outside the marketing department, for example customer retention may be influenced by customer service.

Assume you're a marketing manager for the credit card division of a large bank. You are running a campaign to existing customers to sign them up for a new credit card. As you begin your campaign, you suspect the following:

- Only 40% of your bank's customers are profitable.
- You don't know who those profitable customers are.
- Your goal is to market to this 40%.

How can you identify the profitable customers?

Under traditional cost accounting, you can establish what resources your company allocated to staff all customer interactions, but you're unable to establish what individual customer interactions cost. Under ABC, each customer activity (related to identified cost-drivers) is recorded and attributed its actual cost. This makes it possible to establish the total cost for each customer. Combining this with the revenue each account brings in gives a profit (or loss) figure for each customer.

ABC and CPA requires close partnership between the accounting and marketing functions, including information systems (for example both should work from the same customer database).

Marketing should also partner with the production function to ensure that the products you're about to do a promotion on are actually available, or to help decide which products to promote, based on inventory levels. The most creative campaigns in the world are doomed from the start if they aren't built using relevant information from around the company.

5.3 ABC and service businesses

Many service businesses have **characteristics** similar to those required for the successful application of ABC.

- A highly competitive market
- Diversity of products, processes and customers
- Significant overhead costs not easily assigned to individual types of service
- Demands on resources such as customer services which are not directly proportional to volume

If ABC were to be used in a hotel, for example, attempts could be made to identify the activities required to support each guest by category and the cost drivers of these activities. The cost of a one-night stay midweek by a businessman could then be distinguished from the cost of a one-night stay by a teenager at the weekend. Such information could prove invaluable for CPA.

Many of ABC's supporters claim that it can assist with **decision making** in a number of ways.

- Provides accurate and reliable cost information
- Establishes a long-run product cost
- Provides data which can be used to evaluate different ways of delivering business.

ABC is therefore particularly suited to the following types of decision.

- Pricing
- Promoting or discontinuing products or parts of the business
- Redesigning products and developing new products or new ways to do business

5.4 Cost improvement

Cost improvement (performing the same function to the same standard for lower cost) is one way of improving performance. Activity-based costing facilitates cost control and improvement by focusing attention on cost drivers. With ABC, it is possible to control or manage costs by implementing key performance indicators (covered in the next section) based on cost drivers. For example, the level of returns was an important cost-driver in our ABC example, so a key performance indicator could be established that measures returns as a percentage of orders.

Business process re-engineering (covered in the next chapter) is another technique that may be applied to achieve cost improvement.

The Core Text 'Accounting for Managing for Managers' (Collier) includes a good section on Activity Based Costing in Chapter 13.

ASSIGNMENT TIP

application

Is Activity Based Costing applied to marketing activities in your workplace? If not, could it be?

---

6 Critical success factors (CSFs) and key performance indicators (KPIs)

The use of **critical success factors (CSFs)** can help to determine the information requirements of an organisation.

6.1 Critical success factors (CSFs)

KEY CONCEPT

concept

A **critical success factor** is an element of organisational activity that is key or central to the organisation's future success.

Stated in a slightly different way, **critical success factors** are a small number of key **operational areas** vital to the success of an organisation. CSFs are **measured by key performance indicators** (KPI) – which are explained later in this section.

The philosophy behind this approach is that managers should focus on a small number of objectives, and information systems should be focused on providing information to enable managers to monitor these objectives.

Two separate types of critical success factor can be identified.

- **Monitoring** CSFs are important for maintaining business. A monitoring CSF is used to keep abreast of existing activities and operations.
- **Building** CSFs are important for expanding business. A building CSF helps to measure the progress of new initiatives and is more likely to be relevant at senior executive level.

6.1.1 Data sources for CSFs

In general terms Rockart (1979) identifies **four general sources** of CSFs.

- The **industry** that the business is in.
- The **company** itself and its situation within the industry.
- The **environment**, for example consumer trends, the economy, and political factors of the country in which the company operates.
- Areas of corporate activity which currently represent a **cause of concern**, for example, low customer satisfaction ratings.

More specifically, possible internal and external data sources for CSFs include the following.

- **Customer service department**. This department will maintain details of complaints, refunds, customer enquiries and satisfaction ratings.
- **Customers**. If such information isn't routinely collected, a survey of customers should be undertaken to identify (or confirm) areas where satisfaction is high or low.
- **Competitors**. Competitors' operations, pricing structures and publicity should be closely monitored.
- **Accounting system**. The **profitability** of various aspects of the operation is probably a key factor in any review of CSFs.
- **Consultants**. A specialist consultancy might be able to perform a detailed review of the system in order to identify ways of satisfying CSFs.

6.1.2 Determining CSFs

One approach to determining the factors which are critical to success in performing a function or making a decision is as follows.

Step 1 List the organisation's corporate objectives and goals.

Step 2 Determine which factors are critical for accomplishing the objectives.

Step 3 Determine a small number of key performance indicators for each factor.

6.1.3 Example CSFs which cover both financial and non-financial criteria

Sphere of activity	Critical factors
Marketing	Sales volume Market share Gross margins
Production	Capacity utilisation Quality standards
Logistics	Capacity utilisation Level of service

6.1.4 Example CSFs which relate to specific elements of the marketing mix

Activity	CSF
New product development	Trial rate
	Repurchase rate
Sales programmes	Contribution by region, salesperson
	Controllable margin as percentage of sales
	Number of new accounts
	Travel costs
Advertising programmes	Awareness levels
	Attribute ratings
	Cost levels
Pricing programmes	Price relative to industry average
	Price elasticity of demand
Distribution programmes	Number of distributors carrying the product

6.2 Key performance indicators (KPIs)

KEY CONCEPT

concept

Key performance indicators are measures that help an organisation determine if it is reaching its performance targets and operational goals. KPIs can be financial and non-financial.

We'll look at the relationship between critical success factors and key performance indicators using an example.

One of the **objectives** of an organisation might be to maintain a high level of service direct from stock without holding uneconomic stock levels. This is first quantified in the form of a **goal**, which might be to ensure that 95% of orders for goods can be satisfied directly from stock, while minimising total stockholding costs and stock levels.

CSFs might then be identified as the following.

- Supplier performance in terms of quality and lead times
- Reliability of stock records
- Forecasting of demand variations

6.2.1 Determining KPIs

The determination of **key performance indicators** for each of these CSFs is not necessarily straightforward. Some measures might use factual, objectively verifiable, data, while others might make use of 'softer' concepts, such as opinions, perceptions and hunches.

For example, the reliability of stock records can be measured by means of physical stock counts, either at discrete intervals or on a rolling basis. Forecasting of demand variations will be much harder to measure.

Where measures use **quantitative** data, performance can be measured in a number of ways.

- In physical quantities, for example units produced or units sold
- In money terms, for example profit, revenues, costs or variances
- In ratios and percentages

Sequence	Explanation	Example 1 UK National Health Service	Example 2 Mobile phone operator
Organisational goal	Overall strategy	Improve health care	Increase sales by entering new markets
Critical success factors (CSFs)	Operational goal: must be achieved for the overall strategy to be on track	Measurable reduction in time between booking an operation and receiving it	Establish network coverage in two countries in a year's time
Key performance indicators (KPIs)	Data sharing performance on CSF	For example % patients seen after waiting less than 1 month less than 3 months less than 6 months more than 6 months	% of country covered and date, reported monthly
Critical information requirements	Information requirements to generate KPI	Booking and operations data to enable accurate KPI to be completed	Information about masts installed

ACTIVITY 4

application

An organisation has an objective to fill orders quickly and effectively from stock held, but also not to hold excessive amounts of stock. This has been quantified in the form of a goal, 'to ensure that 95% of orders for goods can be satisfied directly from stock, while minimising total stockholding costs and stock levels'.

Three Critical Success Factors in this situation have been identified as:

- Supplier performance (as if suppliers fill our orders quickly we can hold less stock ourselves).
- Stock records reliability (as we need to be able to rely on stock figures to trigger reorders at the appropriate time)
- Accurate demand forecasting (to enable us to order an appropriate amount of stock in advance)

These CSFs are shown in the table below.

CSF	KPI
Supplier performance	
Stock records reliability	
Accurate demand forecasting	

Required

Complete the table by identifying appropriate KPIs.

ASSIGNMENT TIP

application

Are key performance indicators used in your organisation? If not, should they be introduced?

Learning objective review

Learning objectives	Covered
1 Establish effective cost management processes for marketing operations	☑ Cost management: general principles ☑ Activity based costing ☑ Variance analysis ☑ Ratio analysis ☑ Monitoring marketing mix effectiveness ☑ Critical success factors and key performance indicators
2 Understand how activity based costing may be used to identify and manage factors that drive marketing expenditure	☑ Activity based costing
3 Identify and reconcile budget variances	☑ Variance analysis
4 Identify the causes of budget variances (both internal and external) and recommend corrective actions where appropriate	☑ Variance analysis
5 Establish systems to monitor, evaluate and report upon the financial performance of marketing operations and associated activities	☑ Cost management: general principles ☑ Activity based costing ☑ Variance analysis ☑ Ratio analysis ☑ Monitoring marketing mix effectiveness ☑ Critical success factors and key performance indicators
6 Understand the concepts of critical success factors and key performance indicators	☑ Critical success factors and key performance indicators
7 Suggest appropriate key performance indicators in a marketing context	☑ Critical success factors and key performance indicators

Quick quiz

1 The three steps of a control process, in order, are:

A Measure and evaluate actual performance; Set standards or targets; Take corrective action.
B Take corrective action; Set standards or targets; Measure and evaluate actual performance.
C Set standards or targets; Measure and evaluate actual performance; Take corrective action.
D Set standards or targets; Take corrective action; Measure and evaluate actual performance.

2 The difference between planned, budgeted, or standard cost and the actual cost incurred is referred to as a:

A Standard
B Driver
C Ratio
D Variance

3 If revenue is £200,000 and related advertising spend £20,000, the ratio of advertising spend to revenue (**not** as a percentage) is:

A 1:10
B 1:100
C 10:1
D 100:1

4 The performance of the sales team or an individual sales person should be based on sales alone.

True ☐

False ☐

5 What are the two factors compared in the A/S ratio?

6 List three ways in which an organisation may attempt to restrict sales promotion costs.

7 Critical success factors and key performance indicators are the same thing.

True ☐

False ☐

1 Here are some possible disadvantages of using money as the sole measure.

(a) Looking only at monetary figures ignores the reasons for the result (for example changes in competitor activity).

(b) Taking corrective action (if required) is only possible if the reasons for the monetary result is understood.

(c) Monetary variances from budget may simply be the result of timing changes – for example expenditure budgeted for later in the year may have been brought forward.

(d) Focussing solely on money ignores other important aspects (for example market share and customer satisfaction).

2 There are many reasons why a standard or target set may eventually prove to be unrealistic. Two possible reasons are:

(a) The assumptions or information used to calculate the standard or target were flawed. For example, if the sales revenue budget included revenue based on a 5% response rate to a direct mail campaign but the actual response rate was 1%, the 5% assumption was probably always over optimistic.

(b) The future operating environment can't be predicted accurately. For example, if competitors unexpectedly introduce heavy discounting, the organisation will probably have to follow suit to preserve market share – but revenue will be below budget.

3

Activities	Possible cost driver
Advertising	Air time; Ad size; Ad frequency
Selling	Number of salespeople
Marketing administration	Systems used; Number of staff

4

CSF	KPI
Supplier performance	Average order lead time
Stock records reliability	Number of discrepancies found
Accurate demand forecasting	Difference between forecast and actual demand

Quiz answers

1 C. Set standards or targets; Measure and evaluate actual performance; Take corrective action.

2 D. The difference between planned, budgeted, or standard cost and the actual cost incurred is referred to as a variance.

3 A. Advertising spend (£20,000) to Revenue (£200,000) is a ratio of 1:10 (which would usually be expressed as 10%).

4 False. Profitability should also be considered (sales at an unprofitable price may not be desirable). Also, sales on credit to customers who may not be able to pay should be discouraged.

5 The A/S ratio compares advertising spend and sales revenue.

6 The three ways identified within the chapter were:

(a) Setting a time limit to the campaign.

(b) Restricting the campaign to certain areas or outlets.

(c) Restricting the campaign to specific goods.

7 False. Critical success factors are a small number of key operational areas vital to the success of an organisation. Key performance indicators measure progress in these areas (so a KPI may indicate how an organisation is performing in an important area or towards a key goal such as a CSF).

References

Collier, P. (2008) Accounting for Managers, (2nd edition), John Wiley & Sons, Chickester.

Drucker, P. (1954) The Practice of Management, Harper & Row, New York.

Emmanuel, C. and Otley, D. and Merchant, K. (1990) Accounting for Management Control. (2nd edition), Chapman Hall, London.

Rockart, J. (1979) Chief Executives Define Their Own Information Needs, Harvard Business Review, Vol. 57, No. 1, pp 81–93.

Chapter 12
Other tools and approaches

Topic list

1 Cost-benefit analysis
2 Breakeven analysis
3 Sensitivity analysis
4 The balanced scorecard
5 Value chain analysis
6 Business process re-engineering (BPR)

Introduction

In this, the final chapter covering the Finance section of the syllabus, we look beyond budgeting to other tools that may be used to monitor, control and improve marketing performance.

These tools require information that is both qualitative (subjective, relating to qualities) and quantitative (numeric, relating to quantities). Think about the information required and possible sources as you read through the chapter.

Remember there is no single 'best' tool or technique to monitor or improve performance. Also remember that in the real world, these theories and techniques may be used in part rather than being adopted in full. For example, an organisation may examine how different activities contribute to the success of the organisation without referring specifically to the value chain. The same may be said of business process re-engineering – an organisation may use aspects of this to improve efficiency without referring to the initiative as 'business process re-engineering'.

However, it is important that you understand exactly what is involved in the techniques covered in this chapter, and how they could be applied to improve the efficiency and effectiveness of marketing operations. The theories and techniques provide a framework for discussion (perhaps for your work based assignment) even if in the business world they are rarely referred to by name or implemented 'in full'.

Syllabus linked learning objectives

By the end of the chapter you will be able to:

Learning objectives		Syllabus link
1	Undertake cost-benefit analysis of marketing activities and use the results of the analysis to establish priorities	3.5
2	Understand the balanced scorecard as a means of setting targets and of managing and measuring performance	3.5
3	Apply the balanced scorecard to marketing operations and activities	3.5
4	Understand value chain analysis	3.5
5	Apply value chain analysis in a marketing context	3.5
6	Understand and be able to apply the concept of break-even analysis	3.5
7	Understand and be able to apply the concept of sensitivity analysis	3.5
8	Establish effective cost management processes for marketing operations	3.6
9	Understand business process re-engineering	3.6
10	Apply business process re-engineering to improve efficiency and effectiveness in processes relevant to marketing operations	3.6

1 Cost-benefit analysis

1.1 Cost-benefit analysis – meaning and a simple example

KEY CONCEPT

concept

Cost-benefit analysis (or CBA) is a technique used to determine the feasibility of an activity, project, decision or plan by quantifying its costs and benefits.

Cost-benefit analysis may be used to decide whether to make a change or to establish the value of an activity, course of action or a project.

In its simplest form, a cost-benefit analysis **adds up** the value of the **benefits** of a course of action, an activity or a project, and **subtracts** the **costs** associated with it.

1.1.1 Payback period

The payback period is the amount of time taken to break even on a project or investment, or stated another way, the time taken for benefits received to equal costs.

Example: cost-benefit analysis and payback

The marketing director is considering a new computer-based contact management and sales processing system. The new system would enable sales and marketing staff to contact more customers more regularly, and provide higher quality service to those customers.

Costs:

New computer equipment:

- 10 network-ready PCs with supporting software @ £1,500 each
- 1 server @ £2,500
- 3 printers @ £250 each
- Cabling and installation @ £3,500
- Sales support software @ £7,250

Training costs:

- PC basics training - 8 people @ £400 each
- Sales support training - 12 people @ £500 each

Other costs:

- Lost time: 40 staff days @ £250 / day
- Lost sales through disruption: estimate: £20,000

Total costs: £68,200

Note: We have ignored on-going system maintenance costs on the basis these can be met without additional resource.

Benefits:

- Increased mail shot capacity: estimate: £10,000 / year
- Ability to sustain telesales campaigns: estimate: £5,000 / year
- Improved efficiency and reliability of follow-up: estimate: £5,000 / year
- Improved customer service and retention: estimate: £15,000 / year
- Improved accuracy of customer information: estimate: £10,000 / year
- More ability to manage sales effort: £10,000 / year

Total Benefits: £55,000/year

Payback time: £68,200 / £55,000 = 1.24 years = approx. 1 year 3 months

1.2 Cost-benefit analysis in marketing context

The costs and benefits from marketing activities should be calculated and evaluated to enable informed decisions to be made about how resources should be allocated.

Some of the techniques covered elsewhere in the Finance chapters of this Text may help when preparing a cost-benefit analysis. For example, the advertising to sales ratio (A/S ratio) calculation includes advertising expenditure - the advertising expenditure figure used in this calculation could also be used as the cost element of a cost-benefit analysis of all advertising expenditure (not just a single campaign). The difficulty would be establishing a value for the revenue attributable to advertising expenditure - it's unlikely that all sales could be attributed to advertising, so the total sales figure used in the A/S ratio calculation would not be appropriate.

1.2.1 Costs

In many situations, the cost element of a cost-benefit analysis can be obtained from the accounting records. This should be a relatively simple task, assuming all expenditure has been recognised and coded correctly in the accounting system.

For example, the costs of a specific marketing event or campaign should be coded appropriately in the accounting system to enable easy identification and reporting.

1.2.2 Direct benefits

Direct benefits include the increased sales, contribution and profit directly attributable to the specific marketing activity. These can be difficult to quantify, as many factors influence sales levels.

1.2.3 Intangible benefits

Many benefits of marketing activity are intangible and difficult to value.

- Greater customer satisfaction and loyalty, arising from brand awareness.
- Improved staff morale and staff retention from working in a well-known, reputable company.
- Willingness of other organisations to do business with us due to our reputation.
- Benefits accruing from gaining competitive advantage.
- The fact that so many of the benefits of marketing activities are intangible means that it is difficult to construct a meaningful cost-benefit analysis.

There are three possible approaches to dealing with this problem.

Approach	Comment
Calculate a value for the benefits	We could estimate the worth of each of the intangible benefits and allocate an appropriate cash value. The problem with this approach is that realistically it is nothing more than guesswork.
Ignore the 'too intangible' benefits	Allocate a value to those intangible benefits we are able to estimate a realistic value for and ignore other intangible benefits. This approach will significantly undervalue marketing activities.
Adopt a qualitative approach	Find a reasonable non-financial way of stating intangible benefits. For example customer brand-recognition ratings could be established through questionnaires, market share could be used to assess competitive advantage. The problems with this approach are: • Determining appropriate measures • Isolating the effect of the specific activity from other factors

2 Breakeven analysis

2.1 Breakeven analysis

KEY CONCEPTS

Breakeven analysis is a tool used to calculate the **breakeven point**. The breakeven point is the sales volume at which the variable and fixed costs of producing your product or service will be recovered – so there is neither a profit or a loss.

Breakeven analysis is an adaptation of the cost-volume-profit analysis technique we discussed in an earlier chapter. Breakeven analysis uses cost-volume-profit analysis to find the point at which an organisation or an activity makes neither a loss or a profit.

Breakeven analysis and cost-volume-profit (CVP) analysis study the interrelationships between costs, volume and profit at various levels of activity.

This relationship can be shown in the formula:

Net profit = [Selling price per unit x units sold] **-** [Total fixed costs + (variable cost per unit x units sold)]

For example, assume the following:

- Fixed costs £2,580
- Sale price per unit £40
- Variable costs per unit £10
- Units sold 100

Net profit	=	£40 x 100	-	£2,580 + (£10 x 100)
	=	£4,000	-	£3,580
	=	£420		

2.1.1 Contribution

Contribution is fundamental to CVP and breakeven analysis. Contribution per unit is the difference between selling price per unit and variable costs per unit.

Contribution per unit = Selling price per unit – variable costs per unit

Continuing our example above, the contribution per unit is £40 - £10 = £30. The 100 units sold means £3,000 (100 x £30) is available to be 'contributed' towards fixed costs and (after fixed costs are covered) profit.

As fixed costs were £2,580, profit (at a sales level of 100 units) is £420 (calculated as total contribution of £3,000 less fixed costs of £2,580).

2.1.2 The breakeven point

The level of activity at which there is neither a profit nor a loss is known as the breakeven point.

The breakeven point (BEP) is calculated using the formula shown below.

Breakeven point = The number of units of sale required to break even

$$= \frac{\text{Total fixed costs}}{\text{Contribution per unit}}$$

Continuing the example from above, the breakeven point is calculated as £2,580 ÷ £30 = 86 units.

Another example follows.

Example: breakeven point

Expected sales	10,000 units at £8 = £80,000
Variable cost	£5 per unit
Fixed costs	£21,000

Required

Compute the breakeven point.

Solution

The contribution per unit is £(8–5)	=	£3
Breakeven point (BEP) is where total contribution equals fixed costs	=	£21,000
Breakeven point (BEP)	=	21,000 ÷ 3
	=	7,000 units
In revenue, the BEP is	=	(7,000 × £8) = £56,000

Sales above £56,000 will result in profit of £3 per unit of additional sales and sales below £56,000 will mean a loss of £3 per unit for each unit by which sales fall short of 7,000 units. In other words, profit will improve or worsen by the amount of contribution per unit.

	7,000 units	*7,001 units*
	£	£
Revenue	56,000	56,008
Less variable costs	35,000	35,005
Contribution	21,000	21,003
Less fixed costs	21,000	21,000
Profit	0 (= breakeven)	3

2.2 Profit/volume ratio and breakeven point

The **Profit/volume ratio** (P/V ratio) or **Contribution/sales ratio** (C/S ratio) is a measure of how much contribution is earned from each £1 of sales.

An alternative way of calculating the breakeven point is shown below.

Breakeven point = Sales revenue required to break even

$$= \frac{\text{Fixed costs}}{\text{P/V ratio}}$$

Example: P/V ratio

In the earlier example the P/V ratio $= \frac{£3}{£8} = 37.5\%$

Breakeven is where sales revenue $= \frac{£21{,}000}{37.5\%}$ = £56,000. At a price of £8 per unit, this represents 7,000 units of sales.

The P/V ratio of 37.5% in the above example means that for every £1 of sales, a contribution of 37.5p is earned. Thus, in order to earn a total contribution of £21,000 and if contribution increases by 37.5p per £1 of sales, sales must be:

$$\frac{£1}{37.5\text{p}} \times £21{,}000 = £56{,}000$$

ACTIVITY 1

application

The P/V ratio of product W is 20%. IB, the manufacturer of product W, wishes to cover fixed costs of £25,000 and make a profit of £25,000.

If the selling price is £10 per unit, the number of units of W that must be sold is

2.3 Limitations of breakeven analysis

Breakeven analysis and CVP analysis are useful techniques that provide relatively simple and quick estimates. As with all management tools and techniques, they should be used with an awareness of their limitations.

Limitations of these techniques include:

- They only apply to a single product or a single mix of a group of products.
- They assume fixed costs are constant at all levels of output.
- They assume variable costs are the same per unit at all levels of output.
- They assume that selling prices are constant at all levels of output.
- They assume everything that is produced is sold (inventory levels are ignored).

The Core Text 'Accounting for Managers' (Collier) provides another perspective on CVP analysis in Chapter 10.

3 Sensitivity analysis

KEY CONCEPT

concept

Sensitivity analysis investigates how projected or expected performance would vary with changes in one or more of the assumptions or variables that influence performance.

One way of taking into account the uncertainty of revenue or other benefits is to use sensitivity analysis. This involves:

- **Identifying** the main factors or variables that the benefits the activity could bring are dependent upon (eg customer acceptance, budgetary control, product availability etc).
- **Assessing** the effect on the benefits if a variable was amended by 'x%' up or down.

Sensitivity analysis therefore involves asking 'what if?' questions. By changing the value of different variables a number of different scenarios can be tested. This enables the variables which are most likely to have a significant effect on realising the benefits to be identified.

Once the most critical variables have been established, stringent monitoring and controls can be applied to these variables - or another approach would be to change the plan to reduce the dependence on these critical variables. For example, if management is worried that there will be insufficient stock to meet demand, a marketing campaign could be scaled down (or if feasible, production could be scaled up). A third possible approach would be to increase the selling price to reduce demand while at the same time increasing profit on the units that are sold.

Example: sensitivity analysis showing effect of an increase in variable costs

Let's return to an earlier example, shown below.

Remember, Net profit = [Selling price per unit x units sold] - [Total fixed costs + (variable cost per unit x units sold)]

Assume:

- Fixed costs £2,580
- Sale price per unit £40
- Variable costs per unit £10
- Units sold 100

Net profit	=	£40 x 100	–	£2,580 + (£10 x 100)
	=	£4,000	–	£3,580
	=	£420		

Now assume the variable costs per unit increase by 20%. Assuming all other variables remain the same, what would the effect be on profit?

Net profit	=	£40 x 100	–	£2,580 + (£12 x 100)
	=	£4,000	–	£3,780
	=	£220		

Therefore, a 20% increase in variable costs (from £10 per unit to £12) has resulted in a 47.6% drop in profit (from £420 to £220).

4 The balanced scorecard

KEY CONCEPT

concept

The **balanced scorecard** is: 'a set of measures that gives top managers a fast but comprehensive view of the business. The balanced scorecard includes financial measures that tell the results of actions already taken'. (Kaplan and Norton, 1996)

According to Kaplan and Norton (1996), the balanced scorecard complements traditional financial measures with **operational measures** on customer satisfaction, internal processes, and the organisation's innovation and improvement activities.

Rather than focussing solely on traditional financial measures, the balanced scorecard provides a more holistic view of an organisation, better representing the organisation's strategic vision and plan.

4.1 The four perspectives

The balanced scorecard allows managers to look at the business from four perspectives:

- Customer
- Internal business
- Financial
- Innovation and learning

Financial Perspective	
GOALS	**MEASURES**
Survive Succeed	
Prosper	Increase market share and ROI

Customer Perspective	
GOALS	**MEASURES**
New services	Percentage of sales from new services
Responsive services	Meeting customer service satisfaction targets
Customer partnership	Number of cooperative service initiatives and projects

Internal Business Perspective	
GOALS	**MEASURES**
IT capability	Meeting IT implementation targets
Operations excellence	Achieving operations management targets
New service introduction	Actual implementation schedule vs plan

Innovation and Learning Perspective	
GOALS	**MEASURES**
Technology leadership	Time to develop next generation of services
Service learning	Training to develop staff skills
Service focus	Percentage of services that equal 80% sales
Time to market	New service introduction vs competition

4.1.1 Customer perspective

Given that many company mission statements identify customer satisfaction as a key corporate goal, the balanced scorecard translates this into specific measures. Customer concerns fall into four categories.

Time	Lead time is the time it takes a firm to meet customer needs from receiving an order to delivering the product.
Quality	Quality measures not only include defect levels - although these should be minimised by TQM – but accuracy in forecasting.
Performance of the product	Does the product perform up to expectations and advertising claims? For example, how often does the photocopier break down?
Service	How long will it take a problem to be rectified? If the photocopier breaks down, how long will it take the maintenance engineer to arrive?

In order to view the firm's performance through customers' eyes, firms hire market researchers to assess how the firm performs. Higher service standards and higher quality may actually reduce costs in the long term, as less time is spent dealing with complaints and putting things right.

4.1.2 Internal business or business process perspective

The internal business perspective identifies the business processes that have the greatest impact on customer satisfaction, such as quality and employee skills.

- Companies should also attempt to identify and measure their distinctive competences and the critical technologies they need to ensure continued leadership. At which processes should they excel?
- To achieve these goals, performance measures must relate to employee behaviour, to tie in the strategic direction with employee action.
- An information system is necessary to enable executives to measure performance. An executive information system enables managers to drill down into lower level information.

4.1.3 Innovation and learning perspective

The question is **'Can we continue to improve and create value?'** While the customer and internal process perspectives identify the current parameters for competitive success, the company needs to learn and to innovate to satisfy **future** needs.

- How long does it take to develop new products?
- How quickly does the firm climb the experience curve to make new products?
- What percentage of revenue comes from new products?
- How many suggestions are made by staff and are acted upon?
- What are staff attitudes?
- Can we identify measures for training and long-term investment?

4.1.4 Financial perspective

'How do we appear to shareholders?' Financial performance indicators indicate 'whether the company's strategies, implementation, and execution are contributing to bottom line management.'

Measure	For	Against
Profitability	Easy to calculate and understand.	Ignores the size of the investment.
Return on investment (profit/ capital)	Accounting measure: easy to calculate and understand. Takes size of investment into account. Widely used.	– Ignores risk – Easy to manipulate (eg managers may postpone necessary capital investment to improve ratio) – What are 'assets'? (eg do brands count?)
Residual income	Head office levies an interest charge for the use of asset.	Not related to the size of investment except indirectly.
Earnings per share	Relates the firm's performance to needs of its shareholders	Shareholders are more concerned about future expectations; ignores capital growth as a measure of shareholders' wealth.
DCF measures	Relates performance to investment appraisal used to take the decision; cash flows rather than accounting profits are better predictors of shareholder wealth.	– Practical difficulties in predicting future cash flows of a whole company. – Difficulty in separating cash flows for products which share resources.

4.2 Setting up a balanced scorecard

4.2.1 Kaplan suggests the following methodology

- Identify the key outcomes critical to the success of an organisation.
- Identify the key processes that lead to these outcomes.
- Develop Key Performance Indicators (KPIs) for these processes (covered later in this chapter).
- Develop reliable data capture methods and measurement systems.
- Enact improvement programmes.

From a marketing point-of-view, the balanced scorecard enables all the vital perspectives – not just the financial ones – to be taken into account. In fact two of the main perspectives, customer and innovation, often relate directly to marketing.

MARKETING AT WORK

application

How to Prepare for Balanced Scorecard Implementation

The Balanced Scorecard is used to measure and manage the performance of a company in order to determine if the company's objectives are being met. To prepare for balanced scorecard implementation, there is a need to understand what its purpose is.

The scorecard covers four aspects: finance, customers, internal business processes, and learning and growth. The combination of these aspects determines whether or not a company is performing well. There must be a balance between the four aspects to ensure achievement in all areas, and to maintain stability.

A successful implementation requires a clear strategy and the support of management. The implementation must not be rushed, time is not of the essence here, management can take all the time that is needed to ensure the right things are selected to be measured. The implementation plan should list the steps to be taken clearly and be communicated to all stakeholders.

There must be a definite, concrete method to quantify the results of each area of observation to give meaning to the values obtained. To be of use, the measures obtained must be communicated to those able to act upon them – the recipients of the scorecard report (or those able to access the on-screen scoreboard dashboard) should therefore be considered as part of the implementation plan.

Adapted from an article by Sam Miller, *ezinearticles.com*, 26 October 2008

ASSIGNMENT TIP

application

Could the balanced scorecard be applied in your organisation? What measures would you choose to best monitor progress and success?

5 Value chain analysis

KEY CONCEPT

concept

The value chain depicts the main activities carried out by an organisation. Each of the activities in the chain adds value to the product (or service) being produced.

The value chain model, developed by Michael Porter, offers a bird's eye view of an organisation, of what it does and the way in which its business activities are organised. The purpose of the value chain is to show how organisations create value for their customers. The nine activities shown on the model procure inputs, process them and add value to them in some way, to generate outputs for customers.

Porter's Value Chain

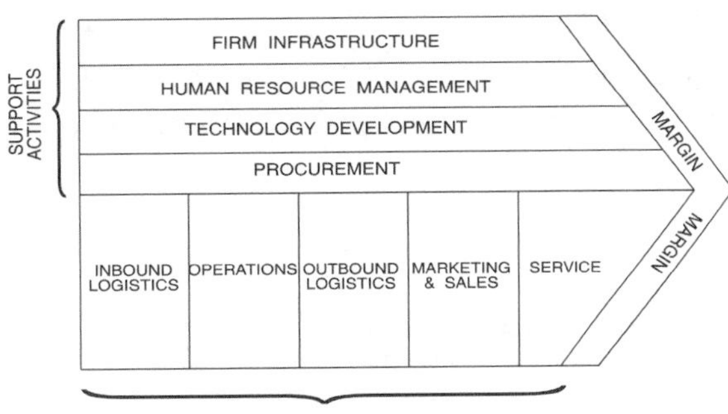

Activities are the means by which an organisation creates value in its products. It is important to realise that business activities are not the same as business functions.

- Functions are the familiar departments of an organisation (production, finance and so on). They reflect the formal organisation structure and the distribution of labour.
- Activities are what actually goes on, and the work that is done. A single activity can be performed by a number of functions in sequence. Activities are the means by which an organisation creates value in its products.

Activities or value activities can be categorised as primary or support.

5.1 Primary activities

Primary activities are directly related to production, sales, marketing, delivery and service.

Activity	Comment
Inbound logistics	Receiving, handling and storing inputs to the production system (warehousing, transport, inventory control and so on)
Operations	Converting resource inputs into a final product. Resource inputs are not only materials. 'People' are a 'resource' especially in service industries.
Outbound logistics	Storing the product and its distribution to customers (packaging, warehousing, testing and so on)
Marketing and sales	Informing customers about the product, persuading them to buy it, and enabling them to do so (advertising, promotion and so on)
After sales service	Installing products, repairing them, upgrading them, providing spare parts and so on

5.2 Support activities

Support activities provide purchased inputs, human resources, technology and infrastructural functions to support the primary activities.

Activity	Comment
Procurement	Acquiring the resource inputs to the primary activities (such as purchase of materials, subcomponents and equipment)
Technology development	Designing products, improving processes and/or resource utilisation
Human resource management	Recruiting, training, developing and rewarding people
Firm infrastructure	Planning, finance, quality control (Porter believes they are crucially important to an organisation's strategic capability in all primary activities.)

The ultimate **value** an organisation creates is measured by the amount customers are willing to pay for its products and services above the cost of carrying out value activities.

- **Customers 'purchase' value**, which they measure by comparing an organisation's products and services with similar offerings by competitors.
- **An organisation 'creates' value** by carrying out its activities either more efficiently than other organisations, or by combining them in such a way as to provide a unique product or service. We continue this point in the activity below.

ACTIVITY 2

application

Outline five different ways in which a restaurant can 'create' value.

5.3 The value chain and competitive advantage

According to Porter (1985), an organisation can develop sustainable competitive advantage by following one of two strategies.

- **Low-cost strategy.** Essentially this is a strategy of cost leadership, which involves achieving a lower cost than competitors via, for example, economies of scale and tight cost control. Hyundai (in cars) and Timex (wrist watches) are examples of organisations that have followed such a strategy.
- **Differentiation strategy.** This involves creating something that customers perceive as being unique via brand loyalty, superior customer service, product design and features, technology and so on. Mercedes Benz (in cars) and Rolex (wrist watches) are examples of organisations that have followed such a strategy.

An organisation's ability to develop and sustain **cost leadership** or **product differentiation** as a means of **competitive advantage**, depends on how well it manages its own value chain relative to competitors.

Competitive advantage is gained either from providing better customer value for equivalent cost or equivalent customer value for lower cost. Value chain analysis can be used to determine the activities within an organisation's value chain that could be improved by either lowering costs or enhancing value.

5.3.1 Cost management and the value chain

Shank and Govindarajan (1992) explained how the value chain framework can be used with a view to lowering costs and enhancing value.

They suggest a three-step approach.

Step 1 Build up the industry's **value chain** to determine the activities in the chain and to allocate operating costs, revenues and assets to individual value activities.

Step 2 Establish the **cost drivers** of the costs of each value activity.

Step 3 Develop sustainable **competitive advantage**, by **controlling these drivers better** than competitors. For each value activity, sustainable competitive advantage can be developed by reducing costs whilst maintaining value (sales) and/or increasing value (sales) whilst maintaining costs.

ACTIVITY 3

application

The examples below are based on two supermarket chains, one concentrating on **low prices**, the other differentiated on **quality and service**.

Identify the 'low price' chain and the 'high quality' chain.

(a)

	INBOUND LOGISTICS	OPERATIONS	OUTBOUND LOGISTICS	MARKETING & SALES	SERVICE
Firm infrastructure	Minimum corporate HQ				
Human resource management		De-skilled store operatives	Dismissal for checkout error		
Technology development	Computerised warehousing		Checkouts simple		
Procurement	Branded only purchases Big discounts	Low cost sites			Use of concessions
	Bulk warehousing	1,000 lines only Price points Basic store design		Low price promotion Local focus	Nil

(b)

	INBOUND LOGISTICS	OPERATIONS	OUTBOUND LOGISTICS	MARKETING & SALES	SERVICE
Firm infrastructure	Central control of operations and credit control				
Human resource management	Recruitment of mature staff	Client care training	Flexible staff to help with packing		
Technology development		Recipe research	Electronic point of sale	Consumer research and tests	Itemised bills
Procurement	Own label products	Prime retail positions		Adverts in quality magazines	
	Dedicated refrigerated transport	In store food halls Modern store design Open front refrigerators Tight control of sell-by dates	Collect by car service	No price discounts on food past sell-by dates	No quibble refunds

The Core Text 'Managing Marketing' (Palmer, Cockton and Cooper) includes an adapted Value Chain, geared towards achieving a marketing orientation, in Chapter 12.

6 Business process re-engineering (BPR)

KEY CONCEPT

Business process re-engineering is 'the fundamental rethinking and radical redesign of business processes to achieve dramatic improvements in critical contemporary measures of performance, such as cost, quality, service and speed'. Hammer and Champy (1993)

The key words in Hammer and Champy's definition are 'fundamental', 'radical', 'dramatic' and 'process'.

- **Fundamental** and **radical** indicate that BPR assumes nothing: it starts by asking basic questions such as 'why do we do what we do', without making any assumptions or looking back to what has always been done in the past.
- **Dramatic** means that BPR should achieve 'quantum leaps in performance', not just marginal, incremental improvements.
- A **process** is a collection of activities that takes one or more kinds of input and creates an output. For example, order fulfilment is a process that takes an order as its input and results in the delivery of the ordered goods.

6.1 Principles of BPR

The *Harvard Business Review* published an article by Michael Hammer in 1990 that presented **seven principles of BPR**.

1 Processes should be designed to achieve a desired outcome rather than focusing on existing tasks.

2 Personnel who use the output from a process should perform the process. For example, a company could set up a database of approved suppliers; this would allow personnel who actually require supplies to order them themselves, perhaps using online technology, thereby eliminating the need for a separate purchasing function.

3 Information processing should be included in the work which produces the information. This eliminates the differentiation between information gathering and information processing.

4 Geographically-dispersed resources should be treated as if they are centralised. This allows the benefits of centralisation to be obtained, for example, economies of scale through central negotiation of supply contracts, without losing the benefits of decentralisation, such as flexibility and responsiveness.

5 Parallel activities should be linked rather than integrated. This would involve, for example, co-ordination between teams working on different aspects of a single process.

6 'Doers' should be allowed to be self-managing. The traditional distinction between workers and managers can be abolished: decision aids such as expert systems can be provided where they are required.

7 Information should be captured once at source. Electronic distribution of information makes this possible.

6.1.1 Re-engineered processes

A re-engineered process has certain **characteristics**.

- Often several jobs are combined into one
- Workers often make decisions
- The steps in the process are performed in a logical order
- Work is performed where it makes most sense
- Checks and controls may be reduced, and quality 'built-in'
- One manager provides a single point of contact
- The advantages of centralised and decentralised operations are combined

6.2 BPR – possible limitations

Many BPR projects fail to bring the benefits expected. To succeed a BPR initiative requires sustained management commitment and leadership, realistic scope and expectations, and a willingness to change.

The wording of the title of Hammer's 1990 article: 'Don't Automate, Obliterate' was misinterpreted by many and became something of a war-cry in the early 1990s that led to a 'downsizing' wave. Rather than re-designing processes, as Hammer had intended, many companies sought to simply remove workers.

As a result, BPR has become associated with narrow targets such as reductions in staff numbers and other cost-cutting measures. However, a process that is not significantly redesigned, but instead is simply performed using fewer people, has not been re-engineered.

Hammer (1990) suggests that management itself should be re-engineered. Managers are not used to thinking in systems terms, so, instead of looking at the whole picture (which might affect their own jobs), they tend to seize on individual aspects of the organisation.

Business process re-engineering is really only part of a wider picture. **Four sets of changes** are regarded as being important in transforming from a company which satisfies customers, to a company that **delights** them – and from a company which is competent to a company which is the best in its industry.

- Breaking down barriers between different disciplinary specialists and business units
- Developing an explicit set of values and behaviour guidelines which are subscribed to by everyone in the organisation
- Redefining the role of management in order to foster empowerment, responsibility and decisiveness at every level
- Openness and trust among managers and employees

MARKETING AT WORK

The Leeds City Council undertook a Business Process Reengineering (BPR) project. Among the areas it looked at were:

Recruitment

The BPR Team identified £3m of projected savings over five years – £2m of which were purely on advertising costs by designing a more efficient way for advertising roles. It also took the 'average time to recruit' figure from 110 days to just 12.

Transforming the Housing Advice Centre

This project took a 'service in crisis' and transformed the experience for customers, involving and developing the staff and laying a solid foundation for closer partnerships between a raft of different agencies dealing with different aspects of homelessness.

The whole team benefited from the experience. [The analysts] spent a lot of time with the staff, and they really appreciated the fact that, stuck away in an old building, people were finally paying them attention. People had come in before and made promises but disappeared, whereas [the analysts] saw it through to the end, and everybody has seen the results.

Source: Leeds City Council Corporate ICT Services www.leeds.gov.uk

ACTIVITY 4

evaluation

An organisation produces books and magazines. It employs 360 staff in seven different locations.

Most of the processing systems used in the organisation were computerised 10 years ago, although generally this involved simply automating existing processes. Computerised systems currently include:

- Production – inventory control including real-time inventory and finished goods levels
- Sales – historical record of books and magazines sold for the last 10 years
- Finance and administration – all accounting ledgers including debtors and creditors
- Human resources – employee records
- Recent changes in the senior management of the organisation mean that BPR is currently being considered.

Required:

Explain how business process re-engineering can benefit an organisation, making reference to the situation in the organisation described above.

Learning objective review

Learning objectives	Covered
1 Undertake cost-benefit analysis of marketing activities and use the results of the analysis to establish priorities	☑ Cost-benefit analysis
2 Understand the balanced scorecard as a means of setting targets and of managing and measuring performance	☑ The balanced scorecard
3 Apply the balanced scorecard to marketing operations and activities	☑ The balanced scorecard
4 Understand value chain analysis	☑ Value chain analysis
5 Apply value chain analysis in a marketing context	☑ Value chain analysis
6 Understand and be able to apply the concept of break-even analysis	☑ Break-even analysis
7 Understand and be able to apply the concept of sensitivity analysis	☑ Break-even analysis
8 Establish effective cost management processes for marketing operations	☑ Cost-benefit analysis ☑ The balanced scorecard ☑ Value chain analysis ☑ Break-even analysis ☑ Business process re-engineering ☑ And all Finance chapters in this Study Text
9 Understand business process re-engineering	☑ Business process re-engineering
10 Apply business process re-engineering to improve efficiency and effectiveness in processes relevant to marketing operations	☑ Business process re-engineering

Quick quiz

1 The main purpose of a cost-benefit analysis is to:

A Attempt to reduce the cost of an activity
B Establish the breakeven point
C Establish suitable key performance indicators
D Compare costs with benefits to establish the value of an activity or a decision

2 Which one of the following is **not** a valid approach to dealing with intangible benefits of marketing activity?

A Reduce associated costs by an estimated value of the benefits
B Attempt to calculate a value for the benefits
C Ignore the 'too intangible' benefits
D Adopt a qualitative approach

3 Contribution per unit is the difference between selling price per unit and variable costs per unit.

True ☐

False ☐

4 If contribution per unit is £5 and fixed costs are £2,500, what is the breakeven point (in units)?

5 Sensitivity analysis aims to:

A Ensure marketing material doesn't cause offence
B Identify the variables most likely to significantly influence results
C Ensure all marketing staff feel valued
D Calculate an exact value for intangible benefits

6 What are the four perspectives of a balanced scorecard?

7 Which one of the following is **not** a primary activity in Porter's value chain?

A Operations
B Marketing and sales
C Human resource management
D Inbound logistics

8 Which one of the following is **not** a word associated with business process re-engineering?

A Radical
B Dramatic
C Fundamental
D Gradual

Activity debriefs

1 The number of units that must be sold is | 25,000 |.

Workings

$$\frac{\text{Required contribution}}{\text{P/V ratio}} = \frac{\text{£}50{,}000}{20\%} = \text{£}250{,}000$$

∴ Number of units = £250,000 ÷ £10 = 25,000

2 Here are some ideas. Each of these options is a way of organising the activities of buying, cooking and serving food in a way that (some) customers will value.

(a) It could become more efficient, by automating the production of food, as in a fast food chain.

(b) The restaurant could develop commercial relationships with growers to obtain the best quality fresh produce.

(c) They could decide to specialise in a particular type of cuisine (such as French or Thai).

(d) The restaurant could be decorated in a particular style for those customers who value 'atmosphere' and a sense of occasion

(e) The restaurant could focus on a particular segment such as young families who may feel unwelcome at other restaurants, for example by providing excellent facilities for small children.

3 The two supermarkets represented are based on the following.

(a) The value chain in (a) is similar to that of Lidl, a 'discount' supermarket chain which sells on price. This can be seen in the limited product range and its low-cost sites.

(b) The value chain in (b) is based on Marks and Spencer, which seeks to differentiate on quality and service. Hence the 'no quibble' refunds, the use of prime retail sites, and customer care training.

4 Some of the main benefits business process re-engineering (BPR) can bring are explained below.

Keep up with competitors

If competitors improve their processes they are likely to be in a stronger position, which may threaten the very existence of a competing organisation. For example, a competitor could innovate leading to reduced costs, and may then be in a position to undercut prices. Improving processes in line with competitors may be necessary simply to survive.

Competitive advantage

Competitors may not be in a position to copy the innovated processes (eg they may not have the funds required to invest in the required IT). For example, the organisation may invest funds developing a website that allows it to sell books direct to consumers. If the organisation's competitors lack the will or funds to provide a similar service, this will provide a competitive advantage.

Effective utilisation of technology

Some BPR might become necessary when technological change means existing processes have become archaic. For example, it is likely that 30 years ago the organisation operated a manual paper-based transaction processing system.

Potential for time and cost savings

Often, the re-engineered process will result in cost or time savings, due to a more efficient and effective way of working.

Better decision making

Better quality internal systems and processes should result in the capture and availability of better quality information. This should lead to better quality decision making. For example, a database of historical sales information may allow better sales forecasting, allowing more effective production planning.

Quiz answers

1 D. The main purpose of a cost-benefit analysis is to compare costs with benefits to establish the value of an activity or a decision.

2 A. The three valid approaches to dealing with intangible benefits are shown in options B, C and D.

3 True. Contribution per unit is the difference between selling price per unit and variable costs per unit.

4 500 units (500 units x £5 = £2,500).

5 B. Sensitivity analysis aims to identify the variables most likely to significantly influence results.

6 Customer; financial; internal business; innovation and learning.

7 C. Human resource management is a support activity in Porter's value chain.

8 D. Gradual is not a word associated with business process re-engineering.

References

Hammer, M. (1990) *'Reengineering Work: Don't Automate, Obliterate'*, Harvard Business Review Vol. 68(4), pp111-118.

Hammer, M. and Champy, J. (1993) Reengineering the Corporation, Nicholas Brealey Publishing, London.

Kaplan, R.S. and Norton, D. P. (1996) The Balanced Scorecard: Translating Strategy into Action, Harvard Business School Press, Boston.

Porter, M. (1985) Competitive Advantage: Creating and Sustaining Superior Performance, The Free Press, New York.

Shank, J. K. and Govindarajan V. (1992) Strategic cost management: The value chain perspective, Journal of Management Accounting Research (4), pp179-197.

Key concepts

Activity based costing 324
Advertising to sales ratio 322
Assertiveness 199
Assets... 77
Authority... 4

Balanced score card 342
Balance sheet... 76
Benchmarking 52, 93
Breakeven analysis 339
Budget 275, 289
Budgetary control 276
Business process re-engineering 348

Capital.. 77
Competence... 149
Conflict 254
Control... 274
Co-ordination 21
Cost behaviour 277
Cost-benefit analysis 337
Cost management 313
Counselling 231
Critical success factors 327
Customer lifetime value 82
Customer profitability analysis 326

Delegation.. 194
Discipline 233
Diversity 245
Divisionalisation.. 16

Empowerment.. 193
Equal opportunities... 157

Grievance 259

Induction 162
Influencing... 202
Information.. 296
Internal marketing..................................23, 234
Interpersonal behaviour 196

Job analysis.. 148
Job description 150
Job design 164

Key performance indicators 329

Leadership style 114
Liability.. 77

Management...101
Management accounting 73
Market share.. 71
Marketing information system 298
Metric.. 70

Non-verbal communication 198

Organisation culture... 28
Organisation structure 3
Outsourcing 167

Person specification...151
Planning 273
Power.. 4
Productivity.. 80
Profit and loss account...................................... 75
Published accounts... 73

Quality 37
Quality assurance... 41
Quality circle.. 44
Quality control 41
Quality management 40
Quality management ststems 42

Ratio analysis 318

Sensitivity analysis 341
Service 57
Share of voice...294
Standard costs 313
Strategic business unit...................................... 16

Talent management...160
Team 137
Time series... 92

Total Quality Management 43
Training 221

Value chain 345
Variance analysis 316

Index

360-degree appraisal, 218

A/S ratio, 322
ABC, 324, 325, 326
Abilene paradox, 138
Absorption costing, 325
Accommodating, 258
Accountability, 70
Accounting measures of performance, 73
Accounting rate of return (ARR), 305
Accounting records, 296
Action learning, 226
Action-centred leadership, 121
Active listening, 198, 203
Activists, 127
Activities, 346
Activity based costing, 324, 325
Activity cost driver, 325
Activity level, 278
Ad hoc structure, 7
Ad hocracy, 20
Adair, 121
Adaptation, 262
Adaptive organisation, 18
Administration expenses, 76
Advertising, 321, 322
Advertising budget, 303
Advertising services, 168
Advertising to Sales Ratio, 322
Affluent Worker research, 191
Affordability, 291
After sales service, 346
Aggressive behaviour, 199
Analysing performance information, 92
Analysis the current position, 127
Annual report and accounts, 74
Anthony, Robert, 274
Appraisal, 215, 220
Appraisal interview, 219
Appraisal procedures, 87
Appraisal report, 217
Appraisal system, 87
Arbitrary estimation, 290
Ashridge Management College, 115
Assertiveness, 199
Assessment centres, 156
Attitude, 230
Authority, 4, 255, 269
Avoidable cost, 84
Awareness training, 253

Back and Back, 199
Balance sheets, 74, 77, 78
Balanced scorecard, 342, 344
Balanced team, 143
Basic marketing measures, 71
Behavioural incident methods, 216
Behavioural/personal competences, 150
Belbin, 141
Belbin's team role, 141
Benchmarking, 52, 93
Benchmarking process, 54
Benefit schemes, 192
Blake and Mouton, 116
Bottom-up budgets, 289
Boundaryless structures, 19
BPR, 348
BPR limitations, 349
BPR principles, 348
BPR process characteristics, 349
Brand, 78
Brand structure, 14
Breakeven analysis, 339
Breakeven analysis limitations, 341
Breakeven point, 339
Brech, 101
Buchanan and Hyczynski, 296
Buckley and McKenna, 276
Budget, 275, 276, 289, 296, 300, 301, 302, 319
Budget committee, 301
Budget cycle, 304
Budget factor, 302
Budget information, 296
Budget manual, 301
Budget negotiation, 300
  techniques, 300
Budget objectives, 275
Budget period, 302
Budget preparation, 301
Budget setting, 289, 290
Budgetary control, 79, 276
Budgeting, 275, 277, 296
Budgeting purpose, 275
Bureaucracies, 18
Burns and Stalker, 18
Business case for quality management, 39
Business case justification, 305
Business case report, 306
Business Excellence Award, 48
Business plan, 211
Business Process Reengineering, 261, 348
Business process re-engineering limitations, 349
Business process re-engineering principles, 348
Business processes, 343
By a business to another person, 78

C/S ratio, 340
Capital and reserves, 79
Capital items, 76
Carbon footprint, 51
Career development, 227
Cash flow, 79
Cash flow statement, 74
Causes of variances, 317
Centralisation, 5
Chairperson, 185

Change, 108, 255, 261, 269
Change experience, 262
Change management styles, 265
Channels of distribution, 323
Charisma, 114
Chunking, 137
Climate change, 51
Coaches, 267
Coaching, 226
Coca-Cola, 80
Cohesion, 178, 183
Collaborating, 259
Collaboration, 164
Communication, 178, 184, 196, 207, 273
Communication channels, 11, 22
Communication process, 197
Communication tools, 184
Communications, 235
Communications budget, 290
Competence, 149
Competence analysis, 149
Competence profiles, 151
Competencies, 212
Competition, 255, 269
Competitive advantage, 39, 347
Competitive parity, 291
Competitor benchmarking, 52
Compliance, 39
Compromising, 259
Conflict, 183, 254
Conflict handling styles, 258
Conflict management, 258
Conformance, 37
Conformity, 138
Consultants, 297
Contingency models, 119
Contingency planning, 315
Contingency theories of leadership, 113
Continuous improvement, 44, 220
Continuum of leadership styles, 117
Contribution, 339
Contribution profiling, 184
Contribution/sales ratio, 340
Control, 3, 21, 22, 274, 313, 315, 319
Control cycle, 275
Controllable costs, 84
Co-operation, 27
Co-ordination, 3, 21, 22, 138, 164, 276
Core competences, 167
Core job dimensions, 165
Corporate finance, 74
Corrective action, 315
Cost behaviour, 277, 278, 281
Cost benefit analysis, 337, 338
Cost control, 313
Cost drivers, 324, 347
Cost improvement, 327
Cost leadership, 347
Cost management, 313, 347
Cost of quality, 38
Cost per unit, 281
Cost pools, 325
Cost-benefit analysis, 305
Costs, 338
Cost-volume-profit analysis, 294
Counselling, 230, 232
Counselling process, 232
CPA, 326
Creativity, 10, 262
Credit control departments, 79
Creditors, 77
Critical incidents, 57, 122
Critical success factors (CSF), 327, 328
Crosby, 38, 42
Cross-cultural competence, 252
Cross-function co-ordination, 237
Cross-functional co-operation, 21
Cross-functional relations, 230
Cross-functional teams, 111, 139
CSF, 328
Cultural change, 29
Cultural differences, 248, 251
Cultural incompatibility, 255
Cultural strength, 29
Cultural web, 28
Culturally diverse team, 252
Culture, 62
Current assets, 78
Current liabilities, 78
Customer appraisal, 218
Customer communications, 85
Customer feedback, 62
Customer lifetime value, 82
Customer loyalty, 81
Customer orientation, 236
Customer perspective, 343
Customer profitability analysis (CPA), 326
Customer retention, 82
Customer satisfaction, 81
Customer type, 14
Customer value, 63

Danone, 161
Data, 296
Debtors, 78
Decentralisation, 5
Decisional role, 105
Decision-making, 183
Delegated budgets, 301
Delegation, 194
Demarcation disputes, 151
Deming, 38
Deming cycle, 55
Demotivation, 187
Departmentation, 3, 11
Detailed planning, 273
Development, 221, 226
Developmental feedback, 201
Dibb, 298
Differentiation strategy, 347
Dimensions of quality, 37
Direct benefits, 338
Direct discrimination, 158
Direction, 110
Directive leadership, 115
Disability Discrimination Act, 157
Disciplinary procedures, 230, 233
Disciplinary sanctions, 234
Disciplinary situations, 233

Discipline, 233
Discounts, 323
Discrimination, 158
Disseminator, 105
Distinctive competences, 343
Distribution channels, 323
Disturbance handler, 105
Diversity, 245
Diversity policy, 246
Divisional structure, 7
Divisionalisation, 16
Divisions, 16
DMAIC, 54
Dorming, 181
Drucker, 316

Education and communication, 266
Effective and **ineffective**, 177
Effective meetings, 186
EFQM, 46
EFQM Quality Award, 48
Elasticity of demand, 323
E-learning, 225
Electronic Point of Sale (EPOS), 297
Emmanuel et al, 315
Emotional competences, 113
Employability, 227
Employee attitude, 87
Employee commitment, 27
Employee involvement, 194
Employee participation, 194
Employee satisfaction, 40
Employee voice, 194
Employer brand, 245
Employment Equality (Age) Regulations 2006, 158
Employment Equality (Religion or Belief) Regulations 2003, 157
Employment Equality (Sexual Orientation) Regulations 2003, 157
Employment law, 157
Empowerment, 166, 193
Empowerment structure, 193
Entrepreneur, 105
Environmental Management Systems (EMS), 50
Environmental scanning, 296
Episodes, 57
EPOS, 297
Equal opportunities, 157, 247
Equal Pay (Amendment) Regulations 1984, 157
E-recruitment, 146
Ethical influencing, 202
Evaluating recruitment, 159
Evaluation and control, 276
Evaluation of training, 227
Evolutionary change, 261
Excellence Model, 46
Exchange rates, 297
Executive information system, 343
Expectancy, 190
Expectancy theory, 190
Expense budgets related to marketing, 303
Experiential learning cycle, 124
Experiment and testing method, 295
Expert power, 4, 108
Explicit knowledge, 296
Extended (service) marketing mix, 58
External data sources, 299
External failure costs, 39
External recruitment channels, 146
External stakeholders, 112

Facilitative style, 115
Fayol, 101, 102
Feedback, 122, 197, 201, 215
Feedback mechanisms, 215
Figurehead, 104
Finance manager's role, 273
Financial accounting, 74
Financial perspective, 344
Financial ratios, 318
Firm infrastructure, 346
Fitness for purpose, 37
Five Point Pattern, 151
Fixed asset, 78
Fixed costs, 84, 279
Flat structures, 19
Flexibility, 19, 245
Flexible organisation, 18
Flexible working, 166
Flexi-time systems, 166
Followership, 107
Follow-up, 219
Force field analysis, 262
Forecast, 275, 302
Forecasting, 273
Forming, 180
Founder, 29
Franchising, 24
French & Raven, 4
Functional authority, 4
Functional flexibility, 20
Functional organisation, 12
Functions of management, 102

Gap analysis, 306
Geographic departmentation, 15
Get it right first time, 43
Global warming, 51
Goal incompatibility, 255
Goals down plans up, 290
Grading, 216
Great Place to Work Institute, 161
Greenhouse gas (GHG) emissions, 51
Grievance, 260
Grievance interview, 260
Grievance procedures, 260
Group, 183
Group dynamics, 137
Group selection methods, 156
Groups, 137, 164
Groupthink, 183
Growth, 262
Guided assessment, 216

Hall's communication model, 250
Hammer and Champy, 348
Handy, 21, 179
Harassment, 158
Headcount, 297
Hersey and Blanchard, 119
Herzberg, 103, 165, 190
Hierarchical structure, 193
Hierarchy, 3
Hierarchy of needs, 188
High performance teams, 178
Historical basis, 292
Hofstede model, 249
Horizontal alignment, 211
Horizontal structure, 17, 19
House (1976), 114
HR specialists, 144
Huczyinski & Buchanan, 3
Human capital management, 160
Human relations, 103
Human resource management, 346
Human resource planning, 145
Hybrid structures, 16
Hygiene factors, 190

Ideologies of conflict, 256
Impact of change, 261
Impact of conflict, 256
Implementation milestones, 315
Imposition, 262
Improving recruitment, 160
Inbound logistics, 346
Incomplete information, 297
Indirect discrimination, 158
Individual objectives, 213
Induction, 162
Influences on organisation structure, 8
Influencing, 202
Informal groups, 137
Informal organisation, 27
Information, 296
Information and Communication Technology (ICT), 8, 140
Information overload, 297
Information sources, 296, 298
Informational role, 105
Innovation and learning measurement, 90
Innovation and learning perspective, 344
Innovation audit, 90
Inspection, 41
Intangible benefits, 338
Intangible fixed asset, 78
Integration, 21
Intelligence, 296
Intercultural communication, 253
Inter-departmental relations, 22
Interdependence, 255, 269
Internal business perspective, 343
Internal Communications, 89
Internal customer relations, 237
Internal failure costs, 39
Internal marketing, 23, 62, 111, 193, 234, 237
Internal marketing mix, 238
Internal measures, 86
Internal rate of return (IRR), 305
Internal records system, 299
Internal recruitment channels, 146
International Organisation for Standardisation (ISO), 49
International structures, 25
International teams, 248
Interpersonal behaviour, 196
Interpersonal role, 104
Interpersonal skills, 196
Interviews, 154, 158
Intrinsic rewards, 190
Involvement, 194
Ishikawa, 38
Ishikawa diagrams, 55
ISO 14001, 50
ISO 9001, 49

Job analysis, 145, 148, 165
Job description, 145
Job design, 190
Job enlargement, 165
Job enrichment, 165
Job requisition, 146
Job roles, 6
Job rotation, 165, 226
Job satisfaction, 165, 187
Joint venture, 24
Juran, 38

Kaizen, 44, 261
Kanal 5, 161
Kanter, 105, 106
Kaplan, 344
Kaplan and Norton, 342
Katz and Kahn, 108
Katzenbach & Smith, 137
Key Performance Indicators, 213, 327, 329
Key result areas, 212
Knowledge, 296
Knowledge management, 296
Knowledge sharing, 27
Kolb, 124
Kotter (2001), 108
KPIs, 327, 329
Kraft Foods, 161

Leader, 104
Leadership, 29, 107
Leadership skills, 112
Leadership style, 114
Leadership theories and models, 113
Leadership traits, 114
Learning opportunity, 122
Learning organisations, 10
Learning style, 126
Legitimate or position power, 4, 108
Liability, 77, 78
Liaison, 104
Liberation Management, 19
Licencing, 24
Limitations of pay as a motivator, 192

Line authority, 4
Line, staff and functional authority, 11
Listening, 198
LL Bean, 235
Long-term liabilities, 79
Low-cost strategy, 347
Loyalty, 72
Loyalty-based cycle of growth, 40

Machine structure, 7
Maier, 219
Make/do or buy, 167
Management, 101
Management accounting, 74
Management tasks, 103
Managerial (or leadership) grid, 116
Managerial role, 104
Managerial support, 231
Managing change, 261
Managing diversity, 245
Managing meetings, 185
Managing service quality, 62
Market management, 14
Market share, 71, 294
Market share analysis, 314
Marketing and sales, 346
Marketing budget, 277
Marketing change, 265
Marketing communications budget, 304, 319
Marketing concept, 21
Marketing costs, 85
Marketing decision support system, 299
Marketing departments, 139
Marketing expenses, 76
Marketing information system (MkIS), 298
Marketing intelligence system, 299
Marketing manager, 144
Marketing manager's role, 273
Marketing mix effectiveness, 319, 320
Marketing organisation, 9, 314
Marketing project teams, 139
Marketing research system, 299
Marketing services, 168
Marketing structure, 13, 15
Marketing success, 264
Marketing team, 277
Marketing triangle, 235
Masculinity, 250
Maslow, 103, 188
Master budget, 304
Matrix organisation, 17, 23
Matrix structures, 17
Mayo, 103
McClelland, 189
McGregor, 188
Measures, 314
  Relationship/customer, 81
Mechanistic and organic organisation, 18
Meetings, 185
Mentors, 267
Merger, 24
Metric, 70
Middle line, 7
Mintzberg (1989), 104
Mintzberg's organisational components, 6
Mixed costs, 280
MkIS, 298
Model, 141
Modelling and simulation method, 295
Moments of truth, 57
Monitor, 105
Monitoring and review, 211
Motivation, 163, 179, 187, 230, 236, 276
Motivation needs theory, 189
Motivation theories, 188
Motivational feedback, 201
Motivator factors, 190
Mourning/adjourning, 181
Multi-disciplinary teams, 140
Multinational structures, 25
Multi-skilled teams, 140
Multi-skilling, 20, 141
Multi-source appraisal, 218
Multi-source feedback, 217

Natural wastage, 163
Negotiating, 201
Negotiating the marketing budget, 300
Negotiation, 266
Negotiator, 105
Network organisation, 24
Networking, 23, 111
New products, 90, 344
Noise, 197
Non-financial ratios, 318
Non-financial rewards, 192
Non-linear variable costs, 278
Non-verbal communication, 198
Norming, 180
N-step change models, 264
Numerical flexibility, 20

Objective and task, 292, 293
Objective setting, 273
Objectives, 213, 315
Off-the-job training, 225
On-boarding, 162
One-to-one interviews, 154
On-the-job training, 226
Operating core, 7
Operating statement, 317
Operations, 346
Organic structures, 19
Organisation, 296
Organisation charts, 10
Organisation culture, 7, 27, 28
Organisation structure, 3, 6, 8, 230
Outbound logistics, 346
Outsourcing, 24, 167, 297

P/V ratio, 340
Panel interviews, 154
Participation, 266
PAS 2050, 51
Passive behaviour, 199
Patent rights, 78

Pay as a motivator, 191
Payback, 337
Payback period, 305
Payment systems, 191
PDCA cycle, 55
Peer appraisal, 218
Penetration prices, 323
People, 58
Perceived service quality, 59
Percentage of sales, 292
Performance, 343
Performance agreement, 211, 212
Performance appraisal, 215
Performance incentives, 191
Performance indicators, 329
Performance management, 163
performance measurement, 70
Performance measures, 213, 314, 320
Performance measures for advertising, 321
Performance monitoring, 214
Performance problems, 228
Performance standards, 213
Performing, 181
Person specification, 145, 151
Personal development, 227
Personal Development Journal, 124
Personal development planning, 122, 127, 211
Personal Portfolio, 123
Personal selling, 320
Personality, 180
Persuasion, 202, 203
Peters, 19
Peters & Waterman, 104
Physical, coercive power, 108
Physicals, 58
Plan-Do-Check-Act, 55
Planned change model, 263
Planning, 273, 276, 277
Poor performance, 228
Poor team performance, 178
Porter, 347
Positioning, 323
Positive action, 159
Post-testing, 321
Power, 4, 108, 202
Power distribution, 255
Pragmatists, 127
Predictive model, 315
Predictive validity, 153
Preparing the budget, 301
Pricing, 323
Primary activities, 346
Principal budget factor, 302
Prioritisation, 212
Problem-solving approach, 219
Procedures, 179
Process, 58, 153
Process alignment, 43
Processes, 179
Procter & Gamble, 297
Procurement, 346
Product differentiation, 347
Product structure, 13
Productivity, 80
Product-market strategy, 323
Professional development, 227
Professional structure, 7
Profex, 104
Proficiency tests, 156
Profit and loss, 75
Profit and loss account, 74
Profit/volume ratio, 340
Profitability, 72
Progressive discipline, 233
Project management, 17, 19
Provisional budgets, 301
Prudence concept, 73
Psychometric testing, 156
Psychometric tests, 156

Qualitative approach, 338
Qualitative targets, 314
Quality, 37
Quality assurance, 41
Quality chains, 43
Quality circles, 38, 44
Quality control, 41
Quality culture, 43
Quality gaps, 37
Quality improvement, 52
Quality in stockbroking, 61
Quality management, 40, 44
Quality management principles, 50
Quality management standards, 46
Quality management strategies, 40
Quality management systems (QMS), 42
Quantitative targets, 314

Race Relations Act 1996, 157
Rapport-building, 203
Rating scales, 216
Ratio analysis, 318
Reconciling budget variances, 317
Recruit or develop/promote, 148
Recruitment, 86
Recruitment advertising, 146, 158
Recruitment and selection, 144
Recruitment policy, 148
Recruitment process, 145
Redundancies, 163
Referent (personal) power, 4
Referent power, 108
Reflection, 122
Reichheld, 236
Relationship marketing, 14, 22, 39, 63
Relationships, 6
Relevant range, 282
Remote teams, 248
Reputation management, 39
Resistance to change, 261
Resource cost driver, 325
Resource power, 108
Responsibilities in recruitment and selection, 144
Responsibility, 276
Responsiveness, 19
Results-orientated, 216
Retention, 163
Return on investment (ROI), 305

Revenue items, 76
Reward (or resource) power, 4
Reward systems, 220, 247
Rewards, 190
Risky-shift phenomenon, 138
Robert Anthony, 274
Rockart, 328
Role definitions, 151
Role profiling, 212
Roles, 6

Sales analysis, 314
Sales budget, 302
Sales figures, 297
Sales promotion budget, 304
Sales promotions, 322
Sales volume, 323
Scarcity of resources, 255
Scenarios, 341
Schroer, 294
Scientific management, 102
Secondary data, 299
Secondments, 166
Segmental analysis, 83
Segmentation, 83
Segmentation of internal customers, 238
Selection, 146, 153
Selection techniques, 153
Selection testing, 156
Self appraisal, 217
Self-development, 226
Self-managed teams, 141
Selling and distribution expenses, 76
Selling expenses budget, 303
Semi-fixed costs, 280
Semi-variable costs, 280
Sensitivity analysis, 341
Service, 57
Service encounters, 57
Service gaps, 59
Service quality, 57
Service recovery', 62
Services, 326
SERVQUAL, 61
Seven Point Plan, 151
Sex Discrimination Act 1986, 157
Shamrock, 20
Shamrock organisation, 19
Shank and Govindarajan, 347
Share of market, 294
Share of voice, 294
Shared objectives, 182
Simple (or entrepreneurial) structures, 7
Situational leadership, 119
Six Markets Model, 235
Six Sigma, 54
Skimming prices, 323
Social facilitation, 138
Specialisation, 3
Spokesperson, 105
Staff authority, 4
Staff retention, 89
Stages of team development, 180
Standard cost, 313
Standards, 313, 314, 320
Standing aims and objectives, 213
Standing objectives, 213
Step cost, 280
Stock, 78
Storming, 180
Strategic alliance, 24
Strategic apex, 7
Strategic Business Unit, 16
Strategic objectives, 8
Style theories of leadership, 113
Subcontracting, 24
Support, 231, 266
Support activities, 346
Support staff, 7
Symptoms of conflict, 256
Synergy, 137
System audits, 49

Tacit knowledge, 296
Tageuchi, 38
Talent management, 160, 163
Tangible fixed asset, 78
Tannenbaum and Schmidt, 117
Tansformational change, 264
Targets, 313, 314, 316, 320
Task allocation, 194
Taylor, 102, 165
Team, 137, 255
Team communication, 184
Team dynamics, 230
Team effectiveness, 177
Team formation and development, 180
Team identity, 182
Team leadership, 178
Team meetings, 185
Team membership, 141
Team roles, 141
Team solidarity, 182
Team structure, 139
Team working, 138
Team-building exercises, 182
Teams, 43, 137
Technical support, 231
Technology, 229
Technology development, 346
Technostructure, 7
Teleworking, 140
Telford & Wrekin Borough Council, 166
Tell and listen method, 219
Tell and sell method, 219
Territorial structure, 15
The balanced scorecard, 342
Theorist, 126
Theory X and Theory Y, 188
Thomas, 258
Thomas Cook, 58
Time series, 92
Timpson, 161
Tom Peters, 19
Top-down budgets, 289
Total cost, 281
Total Quality Management (TQM), 38, 43
Trade creditor, 78

Training, 221
Training and development, 164
Training needs analysis, 223, 230
Training plans, 225
Trait theories of leadership, 113
Trait theory, 114
Transactional, 109
Transactional leaders, 109
Transformation, 109, 261
Transformational leaders, 109
Transformational leadership, 112
Trompenaars, 28
Trompenaars model, 250
Tuckman, 180
Two-factor theory, 190

Unavoidable cost, 84
Uncertainty, 255
Uncertainty avoidance, 249
Uncontrollable costs, 84
Unfreeze-movement-refreeze, 263
Unglued structures, 20
Unit cost, 281
Upward appraisal, 218
Upward management, 111

Vaill, 178
Valence, 190
Value activities, 346
Value chain, 347
Value chain analysis, 345
Variable costs, 84, 278
Variance, 316
Variance analysis, 316
Variance causes, 317
Variances operating statement, 317
Vertical alignment, 211
Virgin Atlantic, 194
Virtual teams, 140, 166
Virtual team working, 253
Vroom, 190

Whetten and Cameron, 186
Whole-organisation marketing, 22
Work life balance, 166
Work-based/occupational competences, 150
Workset, 149

Zaleznik(1992), 108
Zero defects, 43

Review form & Free prize draw

All original review forms from the entire BPP range, completed with genuine comments, will be entered into one of two draws on 31 January 2011 and 31 July 2011. The names on the first four forms picked out on each occasion will be sent a cheque for £50.

Name: ______________________ **Address**: ______________________

____

____

1.How have you used this Text?
(Tick one box only)

☐ Self study (book only)

☐ On a course: college______________

☐ Other ______________

2. During the past six months do you recall seeing/receiving any of the following?
(Tick as many boxes as are relevant)

☐ Our advertisement in *The Marketer*

☐ Our brochure with a letter through the post

☐ Saw website

3. Why did you decide to purchase this Text?
(Tick one box only)

☐ Have used companion Assessment workbook

☐ Have used BPP Texts in the past

☐ Recommendation by friend/colleague

☐ Recommendation by a lecturer at college

☐ Saw advertising in journals

☐ Saw website

☐ Other ______________

4. Which (if any) aspects of our advertising do you find useful?
(Tick as many boxes as are relevant)

☐ Prices and publication dates of new editions

☐ Information on product content

☐ Facility to order books off-the-page

☐ None of the above

	Yes		No	
5. Have you used the companion Assessment Workbook?	Yes	☐	No	☐
6. Have you used the companion Passcards?	Yes	☐	No	☐

7. Your ratings, comments and suggestions would be appreciated on the following areas.

		Very useful	*Useful*	*Not useful*
Introductory section (How to use this text, study checklist, etc)		☐	☐	☐
Introduction		☐	☐	☐
Syllabus linked learning outcomes		☐	☐	☐
Activities and Marketing at Work examples		☐	☐	☐
Learning objective reviews		☐	☐	☐
Magic Formula references		☐	☐	☐
Content of suggested answers		☐	☐	☐
Index		☐	☐	☐
Structure and presentation		☐	☐	☐
	Excellent	*Good*	*Adequate*	*Poor*
Overall opinion of this Text	☐	☐	☐	☐

8. Do you intend to continue using BPP CIM Range Products? ☐ Yes ☐ No

9. Have you visited bpp.com/lm/cim? ☐ Yes ☐ No

10. If you have visited bpp.com/lm/cim, please give a score out of 10 for it's overall usefulness **/10**

Please note any further comments and suggestions/errors on the reverse of this page.

Please return to: Rebecca Hart, BPP Learning Media, FREEPOST, London, W12 8BR.

If you have any additional questions, feel free to email cimrange@bpp.com

Please note any further comments and suggestions/errors below.

Free prize draw rules

1 Closing date for 31 January 2011 draw is 31 December 2010. Closing date for 31 July 2011 draw is 30 June 2011.

2 Restricted to entries with UK and Eire addresses only. BPP employees, their families and business associates are excluded.

3 No purchase necessary. Entry forms are available upon request from BPP Learning Media. No more than one entry per title, per person. Draw restricted to persons aged 16 and over.

4 Winners will be notified by post and receive their cheques not later than 6 weeks after the relevant draw date. List of winners will be supplied on request.

5 The decision of the promoter in all matters is final and binding. No correspondence will be entered into.